KYOTO AREA STUDIES ON ASIA
CENTER FOR SOUTHEAST ASIAN STUDIES, KYOTO UNIVERSITY
VOLUME 30

Money-lending Contracts in Konbaung Burma

KYOTO AREA STUDIES ON ASIA

CENTER FOR SOUTHEAST ASIAN STUDIES, KYOTO UNIVERSITY

The Nation and Economic Growth:
Korea and Thailand
Yoshihara Kunio

One Malay Village:
A Thirty-Year Community Study
Tsubouchi Yoshihiro

Commodifying Marxism:
The Formation of Modern Thai Radical Culture, 1927–1958
Kasian Tejapira

Gender and Modernity:
Perspectives from Asia and the Pacific
Hayami Yoko, Tanabe Akio and Tokita-Tanabe Yumiko

Practical Buddhism among the Thai-Lao:
Religion in the Making of a Region
Hayashi Yukio

The Political Ecology of Tropical Forests in Southeast Asia:
Historical Perspectives
Lye Tuck-Po, Wil de Jong and Abe Ken-ichi

Between Hills and Plains:
Power and Practice in Socio-Religious Dynamics among Karen
Hayami Yoko

Ecological Destruction, Health and Development:
Advancing Asian Paradigms
Furukawa Hisao, Nishibuchi Mitsuaki, Kono Yasuyuki and Kaida Yoshihiro

Searching for Vietnam:
Selected Writings on Vietnamese Culture and Society
A. Terry Rambo

Laying the Tracks:
The Thai Economy and its Railways 1885–1935
Kakizaki Ichiro

After the Crisis:
Hegemony, Technocracy and Governance in Southeast Asia
Shiraishi Takashi and Patricio N. Abinales

Dislocating Nation-States:
Globalization in Asia and Africa
Patricio N. Abinales, Ishikawa Noboru and Tanabe Akio

People on the Move:
Rural–Urban Interactions in Sarawak
Soda Ryoji

Living on the Periphery:
Development and Islamization among the Orang Asli
Nobuta Toshihiro

Myths and Realities:
The Democratization of Thai Politics
Tamada Yoshifumi

KYOTO AREA STUDIES ON ASIA

CENTER FOR SOUTHEAST ASIAN STUDIES, KYOTO UNIVERSITY

East Asian Economies and New Regionalism
Abe Shigeyuki and Bhanupong Nidhipraba

The Rise of Middle Classes in Southeast Asia
Shiraishi Takashi and Pasuk Phongpaichit

Farming with Fire and Water:
The Human Ecology of a Composite Swiddening
Community in Vietnam's Northern Mountains
Trần Đức Viên, A. Terry Rambo and Nguyễn Thanh Lâm

Re-thinking Economic Development:
The Green Revolution, Agrarian Structure and Transformation in Bangladesh
Fujita Koichi

The Limits of Tradition:
Peasants and Land Conflicts in Indonesia
Urano Mariko

Bangsa and Umma:
Development of People-grouping Concepts in Islamized Southeast Asia
Yamamoto Hiroyuki, Anthony Milner, Kawashima Midori and Arai Kazuhiro

Development Monks in Northeast Thailand
Pinit Lapthanon

Politics of Ethnic Classification in Vietnam
Ito Masako

The End of Personal Rule in Indonesia:
Golkar and the Transformation of the Suharto Regime
Masuhara Ayako

Grassroots Globalization:
Reforestation and Cultural Revitalization in the Philippine Cordilleras
Shimizu Hiromu

Conceptualizing the Malay World:
Colonialism and Pan-Malay Identity in Malaya
Soda Naoki

Violence and Democracy:
The Collapse of One-Party Dominant Rule in India
Nakamizo Kazuya

Bali and Hinduism in Indonesia:
The Institutionalization of a Minority Religion
Nagafuchi Yasuyuki

At the Edge of Mangrove Forest:
The Suku Asli and the Quest for Indigeneity, Ethnicity, and Development
Osawa Takamasa

Money-lending Contracts in Konbaung Burma:
Another interpretation of an early modern society in Southeast Asia
Saito Teruko

KYOTO AREA STUDIES ON ASIA
CENTER FOR SOUTHEAST ASIAN STUDIES, KYOTO UNIVERSITY
VOLUME 30

Money-lending Contracts in Konbaung Burma

Another interpretation of an early modern society in Southeast Asia

Teruko Saito

Professor Emeritus,
Tokyo University of Foreign Studies

Kyoto University Press

TRANS PACIFIC PRESS

Money-lending Contracts in Konbaung Burma: Another interpretation of an early modern society in Southeast Asia. Published in 2024 jointly by:

Kyoto University Press
69 Yoshida Konoe-cho
Sakyo-ku, Kyoto 606-8315, Japan
Telephone: +81-75-761-6182
Fax: +81-75-761-6190
Email: sales@kyoto-up.or.jp
Web: http://www.kyoto-up.or.jp

Trans Pacific Press Co., Ltd.
PO Box 8547
#19682
Boston, MA, 02114, United States
Telephone: +1-6178610545
Email: info@transpacificpress.com
Web: http://www.transpacificpress.com

© Teruko Saito 2024
Copyedited by Cathy Edmonds, Kyneton, Victoria, Australia
Designed and set by Ryo Kuroda, Tsukuba-city, Ibaraki, Japan

Distributors

USA and Canada
Independent Publishers Group (IPG)
814 N. Franklin Street
Chicago, IL 60610, USA
Telephone inquiries: +1-312-337-0747
Order placement: 800-888-4741 (domestic only)
Fax: +1-312-337-5985
Email: frontdesk@ipgbook.com
Web: http://www.ipgbook.com

Europe, Oceania, Middle East and Africa
EUROSPAN
Gray's Inn House,
127 Clerkenwell Road
London, EC1R 5DB
United Kingdom
Telephone: +44-(0)20-7240-0856
Email: info@eurospan.co.uk
Web: https://www.eurospangroup.com

Japan
For purchase orders in Japan, please contact any distributor in Japan.

China
China Publishers Services Ltd.
718, 7/F., Fortune Commercial Building,
362 Sha Tsui Road, Tsuen Wan, N.T.
Hong Kong
Telephone: +852-2491-1436
Email: edwin@cps-hk.com

Southeast Asia
Alkem Company Pte Ltd.
1, Sunview Road #01-27, Eco-Tech@Sunview
Singapore 627615
Telephone: +65 6265 6666
Email: enquiry@alkem.com.sg

Library of Congress Control Number: 2024900878

All rights reserved. No reproduction of any part of this book may take place without the written permission of Kyoto University Press or Trans Pacific Press.
ISBN 978-1-920850-40-1 (hardback)
ISBN 978-1-920850-41-8 (paperback)
ISBN 978-1-920850-42-5 (eBook)

Contents

List of illustrations viii

Explanatory notes x

Abbreviations xiv

Acknowledgements xv

Introduction: *thet-kayit*s as important historical documents 1

I. Money-lending Contracts and Their Background 15

    Chapter 1: Climate, Demographic Changes, and Foreign Wars 17

    Chapter 2: The Konbaung Era in Burmese Monetary History 49

II. Humans as Collateral for Debt 69

    Chapter 3: Human-mortgage Contracts in the Eighteenth and
             Nineteenth Centuries 71

    Chapter 4: Human-mortgage Contracts in the Salin Region 101

III. Land as Collateral for Debt 131

    Chapter 5: Land-mortgage Contracts in Byangya Village 133

    Chapter 6: Land-mortgage Contracts in the Central Plains 161

IV. How to Characterize Early Modern Burma? 189

    Chapter 7: Early Modern Burma as a Contractual Society 191

    Chapter 8: Mediation of Disputes over Pledged Land 211

Conclusion 233

Notes 243

Bibliography 273

Index 291

List of illustrations

Photos

0.1: *Para-baik*s and *pe-sa*s collected by librarians and students of Meiktila University 2

0.2: Money-lending contracts written in *para-baik*s: human-mortgage contract, 1881, in the royal capital Mandalay, and paddy field mortgage contracts written during several years from 1816 in the Wundwin area 3

0.3: Royal edict written in a *pe-sa*: an appointment letter for the village head 4

4.1: Irrigation system in Salin 105

4.2: The mansion of Salin *Thugaung* 106

Figures

1.1: Annual rainfall in the central lowlands 20

1.2: Places where *thet-kayit*s were collected 21

1.3: Trends in the number of debt contracts (1752–1885) 36

2.1: Movement of paddy prices in the Konbaung period 59

2.2: Chronological distribution of Salin *Thugaung* money-lending contracts (1772/75–1896/1900) 61

2.3: Paddy prices in Lower Bruma (1848/49~1855/56) 66

4.1: Salin and its neighboring areas 104

4.2: Irrigation systems in Minbu 104

4.3: Poza and Taungzin families and marriage relations 110

5.1: The location of Byangya village 134

6.1. Distribution of three forms of debt (1752–1885) (nos.) 166

Tables

0.1: Types of written *thet-kayit* contracts in the Konbaung period (1752–1885) 8

1.1: Irrigation systems in the central plains 22

1.2: H. Burney's estimate of the 1783 population 26

1.3: Number of households in 1783 and 1802 *sit-tan*s 27

1.4: Household numbers in each administrative unit in 1826 28

List of illustrations   ix

1.5: Comparison of 1783, 1802, and 1826 *sit-tan*s (household numbers) 28

1.6: Major wars in the Konbaung era (1752–1885) 33

1.7: Permanent markets and market tax per year (in *kyat*s) 38

1.8: Imports from British Lower Burma, 1854~55 (1 year) 44

2.1: Silver-copper alloys circulated as currencies during
the Konbaung period (1752–1865) 53

2.2: Description of items relating to Bodawhpaya's monetary reform 58

2.3: New silver coins; denomination, weight, and
equivalent British Indian rupee 65

2.4: Approximate output of silver coins at the Mandalay mint (1865~1885) 67

3.1: Chronological distribution of debt-slave contracts 73

3.2: Geographic distribution of debt-slave contracts 74

4.1: Breakdown of contracts (Salin *Thugaung* debt-slave contracts) 108

4.2: Creditors in debt-slave contracts 111

4.3: Body price and added debt (1878–1885) 123

4.4: Nga Shwe's debt history 126

5.1: Assayers and weighers of currencies (Byangya) 137

5.2: Land-related *thet-kayit*s in Byangya village (1776–1812) 138

5.3: Land-related *thet-kayit*s in Byangya village (1827–43) 140

5.4: The contents of *thet-kayit*s of Byangya village 142

6.1: Breakdown of money-lending *thet-kayit*s in KUMF (nos.) 164

6.2: Breakdown of money-lending *thet-kayit*s in DMSEH 165

6.3: Types of agricultural land pledged (DMSEH) (nos.) 168

6.4: Regional distribution of farmland-selling *thet-kayit*s in DMSEH (nos.) .. 172

6.5: Distribution of farmland-selling *thet-kayit*s by period (nos.) 174

6.6: Paddy field mortgage and additional loan on the same field 180

8.1: Court changes in the case of the paddy fields called Pauk-yin-daw 224

8.2: Nga Yin's expenses in the Leik-kya-daw paddy fields lawsuit,
April 2, 1848 229

8.3: Nga Yin's expenses in the Pauk-yin-daw paddy fields lawsuit
(date unknown, c. December 1856) 230

Explanatory notes

In this book, for the sake of convenience and continuity with previous studies, I use the common name Burma, which is used widely in historical studies for the area under the rule of the Konbaung dynasty (1752–1885). In Burmese, the current official name of the country is Pyidaungzu Thamada Myanmar Naingan-daw, and its English translation is the Republic of the Union of Myanmar, which is widely referred to as Myanmar. The Konbaung dynasty is considered to be the first Burmese dynasty to successfully integrate politically in an area that roughly overlaps modern-day Myanmar, but the areas under its influence are variable and fluctuating at different times.

Notation of names

The names of places and people are written as close as possible to the local sounds; however, there are many difficulties because of the differences in pronunciation among speakers, and it is also difficult to distinguish between anaerobic and aerial sounds in Burmese and to express, in the English alphabet, the tone of voice.

Burmese names do not have surnames, but they are preceded by honorary titles that distinguish between gender and old and young. Among males, the same titles (at present) are found in order from the oldest to the youngest, such as U, Ko, and Maung. However, the most common one is Nga, which is less common nowadays and is used by both young and old alike. Among females, Shin, Me, Ma, and Mi are common, but Daw, which is currently used for older women, is not found at all in the Konbaung manuscripts.

Weights and measures in debt documents
Weight

The unit of weight was also used as a monetary unit:

- *beita* (*viss*): 1 *beita* = 100 *kyats*, approx. 1.63 kg
- *kyat*: 1 *kyat* is approx. 16.3 g
- *mat*: 1 *mat* = 1/4 *kyat*, approx. 4.1 g
- *mu*: small *mu*: 1 mu = 1/10 *kyat*, approx. 1.63 g
- large *mu*: 1 *mu* = 1/2 *mat* = 1/8 *kyat*, approx. 2 g
  (the large *mu* was used after the monetary reform in 1865)
- *pe*: 1 *pe* = 1/2 *mu*, approx. 0.8 g
- *ywe*: 1 *ywe* = 1/4 *pe*, approx. 0.2 g

Therefore:

- 1 *kyat* = 4 *mat* = 8 large *mu* = 16 *pe* = 64 *ywe*, or
- 1 *kyat* = 4 *mat* = 10 small *mu* = 20 *pe* = 80 *ywe*

As described above, there was a mixture of decimal and divisional systems. In *thet-kayit* manuscripts, all units of weight are denoted by abbreviations, as follows (⊙ represents a number):

- *kyat*: ⊙
- *mat*: ⊙
- *mu*: ⊙
- *pe*: ⊙
- *ywe*: ⊙

Length

- *letma*: length of the width of the thumb, 1 *letma* = approx. 2.5 cm
- *twa*: length from the tip of the thumb to the tip of the middle finger when fingers are spread, 1 *twa* = approx. 22~23 cm
- *taun*: length from the elbow to the tip of the middle finger, 1 *taun* = approx. 45 cm
- *tar*: approx. 2.8 meters, 1 *tar* = 7 *tauns*
- *tain*: approx. 2.8 km, 1 tain = 1,000 *tars*

Grain weight

- *tin*: baskets, varying in size, but one basket of paddy can weigh around 21 kg
- *seik*: 1/4 basket
- *pyi*: 1/16 basket, 1 *pyi* is 1/4 *seik* = 1/16 basket of paddy
- *sale*: 1/64 basket, 1 *sale* of paddy = 1/4 *pyi* = 1/16 *seik*

In *thet-kayit* documents, these units of grain weight are described as follows (⊙ represents a number):

- *tin*: ⊙
- *seik*: ⊙
- *pyi*: ⊙
- *sale*: ⊙

Area

- *pe:* there are two types of *pe:* the Bagadi *pe* (original *pe, pe* of the poor) and the Min *pe* (king's *pe*). The Bagadi *pe* was considered to be the size of a square measuring 25 *tar* on all sides. In British times, a *pe* was approximately 1.75 acres. The Min *pe* is estimated to have been about twice as much as the Bagadi *pe*. However, in most provinces the area of a field was expressed in terms of the amount of labor, yield, and sowing.

Burmese calendar

There are three calendars in use in Myanmar today—the Gregorian calendar (Western calendar), the Burmese calendar, and the Buddhist calendar—but the Burmese calendar was the only one used in private contracts during the Konbaung period. The Gregorian calendar was introduced under British colonial rule, and its use spread from official areas such as administration. The Buddhist calendar is still in use today for festivals related to Buddhism.

The Burmese calendar has a starting point of 638 A.D.—year 0 of the Burmese Era (B.E.) calendar—and the beginning of the year is based on the time of the descent and return of the god Indra, who was placed at the top of the indigenous gods, known as Thagyamin, for two days, which often fall in mid-April. However, it is not constant every year.

It is believed that the Burmese calendar follows the lunar calendar tradition for the months, and that it follows the solar calendar tradition for the years. The year consists of 12 months, with 29 days and 30 days repeating in sequence as follows: Tagu (29 days), Kason (30 days), Nayon (29 days), Wazo (30 days), Wagaung (29 days), Tawthalin (30 days), Thadingyut (29 days), Tazaungmon (30 days), Nadaw (29 days), Pyatho (30 days), Tabodwe (29 days), Tabaung (30 days).

The total number of days in these months is 354 days, which is a considerable deviation from the solar calendar year. In order to compensate for the difference, it is customary to add a second Wazo month between Wazo and Wagaung seven times in 19 years, and to add a day to the month of Nayon once every few years (which is about seven times in 38 years).

Each month is divided into two halves, the first half and the second half, according to the phases of the moon, called the white equinox (the period of fullness of the moon, *lazan*) and the black equinox (the period of absence of the moon, *lazo*). The fifteenth day of *lazan* is called *labye* (full moon), and the next day begins the day of the black equinox. The end of the black equinox (fourteenth or fifteenth day) is the day of the dark night or new moon, called *lagwe*, and this day marks the end of the month. The Burmese calendar is still used for public holidays and events, and newspapers show both the Western and Burmese calendars.

In the money-lending contracts of the Konbaung period, the word *thet-kayit* (Burmese calendar) appears at the beginning of the certificate, and the date when the contract was concluded is written first. For example, if it starts with '*Thet-kayit* 1170, the 14th day of the month of Thadingyut-…', we can know that it was made on August 3, 1808, when converted to the Western calendar. However, it is almost impossible to convert from the Burmese calendar to the Western calendar according to a certain formula because of the complicated Burmese calendar mentioned above. For this reason, several conversion tables for the Burmese and Western calendars of the period have been published, and I refer to four of them (see the bibliography).

Kings of the Konbaung dynasty (1752–1885)

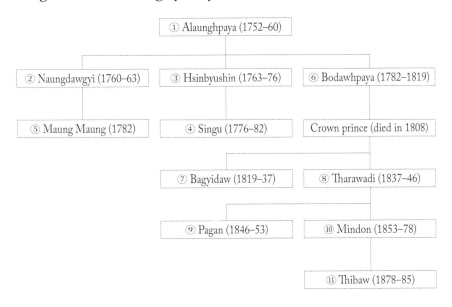

Abbreviations

B.E.   Burmese Era

C-DATS *Thet-kayit* collection in the Centre for Documentation & Area Studies, Tokyo University of Foreign Studies

DMSEH Documents of Myanmar Socio-Economic History (Aichi University, Volumes 1–11)

GUBSS *Gazetteer of Upper Burma and the Shan States* (five volumes)

KBZ   *Konbaung hset Maha Yazawin-daw-gyi* (Maung Maung Tin, three volumes)

KLT   *Konbaung Hkit Leya Thet-kayit Pa Luhmu Sibwayei Thamaing* (Toe Hla, two volumes)

KLT-Bc KLT, Byangya collection

KUMF   Microfilmed Materials on Myanmar History (Kagoshima University, in 114 volumes)

M.E.   Myanmar Era

MMOS   *Myanmar Min Ok-chok-pon Sadan* (U Tin, five volumes)

MTC   Meiktila *Thet-kayit* Collection

ROB   Royal Orders of Burma (edited by Than Tun, ten volumes)

STM-KT Salin *Thugaung* Manuscripts, '*Ko-nei Thet-kayits*' (Volume 10)

UCL   Universities' Central Library (Yangon)

Acknowledgements

This book has only been possible thanks to the work of many historians, librarians, and archivists in Myanmar who discovered, collected, restored, and investigated thet-kayits. A thet-kayit is a contractual deed exchanged by people of all social strata, which have been considered non-existent in early modern Southeast Asian societies. These manuscripts show in vivid detail the lives of people who lived in eighteenth- and nineteenth-century Burma, as well as various problems that arose in their lives and how they could or could not cope with these problems.

The author will refrain from listing the names of the many academic benefactors who contributed to her study, but would like to dedicate these research findings to them as a token of her sincere gratitude.

The author would also like to express her sincere gratitude to the Global Collaborative Research Program of the Center for Southeast Asian Studies and Asian Studies Fund at Kyoto University for a grant for publication, and to Kyoto University Press and Trans Pacific Press for changing the manuscript, which contained not a few errata, into a beautiful book through great editing skills.

Introduction: *thet-kayit*s as important historical documents

The term *thet-kayit* must once have been totally unfamiliar to non-Burmese historians. Moreover, even in Burma, it has been forgotten that *thet-kayit* had a special meaning in early modern Burmese society. In the present day, this word is used only to denote the Burmese calendar year. For example, '*thet-kayit* 1382' means the year 1382 in the Burmese calendar, which roughly corresponds to the year 2020 in the Western calendar.

However, this word had another important message in eighteenth- and nineteenth-century Burma. In historical documents related to the socioeconomics of the Konbaung period, we often find such phrases as 'according to the description of *thet-kayit*' or 'the court ordered to submit the original *thet-kayit*'. These imply that the word *thet-kayit* represented the transactional documents of various kinds exchanged among the people.

The reason why these documents were called *thet-kayit*s is thought to have been because they always started with the word *thet-kayit*.[1] It was customary to write at the beginning of the document the date[2] when the parties concerned reached an agreement and made the document. Although other documents started with the word *thet-kayit*, such as royal orders and stone inscriptions in early modern Burma, these documents were never called *thet-kayit*, but had separate names such as *amein-daw* (royal edict) or *kyauk-sa* (stone monuments). The term *thet-kayit* was confined to the contracts exchanged between private individuals.

Para-baik and *pe-sa*: transcription medium of *thet-kayit*s

*Thet-kayit*s had their own writing style as contractual documents, and at the same time the writing medium was unique. The most common material for writing *thet-kayit*s was a kind of notebook called a *para-baik*, made of thick paper folded like an accordion for convenient storage and carrying.[3] Another medium was *pe-sa*, dried and trimmed palm leaves. The paper was mainly made from the trunks of mulberry trees on the Shan Plateau, but a cheaper paper was also made from a mixture of wood and bamboo chips.[4]

There are two types of *para-baik*: the relatively inexpensive black *para-baik*, which is made of paper soaked with black ink, and the white *para-baik*, which is made of higher quality paper used mainly in the royal

Photo 0.1: *Para-baik*s and *pe-sa*s collected by librarians and students of Meiktila University

palaces. In the black *para-baik*, people wrote white letters using a soft soap stone. When there was no longer a need to save the writing, the *para-baik* was sometimes reused by repainting black ink. On the other hand, white *para-baik*s contain not only letters but also colored illustrations and drawings, and there are many beautiful manuscripts recorded in the hands of professional scribes and painters, but private testimonies such as *thet-kayit*s are rarely found on white *para-baik*.

Paper for *para-baik*s was carried by peddlers from the Shan Plateau and processed into *para-baik*s of various sizes from 8 x 15 cm to 15 x 40 cm, and with thicknesses from a single sheet of paper to one with 64 folds, according to the intended use.

Many *para-baik*s are found not only in the central semi-arid plains and northern part of Burma, but also in Thailand and Laos, mainly in the northern part of mainland Southeast Asia. However, historians have not yet found contractual documents in *para-baik*s in places other than Burma. It is not clear whether these regions produced testimonies but did not write them in *para-baik*s, or whether there was not much custom of keeping contractual testimonies in writing. As it was only a few decades ago that Burmese scholars and librarians came to know of the existence of

Photo 0.2: Money-lending contracts written in *para-baik*s: human-mortgage contract, 1881, in the royal capital Mandalay (above), and paddy field mortgage contracts written during several years from 1816 in the Wundwin area (bottom)

records of private transactions in *para-baik*s, the possibility of finding such documents in other neighboring Southeast Asian regions in the future cannot be ruled out.

*Pe-sa*s made of dried palm leaves are considered to have spread from India to various parts of Southeast Asia and were widely used as a writing medium in both the mainland and the islands, where they were called *lontar* in Bali and *bai-lan* in Thailand. In central Burma, records were scribed in a *pe-sa* by a stylus or a slate pencil, then soaked in crude oil from oil wells near Yenan-kyaung, and then wiped with a dry cloth to leave characters. Unlike *para-baik*s, which could be written or erased easily by anyone, the palm leaves had to be inscribed by specialists, and could not be modified, once written. In the *para-baik*s, we find some beautiful characters, and they are full of idiosyncratic characters and scribbles as well. *Para-baik*s also contain many regional dialects used only in specific regions.

There are some differences between the written contents of *para-baik*s and *pe-sa*s, although there is much overlap between them. The contents of *pe-sa*s include sutras, customary law, royal orders, astrology, contractual

4 Introduction

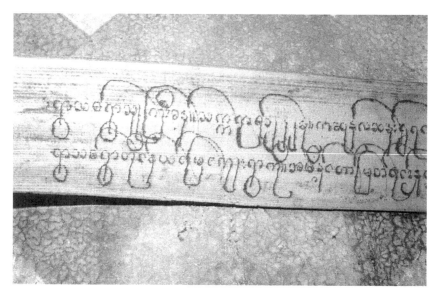

Photo 0.3: Royal edict written in a *pe-sa*: an appointment letter for the village head

documents, indigenous medicine, temple omens, various poems, and royal chronicles. Royal orders were inscribed in special *pe-sa*s whose palm leaf tips were left uncut, and they were sent all over the country in cylindrical metal containers.

In the *para-baik*s, people wrote records much more familiar to daily life, such as lists of taxes, irrigation water charges, village maps, *sit-tan*,[5] commodity prices, and so on, and similar records are found in the *pe-sa*s.

Where can we find *thet-kayit*s?

Despite the widespread use of *para-baik*s in society, these documents are now rarely found in private homes. In rare cases of long-lasting hereditary landlords and other influential local families who have inherited wealth built up over generations, *thet-kayit* documents have been passed down from generation to generation. However, they are rarely found in the homes of ordinary farmers or commoners. Common people's houses in rural areas were extremely simple, made of bamboo, wood, and thatch, and were vulnerable to fire, as well as water and wind damage. Moreover, people did not live in the same house for two or three generations, so it is unlikely that they were suitable places for storing important documents.

Another reason why a *thet-kayit* has rarely been found in an individual house is due to the history that Burma has experienced since the colonial period. During the British colonial period, the custom of writing *thet-kayits* was gradually lost because only contracts written on official paper with the portrait of the British king were made legal.[6] Furthermore, after independence, the Burmese government enacted the Land Nationalization Act and made the farmland-mortgage contracts irrelevant, even though they were the majority of the debt documents of the Konbaung era. However, the effect of the land nationalization law was limited to a few cases, mainly due to the political unrest that began immediately after independence.

After 1962, however, the Land Nationalization Act was revived when the Burmese socialist military regime took over power. Consequently, the Land Nationalization Act was strictly enforced, making it almost impossible for farmers to transact their farmland. Consequently, *thet-kayits* lost their practical meaning, even in the families of the great landowners of the old days who had maintained the customary deals for generations. During the Konbaung period, *thet-kayits* had been handed down for two, three, or more generations, and descendants often fought for land on the basis of the old *thet-kayits*. However, the *thet-kayit* itself is almost forgotten nowadays.

Where, then, can we find these *thet-kayits* written during the eighteenth and nineteenth centuries? The largest numbers of *thet-kayits* were found in monasteries across Upper Burma. The monastery was an essential institution and spiritual center for Burmese Buddhists. Therefore, in the Konbaung era, when people built a village, they first secured a piece of land for a monastery on the east side of the village, or on a slightly elevated site. Even if they could not afford to build a monastery at the same time as the village, it was almost essential for them to build one that was as solid and magnificent as possible.[7]

Well-known monasteries in the royal capitals and relatively large provincial cities constructed separate buildings, called *bidakat-taik*, for the purpose of storing the Buddhist scriptures and a large number of sutras and documents. It is highly likely that monasteries were also used as repositories for not only Buddhist scriptures, but also other important documents and testimonies, and a monastery's *bidakat-taik* must have played a role as an archive for the local community. U Toe Hla mentions

6 Introduction

an idiom that 'the document, the monastery, and the village are eternally inseparably united as one body' and gives the following example of a fierce dispute between village elders and a monk during the reign of King Mindon over the ownership of a monastery's documents:

> During the reign of King Mindon, the *saya-daw* (the chief priest) of the village of Kadaw-zeik appointed one of his disciples, a monk named Shin Thirima, to succeed him after his death and entrusted him with all the aftermath of the temple and his belongings. When the *saya-daw* passed away, Shin Thirima attempted to transfer all the documents to the monastery where he lived, but the village elders tried to prevent this and a fierce battle ensued. The dispute was left to the adjudication of a specially organized Buddhist court of elder monks, who ordered all the documents to be returned to their original monastery. In other words, the court ruled that the sutras and other documents stored in the scripture chests of the village monastery did not belong to the chief priest of the monastery or to a particular monk, but had a strong connection to the village and its inhabitant.[8]

*Bidakat-taik*s were built from the eleventh-century Pagan period. During the Konbaung period, the word *bidakat-taik* was used not only for monasteries' archives but also for archives of kings and individuals.[9] In addition to the Buddhist scriptures, a wide variety of records and documents were stored in these archives, including court traditions, administrative records, poetic works, literature, chronicles, customary law, traditional medicine, astrology, prophecy, contractual documents, and other court records. Even in the colonial period, the word *bidakat-taik* continued to be used for a long time to refer to the library.

While there is no doubt that many *thet-kayit*s have been lost, a significant portion of these documents, which were preserved in *bidakat-taik*s or by influential local families, are now available in the form of microfilm or digitalized databases. The advent of digitalization of archives on the web has led to dramatic improvement in the research environment in recent years.[10]

Types of *thet-kayit*s

A look at the general picture of the kinds of contracts (collectively called *thet-kayit*s) exchanged between individuals shows us cases in which people in eighteenth- to nineteenth-century Burma thought it necessary to make written contracts instead of verbal promises.

The meaning of the Burmese word *paun* is closest to that of 'pawn' in English, but it does not distinguish between cases where the usufruct of the collateral is transferred to the creditor and cases where it is not. Most secured debts in the Konbaung era were basically secured by transferring the usufruct to the creditor in lieu of interest, whatever the collateral. However, in a few cases the debtor continued to cultivate the mortgaged land as before and paid part of the harvest to the creditor in lieu of interest. Thus, the term 'mortgage' seems to be more appropriate to the situation than the term 'pledge', as the mortgage in a broader sense includes both mortgages with usufruct and mortgages without transferring usufruct.

Among things offered as collateral for a debt, it is noteworthy that in some cases the right to govern or control a certain territory was offered to the creditor in lieu of a debt. In very hard times, it happened that the head of a *myo* (city, township) or *ywa* (village) had to borrow money and pledge his *myo* or *ywa* to the money-lenders in order to pay taxes.[11] There were also cases of pledges of management rights over the irrigation canals (with the right to collect water rates from the beneficiary of the canals) and rights to collect tolls at piers as collateral for loans.[12]

Unsecured debts bore interest and were called by various names depending on how the interest was paid. In some cases, the principal was paid back in cash and interest was paid in kind, or both the principal and interest were paid in the form of specific labor, or in paddy. When both principal and interest were repaid in cash, interest rates as high as 5% per month were charged in most areas.

People also made written contracts when borrowing goods, among which paddy was most commonly borrowed. In these cases, both principal and interest were repaid in paddy, or were converted into cash and repaid in money.

A selling contract was prepared when the sale of goods took place and there was a time lag between delivery of the goods and the payment of the price. If the delivery and payment of the goods were made at the same time, there was no need to make a written contract. In sales contracts,

8 Introduction

Table 0.1: Types of written *thet-kayit* contracts in the Konbaung period (1752–1885)

1	Money-lending *thet-kayit* a) Loan with mortgage pledges	Agricultural land, human, cattle Mango tree, sugar palm tree Jewelry, gold or silverware Jurisdiction over a town or village Irrigation canal, landing jetty
	b) Loan without mortgage	Repay both principal and interest by cash Repay both principal and interest by labor Repay by crops, especially by paddy Repay interest by labor, principal by cash
2	Borrowing *thet-kayit*	Paddy borrowing, cattle borrowing
3	Selling *thet-kayit*	Sale on credit, etc.
4	Tenancy *thet-kayit*	*lo'hpet* (share-cropping tenancy)
5	Inheritance *thet-kayit*	Division of inheritance among the heirs
6	Promising *thet-kayit*	Present for wedding, or for entering priesthood
7	Other *thet-kayit*	Putting new debt on the same pledge Confirmation of repayment Guarantor's oath to repay for runaway slaves, etc.

prepayment *thet-kayit*s were written in the case of marketable crops such as paddy, sesame, maize, chickpeas, and dates. For post-payment, namely selling on credit, *thet-kayit*s were prepared for high-priced goods such as horses, cattle, land, timber, boats, oil, medicine, and bricks. There were also *thet-kayit*s where credits were the subject of a sale. This was typical when debt contracts, such as land-mortgage contracts, were sold to a third party by a creditor who was in need of cash.

What is clear from Table 0.1 is the nature of tenancy agreements—namely, the so-called share-cropping contract known as *lo'hpet* or *pet-sa*, meaning joint working. The idea was that the landowner and the tenant would bring together the means of production necessary for farming (land, seed, labor, and cattle for plowing, etc.) and confirm the rights over the harvest in proportion to their respective contributions. In most cases, the landowner provided land, seeds, and so on, and the tenant provided necessary labor for cultivation, and the total harvest was divided fifty–fifty between them. The modern Burmese word *thi-sa*, meaning tenant farmer, is not found in *thet-kayit*s, and the word *lo'hpet*, meaning working companion or partner, was used in the Konbaung period.

A written oath or covenant was literally a promise by the parties, in the presence of witnesses, to perform obligations. However, in most cases, there was a preceding contractual instrument, and it was made anew if the matter was not carried out as stated. If a debt was not repaid by the due date, a covenant was made with a new deadline. In the case of a fugitive debt-slave, a covenant was made that stipulated how the guarantor of the debt-slave should repay the total amount of the debt and the labor that was not performed.

An agreement on an inheritance distribution was also called a *thet-kayit*. After the death of a family member, the distribution of property was decided by the elders and other adjudicators, and an agreement on how to distribute the property among the heirs was compiled as a promise in the presence of witnesses. A list of contributions to the monastery was also specified as a deed with witnesses to ensure their fulfillment.

Other *thet-kayit*s included repayment deeds that were made when the debt was cleared, and additional debt contracts that were made when additional debts were put on the security of the first debt. In this way, in Burmese society during the Konbaung era, transactions and promises in a wide range of fields were documented in a certain format, and the term *thet-kayit* was used as a generic term for these contract documents between private individuals.

The history of *thet-kayit* studies and research subjects

The importance of *thet-kayit*s as historical documents in Burma was first pointed out by U Thaung, a local historian living in Shwebo. From the late 1960s to the 1970s, he wrote several articles in the daily newspaper *Loktha Pyithu Neizin* (Workers' Daily) about *thet-kayit*s written in *para-baik*s as important sources about life in Upper Burma during the Konbaung period. However, it was U Toe Hla, then a lecturer in the Department of History at Mandalay University, who initiated the systematic excavation of the materials. U Toe Hla wrote about his encounter with *thet-kayit*s as follows:

> I first came across *thet-kayit*s in 1967, when I was asked to accompany Dr. Than Tun to the Taungwin Buddhist Headquarters in Mandalay to

copy the *para-baik*s in the Sanzang Sutra Archives for the Department of History of our university...I was going to start by looking through all the *para-baik*s and have copied only those documents whose handwriting was clear and legible.

The first manuscript I worked on was the *para-baik* of Minfla-Min-Tin-Kyaw, the Deputy Minister and the Myo-sa of Poppa,[13] which contained *thet-kayit*s relating to borrowing, mortgaging, sale, and litigation. People from different social classes of the time appeared in the manuscript, describing the reasons for borrowing, mortgaging, and selling, as well as the promises they made to each other. There were also records of the coins and weights in use at the time, and incidents of broken promises that resulted in lawsuits. All information showed us the daily life of that time as it was, and I realized that the historical value of *thet-kayit*s is very great.[14]

U Toe Hla copied 1,055 *thet-kayit* manuscripts in handwriting and later typeset and printed them in two unpublished volumes.[15]

The first person who introduced *thet-kayit*s in Japan was Mr. Toru Ohno, a pioneer of Burmese studies in Japan as a linguist, as well as an expert in Burmese area studies. He wrote an introductory essay, 'Financial forms of rural Burma in the 18th and 19th centuries', focusing on the money-lending *thet-kayit*s collected and microfilmed by the Kagoshima University's Research Group on Burmese Archives.[16]

U Toe Hla's *thet-kayit* work resulted in a doctoral dissertation, 'Money-lending and contractual "*thet-kayit*": A socio-economic pattern of the later Kon-baung period, 1819–1885', submitted to Northern Illinois University,[17] which is a fascinating study that vividly highlights previously unknown socioeconomic aspects and peoples' life during the late Konbaung period. In this study, he attempted to interpret the socioeconomic character of the late Konbaung period in his own way, which was something new to Burmese historical studies. Traditional studies were based on thoroughgoing objectivism in writing a historical narrative, where scholars tried to accumulate primary sources as much as possible and to maintain 'objectivity' by excluding the interpretation of individual historians.[18] It was a step forward, and in addition to new *thet-kayit* materials, his study marked a new phase in terms of the nature of historiography. This study made me turn to the study of Burmese history in the early-modern period, feeling that a new and fertile ground for precolonial socioeconomic studies was opening.

As I read increasing numbers of *thet-kayit*s, however, I came to feel that there were a few contradictions between the socioeconomic reality of Burma in the eighteenth and nineteenth centuries, as revealed in the manuscripts, and the overall socioeconomic picture that U Toe Hla described for this period. For example, he tried to understand the period on the basis of the absoluteness of royal power, and saw Burmese society in the Konbaung period as a two-tiered society consisting of a king with absolute power and the rest of the population. He cited John Nisbet and H. Fielding Hall, who experienced colonial Burma in the late nineteenth and early twentieth centuries, as a scholar and a novelist respectively, and agreed with their views that there was no landed aristocracy or landed gentry in Burma's past[19] and no middle class between the king and the villagers.[20] So, U Toe Hla was skeptical about V. Lieberman's assertion that local hereditary chiefs, *myo-thugyi*s (hereditary rulers of *myo*s), and *ywa-thugyi*s (chiefs of *ywa*s) were the gentry in sixteenth- to eighteenth-century Burma.[21]

The spectacle that emerges from the money-lending contracts shows that private right over land was established effectively in the kingdom and people enjoyed not only the right to use land but also the right of disposal at the time of need. In fact, land was pledged as collateral for debts, or even sold, and the documents of these transactions were freely recorded as contracts without the need for notification to the central, as well as local, authority.

The importance of *thet-kayit*s as historical documents lies in the fact that they were time- and place-specific records of agreements made by all strata of society, including the common people, whose daily life rarely appeared in recorded history. *Thet-kayit*s, which described agreements or promises made between individuals, recorded not only the parties involved, but also the names of witnesses, assayers, and weighers, scribes, and draft writers, as well as dates, places, quantities of money borrowed, and brokerage if any. The fact that such contractual documents were widely and massively produced seems to have prompted us to question the conventional precolonial socioeconomic picture and to draw a new picture for premodern Burmese society.

12 Introduction

After U Toe Hla, using *thet-kayit*s collected in the Meiktila region, Thu Nandar wrote a dissertation based on a detailed analysis of land-mortgaging contracts in the region.[22] She showed that, in Meiktila, the strong persistence of the practice of an equitable inheritance system among all children led to a high number of farmland-related lawsuits. However, apart from this study, even though circumstances for the study of *thet-kayit*s has greatly improved, research has been very slow to move forward.

Themes of this study

The starting point of my *thet-kayit* research was my surprise at the sudden appearance of contractual documents between private individuals not only for those at the upper echelons of society, but also for ordinary people who were otherwise buried in history and hardly visible in their own right. As I read the material and imagined the lives of people in eighteenth- to nineteenth-century Burma, I began to see a contradiction between the historical picture drawn up in the past and what *thet-kayit* manuscripts tell us about the life of people in the Konbaung period. What I saw was not a view of history that is influenced by the 'oriental tyranny' theory of the absoluteness of kingship in the control of resources, but a dynastic society that was already in the process of modernization before it was subjected to colonial rule, a view which I myself had held in the past[23] but that now seemed irrelevant. I came to notice the deficiencies of this perspective, as it often happens that what looks to be a modernization process in eighteenth- to nineteenth-century Southeast Asia was often carried out by intentions and ideas different from so-called modern thought. What is obscured by applying the framework of modernization is actually important for understanding a society at that time. In this context, the objectives of my research are naturally summarized in the following two issues.

My first objective was to read *thet-kayit* manuscripts as widely and intensely as possible to capture the socioeconomic changes underway in eighteenth- and nineteenth-century Burma and to clarify their background and historical significance. The second objective was to answer the question that always sticks in my mind, why a *thet-kayit* was socially recognized as a contract and was able to urge both parties to perform it. In answer to this question, there might be an important clue to understanding the specific character of Konbaung Burmese society.

*thet-kayit*s as important historical documents   13

During the second Taungoo period in the seventeenth and eighteenth centuries, the royal government was nervous about the fact that not a few people in the hereditary service groups to the Crown were beholden in the private sector through debt-slave contracts. However, during the Konbaung era, the royal government showed little willingness to intervene in these contracts. What socioeconomic conditions were behind the drastic changes in the response of the seventeenth- to eighteenth-century king's government and the Konbaung king's government to private contracts?

With these two central thoughts in mind, this book takes up several issues that lead to different conclusions from previous studies, as these issues also become unavoidable in the course of the discussion. The structure of this book is as follows.

Part I discusses the background of the rapid increase in money-lending contracts from the middle of the eighteenth century in the core area of Konbaung Burma. The first chapter examines the role of climatic conditions, especially the dry savanna weather and the irrigation networks built and maintained by the central royal authority over the centuries. As further background, I focus on foreign wars and trade between Burma and the outside world, and examine the socioeconomic impact on the daily life of the people. The second chapter deciphers the complicated monetary system in eighteenth- to nineteenth-century Burma by placing it in the context of the long history of Burmese currency.

Part II, which focuses on human-mortgage contracts, analyzes 309 debt-slave contracts collected from all over the central plain and depicts the actual state of debt-slaves in the period. I then analyze 104 debt-slave contracts written in the Salin region, and examine in detail the causal factors attributable to make people debt-slaves and their conditions of work, as well as the possibility for liberation. The results show that the historical significance of debt-slavery in eighteenth- to nineteenth-century Burma was quite different from that of debt-slaves in the seventeenth to eighteenth centuries.

Part III deals with land-mortgage contracts, which had been increasing rapidly since the middle of the Konbaung period in place of human mortgages. Chapter 5 traces mortgaged paddy fields from 61 *thet-kayit*s of Byangya village in the Shwebo region. In this area all land, regardless of its type (private, granted, or monastery), was treated in the same way and was mortgaged and even sold amid the unstoppable increase in land-mortgage contracts.

Chapter 6 provides an overview of all available land-mortgage contracts collected from the whole central plain, and finds that progression from mortgaging to selling of farmland, as seen in Byangya village, was not a common phenomenon. In other regions, a strong power worked to prevent the sale of farmland.

In Part IV, in examining the question of how the effectiveness of a *thet-kayit* as a contract was secured in the society, I first focus on the significance of the presence of witnesses, which is considered to be particularly important. Second, I examine how a *thet-kayit* exchanged between private parties was handled in the civil courts at each level from villages to the royal capital. Third, I examine the interventions that the central kingship and local rulers made or did not make in relation to contracts between private individuals, and from this I clarify the relationship between the governing power and private contracts.

Chapter 8 looks at how land disputes were resolved by the courts at various levels, taking up a few cases as examples that occurred during the Konbaung period. It shows that Burmese civil courts were based on very different principles and methods from those of the colonial courts. A *thet-kayit* seems to have been similar to a modern contract between independent individuals, but it was nurtured in a different culture and practice from what we call modernity.

Part I

Money-lending Contracts and Their Background

Chapter 1

Climate, Demographic Changes, and Foreign Wars

In this chapter, I examine the causes of the rapid increase of debt contracts, especially land-mortgage contracts in the Konbaung period, from two perspectives. The first aspect is the climate of the central plains, the core area of Konbaung Burma, which is the most arid area in the inland savanna belt of mainland Southeast Asia. Since the ancient Pyu (first to ninth centuries) and Pagan (eleventh to thirteenth centuries) periods, royal governments had constructed large irrigation systems in order to make rice cultivation possible in this dry area. Although the royal irrigation networks had contributed to the expansion of land under rice cultivation, the expansion was limited due to several reasons, such as budget and technological constraints.

It is only when farmland becomes a scarce resource under any economic system that people treat agricultural land as a more valuable and secure collateral for debt than human labor, or any other form of asset. In this sense, the large-scale irrigation systems in the central plains prepared the basic conditions for the land scarcity.

The second aspect concerns the socioeconomic changes in eighteenth- to nineteenth-century Burma. Although the climate and the irrigation systems created the conditions for enhancing the scarcity value of agricultural land, most of the irrigation networks functioned in a cycle of rises and falls over the centuries. Therefore, the existence of irrigation networks alone cannot explain why land-mortgage contracts started increasing rapidly from the middle of the eighteenth century among people of all social strata.

The Konbaung period was a time when major changes in the system of resource collection and allocation were taking place. To borrow K. Polanyi's

17

terms, the socioeconomic emphasis had shifted from a system based on the redistribution of economic resources to a system of exchange that depended largely on the market.[1] The background of these socioeconomic changes was the upheaval of foreign relations in Konbaung Burma, especially in regard to the foreign trade and the wars against outside forces. Although these two indicators alone cannot fully explain the socioeconomic changes of the period, they seem to be the most important variables to explain the socioeconomic characteristics of Burmese society in the eighteenth and nineteenth centuries and the direction of its changes.

Central plains climate: irrigation systems in the savanna

The image of farmland scarcity might be quite different from the commonly held one of premodern Southeast Asia as a world of small population.[2] The entire population of Southeast Asia at the beginning of the seventeenth century is estimated at 20.8 million people—six people per square kilometer in continental Southeast Asia, and four on the islands—which was only one-sixth or even one-seventh of the population of India and China at that time.[3] Until the end of the eighteenth century, a significant portion of the small population was concentrated in trading cities at the mouths of rivers or in the rice cultivating flatlands, which had been cleared and settled from a relatively early date, while the rest of the area was covered with extensive tropical and subtropical forests, where people made their living by shifting cultivation and gathering forest products. As this state of affairs continued up to the eighteenth century, the overall population growth rate in Southeast Asia was minimal. It was only after colonial rule in all regions that the population curve began to show a clear upward curve, a phenomenon that began to occur after the mid-eighteenth century in the islands and after the second half of the nineteenth century on the continent.[4] The main reasons for this were the suppression of inter-kingdom and inter-regional warfare under strong colonial power, which reduced the devastation caused by warfare, and the progress of settlement in the midst of colonial development.

In the context of pre-eighteenth-century Southeast Asian societies characterized by large tracts of uncultivated land, small populations, and high population mobility, the central plains of Burma, along with the Tonkin Delta in Vietnam, Central Java, and Bali, were long established paddy cultivation areas (i.e., relatively densely populated) in Southeast Asia. However, what is different from the Tonkin Delta and Central Java is that the inland central plains where Konbaung Burma was based were significantly drier than these areas, mainly due to the very low impact of monsoon rainfall.

The vast valley floor plains formed by the Ayeyarwady River, which runs through Burma from north to south, and the Sittaung River, which originates near Yamethin and runs parallel to its east and flows into the Gulf of Martaban, are divided into two regions, roughly bordered by the nineteenth parallel north latitude between Taungoo and Pyi. The northern region is known as Upper Burma and the southern region as Lower Burma. The climatic conditions of the two regions differ greatly, the former being a semi-arid savanna and the latter being a tropical rainforest. This great climatic variance is mainly due to the mountainous region which surrounds Burma like a screen, and to two monsoon patterns. During the rainy season from May to October, the southwest monsoon, which pours up from the Indian Ocean, brings 2,000–5,000 mm of rain to Arakan and the vast delta area downstream of the Ayeyarwady and Tenasserim region, which stretches towards the Malay Peninsula. However, the Arakan Mountains block this monsoon, which brings only a small amount of rainfall to the Upper Burma central plains that stretch inland. During the dry season, from November to April, the northeast monsoon, which blows down from the East China Sea, has little effect on the rainfall of Burma, which is located on the western edge of Southeast Asia, except in the northeastern mountainous region. As a result, the central plains in Upper Burma, far from the coast and surrounded by mountains and plateaus, become the driest of the tropical monsoon savanna plains in Southeast Asia, with annual rainfall of around 800 mm.

Since the Pagan period, except for the Taungoo dynasty, all the Burmese dynasties were located in these central plains in Upper Burma. The Pagan (1044–1299), Nyaung Yang (1604–1752),[5] and Konbaung (1752–1885) dynasties had their bases in the Upper Burma plains, while the Taungoo dynasty (1531–1599) was founded in Taungoo, on the border between Upper and Lower Burma, and in 1539 it moved its capital in the port city of Pegu in Lower Burma.

Figure 1.1 divides the central lowlands of the Ayeyarwady and Sittaung rivers by annual rainfall. Except for the first royal capital of the Konbaung

20   Chapter 1

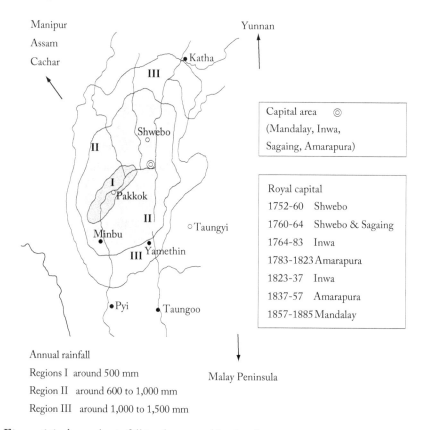

Figure 1.1: Annual rainfall in the central lowlands

dynasty, Shwebo, which is situated slightly north, other successive royal capitals (i.e., Sagaing, Ava, Amarapura, and Mandalay) are concentrated in a very narrow area within Region II in the figure, with an annual rainfall of around 800 mm. The main areas of the dynasty were located in the arid and semi-arid plains with annual rainfall of 500 to 1,000 mm in Regions I and II, where wet-rice cultivation is very difficult without irrigation facilities. The irrigation systems which were under the direct control of successive kings' governments are concentrated in these regions.

Region III lies between the mountains and the central plains, where many alluvial fans are created by the rapid streams flowing out of the mountainous regions. Almost all royal river irrigation systems take water from the large weirs built in such rivers on the alluvial fans and distribute water by the numerous canals to downstream paddy fields.

Figure 1.2: Places where *thet-kayit*s were collected

Figure 1.2 shows the locations where the debt contracts discussed in this volume were found and collected. Most were found in the arid and semi-arid areas of Regions I and II. Although a few debt contracts were found in Region III (i.e., alluvial fans and hilly areas with annual rainfall of 1,000–1,400 mm), the number is very small.[6] In the tropical rainforest area, south of the line between Taungoo and Pyi, including the vast delta in Lower Burma, there are very few *thet-kayit*s, almost none, especially land-mortgage *thet-kayit*s that were the mainstream of debt in the Konbaung period.[7] As a rainforest area, Lower Burma, like many other parts of Southeast Asia, was characterized by a small population and the abundance of uncultivated land. When the British annexed Lower Burma in 1852, there was rain-fed rice cultivation in the northern parts of the upper delta, and the middle and lower reaches of the delta had scattered

22 Chapter 1

Table 1.1: Irrigation systems in the central plains

	Region	Origin	System	Facilities	Irrigated area (acres)
River irrigation	Kyaukse	Pagan	Zawgyi River Panlaung River	Weir, canal	105,000~161,722
	Minbu	Pagan	Salin River Mon River Man River	Weir, canal	22,132 7,000~10,000 28,252
	Shwebo	Pagan	Mu River	Weir, canal, tank	300,000
Tank irrigation	Meiktila	Pyu	3 big tanks and 60 small tanks	tank, canal	33,000
	Yamethin		Kyaukse Pond Yamethin Lake		5,000 5,000
River and tank	Mandalay	Pagan (relic) Konbaung		Weir, canal, tank	74,341

Note: the estimated irrigated area is based on Michael Aung-Thwin, *Irrigation in the Heartland of Burma*, Northern Illinois University, Occasional Paper No. 15, 1990, pp. 14–32. The origin of each system might be changed by future archeological research.

evidence of shifting cultivation, where rice was grown in the tropical forest and the land abandoned after two or three years of harvest.[8] The idea of land ownership hardly existed, and the conditions under which land itself could be treated as a good for transaction was almost non-existent.

Table 1.1 shows the large-scale irrigation systems under the direct control of the royal governments that were in use during the Konbaung period. River irrigation systems were constructed in Kyaukse, Minbu, and Shwebo. The headworks of these systems were built at the top of alluvial fans in Ayeyarwady tributary rivers that run through the valleys of surrounding mountains and hills, where rainfall was high and water never ran dry. In each system, several main canals and numerous small distributaries sent water to the downstream paddy fields.

In Meiktila and Yamethin, where there is no such perennial river, the reservoir irrigation systems with a big reservoir and a number of small and medium-sized reservoirs have been developed since ancient times. In Mandalay, a combined irrigation system of river irrigation and reservoir irrigation was constructed in the Pagan period. It was rebuilt under the Konbaung kings on an enlarged scale.

These systems have served as the foundation for agricultural production in Upper Burma to the present day, with constant repairs and expansions

Climate, Demographic Changes, and Foreign Wars   23

under the central dynasty government to the British colonial administration and then to post-independent governments. I have visited all the systems except for Yamethin and walked around from the headworks to the end plots, and was strongly impressed by the large scale of the systems, as well as their elaborate design, which was based on a careful reading of the climate and topography. The irrigation canals excavated along the contour lines create a landscape like a natural river and make oases of greenery in the arid region of Upper Burma.

Most of the systems listed in Table 1.1 are traditionally thought to have originated in the Pagan period, but the possibility that at least some of them were built during the ancient Pyu period cannot be ruled out.[9] In particular, the construction of Lake Meiktila, the mainstay of the Meiktila reservoir system, is likely to date back to the Pyu period.[10]

The reason these systems were under the direct control of the royal governments was that only by royal orders could a large amount of labor be mobilized in order to build huge reservoirs or to dam big rivers and excavate irrigation canals for the systems, which are each hundreds of kilometers in length.[11] Along with the generous donations as a protector of Buddhism, the king's irrigation projects were inscribed and recorded in the royal chronicles, which shows that irrigation projects to secure water and set up a foundation for the production of the main grain were the most important tasks of the royal government.

It is also noteworthy that the prototype of the irrigation system under the direct control of the royal authority finalized its basic form at least during the Pagan period and did not change until the last dynasty, Konbaung.[12] Although some existing facilities were renovated or expanded, there was no new development in other areas. The major reasons are attributed to natural constraints in terms of the availability of suitable rivers and other topographical problems. Under these circumstances, it was not easy, even for royal governments, to expand the area of irrigated paddy fields and almost impossible for individual cultivators. The paddy field, with a stable water supply from the irrigation system constructed through huge investment in the form of labor and capital, was not an inexhaustible resource that could be obtained simply by reclaiming land, but a rare and limited resource. Although expressions such as 'plentiful or inexhaustible land and scarce population' have often been used to describe characteristics of precolonial Southeast Asian societies, they were not applicable to the

24   Chapter 1

central plains, the core area of Konbaung Burma, along with the Tonkin Delta in Vietnam and the densely populated paddy fields in Java.

Demographic changes in the Konbaung period

The previous section discussed limited irrigation as one factor attributable to the increasing scarcity value of land. However, we should not ignore the other factor, namely the increasing demand for land due to demographic change, which is closely related to food production and consumption. However, due to the limitation of data, it is not possible to trace a detailed demographic profile of the entire Konbaung period. Yet, a certain amount of data is available for the period from the 1780s to the 1820s, when important socioeconomic changes were in progress.

The demographic trends in eighteenth- and nineteenth-century Burma were influenced by natural and socioeconomic conditions such as famine, wars, insecurity, and excessive demands of the Crown for taxes and public dues, as opposed to the ever-increasing population curve that began in the postcolonial period.

The most important source of information on population during the Konbaung period are reports called *sit-tan*s, which were submitted to the royal government by the local chiefs or the heads of *ahmudan* groups.[13] *Sit-tan*s covered a wide range of topics, including dates, names of respondents, ages, days of birth, genealogy of the chiefs, the extent and boundaries of their rule, agricultural land in the area, taxes and dues and their amounts, the existence of monastery estates, products and labor offered by people to the lord or officials, and the ceremonial privileges granted to the chiefs. A list of households living in the area under the jurisdiction of the chief was attached to each report and provides a valuable source of information on the population.

The oldest *sit-tan* is said to have been compiled in the early fourteenth century, but this *sit-tan* was lost completely.[14] In the Konbaung period, *sit-tan*s were implemented four times, in 1765, 1782/83, 1802, and 1826. Among them, the *sit-tan* of 1765 was almost lost except for the data of the Pagan region, but the other *sit-tan*s contain some useful information about population, even though there are lots of missing data. Since 1826, the tradition of the royal government implementing *sit-tan*s all over the country seems to have been abandoned.[15] This was a time when Burma fought against British invasion three times and was defeated in all wars, losing two coastal provinces, Arakan and Tenasserim, in 1826 and, in the next stage, losing the whole of Lower Burma and becoming a land-locked kingdom. In 1885, the Kingdom of Burma ceased to exist as a result of the defeat in the Third Anglo–Burmese War, and the whole country was annexed to British India as the Province of Burma. Any data on the population for this period have not yet been found.

King Bodawhpaya's *sit-tan* of 1145 B.E. (Burmese Era)—that is, 1782/83 A.D. —is said to be the most thoroughly implemented and provides us with reliable information.[16] However, the next *sit-tan* implemented by the same king in 1802 is only partially reliable, as many data on population in southern peripheral regions were simply a repetition of the figures of the previous *sit-tan*. It shows the declining authority of the royal government after the crushing defeat in the war against Siam in 1785, especially in the southern peripheral regions.

As for the population of the whole kingdom, H. Burney, an emissary of the British India Company stationed in Ava during 1830–40, obtained the *sit-tan* of the year 1145 B.E. (1783 A. D.) through an official of the court, and mixed it with other information to arrive at the following estimates. The number of households living in the broad plains of the Ayeyarwady and Sittaung river basins[17] was estimated at 295,967 and the total population was 2,280,000, of which 43% were of the *ahmudan* class and 57% were of the other class known as *athi*.[18] As for the population of the whole kingdom, Burney estimated that it had a population of 4,210,000 in 1783.

H. Burney used different sources for his estimations. For the main district of Burma he relied on the *sit-tan* of 1783 and then superimposed estimates of different years and sources for the rest of the country. However, we have not yet found any other estimation of the population for the end of eighteenth-century Burma. The *sit-tan*s of 1782/83 and 1802 have been examined in detail by W. Koenig, so we can use the results of his study to compare demographic changes during nearly two decades interspersed with the eighteenth and nineteenth centuries. As for the data of 1826, a few data collected and compiled by U Htun Yee are available. Estimated demographic changes over the years from 1783 to 1826 are shown in Tables 1.3, 1.4, and 1.5.

As the existing data of *sit-tan*s in 1783 and 1802 differ in their coverage, Koenig extracted and compared the areas included in both *sit-tan*s

26   Chapter 1

Table 1.2: H. Burney's estimate of the 1783 population

Region	Population	Source
Burma Proper	2,280,000	(Household nos. in 1783 *sit-tan* + 10%) x 7
Yey, Tavoy, Mergui	30,000	Census data in 1833 carried out by Mr. Maingy
Highland area	830,000	Estimation by J. Crawfurd
Shan States	1,070,000	1800 military conscription list
Total	4,210,000	

Source: Burney, 1941, pp. 19–32.
Notes: in Burma Proper's population estimates, Burney calculates household members per household as 7, and the population omitted from the *sit-tan* (i.e., ordained priests, domestic slaves, servants, pagoda slaves, and the fluid population combined) as 10% of the population. Regional divisions and placenames are based on the British administration. Burma Proper refers to Upper and Lower Burma in the Central Low Plain, excluding the surrounding mountainous areas and Arakan and Tenasserim. Tavoy and Mergui are now written as Dawei and Myeik, respectively.

to measure the demographic change. Table 1.3 is a reconstruction of the results, covering only the royal capital, north, northwest, central, and Prome areas, which cover the whole Upper Burma. The table does not cover the Taungoo, Ayeyarwady Delta, and Martaban regions because most of the population figures in these areas were just repetitions of the figures in the *sit-tan*s of 1783. Similarly, in the Prome area, we see the repetition of the same figures in seven regional units out of ten, and it makes the credibility of the population figure in Prome questionable. In the figures for other regions (i.e., the royal capital, the north and northwest, and the central region), about a quarter of the response units showed repetition of the same figures but, as a whole, the results of these regions are the most reliable in the *sit-tan* of 1802.

The population in the central region of Konbaung Burma, as seen in this table, shows a severe decline at the beginning of the nineteenth century compared to 1783. While the number of households increased only in the area surrounding the capital, the rest of the country experienced a continuous decline, notably in the north and northwestern regions (resulting in a loss of 38% of households), where the core of the kingdom's standing army, including the cavalry, was located as the main line of defense.

While the *sit-tan* of 1783 was carried out under the ambitious and energetic King Bodawhpaya, who had just ascended the throne and was determined not to allow any false reports from the provinces, the figures in the 1802 *sit-tan* seem to have been underreported not only in the peripheral

Climate, Demographic Changes, and Foreign Wars   27

Table 1.3: Number of households in 1783 and 1802 *sit-tan*s

Region	1783	1802	Increase or decrease (%)
Royal capital	20,075	22,428	12
North/Northwest	69,058	42,751	–38
Central	57,637	47,638	–17
Prome (Pyi)	30,189	28,786	–5
Total	176,959	141,603	–20

Source: Koenig, 1990, p. 59, Appendix 1, pp. 241–243.

Notes: the names of *myo*s in each region are as follows. Royal capital: Ava, Amarapura, Sagaing, Pinya. North/Northwest: Tabayin, Alon, Myedu, Amyin, Kanni, Mokshobo, Ngasingu, Htantabin, Pyinzala 5 Myo, other *myo*s. Central: Meiktila, Yindaw, Yamethin, Nyaunyan, Kyaukhse, Pindale, Pyinzi, Kyaukhsauk, Pin, Kyaukpadaun, Talok, Pagan, Salin, Pyinzi, Pahkangyi, Taundwingyi, Magwe, Myingun, other *myo*s. Prome: Sagu, Malun, Myede, Kama, Prome, Padaung, Kanaung, Legain, other *myo*s.

areas, but also in the central areas, reflecting the weakening of prestige and administrative capacities of the monarchy. However, this is not enough to explain the severe decline in population. As we will see later, the repeated defeats of the Siamese expeditions at the end of the eighteenth century and the endless mobilization of labor to build the world's largest pagoda in Mingun, which began in 1790 and continued to the 1810s, are thought to have contributed to this situation.[19] According to Toe Hla, the year 1800 was a year of fire, floods, and other disasters that caused many villages to be abandoned.[20] In addition, during the early 1810s, whole Upper Burma regions were devastated because of a prolonged and severe famine. We can safely assume that the population of Upper Burma in the 1810s had declined considerably compared to that of 1802.

The *sit-tan* in 1826, which was carried out by King Bagyidaw (r. 1819–37), was accommodated in a collection of various tables of the Konbaung period compiled by Htun Yee. However, this was not the original *sit-tan*, but a record, probably a memorandum, of a court official.[21]

If we compare the total number of households of 295,967 in 1783 (Burney's estimate) with the figure of 301,963 in 1826 (Htun Yee's estimate), we can see an increase in the number of households of about 2% for the period. This shows that the population recovered in 1826 to a level slightly over the level of 1783. As noted before, from 1783 to 1802, there was a sharp decline in the number of households, estimated at a loss of 17% in the core area of the kingdom (i.e., the central plains). In 1810–12, another crisis

28   Chapter 1

Table 1.4: Household numbers in each administrative unit in 1826

Myo (145)	Athi	150,690
	Ahmudan	107,300
Taik (12)	Athi	11,384
	Ahmudan	6,665
Cavalry (5)	Athi	7,922
	Ahmudan	3,143
Special Tax Unit	Athi	0
	Ahmudan	14,859
Total		301,963

Source: Htun Yee, 2003, vol. 1, pp. 27–29, 115–118.
Notes: *myo:* a district comprising a main town and small towns and many villages. *Taik:* an administrative unit comprising a number of villages. Special Tax Unit: a unit comprising *ahmudans* working in gold and silver mining.

Table 1.5: Comparison of 1783, 1802, and 1826 *sit-tans* (household numbers)

1783		1802		1826	
145 *myos*	228,533	141 *myo*	178,806	145 *myo*	257,990
12 *taik*	43,506		–	12 *taik*	18,049
6 departments	23,926		–	5 cavalry	11,065
				Special Tax Unit	14,859
Total	295,967		178,806		301,963

Source: Htun Yee, 2003. Koenig, 1990, p. 110.

hit the central plains—namely, the worst famine in the history of Burma. Although we have no demographic records for this period, a few written verses depicted the dismal state, such as numerous abandoned villages and countless deaths from starvation. It is certain that the famine caused another sharp decline in population. From the late 1810s to the mid-1820s, there is no record of any major famine, and the population seems to have recovered gradually.

The ratio of *ahmudan* to *athi* in 1826, based on Table 1.4, was 44:56, which is very close to the 43:57 estimated by Burney for 1783; since the decline in the *ahmudan* population was greater than that of *athi* in 1803, it is likely that the reinforcement of the *ahmudan* population was promoted during the period.[22]

Even with this rough sketch, it is clear that the population of the Konbaung period did not show a stable trend of growth but, rather, a large range of short-term fluctuations. Therefore, the conditions for farmlands to become scarce goods and flow as economic resources were not simply due to an increase in population pressure over time. Rather, natural and social disasters such as famines, fires, foreign wars, and social disruptions seem to have played a major role, as discussed below.

Threats in the arid areas—famine and fire

M. Aung-Thwin's work on the precolonial Burmese irrigation systems is useful for learning about the old irrigation works, but his conclusion that the production capacity of rice in Upper Burma was not only substantial but also stable, even without depending on rice from Lower Burma, might leave room for reconsideration.[23]

It is true that if the irrigation networks had been well maintained and the rains had been normal, the shortage of staple crops would not have occurred in Upper Burma regions. In addition, even if the harvest was insufficient in Upper Burma and if the rice from Lower Burma had been brought in without delay, as a tax in kind or as a commodity for sale, there would not have been a serious situation. However, it should be noted that severe rice shortages and famines had struck Upper Burmese societies on several occasions during the Konbaung period, although the frequency was not high. Famine has never been a big issue in Burmese historical studies, and is not given much weight as a factor that moves the history. According to V. Lieberman, there were repeated shortages of food and one or two severe famines in Burma during the Taungoo period (1580–1635 A.D.). At the end of the second Taungoo period (1741–43), he pointed out that the famine was so prolonged that people scavenged for dogs and even human flesh.[24]

What was the situation during the Konbaung period? Even in its founding period, the conquest of Lower Burma by King Alaunghpaya caused a great number of Mon to flee to the Siam side and, as a result, the total grain production in Burma was considerably reduced. During the expeditions to Manipur in 1758 and to Ayuttaya in 1758, it was reported that many people who sent their sons or husbands to the expeditions became heavily indebted to sustain their lives.[25] However, the word 'famine' is not used to depict the situation in this period. During the great famine that occurred throughout central Burma in the early 1810s, drought-driven exiles, including those in the granary belts with irrigation networks, wandered the countryside and abandoned the villages, where dead bodies

30   Chapter 1

filled fields and roads. The prolonged famine increased the amount of debt both with human mortgage and farmland mortgage, and became the starting point for a massive liquidation of farmland; in some regions, village chiefs pledged entire villages as collateral to borrow money. Stories of this famine have been passed down generation to generation and it is remembered as the worst famine in the history of Burma.[26]

In 1826, there was another famine in central Burma. However, this was not mainly due to drought, but to the mobilization of a large number of adult males for military service at the outbreak of the First Anglo-Burmese War (1824–26). After the defeat in the Second Anglo-Burmese War (1852), the whole Lower Burma was annexed to British India and the number of famines and severe rice shortages increased noticeably. In 1864 and again in 1866, the country suffered severe food shortages.[27] In addition to the drought, the difficulty in purchasing rice in Lower Burma by the royal government resulted in the rapid flow of immigrants from the kingdom of Upper Burma southward to British Burma. M. Adas also cited these famines in Upper Burma as one of the main causes of immigration.[28]

Famine was caused not only by weather conditions such as drought, as we have seen above, but also by social conditions such as the reduction of cultivators due to the military conscription and the abandonment of cultivation, as well as maintenance of irrigation facilities during the breakdown of social order. The premise that rice shortages in the central regions would not lead to major famine, if the social order was maintained and rice could be transported from surplus regions, was often violated and the balance was lost; the great famine of the early 1810s was also caused by prolonged drought, as well as foreign wars with Arakan and Siam and, in addition, popular exhaustion caused by mobilization for public works projects such as the construction of the Gigantic Pagoda in Mingun.

The natural conditions of the semi-arid land posed another major threat to society, namely fire. Houses, whether in the palace or in the village, were basically built of wood, bamboo, thatch, and other flammable materials, and they were also built in dense clusters in the royal palace, in the commercial and residential areas of the capital, and even in the residential areas of the villages, so that once a fire broke out, a combination of strong winds and dryness could cause a major fire. The danger of fires to the socio-economy was well recognized by the administrators, and fire prevention was an important duty for both officials and the public. King

Alaunghpaya, the founder of the Konbaung dynasty, issued a royal edict urging the public not to be negligent in preparing against fires, and also set out detailed rules on fire prevention measures.[29] In January and February, when the weather is extremely dry and strong winds blow, the royal edict often urged people to be prepared for fire.[30]

There are many records of fire in the royal chronicles as follows. In February 1788, a fire broke out in the palace guardhouse and spread over the whole of the capital.[31] In March 1810, a fire in the royal palace spread to the residences of the royal family and courtiers and destroyed many temples and pagodas.[32] In February 1856, a fire on the western outskirts of the capital destroyed more than 2,000 houses.[33] On April 15, 1866, a fire on the west side of the capital destroyed more than 3,800 houses, including the moat fence of the royal palace, the marketplace, the quarter for officials and wealthy people, the quarter for pottery makers and ironsmiths, the quarter for rice shops and bamboo stores, and so on.[34] On March 25, 1885, a fire broke out on the northeast side of the capital, destroying more than 3,800 houses. The fire became huge and destroyed a number of monasteries, the southwest approach to Mandalay Hill, and the buildings on the summit.[35]

As for government relief measures, there are a few examples. In 1788, after the fire in the capital area, the government distributed two baskets of paddy, pots and pans, and water jars for fire prevention to the affected households from the royal treasury. In 1810, after a big fire, the paddy left over in the half-damaged royal granary was distributed to victims.[36]

Ministers and courtiers were obliged to come straight to the palace when a fire broke out in the capital, and if anyone failed to do so, he was subjected to severe physical punishment.[37] As the royal capital was located in a particularly arid area of the region, fire was a serious threat to the government, and it is evident that every precaution was taken to avoid a serious financial crisis.

The years of the major fires, as confirmed by the royal edicts and chronicles, almost always coincided with the onset of famine and severe rice shortages. Under the conditions of well-functioning government and with no shortage of grain, a major fire, even the largest, would not be enough to shake a society. In villages where fires occurred, it was not so difficult to rebuild the inhabitants' simple dwellings, which were made of wood, bamboo, and thatch, and recovery was relatively easy and quick. But when other crises struck in combination, such as drought, disruption of

32   Chapter 1

social order, or depletion or exhaustion of the labor force, a big fire could be a devastating blow to the society and also to the kingdom.

Changes in external relations and their impacts

Trends in foreign wars and their impacts

The Konbaung period began amidst warfare. The Hanthawady Mon Kingdom in Pegu in Lower Burma had been destroyed by King Tabinshwehti, founder of the Taungoo dynasty, and was rebuilt in 1740 and quickly expanded its sphere of influence. When the Mon forces attacked Upper Burma in 1752, the second Taungoo dynasty, being weakened by the civil wars and revolts, was overthrown after the capture of the royal capital Ava. However, not long afterwards, Aung Zeya, the local chieftain of Shwebo, declared himself as King Alaunghpaya (Future Buddha), and rallied the surrounding forces and regained Ava in 1754 from the hands of the Mon. Furthermore, he marched to Lower Burma against the Hanthawady Mon and destroyed the Mon kingdom and brought Lower Burma under his control.

There were 25 major foreign wars during the Konbaung period, as shown in Table 1.6, until the fall of the kingdom in 1885. The scale and consequences of these wars had a significant impact on the economy of the Kingdom of Burma, and also on the number of debt contracts because wars affected the livelihoods of people in no small way. Looking at the foreign wars, there were four major phases during the Konbaung period.

The first phase was the period from 1752 to 1784, from the time of Alaunghpaya's accession to the annexation of the Arakan Kingdom by King Bodawhpaya. In this period, there were 13 foreign wars and expeditions, which accounted for more than 50% of all the wars during the Konbaung period. With the exception of the Ayutthaya expedition in 1759, which was interrupted by the accidental death of King Alaunghpaya during the expedition, Burma won all other wars.[38]

As a result of the successful campaign against Manipur in 1758–59, Manipur had to promise to send Burma 10 *viss* (16.3 kg) of gold, 100 horses, 5,000 bows with poisoned arrowheads, and 1,000 *viss* of dye resin every year, and in the event of a Burmese military campaign, to send 1,000 cavalrymen and 1,000 archers to work under the Burmese commanders.[39] The number of war captives taken from Manipur, Assam, and Cachar[40] is

Climate, Demographic Changes, and Foreign Wars   33

Table 1.6: Major wars in the Konbaung era (1752–1885)

The first phase (from the coronation of Alaunghpaya to war against Arakan)

1752–57	War against the Mon force Recapture of Ava, pacification of Lower Burma Established the third Burman Empire
Nov. 1758	Expedition to Manipur, annexation of Manipur (January 1759)
Jan. 1759	Ayutthaya expedition, Alaunghpaya's death on the way
Mar. 1762	Chiang Mai expedition
Oct. 1764	Expedition to Northern Shan and Vientiane
Nov. 1764	Ayutthaya expedition, the fall of Ayutthaya (April 1767)
Jan. 1765	Manipur expedition
Mar. 1765	Vientiane expedition
1765–69	Repeated invasion to northeast Shan Plateau by Chinese army
Feb. 1772	Siam expedition
Mar. 1772	Vientiane expedition
Nov. 1774	Siam expedition
Oct.–Dec. 1784	Arakan expedition, annexed Arakan to Burma

The second phase (from the defeat in war against Siam to the First Anglo-Burmese War)

Sep. 1785	Siam expedition
Sep. 1786	Crushing defeat in the war against Siam
Aug. 1787	Chiang Mai expedition resulted in failure
Mar. 1792	Taking back Dawe from Siam
Nov. 1797	Chiang Mai expedition resulted in another failure
Feb. 1814	Expedition to Manipur
1818–19	Expedition to Manipur
Feb. 1822	Expedition to Assam
Jul.–Sep. 1823	Conflict against the British over an island in border area
Feb. 1824	Expedition to Cachar

The third phase (from the First Anglo-Burmese War ~)

Mar. 1824	The First Anglo-Burmese War
Feb. 1826	Yandabo Treaty: cession of Arakan and Tenasserim A large indemnity (10,000,000 rupees) Yield of the suzerainty over Manipur and Assam

The fourth phase from the Second Anglo-Burmese War to the fall of kingdom

1852	The Second Anglo-Burmese War, Burma lost Lower Burma
1885	The Third Anglo-Burmese War, the fall of Konbaung dynasty Annexation of Burma

34   Chapter 1

unknown, but many of them were incorporated into the king's military *ahmudan* groups, especially as cavalry *ahmudan*s, and formed the core of the royal cavalry. Other war captives also organized into non-military *ahmudan* groups and worked as silversmiths, gunsmiths, and silk weavers according to their skills.[41] In the vicinity of the royal capital, some were sent to serve in the residences of royalty and dignitaries as house slaves,[42] while others were engaged in agriculture, fruit growing, and mining, especially in ruby and lead mines in the Shan highlands.

The battle of 1764–67, at which Ayutthaya was destroyed by the forces of King Hsinbyushin (r. 1763–76), was a large-scale military operation that involved the construction of 24 solid brick fortifications surrounding the capital city of Ayutthaya.[43] Ayutthaya was finally burned to ashes in 1767 and many people, including the royal family, were brought to Burma as war captives. However, regarding the number of Thai people taken away to Burma, there remains a big gap between Burmese and Thai records. In the Burmese documents, Letwe Nawyahta, who was a court official and court poet of the same period, mentioned that 106,100 households were taken to Burma as war prisoners.[44] On the other hand, Thai history books mention that the number of people taken away was much smaller. For example, Prince Damrong's *Our Wars with the Burmese* records the number at just over 30,000.[45]

Many Thai people who were taken away were given irrigated farmland, mainly in Kyaukse, and settled there. The abduction of war captives was not only for the accommodation of additional population, but also for the transfer of culture and technology in various fields such as performing arts, military skills, and craftsmanship.

During the Arakan expedition of 1784 under the reign of Bodawhpaya, it is said that the Burmese army led by the Crown Prince destroyed the then independent kingdom of Arakan and took away more than 20,000 war captives to Upper Burma.[46] The gigantic Buddha statue called Mahamuni, now set in the Arakan Pagoda in Mandalay, was also one of the war trophies of that expedition.

The second phase was from the defeat in the war against Siam in 1785 to the outbreak of the First Anglo-Burmese War in 1824. In 1785, Bodawhpaya prepared a large army and attacked Siam from three different routes, but the result was the crushing defeat which Burma experienced for the first time in wars against Siam. Nevertheless, Burma repeated expedition to Siam in 1786, 1787, and 1797 on a much smaller scale, and failed in all campaigns except one, when the Siam-occupied Tavoy region was won back in 1792. With these consequences, the expansionist policy of the Burmese kingdom to the east came to an end.[47] However, the king sent expeditions to Manipur, Assam, and Cachar in 1818–19, 1822, and 1824, respectively, and maintained some influence in East India.

There is no doubt that these nearly four decades of foreign warfare had serious negative consequences in economic terms, both for the kingdom's ruling class and for the common people. An exact figure on the number of soldiers lost in the wars against Siam is not available, but it is roughly estimated that more than 100,000 men were sent to Siam and between one-third and one-half of them were lost or disappeared.

Of the debt contracts in two databases—microfilms in 114 volumes held by the Kagoshima University Burma Research Mission (KUMF) and the Documents of Myanmar Socio-Economic History, Aichi University, Volumes 1–11 (DMSEH)—there are 2,242 debt contracts available for the study of the chronological distribution of debt contracts, if we exclude the duplicated contracts and those whose dates are not legible due to damage, as shown in Figure. 1.3. It is noteworthy that the number of debt contracts in the period before 1785 was quite small, but after 1785 the number had increased rapidly. Even if we consider that older manuscripts are less likely to have survived, the rapid increase of debt contracts after 1785 shows the strong impact of foreign wars, especially the devastating defeat in the war against Siam in 1785.

The third phase was the period from the First Anglo-Burmese War in 1824 to the Second Anglo-Burmese War in 1852. The Treaty of Yandabo, signed after the defeat in the first war, included the cessation of two coastal provinces of Arakan and Tenasserim to the British, the renunciation of suzerainty over Assam, Cachar, and Manipur (which Burma had exercised), and the payment of 10 million rupees as war reparations. The Burmese royal government, suffering from financial depletion, collected temporary silver taxes, as well as gold and jewelry from a wide range of provinces to fund the reparation.[48] This tax burden also caused a large number of people to go into debt, and in the five years following the Treaty of Yandabo, from 1826 to 1830, the number of debt contracts more than doubled compared to the previous five years.

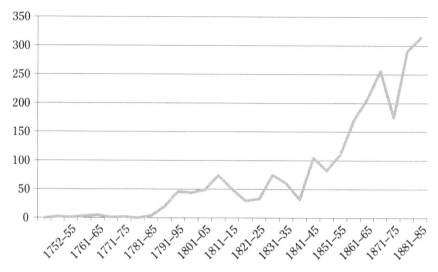

Figure 1.3: Trends in the number of debt contracts (1752–1885)
Sources: 2,242 debt contracts in DMSEH and KUMF.
Note: duplicated contracts and contracts without a date are excluded.

The last phase ran from the Second Anglo-Burmese War of 1852, which resulted in the loss of Lower Burma, to the end of the Third Anglo-Burmese War, when the whole country was annexed to British India. As we will discuss later, the loss of Lower Burma was nothing less than the loss of the vital part of the resource cycle within the kingdom. The rapid increase in the number of debt contracts after 1852, when Lower Burma was lost, is also remarkable, as can be seen in Figure. 1.3.

Thus, the Konbaung dynasty made frequent expeditions to its eastern and western neighbors in the period from its foundation to 1785, and succeeded in getting annual tributes or bringing back large numbers of war captives, arms, ammunition, and precious metals. Many war captives were organized as soldiers or by virtue of their skills into the *ahmudan* organization of the Kingdom of Burma. The best irrigated land was given to them generously because the settlement of war captives was of such importance to the monarchy.

However, after 1785, when Burma was defeated in the war against Siam, the avenues for procuring labor, arms, and treasures from neighboring territories in the east, including Chiang Mai and Vientiane, were closed. The influence over Manipur, Assam, and Cachar, which Burma continued

Climate, Demographic Changes, and Foreign Wars   37

to retain, was decisively lost with the Treaty of Yandabo after defeat in the First Anglo-Burmese War.

Foreign war was a hindrance to the livelihoods of mobilized soldiers and their families, even in the case of victorious war. Soldiers were required to prepare their weapons and rations by themselves, and not a few recruits had to borrow money for that purpose. In the case of a defeated war or when responsibility for war reparations fell directly on the inhabitants, it was inevitable that the debt would spread and become more serious.

The reversal of the balance of power in the foreign wars also forced changes in the way resources were procured and in the fiscal policy of the royal government.

Changes in economic cycles

Among the economic activities of the Konbaung period, agriculture, especially the production of rice, was regarded as the most important. Recognizing that securing rice was the key to the kingdom's stability, the royal government placed the maintenance of large-scale irrigation systems under its own direct control and encouraged the settlement of war captives and the migration of hill tribes to the central plains in order to ensure rice production capacity, while banning the export of rice to other countries. The royal government maintained a monopoly on trade in timber, precious stones, crude oil, rice, gold and silver, and women, but among these the most severe restrictions were imposed on the exportation of gold and silver, women who bore children, and rice.[49]

However, it is not appropriate to view Konbaung Burma as an inland agricultural country. The prominent Burmese economist U Tun Wai pointed out long ago that, compared to the colonial period, when rice production and export came to dominate the economic structure, the weight of commerce and cottage industries was not so small in the whole economy.[50] During the Konbaung period, in addition to rice production for subsistence use, cash crop production for the outside markets was also increasing rapidly. A striking example was the expansion of cotton cultivation for the Chinese market. Exports of Burmese cotton had begun in the sixteenth century during the Taungoo period,[51] but in the eighteenth and nineteenth centuries—when the demand for raw cotton in China was growing rapidly due to increasing demand for cotton textiles and the rise of the cotton industry for export—the number of merchants who came

38   Chapter 1

Table 1.7: Permanent markets and market tax per year (in *kyat*s)

Market	Market tax	Market	Market tax
1. Zaygyodaw	3,600	17. Sathaw	600
2. Nandawshei	1,800	18. Taunggyi	1,200
3. Ywahaing	1,200	19. Amarapura Zaygyo	300
4. Yodaya	1,200	20. Kandwin Zaykun	360
5. Kan U	628.8	21. Dagundaing	1,080
6. Sishe	1,999.2	22. Shwekyawpauk	240
7. Malun	3,000	23. Leitankunzay	1,240
8. Zaygale	300	24. Lettiya	300
9. Seinban	360	25. Ava-myo-dadau	1,200
10. Lehdin	360	26. Zaygyo	720
11. Mingala	960	27. Nandawshei	496
12. Mathe	60	28. Nyaungbin (Sagaing)	180
13. Okbo	120	29. Moza	600
14. Nyaunbin	600	30. Dawei	600
15. Thaye	996	31. Paleik	960
16. Miba	120		
Total market tax			27,340

Source: Htun Yee, 2003, Vol. IV, pp. 320–323.
Note: it is not clear what year the record is for. There are two markets of the same name (Nandawshei), but it is unclear whether they are the same market or two markets of the same name in different regions. There is a discrepancy in the total market tax amount, but it is noted as it appears in the original source.

down via the Yunnan route was growing. Through village chiefs and agents, Chinese merchants paid farmers in advance to encourage them to cultivate cotton. Thus, in the first half of the nineteenth century, cotton cultivation expanded rapidly in wide areas from Pyi to Sagaing.

Next, let us look into the commercial sector. Table 1.7 shows a list of 31 major markets and market taxes in the kingdom during the Konbaung period, the size of which can be estimated from the amount of market taxes paid. The largest permanent market was Zaygyodaw, the central market of the royal capital, followed by Malun, located on the west bank of the Ayeyarwady, south of Minbu, which was notable for paying the second-largest amount of market tax. However, Malun declined rapidly during the colonial period when its function as a landing place was taken over by the east bank of the river. Up to that time, it was a busy trading center for the products of Upper and Lower Burma. Market taxes were also sent to the capital from Taungyi in the eastern part of the Shan Plateau and from the city of Tavoy in Martaban Bay at the base of the Malay Peninsula. It can be assumed that a permanent market was opened at the interface between the densely populated areas around the capital and the zones with different climates and ecosystems, or at the ports on the sea and rivers, where a variety of products were traded.

In addition to the permanent markets, there were also periodic fairs at the border of the mountainous area and the plains, or at key transport hubs, and pagoda bazaars opened annually at the time of pagoda festivals, where people could buy and sell all kinds of daily necessities. In the late Konbaung period, there were 98 pagodas in Upper Burma and Shan State, where the royal government collected taxes on stalls, and the revenue from pagoda festivals amounted to nearly 16,000 *kyat*s a year.[52]

As we saw earlier, interregional trade within the kingdom of Konbaung was an essential component of the eighteenth- and nineteenth-century Burmese economy and society. The three different climate regions—the central savanna plains, the tropical rainforest at the southern exit to the sea, and the mountains and highlands surrounding the central plains—each produced their own specialties. This was also a time when these products became essential necessities, even in the daily life of people. Salt, dried fish, and fish sauce came from Lower Burma, while tea and paper came from the Shan regions. Palm sugar, beans, barley, petroleum, lacquer wear, silk textile, and cotton were produced in Upper Burma. Numerous boats and rafts loaded with these commodities sailed up and down the Ayeyarwady River, which runs north–south through Burma. The Ayeyarwady and its tributaries were the backbone of the transportation system from the mountains to the plains, as well as from Upper Burma to Lower Burma.

It was also during the reign of Bodawhpaya in the late eighteenth and early nineteenth centuries that the fiscal policy of the royal government changed noticeably. This was probably due to the fact that the old practice of supplementing labor and seizing precious metals, treasures, and arms and ammunition through foreign wars had become almost impossible with the defeat of the war against Siam at the end of the eighteenth century. Instead, the idea emerged that revenue from trading activities would be one of the main sources of financial income. Of course, this was not a free trade policy, but rather a policy within the tradition of royal

40   Chapter 1

monopoly over the trade. Competitive bidding for monopoly rights to various commodities, among other things, had been actively adopted since the reign of King Bodawhpaya. In many countries in Southeast Asia, the system of tax farming was introduced with the migration of Chinese merchants in the early nineteenth century, and Burma was no exception. Decrees on the granting of monopoly rights began to be issued one after another. The king also issued a large number of trading charters to the large and small trading boats on the Ayeyarwady River, on condition that a certain number of guns were delivered to the royal government each year.[53] Not only merchants but also officials and military officers of all kinds applied for the licenses, but some surrendered their licenses on the grounds that they were unsuccessful in their business or unable to deliver their guns.[54]

Competition among merchants for the monopoly rights was fierce, as shown in the following example.

> By 1810, Nga Shwei Pu was the sole dealer of cooking oil in the capital. He paid 150 *kyat* of weight of gold a year for this monopoly right. However, he was beaten in 1812 by another merchant who bought this monopoly right by paying 220 *kyat* weight of gold and 220 *viss* of cooking oil to the government per annum. Paddy, varieties of peas, and Indian millet were in 1810 monopolized by two merchants, Nga Shwei Pu and Nga Shwei Kyaw. For this privilege, they paid the government 1,200 *kyat* weight of silver plus 2,160 baskets of unhusked rice a year. But, when they were contested by other merchants, they raised their payment up to 4,500 *kyat* weight of silver for the year 1811 in order not to lose the privilege.[55]

In the later period, foreign merchants and trading companies were prominent in the competition for monopoly rights. The British merchant Henry Gouger obtained a teak concession from King Bagyidaw (r. 1819–37) to cut 1,400 tons of teak for export to Bombay, Java, and Calcutta. One of the most active merchants in the mid-1860s was Moola Ibrahim, an Indian merchant, who had commercial rights in teakwood, oil, cotton, and sesame, as well as the rights to manage the king's steamships and to handle customs duties.[56] In the reigns of King Mindon and King Thibaw, the Bombay-Burma Trading Corporation, Steel Brothers & Company,

McGregor Co., Forker Company, T. D. Findley and Sons Co., and others contested fiercely for teak logging rights. In 1862, the Bombay-Burma Trading Corporation won the rights to cut teak from Ningyang and other timber from all over Upper Burma.[57] In 1880, the company succeeded in getting the rights to cut teak from Chindwin and the Mu River Basin, obtained logging concessions in the Yaw region, and took control of the teak-growing heartland of Upper Burma.[58] Some Burmese merchants were also very active in the battle for teak logging concessions. In 1881, U Mon Thaw and his brother Nga Pauk were granted teak logging concessions in several forests by King Thibaw at the price of 100,000 rupees per year. However, the following year, U Bo Hnin and his son Nga Bo Hmyin joined the auction and offered to pay 250,000 rupees for the concessions. U Mon Thaw and his brother won this competition by offering 500,000 rupees.[59]

As for tax farming, the tax collection rights were often sold to high-ranking officials linked to the royal family, but there were also cases where Chinese merchants won tax farming rights in the upstream regions of the Ayeyarwady and the Chindwin River valley.[60] Compared to the Siamese kingdom, however, Chinese participation in tax farming was very limited.

Foreign trade

During the Konbaung period, there were two main forms of foreign trade: maritime foreign trade via the Yangon port and overland foreign trade with China through Yunnan. When the Konbaung dynasty was established, Pegu, the former Mon capital, was devastated by the Burmese army and also heavy silt had closed it off from the sea. Syliam, the international trading port of the Taungoo period, was in the same situation. Yangon was renamed by Alaunghpaya from the old name of Dagon in 1755, and chosen as the new trading port along with Pathein (Bassein) in the southwest of the delta. By the early nineteenth century, Yangon had become the largest trading port, and foreign traders of various races and ethnicities, including Muslim and Moor traders from India, Parsees (Zoroastrians), Armenians, Persians, and a few English, French, and Portuguese traders, were seen in the town.[61] The port of Yangon became linked by trade with ports in Chittagong, Dacca, Calcutta, Madras, Muslipatam, the Nicobar Islands, Penang, Bombay, and the Persian and Arabian Gulf. According to J. Crawfurd, who was sent to Burma by the British East India Company, the number of square-rigged vessels cleared out of Yangon port was 18–25

42   Chapter 1

before 1811, but increased to an average of 40 during 1817–22, and the number for the year 1822 was 56, when the value of imports and exports were both estimated at £300,000.[62] Burma exported teakwood, catechu, lac, beeswax, raw cotton, ivory, gold and silver, rubies, sapphires, and horses. In return, Burma imported Indian and British cotton piece goods, and British wool fabric, iron, steel, mercury, copper, copper cordage, borax, sulfur, gunpowder, nitrate, firearms, coarse porcelain, English glassware, opium, tobacco, cocoa, areca nuts, sugar, and spirits. In other words, the Kingdom of Burma exported wood, dyes, and other forest products, precious metals, jewelry, raw cotton, and other raw materials, while importing industrial products such as textiles, sundries and processed foods, arms, and gunpowder.

H. Malcolm described Yangon at the end of the 1830s as a city of bamboo huts,[63] and foreigners who visited Yangon for the first time shared the impression of Yangon as a shabby city, except for the majesty of the golden Shwedagon Pagoda on the hilltop.

British merchants and the East India Company repeatedly criticized Burmese royal government trade policies, such as bans on the export of rice and precious metals, high port charges, high tariffs, and the gift-giving practices demanded of foreign merchants and captains, as the greatest impediment to trade. The East India Company later realized a reduction of tariffs and the abolition of the royal monopoly through several rounds of trade negotiations.

Indeed, in the early days of Konbaung, it was customary for foreign ships to pay a port entry tax of 10–500 *kyat*s depending on their tonnage when they entered a port. Custom dues on imports were 10% in kind for the king and 2% for custom officials. During the reign of King Bodawhpaya, who was sensitive to trade interests, port charges and custom dues were reduced to 5% and 1%, respectively, but after the First Anglo-Burmese War (1824–26), successive kings raised custom dues and this caused a certain decline in trade, as free ports in Southeast Asia (such as Singapore, which was occupied in 1819 by the British) had already emerged. Regulations and tariff policies were certainly factors in the stagnation of Yangon's trade volume.

However, a more fundamental reason why sea trade did not make much progress was the relatively low necessity for the Burmese economy in the early and middle Konbaung period to seek foreign goods by maritime trade. The successive royal governments certainly had a strong interest in foreign modern arms, ammunition, and nitrate, which were directly related to military power, and they tried very hard to obtain them, but the British, who were anxious about the military build-up of the Burmese kingdom, prevented the import of arms and ammunition by all means.[64]

Burma had an economic structure in which almost all necessities could be provided for under conditions of unhindered circulation of the products within the territories under the direct or indirect control of the central government. Even the materials for casting monies, gold, silver, copper, lead, and tin all came from within the kingdom, although most of the mines located in the mountainous areas of the Shan Plateau and in areas far from the central plains, such as Tenasserim, were not always under the control of the royal government. When the main raw materials for metal coins were in short supply within the kingdom, gold, silver, and copper were sought mainly from Yunnan and from India.

This situation was shaken up and the self-sufficiency within the kingdom was broken by the loss of Lower Burma in 1852 due to the defeat in the Second Anglo-Burmese War. As a result, the Kingdom of Burma lost its outlet to the sea, and trade by sea was disrupted, but a more serious blow was the loss of the traditional structure of the kingdom's ability to provide for its needs within the kingdom. Table 1.8 shows the items imported from British Lower Burma and their value in Thayetmyo, where customs clearance was placed as a trading point between the kingdom and British Burma. The import value of Lower Burma products was 2,608,028 rupees, which was about six times higher than the import value of tax-free foreign products. The total import value of rice was 1,045,000 rupees, followed by *ngapi*,[65] an essential condiments of the Burmese diet, at 939,000 rupees, and dried fish and salt. All of these were necessities that had traditionally depended on Lower Burma.

On the other hand, the value of exports from the kingdom to British Burma, which also passed through Thayetmyo, was recorded as only 992,259 rupees for the nine months from February to November 1855. Although this is a nine-month figure, if compared to total imports by the kingdom in the year 1854/55, it shows a significant trade deficit in the kingdom.[66] Exports at that time to British Burma included edible oil, palm sugar, silk and velvet from China, teak wood, dyes, and so on, similar to the traditional pattern of foreign trade through the Yangon port.

44   Chapter 1

Table 1.8: Imports from British Lower Burma, 1854~55 (1 year)

At Thayetmyo custom

Article	Weight (tons)	Price (rupees)	Duty levied (%)
Nga Pyi	13,502	939,707	6.2
Paddy	43,000	594,124	9.0
Rice	18,600	451,278	10.1
Dried fish	1,734	297,578	4.0
Salt	7,189	206,091	25.1
Betel nut	716	118,925	7.3
Fish eggs		190	4.2
Leeches		135	3.3
Total		2,608,028	230,053

Tax-free item

Cotton product and yarn		227,539	0
Silk product		76,335	0
Woolen product		27,666	0
Cigar, tobacco		20,588	0
Porcelain		20,511	0
Medicine		10,612	0
Hardware		5,090	0
Glassware		2,844	0
Cacao, die, gold leaf, paper		3,102	0
Miscellaneous		17,593	0
Total		411,885	

Source: Yule, 1968, p. 362.
Note: the total sum of tax-free items in the original text is thought to be incorrect.

Sea trade in the period before the loss of all the coastal regions would have been of keen interest to the Burmese royal government if it had provided a steady supply of modern arms and ammunition; otherwise, there was no reason to be proactive. The most important route for the foreign trade of Konbaung Burma was the trade route from the royal capital to the north by boat or raft along the Ayeyarwady, and then to the mountainous basin of Bhamo, where the goods were transshipped on horses or donkeys and passed to Yunnan. This was called the 'Road of Ambassadors' because it was used for the passage of tribute and gift envoys to and from China, and Burmese envoys went from the royal capital to Bhamo, and then overland to Tengchong, Dali, Yunnan Province, and Beijing, and Chinese envoys came down on the same route in the reverse direction.[67] In addition, there were other trade routes used by Chinese Muslim traders known in Burma as Panthay, who organized caravans and carried goods from basin to basin around Yunnan, northern Thai, and the Shan Plateau. Among them, the route from Tengchong to the west bank of the Ur River, where jade deposits had been excavated since early times,[68] or the route along the Xueli River from Tengchong to Namtu, where many Chinese Islamic miners came to work in the silver mine in the seventeenth century,[69] are noteworthy. These silver mines, or Chinese demand for jade, factored in encouraging trade with Burma, but even more important was cotton.

A large town called Ta-Ming-gye (Great Ming Town, the Burmese name is Bhamo) appeared near the border as a transit point for trade, and merchants from Fujian, Guangdong, Jiangxi, Sichuan, Yunnan, and other provinces thrived in this area.[70] In the seventeenth century, cotton was already a major export from Burma, and large quantities of silk thread and copper coins were brought in from China. The Dutch East India Company, which entered Burma from 1634 to 1680, began to buy Chinese copper coins in large quantities, which were transported by the company to the east coast of India, Ceylon, and Java.[71] The Burmese merchants also bought large amounts of Chinese copper coins to make Ganza, the main currency in the Taungoo period.

During the reign of King Hsinbyushin, China–Burma border trade was often disrupted by the repeated invasion of the Chinese army. However, during the reign of King Bodawhpaya, trade was reopened and thousands of Chinese merchants came to Amarapura, the royal capital, and settled there. Cotton was still the largest export from Burma, but, in addition, amber, ivory, jewelry, swallow's nests, antler, and betel nut imported from Penang were exported to China. Imported goods from China included silk, velvet, gold leaf, jam, paper, and metal household goods.[72] Gold, silver, and copper, which could be used as numismatic material, did not flow only in one direction between China (Yunnan) and Burma, but moved in both directions. Outflows of bullion were often subject to embargoes by the central governments on both sides, but the embargoes were not always complied with in Yunnan, a remote province from the center. Furthermore, if gold was processed into gold leaf, and silver and copper into household utensils and ornaments, the transfer of these products did not cause any problems.

H. Yule, who accompanied A. Phayre, the Commissioner of Pegu,[73] in 1855 to the royal capital to gather comprehensive information on the Kingdom of Burma, estimated that the kingdom's trade with China in the 1850s consisted of an annual export value of £225,000, 95% of which was cotton, and an import value of £187,500, of which 64% was silk.[74]

Later, the border trade routes were often closed due to attacks by the Qing dynasty on the Islamic regime established in Dali in 1856, and the confusion it caused. The overland trade with China, even if influenced by the political turmoil in the border areas, was indispensable in compensating for the shortage of money and materials in the Kingdom of Burma when the supply of money and materials was tight. Cotton cultivation for export spread widely throughout the semi-arid areas of central Burma by the advanced payment system which the Chinese merchants introduced. It played a major role in the penetration of cash crop cultivation and money into the villages.

Compared to the maritime foreign trade, the overland trade with China had a significant influence on structural changes in Burma's socio-economy, although trade with China was haunted by the instability caused by the political situation in the borderlands. The migration of Chinese merchants to the royal capital and their activities promoted the penetration of cash crop cultivation for exports among the Burmese villagers. Government fiscal policies were also influenced by the Chinese merchants' introduction of tax farming and by the sale of trade monopolies which began in the 1800s and 1810s under the reign of Bodawhpaya, when trade with China was reopened.

The climatic conditions of the central plains, the core area of successive Burmese dynasties, is not favorable for cultivation of rice, the staple grain, as it is the driest savanna in mainland Southeast Asia. To overcome the climatic conditions and to make rice cultivation possible, irrigation networks were constructed and maintained under the royal governments from ancient times. This meant, in other words, that there were certain restrictions imposed on the supply of available farmland, which set a precondition for farmland, mainly paddy fields, becoming a scarce commodity, and also becoming the safest collateral for money lending.

Looking at the socioeconomic trends, it is clear that the transition period from the eighteenth to nineteenth century was marked by significant socioeconomic exhaustion and confusion. The first crushing defeat in the war against Siam in 1785 and the mobilization of the labor force for the construction of a pagoda which was intended to be the largest in the world but was never completed, coupled with frequent droughts, resulted in a significant decrease in the population from the beginning of the nineteenth century to the 1810s compared to the 1780s. It was a time when the number of debt contracts began to increase visibly.

In the early years of the Konbaung period, victorious foreign wars brought Burma important resources such as people, arms, and treasures, but from the end of the eighteenth century onwards, foreign wars emerged as a way of losing resources and impeding production. As a result of the defeat of the First Anglo-Burmese War, Burma lost Arakan and Tenasserim in 1826, and the British government demanded 10 million rupees in war reparations. Because of the depletion of the national treasury, the burden was shifted to the inhabitants of widespread areas, and there are testimonies of people borrowing money to pay this special tax. Furthermore, as a result of the Second Anglo-Burmese War in 1852, Burma lost the whole Lower Burma, and the result was the breakdown of the traditional economic cycle built upon internal trade among three different regions, namely the central plains, tropical rainforests, and mountainous highlands. After the war, the royal government had to send officials to British Lower Burma to buy rice and other necessities by competing with foreign merchants.

Thus, the period of crisis that began at the end of the eighteenth century, while sometimes returning to a lull, deepened with the defeats in the three Anglo-Burmese Wars in the nineteenth century, and with it the number of debt documents also increased. These debt documents remind us of the fact that many people from all social strata wrote debt documents and struggled to earn their livelihoods by all means.

However, even after reading many of these debt documents, what remains is not only a serious and tragic impression, but also, as we will see in Part III, a wisdom and a kind of optimism in people's lives, and a flexibility in the customs and culture that surround debt relations, which are examined in more detail in Chapters 7 and 8.

Chapter 2
The Konbaung Era in Burmese Monetary History

One of the great puzzles in Burmese economic history during the eighteenth and nineteenth centuries is the complicated monetary system during the Konbaung period. Up to 1865, a variety of metallic currencies casted freely by individuals were circulating side by side with the gold, silver, copper, and lead bullion. For example, in money-lending contracts of the Konbaung period, we often find such expressions as, 'Please lend me 2 *kyat ke* 15 *kyat*s, 1 *kyat* 2 *mat ke* 8 *kyat*s and 3 *kyat ke* 3 *kyat*, in total 26 *kyat*s.' When we saw such money-lending contracts that appeared for the first time in this period, the wording looked like a cipher too difficult to paraphrase. In fact, the above contract literally suggests that the total amount of 26 *kyat*s would be paid in three kinds of silver-copper alloy; the first alloy with 80% pure silver, the second with 85% pure silver, and the third with 70% pure silver. Yet, there still remains something beyond our comprehension. Does it make any sense to add up the weights of three kinds of metallic currencies that differ in quality?

In order to find an answer to this question, let us examine two dimensions of the issue in this chapter. First, I would like to shed light on the state of money in circulation in the Konbaung period, which looks extraordinarily complicated to our eyes. The main objective is to examine how it was functioning and what kind of system was in place to make it workable. Second, I will compare two monetary reforms introduced by royal governments, one by King Bodawhpaya (r. 1782–1819) at the end of the eighteenth century and the other by King Mindon (r. 1853–1878) in 1865. A comparative analysis of these two reforms aims to unveil factors that have not previously been explored. These reforms, however, brought up completely opposite results, despite the similarity in their objectives and methods.

50   Chapter 2

Money in circulation from the eleventh to eighteenth centuries

Unlike the rulers of the earlier kingdoms such as Pyu, Arakan, and Mon in the region, Burmese kings of the Pagan, Taungoo, and Konbaung dynasties seem to have been indifferent in issuing standard official coins until the end of the eighteenth century. It remains an unsolved question as to why Pagan rulers who had absorbed various cultures and technologies from Mon, Pyu, and Arakan and amalgamated them into the 'Burmese culture' did not follow the monetary tradition of these preceding kingdoms.

In the Pagan period, gold, silver, copper, and lead bullion were used as a medium of exchange along with paddy, salt, and cloth. Inscriptions of the Pagan period suggest also that there were a variety of barter trades, such as exchange of slaves for an elephant or horses, purchase of land in silver, wage payment for workers in the combination of silver, paddy and cloth, and so on.[1] Certainly, silver was the most important medium of exchange of the time and the demand for silver was so high as to make the ratio of gold to silver extraordinarily strong for silver, which varied from 1:5, 1:8, 1:10 to 1:12.[2] The trade route connecting Yunnan–Burma–Bengal had been opened and Burma was able to obtain silver bullion and horses from Yunnan, but it was not sufficient to meet the great demand in Pagan. The silver-producing areas of Shan—the most famous of them being Bawdwingyi (Great Silver Mine)—were not fully under the control of the Pagan kingdom, despite a desire for such. The supply of gold, on the other hand, found in many small rivers in the plain between the Ayeyarwady and the Chindwin, was enough to meet the demand in the kingdom.

During the first Taungoo period (1539–99), copper became the main material of metallic currencies. Cesare Fedrici, a Venetian merchant who visited the royal capital Pegu in 1569, observed that non-barter trade was practiced throughout Lower Burma by using privately produced lumps of copper-lead alloy called *ganza*.[3] Although the shape and weight of each *ganza* was different, it was called *ganza* so long as it was a disk-shaped copper-lead alloy. As such, given the state of money in circulation, it was necessary to have a money assayer and a weigher in each transaction.

The trade route connecting Yunnan–Ava–India had been open since the seventh century[4] and developed different sub-branches during the late thirteenth to the nineteenth centuries.[5] Burma imported copper, silver, ironworks, copper vessels, weapons, tea, and silk from Yunnan and exported raw cotton, along with spices, gems, and salt. The Dutch East India Company made its first foray into Burma when King Thalun (r. 1629–48) of the restored Taungoo dynasty (1597–1752) moved the capital from maritime Pegu to inland Ava in 1634. After the fall of the Ming dynasty in 1644, the Yunnan merchants brought large quantities of Chinese copper coins into Ava. While Burmese brokers and coppersmiths had been using Chinese coins to make *ganza*, the Dutch East India Company had also participated vigorously in the procurement of Chinese copper coins since 1653, as it had very profitable markets in Coromandel and Bengal, where the company's factories were often strapped for cash.[6] In 1655, the ratio of Chinese copper money in the total exports from Burma by the Dutch East India Company reached as high as 78.7%.[7] The company also exported Chinese copper coins to Batavia and Ceylon, where these coins were used as legal tender.[8]

Although we do not have any historical evidence to confirm why Burmese people did not use Chinese copper coins as their currencies, it is highly probable that brokers, assayers, and coppersmiths who often made *ganza* by themselves found that it was more profitable to melt Chinese coins into *ganza* by manipulating its quality to their favor rather than working simply as brokers or assayers.

The quality of *ganza* in general deteriorated greatly as time passed. When compared to the English sterling pound, the comparative value of *ganza* fell from 1 in 1580, when R. Fitch visited Pegu, to 0.5 in 1650 and finally to 0.03 in 1712.[9] *Ganza* was circulated up to the early eighteenth century, but at that time it was no longer copper-lead alloy but almost nothing but a lump of lead. As the value of *ganza* decreased, people had to pay enormous amounts of *ganza* in each transaction. Gradually, silver bullion, which was used in trade with foreign merchants, became a more important means of exchange even in domestic transactions. In the markets of Ava, where paddy prices had been quoted in copper or copper-alloy during the seventeenth century, the prices of paddy and other commodities were quoted mostly in silver or silver alloy in the eighteenth century.[10] There were several silver-producing areas in Shan, Martaban, and Taungoo, but the volume of silver production was not enough to meet the increasing demand in the seventeenth and eighteenth centuries. In addition to the Yunnan silver, the influx of New World silver via the Philippines and India, which had already started from the end of the sixteenth century, filled the increasing demand–supply gap.

Currencies in the Konbaung period

When the founder of the Konbaung dynasty, Alaunghpaya (r. 1752–1760), ascended the throne, copper and copper-alloys were still in use for taxation, as well as transactions, although silver had become the main standard for currency. *Ganza* had already disappeared, and for petty trade of daily commodities, every shop in the markets had baskets full of pieces of lead.[11]

To investigate the state of money in circulation in eighteenth- and nineteenth-century Burma, we can use the important *thet-kayit* historical documents, written contracts of various transactions between private individuals. Among them, money-lending *thet-kayit*s are vast in number and were used widely in central Burma. These money-lending *thet-kayit*s reveal that almost all monies that appeared in these contracts were confined to silver-copper alloys, as seen in Table 2.1.

It is said that there was an implicit assumption that all currencies should contain more silver than copper. *Ngwe*, the Burmese word for silver, acquired new meaning (i.e., currencies in general since the mid-eighteenth century, although *kye* (copper) was still used for money).

However, there were a few exceptions. The most inferior currency found in *thet-kayit*s so far was 7 *kyat ke*, which means the content of silver in alloy was only 30%. According to R. Temple, the worst currency he ever heard of was a silver-copper alloy whose silver content was only 10%.[12] However, these cases were rare. It seems fairly certain that compared to the restored Taungoo period, the so-called Gresham's law that states that 'bad money drives out good' might have been working more slowly in the Konbaung period. Besides the alloys shown in Table 2.1, we find various names of money such as *Kayuba-dain*, *Kayuba-loun*, *Ngwe-kale*, *Ngwe-kwet*, *Ngwe-pyou*, and *Ngwe-loun* in *thet-kayit*s. However, we have no way to know now where they were actually circulated, nor their qualities.

Currencies during the Konbaung period had become much more complicated than in the Taungoo period on account of the wide varieties of alloys and also wide regional differences. To make the situation more complicated, it often happened that money called by the same name had a different quality depending on the region. For example, in many regions, people called 1 *kyat ke* alloy *ywet-ni*, but in another place 1.5 *kyat ke* was called *ywet-ni*, and in some places even 2~5 *kyat ke* alloys were also called *ywet-ni*.[13]

The Konbaung Era in Burmese Monetary History   53

Table 2.1: Silver-copper alloys circulated as currencies during the Konbaung period (1752–1865)

Weight	Copper infused	Name of alloy		Commonly known as	Silver percentage (%)
		Based on 10 *k*	Based on 100 *k*		
10 *k*	2 *mat*	5 *mu kè* / 2 *mat kè*	5 *kyat kè*	*ywet-pwin*	95
10 *k*	1 *k*	1 *k kè*	10 *k kè*	*ywet-ni*	90
10 *k*	1 *k* 2 *mat*	1 *k* 2 *mat kè*	15 *k kè*	*ywet-thei*	85
10 *k*	2 *k*	2 *k kè*	20 *k kè*	*ywet-so* (*ngwe-so*)	80
10 *k*	2 *k* 1 *mat*	2 *k* 1 *mat kè*	22 *k* 5 *mu kè*		77.5
10 *k*	2 *k* 2 *mat*	2 *k* 2 *mat kè*	25 *k kè*		75
10 *k*	3 *k*	3 *k kè*	30 *k kè*		70
10 *k*	3 *k* 2 *mat*	3 *k* 2 *mat kè*	35 *k kè*		65
10 *k*	4 *k*	4 *k kè*	40 *k kè*		60
10 *k*	4 *k* 2 *mat*	4 *k* 2 *mat kè*	45 *k kè*		55

Note: *k* = *kyat* (1 *k* = 16.3 g) *mat* = 1/4 *kyat mu* = 1/10 *kyat*. *kè(ake)* means alloy.
Sources: Toe Hla, 'Konbaung hkit Athapya hnin Alei mya', *Tekkatho Pyinnya Padeitha*, Vol. 15, Part 6, 1981 (November), p. 106. R. C. Temple, 'Notes on currency and coinage among the Burmese', Bombay: The British India Press, 1928 (reprinted from *Indian Antiquary*, Vol. XLVIII, 1919), p. 11.

As mentioned earlier, it was often the case that monies with different qualities were used at the same time in one transaction, as below:

Thet-kayit (Burmese Era) 1174 Month of *Waso*, waxing 6th (AD. 14th June 1812), Shin Nyein said to Shin Nga Htat, 'Please lend me money again and take my 16 plots of paddy field irrigated from South Okpo Canal, sown with 18.5 baskets of paddy and called *Htein-bin- le-taik* as mortgage. Please lend me 60 *kyat*s in *ywet-ni*, 25 *kyat*s in 10 *kyat*s ke, 2 *kyat*s 2 *mat*s in 2 *mat ke ywet-ni*.' According to her request, Shin Nga Htat lent 87 *kyat*s 2 *mat*s and took the mortgage. Maung Hmwe Ang was the writer.[14]

It is certain that the sum of the weight of the alloys did not denote the total amount of the debt; the qualities of three alloys used in the contract were different. How could they settle the debt when the debtor wanted to repay the loan? Did they repay alloys of the same qualities written in the *thet-kayit*, or was there a method to convert each alloy to standard money, if any? According to Toe Hla, the pioneering scholar who introduced *thet-kayit*s to the world, there were two methods to convert a silver-copper alloy to *ywet-ni*: one was to use a calculation formula to compute the *ywet-ni* equivalent, and another was to use the melting method to quantify silver content of the alloys.[15] However, the underlying problem was that the quality of *ywet-ni*, which was treated as a standard currency, varied according to space and time. As seen in Table 2.1, *ywet-ni* was supposed to be a silver-copper alloy that contained silver and copper at the ratio of 9:1 by weight, but in reality there are many *thet-kayit*s in which alloys of inferior quality were also called *ywet-ni*.

Another method adopted was to examine the patterns on the surface of metal currencies which would emerge after the melting process.

> If you infuse 1 *kyat* copper (into silver)
>> Footprints of birds or flowers of jujube would appear.
>> …
>> One forth copper infusion would make
>> Surely patterns of Arabian jasmine.[16]

This song was another device to gauge the quality of metallic currencies. Despite these devices, it was very difficult for ordinary people to know the precise quality of silver-copper alloy currencies. Only those who could cast metallic currencies knew their exact value. Brokers, assayers, weighers, merchants, and some money-lenders would cast silver-copper alloys freely. From time to time, the royal government issued decrees prohibiting the circulation of inferior silver-copper alloys, but these were not sufficiently effective in the capital, and null in the provinces.[17] Since the commission for brokerage was relatively low, somewhere around 1 *mat* (0.25 *kyat*s) or 2 *mu* (0.2 *kyat*s) in one transaction, and the service charges of assayers and weighers were null in most cases, there was persistent temptation to make profits in the process of casting money. Similarly, customers often asked them to cast debased currencies by increasing the ratio of copper.[18]

The monetary reform of King Bodawhpaya

It was King Bodawhpaya who made the first attempt to reform the complicated monetary situation in eighteenth-century Burma. Bodawhpaya was an energetic and ambitious reformist in various fields such as religious organizations and trade promotion, as well as the unsuccessful introduction of the Gregorian calendar as a substitute for the Burmese calendar.

Bodawhpaya introduced the concession system for the extraction of teak and granted monopoly rights over some essential goods to the highest bidder, regardless of their ethnicity. His interests in seaborne trade caused him to provoke wars against two maritime kingdoms: Arakan in 1784 and Siam in 1785–86. Bodawhpaya conquered Arakan, but met a devastating defeat in the war with Siam. For the first time, Burma was defeated in the long history of war with Siam.

The conquest of Arakan by Bodawhpaya's army was one factor in changing the monetary policy of the Konbaung kingdom. Arakan, a kingdom facing the Gulf of Bengal, was one hub of the trade network in the Indian Ocean and had a long tradition of issuing coins by the royal government. Bodawhpaya issued his own coins in Arakan after his conquest, following the model of Arakanese coins. In October 1787, the king issued a decree saying that previous coins in Arakan became invalid as the Arakan kingdom was merged into the Burmese Empire and that people should use only new coins.[19]

In Burma, despite royal orders prohibiting casting and the use of any money except *ywet-ni*, a variety of alloys were still in use in the capital, as well as in the provinces. The royal order issued on October 16, 1783, noted:

> People still cast and circulate deteriorated currencies despite the repeated royal orders in the past that prohibited the use of currencies other than *ywet-so, ywet-thei and ywet-ni*. Town governors, clerks and other officials should monitor carefully. The king knows that some jailors took briberies and released those who committed the offense of casting debased money. He also knows that people circulate such inferior currencies as 25 *kyat ke, wunbwa,* and 30 *kyat ke.*[20]

Furthermore, on July 23, 1784, the king's government issued another royal order as follows:

56   Chapter 2

> People are using various kinds of currencies like *wunbwa*, *ngwe-so*,
> *ywet-thei*, and *ywet-ni*. *Wunbwa*, *ngwe-so* and *ywet-thei* could be used
> only up to the end of *Thet-kayit* 1146 (April 11, 1785) and thereafter,
> only *ywet-ni* shall become the currency to be used in any transaction in
> the kingdom. Any *pwe-sa* [broker] who circulates other kind of silver
> alloys and anyone who accepts them or uses them shall be punished
> severely. Circulate this order in all provinces.[21]

Consequently, Bodawhpaya's monetary policy moved towards a royal
monopoly over the right to issue currency. In 1795, Bodawhpaya requested
Michael Symes, on his second missionary visit at the behest of the Governor of India, to bring minting equipment for his government.

Two years later, Captain Hiram Cox visited Amarapura, bringing
minting equipment, together with a voluminous sample of 1,000,000
copper coins and 20,000 silver coins, from Calcutta.[22] However, there arose
a series of troubles between Cox and the king due to misunderstandings
on both sides. The first precipitating event was that the king ordered the
silver coins to be assayed. This was an ordinary procedure for the Burmese,
as they always had to assay any metal lump currency in each transaction.
However, Cox took this decision as an insult to the Governor-General in
Calcutta, who had ordered the minting of the sample coins requested by
the king's ministers. Bodawhpaya refused to pay for the sample coins as he
thought their quality was poor. When he asked Cox to take the coins back
to Calcutta, Cox answered in anger that he would never do it. Later on,
the king's government paid Cox for the silver coins, but in Cox's words, in
much inferior silver.

It is regrettable that there remain very few Burmese historical records
on the process of this unsuccessful monetary reform by Bodawhpaya. Every
historian writing on the subject so far has relied solely on what Cox wrote
on this issue. Thus, Malcom, Yule, Temple, and Robinson and Shaw[23] replicated almost the same story as follows: King Bodawhpaya issued coins
but fixed the nominal value of his coins at an extraordinarily higher rate
than their value in real terms, and so people naturally refused to accept the
royal coins; the king then banned all other currencies and severely punished those who still traded with silver lump currencies; all trade activities
were suspended for weeks until some ministers persuaded the king to give
up his policy; and finally the king had to abandon his experiment.

All the English writers mentioned above concluded that the failure of the monetary reform by Bodawhpaya was attributable to the methods taken by the king, characterized by his extreme avarice (the debased quality of his coins), despotism (decrees and punishment), and ignorance. Cox wrote in fury, Temple traced the story without hiding his contempt for the king, and others repeated more or less the same story in more moderate terms.

Toe Hla, the Burmese expert in the field of Konbaung socioeconomic history, similarly quoting solely from Cox's text, noted that the king's reform was not successful because people thought that the king took too much profit from the new standard coinage.[24]

Table 2.2 shows the results of an examination of Cox's text and three Burmese texts containing ample records about King Bodawhpaya's administration. There is a sharp contrast between Cox's text and the Burmese ones. All the Burmese texts contain the royal order issued on August 13, 1812, which gave permission to use the lead currencies as before, admitting that official copper coins were not used by the people in their daily petty transactions. As such, it marks the end of the king's attempt to standardize currency in the kingdom. However, the Burmese texts remain silent on all the other items we find in Cox's text. According to Cox, Bodawhpaya started his reform abruptly by orders issued on July 21, 1797, which prohibited the use of currencies circulating in bazaars and ordered the use of copper coins brought from Calcutta.[25] Cox went on to say that he had come to notice the royal regulation regarding currencies the next day, July 22. Based on this regulation and his own assumptions, he calculated the enormous profit of the king, which ranged from 66.6% at the minimum to as much as 589% at maximum.[26]

The next information provided by Cox is the royal order dated August 2, 1797, which permitted the use of *ywet-ni* again,[27] implying that the king gave up his reform to unify the silver currencies in the kingdom. Cox and Temple regarded this royal order as marking the end of the monetary reform and said that the reform lasted only two weeks, in sharp contrast to the Burmese accounts, which asserted that it lasted until 1812.

In both Cox's text and the Burmese texts, we cannot find any data on the amount of coins issued. As for the quality of the royal coins, we have only dubious information based on Cox's calculations. As the available information is so limited, it seems futile to discuss the causes of the reform's failure on the basis of these documents. This is a reason to seek an

58   Chapter 2

Table 2.2: Description of items relating to Bodawhpaya's monetary reform

	Royal order, July 21, 1797	Regulation, July 22, 1797	Permission for *ywet-ni*	Amount of issued coins	Quality of coins	Royal order, August 13, 1812
Cox	+	+	+	-	+ (?)	-
ROB	-	-	-	-	-	+
MMOS	-	-	-	-	-	+
KBZ	-	-	-	-	-	+

Notes: + : mentioned; - : not mentioned; Cox: Journal of a Residence in the Burhman Empire; ROB: Royal Orders of Burma, Vols. V–VII; MMOS: *Myanmar Min Ok-chok-pon Sadan*; KBZ: *Konbaung hset Maha Yazawin-daw-gyi*.

alternative interpretation by examining the socioeconomic background of the monetary reform of Bodawhpaya; namely, to find the king's motive in his attempt at standardizing currencies and the causes for its failure.

Factors behind the reform and its failure

We can set forth a hypothesis that Bodawhpaya had a strong desire to establish a royal monopoly over the issuance of standard currency as quickly as possible under the tight fiscal situation prevalent in the 1790s. In 1782, when the king ascended the throne, he could have given the waiver to all debts incurred by the people from the time of Alaunghpaya, which amounted to 23,000 *viss* of silver and 10 *viss* of gold.[28] It is certain that after the devastating defeat in the war with Siam in 1785–86, the kingdom's power had declined. In 1788, the government launched another war against Siam, with deliberate preparations (such as the imposition of war levies in cash from the people) and the reinforcement of the production of more firearms. However, this campaign did not work.[29] Such campaigns caused an enormous drain on the kingdom's resources in terms of finance, labor, and agricultural production.

Another setback to note was the frequent occurrence of severe drought during the reign of Bodawhpaya. Figure 2.1 shows the trend of paddy prices for the period from 1785 to 1885. Paddy prices rose from 1793 and reached 200 *kyats* for 100 baskets in 1804. Thereafter prices fluctuated widely and soared to 400 *kyats* in 1812, the highest price during the Konbaung period. The years 1810–12 are known as the time when the people suffered from a great famine caused by an unprecedented drought. There were also records

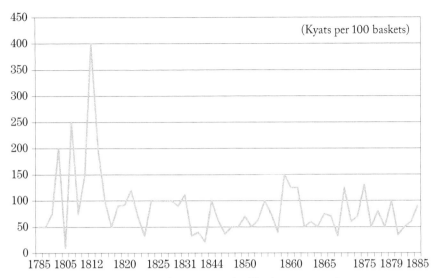

Figure 2.1: Movement of paddy prices in the Konbaung period
Source: Toe Hla, 'Monetary system of Burma in the Konbaung period', *JBRS*, Vol. LXII, Parts I & II, 1979, pp. 74–79.

of droughts before and during the monetary reform. In July 1788, to stop the drought, a Buddhist sutra was recited by the senior monks in a pavilion in front of the *Hluttaw*, the Supreme Court.[30] Testimonies exist in the literature of the time as to what was going on at village level during the time of the great famine in 1810–12. A Reverend Buddhist monk (*saya-daw*), Kyi-gang-shin-gyi, described the situation in the following homily given to the king:

> No hope to settle in this disordered world
>
> The unredeemable debt, the unbearable levies
>
> People flee from one another
>
> If our headmen are helpless to prevent it
>
> There will remain only corpses of villages.[31]

Similarly, another famous monk known as Salin Myo *Saya-daw* wrote in 1812:

Scarce rain and scanty food

In abundance are only war and violence

Such is our time

Prices are soaring, a basket of rice

Goes up to three *kyat*s,

And finally, to fifteen *kyat*s.[32]

The chronological distribution of money-lending contracts during the Konbaung period also shows an increase during the reign of Bodawhpaya (Figure 2.2). Because of the deteriorating economic conditions caused by the extraction of war levies, drought, and frequent recruitments for the military campaigns, people were compelled to borrow money from money-lenders. It is highly probable that the actual numbers of money-lending contracts in the reign of Bodawhpaya, about 200 years ago, might have been much greater than the numbers noted in Figure 1.3, since the old contracts written on *pe-sa* (dried palm leaf) or black *para-baik* (folded paper) do not seem to have lasted for a very long time.

Fortunately, a large collection of money-lending contracts have been well preserved for generations by families known as Salin *Thugaung*. They accumulated vast tracts of lands and many debt-slaves through their money-lending operations, which covered wide areas both on the west and east bank of the Ayeyarwady.

By looking at the chronological distribution of money-lending contracts of Salin *Thugaung*, as shown in Figure 2.2, we come to know that the number of contracts had increased considerably during the 1790s, some ten years after King Bodawhpaya took the throne, and reached its highest point for the whole Konbaung period in 1810. It is certain that the figures in Figure 2.2 are much closer to the actual situation of what was going on in the whole kingdom.

Another peak appears in the latter half of the 1860s, especially in 1867 and 1868, when King Mindon raised the household tax to 10 *kyat*s from the former rate of 1~5 *kyat*s per household.[33] It is noteworthy that the first and second monetary reforms by the royal governments coincided with two peaks in the number of money-lending contracts. During these periods, many people could not help but borrow money from money-

The Konbaung Era in Burmese Monetary History   61

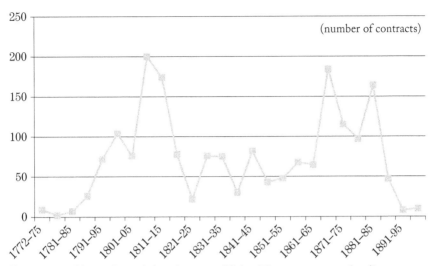

Figure 2.2: Chronological distribution of Salin *Thugaung* money-lending contracts (1772/75–1896/1900)
Source: calculation based on Kyaw Hmu Aung, 'Konbaung Hkit Hnaung Salin Thugaung Thamaing', MA thesis submitted to the History Department, Yangon University, 1992.

lenders by offering their lands or labor as mortgages. Similarly, the royal governments must have tried everything possible to overcome the financial crisis. Bodawhpaya was the first king to introduce an auction sale of trade monopolies and a tax-farming system in order to broaden the revenue base in the Konbaung period. Therefore, it would not be surprising if King Bodawhpaya did actually try to raise revenue by issuing royal coins of debased quality. As cash taxes constituted nearly 70% of recorded local levies from 1752 to 1804, according to Lieberman's estimate,[34] it might have been anticipated that the revenue income would decrease sharply if people were tempted to pay tax with debased currencies under the free play of casting by private hands. The main driving force of the king's reform in the field of currency must have been in response to such economic circumstances.

Then, what were the main causes of the failure of Bodawhpaya's monetary reform? It is certain that we cannot blame only the king's debased coinage, as asserted by Cox and other writers. Despite the rapid penetration of the cash economy into the daily lives of the people, there was no standardized money market for the whole country at that time. The quality of currencies varied according to time and space, and the people had to use an assayer and a weigher for each transaction. Money was circulating in segmented markets, and it was people like the *pwe-sa*s (brokers) or *ngwe-hkan-thu*s (assayers) rather than the market who linked demand and supply. Contemporary observations by Western travelers noted that there were numerous *pwe-sa*s and *ngwe-hkan-thu*s all over the country. In fact, evidence also shows that in a village called Byangya, as many as 13 assayers in 18 money-lending contracts were involved in the period from 1791 to 1812.

As already mentioned, the service charges of assayers (including weighers) were none or very little. Usually they were engaged in other occupations as well, and one of their lucrative businesses was currency casting. It is highly plausible, therefore, that they resisted any attempt to standardize the currency, as it would have deprived them of their most important source of profits. Bodawhpaya's reform was not well prepared for such quiet but persistent resistance; furthermore, the degree of administrative centralization had not reached the stage where the royal government could change the long-lasting tradition of business practices merely by issuing decrees and imposing exemplary punishments.

The monetary reform of King Mindon

After Bodawhpaya's first attempt at monetary reform, three successive kings, Bagyidaw (r. 1819–37), Tharawadi (r. 1837–46), and Pagan (r. 1846–53), made no attempt to reintroduce the monetary standardization, except for minting coins by making use of the equipment brought by Cox. In the royal decree issued on January 29, 1854, King Mindon lamented that the extent of impurity in silver lump currencies was being manipulated with ill intention and that such conduct was nothing but theft deserving punishment in hell.[35] Again, on November 11, 1854, another royal decree noted that the quality of silver, as well as the weights and measures used in transactions, varied so much as to worsen the economic conditions of the country.[36]

Up until the middle of the 1860s, almost all currencies appearing in money-lending contracts throughout the country were silver-copper alloys. However, we find a few exceptional contracts where *dinga* (minted coinage) was used, as in the following transaction:

Thet-kayit[37] 1226, Nadaw 11 (Dec. 24, 1864) Mi Min Tha and sister Mi Bo Sa asked *Thugaung-ma*,[38] the daughter of *Myo-thugyi*,[39] to lend 312 *mu* 1 *pe* in *dinga*, of which 272 *mu* 1 *pe* is to pay Maung Hla Tha as land rent, the rest is for other expenses. They promised to repay the loan within 3 months. Then, *Thugaung-ma* paid 312 *mu* 1 *pe* in 1 *kyat dinga* to Mi Min Tha and Mi Bo Za with the condition of repaying the loan within 3 months...[40]

*Dinga*s were found in contracts in several areas such as Malun (1857), Kyaukka (1859), Legaing (1862), Ngazun (1862),[41] Mandalay (1850s), and Salin (1864~66). Since the use of *dinga* spread widely only after the monetary reform by Mindon's government in November 1865, when the new silver coin known as the peacock coin was issued in large quantities, it would be interesting to know who issued these *dinga*s in the contracts in and before 1865. There are two possibilities. They might have been coins minted by the government of successive kings, or British Indian rupees circulating in Lower Burma. As coins minted by royal governments from the time of Bagyidaw to that of Pagan have not yet been found, it is quite doubtful whether they were actually circulating. Therefore, it is unlikely that these early *dinga*s in the contracts were the coins issued by the royal mint. Considering the economic conditions in the late 1850s and the early 1860s, it is highly possible that they were British Indian rupees.

Lower Burma was annexed to British India in 1852 after Burma's defeat in the Second Anglo-Burmese War. As the two coastal regions of Arakan and Tenasserim had been lost since 1826, Burma lost all its seaports and had become a landlocked country when Mindon ascended the throne in 1853. Products of tropical rainy Lower Burma such as salt, paddy, dried fish, and fish paste were indispensable necessities for everyday life in semi-arid Upper Burma. After the annexation of Lower Burma, these goods, as well as those imported from Europe, were traded in British Indian rupees, which became legal tender in the British territory. Burmese merchants in commercial centers such as Pyi, Mandalay, and Shan adapted themselves to using British Indian rupees in their transactions. Under such circumstances, the royal government started to seriously consider the introduction of monetary reform.

It was William Wallace, a Scottish merchant, who helped procure minting equipment for the government of King Mindon. Wallace accompanied A. Phayre, the first Chief Commissioner of the Province of Burma, who visited Mandalay in 1862 with the purpose of negotiating a trade treaty between Burma and Britain. Wallace succeeded in building a friendly relationship with the king and obtained a concession to extract teak from the best forest in Burma.[42] He negotiated with a company called Ralph Heaton and Sons in Birmingham and sent the equipment with Edward Wyon,[43] the company's engineer, to Mandalay in 1865.

The mint's opening ceremony was held on November 11, 1865, with a gun salute.[44] Gold, silver, copper, iron, and lead coins were minted and, among these, the silver coin was regarded as the most important medium for exchange, while the gold coin was not for circulation. It was a time when the gold to silver ratio in the kingdom jumped to 1:32[45] because of the increasing demand for gold in building the new royal palace in Mandalay and also because of the influx of a large quantity of silver from China due to the export boom of cotton.

The most important point to make in regard to the second monetary reform is that the royal government made the qualities and weights of the new silver coins almost the same as those of the British Indian rupee. According to an assessment by the Calcutta Mint, the average weight of the new *kyat* coins was 180 grains and their purity was 0.912, whereas the British Indian rupee was 180 grains in weight and 0.917 in purity.[46] Furthermore, the scale of weight was changed in conformity to the British Indian rupee, as shown in Table 2.3. In the traditional scale, 10 *mu*s made 1 *kyat*, but was changed to 8 *mu*s.

It was the earnest desire of Mindon's government to retain independence of the country and recover through diplomatic efforts the territories lost in defeats in previous wars. Why, then, was it necessary to alter the traditional monetary system to such an extent that it seemed to have merged into the British Indian monetary system? We assume the answer lies in the loss of Lower Burma.

The economy of the kingdom was working out well through internal trade between the semi-arid plains in Upper Burma, tropical rain-fed Lower Burma, and mountainous areas covered with evergreen forests such as Shan and Kachin. Wide differences in climate and geology contributed to produce unique sets of products in each region, which were traded in marketplaces, at pagoda festivals, or through direct dealings with peddlers. With respect to foreign trade, guns and gunpowder from the West and

Table 2.3: New silver coins; denomination, weight, and equivalent British Indian rupee

Denomination	Weight	Equivalent British Indian rupee	In traditional scale
1 *kyat* coin	1 *kyat*	1 rupee	1 *kyat*
5 *mu* coin	8 *pe*	8 anna	10 *pe*
2 *mu* 1 *pe* coin	4 *pe*	4 anna	5 *pe*
1*mu* coin	2 *pe*	2 anna	2.5 *pe*
1 *pe* coin	1 *pe*	1 anna	1.25 *pe*

Note: in the traditional scale 1 *kyat* = 10 *mu* = 20 *pe*. In the new scale 1 *kyat* = 8 *mu* = 16 *pe* (just like 1 rupee = 16 anna).

metal material for currencies from China were very important. However, it has to be pointed out that Burma could supply almost all necessities from within its own territory until Lower Burma was lost.

After the annexation of Lower Burma by British India, the royal government had to send missions every year to buy paddy from Lower Burma. In 1858/59, total imports from British Burma amounted to 3,726,000 rupees, and in 1867/68 total imports rose to 12,252,000 rupees, while exports for British Burma in the corresponding years were 2,228,000 rupees and 4,491,000 rupees, respectively,[47] which indicated a deteriorating trade balance for the kingdom. The paddy price in Lower Burma increased sharply after the colonial government lifted the ban on rice exports.

Since the traditional metal currencies had lost their validity in trade with British Burma, there was an urgent need for the royal government to have new silver coins similar to the Indian rupee in terms of quality and weight so that they were interchangeable. Thus, a new silver coin almost identical in quality and weight to the British Indian rupee was born. However, the coin was proudly Burmese in its design, with a peacock in full splendor on the obverse and a wreath, the value, and the year when the king ascended the throne on the reverse. King Mindon's government had been under persistent pressure for a reduction of custom duties, free intercommunication between subjects, and the abolition of royal monopolies over various products. As a result of the first and second trade treaties in 1862 and 1867, the British demands were mostly accepted by the royal government. The second monetary reform was carried out under these conditions and the king and his government fully realized their precarious situation.

66   Chapter 2

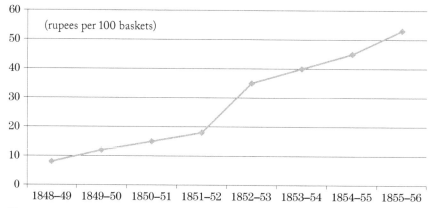

Figure 2.3: Paddy prices in Lower Bruma (1848/49~1855/56)
Source: Government of Burma, *Gazetteer of Burma*, Delhi: Gian Publishing House, 1987 (reprint), Vol. 1, p. 441.

The money-lending contracts show that the new silver currencies were circulating smoothly throughout the whole country.[48] In most of the contracts during the latter part of the 1860s, we find the new silver coins replacing the old metal currencies. The royal government paid salaries to all officials and *ahmudan*s in the new silver coins, and the king used the new currencies for religious donations and for the procurement of cash crops such as cotton and oil seeds. As a result, without issuing any decree to prohibit the use of metal currencies, the royal government achieved the targeted standardization of currencies.

For a few years after the monetary reform, some assayers appeared in money-lending contracts in order to convert old debt in metal currencies into the new currencies. However, they disappeared quickly, as there was no place left for them after the standardization of currency.

Up to 1865, a variety of metallic currencies were freely cast by private individuals and circulated side by side with gold, silver, copper, and lead bullion. In other words, no successive royal governments had ever tried to standardize their own currencies up to that time.

An attempt at standardizing currencies was made by two kings: King Bodawhpaya at the end of the eighteenth century and King Mindon in 1865. Interestingly enough, the first monetary reform was unsuccessful,

Table 2.4: Approximate output of silver coins at the Mandalay mint (1865~1885)

Denomination	Nos.	Value in *kyat*
1 *kyat*s	26,406,000	26,406,000
5 *mu* (1/2 *kyat*)	1,973,000	986,000
2 *mu* 1 *pe* (1/4 *kyat*)	2,866,000	716,500
1 *mu* (1/8 *kyat*)	5,173,000	646,625
Total		28,755,125

Source: Robinson and Shaw, 1980, p. 89.

while the second proved successful, despite the similarity in terms of policy content and methodology.

As far as the former reform is concerned, Captain Cox and other writers attributed its failure to the debased coin by the royal government. However, they failed to inquire into the causes of issuing the debased coin. This chapter has argued that the royal government was driven to do so in order to overcome the financial crisis caused by the defeat in the war with Siam in terms of the resource drain, and also the revenue loss due to the continuous droughts and famine that occurred at the same time. In addition to these factors, we would presume that the authority of the kingdom was not able to control the free play of brokers and assayers in casting currencies, who showed persistent resistance to accept and circulate the king's coins.

As against the failure of the first monetary reform, the second reform in terms of issuing effective standardized coins by Mindon's government was accepted by the people and diffused widely in the country. After examining the factors behind the success, we have reached the conclusion that, ironically enough, it was given a momentum by the loss of Lower Burma in the Second Anglo-Burmese War in 1852. Lower Burma, the important supplier of the rice staple to Central Burma, was annexed to British India. The royal government had to procure necessary staples for the country with the currencies acceptable to British Burma. The only option for the government, in this regard, was to issue a standardized currency similar to the British Indian rupee in terms of quality and weight. Merchants in Upper Burma had to use the new currency in their business transactions. By linking the new currencies to the British Indian currencies, room for the brokers, assayers, and weighers to squeeze profits by casting coin quickly disappeared.

Part II

Humans as Collateral for Debt

Chapter 3

Human-mortgage Contracts in the Eighteenth and Nineteenth Centuries

The place of human-mortgage contracts among debt contracts in the Konbaung period was not very large. Compared to debts with interest, where money was borrowed and principal and interest paid in cash, or debts secured by farmland, which increased rapidly during the Konbaung period, the number of human-mortgage contracts was much smaller, and they were decreasing during the period. For example, a look at the 114 volumes of microfilms of Kagoshima University's Burmese historical documents (KUMF), including a large number of *thet-kayit*s, shows about 600 farmland-mortgage contracts, while the number of human-mortgage contracts is only about 100, or about one-sixth of the number of farmland-mortgage contracts. The difference is even greater in the case of farmland *thet-kayit*s in the Meiktila region, where several systematic collections of *thet-kayit*s were carried out; nearly 800 land-mortgage contracts were found, but the number of human-mortgage contracts was only 18. The ratio of debt contracts with interest, human-mortgage contracts, and farmland-mortgage contracts in the two databases, namely KUMF and DMSEH (Documents of Myanmar Socio-Economic History), is 41%, 9%, and 50% respectively; that is to say, human-mortgage contracts comprise less than 10% of all three types of debt contracts.

These figures, of course, refer to *thet-kayit*s that were fortunate enough to endure and survive for nearly 200 years, suggesting many more contracts must have been written in eighteenth- and nineteenth-century Burma. But, so long as these databases are the most comprehensive ones available, covering the main areas of the central plains, which constitute the core of the kingdom, it seems possible to estimate the changes in debt contracts during the Konbaung period, based on these databases.

72 Chapter 3

During the Konbaung era, borrowing money using people as collateral—in other words, debt-slave contracts or *ko-nei thet-kayit*—occupied rather a small portion of the total debt. Nevertheless, in some areas, this practice of lending money and accepting people as debt-slaves was an important source of agricultural labor for the rich and powerful families who accumulated a lot of farmland, and it was also an important source of labor for the royalty and high-ranking officials of the royal capital to cultivate their lands, as well as to perform all kinds of tasks inside and outside their residences. There was still ample merit in securing debt-slaves, along with hereditary slaves, for these top elite classes.

And for those who were sometimes too poor to eat, debt-slavery was an option to secure food and shelter, even if they fell into a life of subordinate existence. In other words, the debt-slave contract still retained importance as a guarantee of survival in case of emergency, even in the Konbaung period. However, other than a brief introduction by Daw Ohn Kyi,[1] there has been no research on debt-slave contracts and the status of debt-slaves in this period. In this chapter, therefore, I would like to elucidate the nature of debt-slavery in the Konbaung period based on *thet-kayit* documents collected in the central plains, the core area of the Konbaung kingdom, with reference to historical trends and regional variations. In addition, I would like to examine socioeconomic changes in the period from the perspective of debt-slave contracts. The next chapter examines in detail the contents of debt-slave contracts, based on the documents of the Salin *Thugaung*, the powerful families in the west bank of the Ayeyarwady River. I also try to reconstruct, as much as possible, the footprints of those who were trapped in the circumstances of debt-slavery and their families.

What is a *ko-nei thet-kayit*?

The materials used in this chapter are debt-slave contracts, called *ko-nei thet-kayit*, from eighteenth- to nineteenth-century Burma; 103 contracts in KUMF, 185 in DMSEH, and 104 in the Salin *Thugaung* Manuscripts, '*Ko-nei Thet-kayits*' (STM-KT), for a total of 392 contracts. However, 55 of these are duplicates,[2] and a significant number of them were almost impossible to decipher due to damage to the material and worn-out letters. All three groups of documents are classified under the title of *ko-nei*, but the criteria for classification are different in each database, and therefore,

Human-mortgage Contracts in the Eighteenth and Nineteenth Centuries   73

Table 3.1: Chronological distribution of debt-slave contracts

King	Period		Number of debt-slave contracts			
	A.D.	B.E.	DMSEH	KUMF	STM-KT	Total
Bodawhpaya	1782–1819	1144–1181	11	6	0	17
Bagyidaw	1819–1837	1181–1199	10	1	24	35
Tharawadi	1837–1846	1199–1208	9	4	27	40
Pagan	1846–1853	1208–1215	9	1	9	19
Mindon	1853–1878	1215–1240	52	90	23	165
Thibaw	1878–1885	1240–1247	35	0	21	56
Colonial period	1886–	1247–	1	0	0	1
Date unknown			30	1	0	31
Total			157	103	104	364

Source: DMSEH (Documents of Myanmar Socio-Economic History), KUMF (Microfilms on Myanmar history, Kagoshima University), STM-KT (Salin *Thugaung* Manuscripts, '*Ko-nei Thet-kayits*').
Notes: distribution by score, if the same contracts were in different databases, they are also counted.

strictly speaking, they cannot be simply added together.[3]

The difficulties encountered in using these documents include messy handwriting, clumsy characters, and errors in the spelling in original documents, but, more importantly, there are many instances of partial damage and fading or loss of characters in the original documents. Some of the earliest microfilms produced by Kagoshima University have deteriorated to such an extent that the most important information has been lost, such as date, amount of debts, and the names of creditors and debtors. In this chapter, even for the badly damaged documents on microfilm, if they contain some important information, only that part of the microfilm was taken out and used. Tables 3.1 and 3.2 show the chronological distribution of debt-slave contracts in the databases.

A very few debt contracts have survived from the early Konbaung period, and the earliest contract found was one from Magwe district written in 1791, which says, 'Nga Myat Saing and his wife of Einthet village pawned their son to Aung Myat, the donor of the Pagoda corridor and his wife, to repay their debts'.[4] As shown in Table 3.1, all available debt-slave contracts belong to the period from Bodawhpaya's reign to the last King Thibaw. The main reason why contracts written in the earlier period were not found seems to be the durability of the *para-baik* (a kind of traditional

74   Chapter 3

Table 3.2: Geographic distribution of debt-slave contracts

Region	DMSEH	KUMF	STM-KT	Duplicates	Net total
Amarapura	1				1
Mandalay	22	83			105
Shwebo		10			10
Monywa	2				2
Magwe		6			6
Sale	2				2
Salin	74		104	46	132
Sagu		1			1
Meiktila	18				18
Wundwin	2				2
Kyaukpadan	12				12
Pyobwe	1				1
Pyi	22			9	13
Dawe	1				1
Place unknown		3			3
Total	157	103	104		364
Duplicates	55			55	55
Net total	102	103	104		309

Source: same as Table 3.1; DMSEH, KUMF, and STM-KT.

notebook) on which they were written, as *para-baik* rarely remains in good condition for more than 200 years. It is certain that debt-slave contracts were greater in number in the seventeenth and early eighteenth centuries compared to the eighteenth to nineteenth centuries. The relatively large number of contracts from the reigns of kings Mindon and Thibaw cannot be interpreted as a surge in debt-slavery in this period, since the later the period, the more likely the contracts were to survive.

In terms of the geographical distribution of debt-slave contracts, Salin region stands out, with a total of 132 documents, and Mandalay with 105 documents (Mandalay was built during the reign of King Mindon as the royal capital and remained as it was until the collapse of the Konbaung dynasty in 1885). The Salin region was one of the kingdom's largest granary areas, with an elaborate canal irrigation system, and was known for the accumulation of vast farmland and many debt-slaves by the famous local families known as the Salin *Thugaung*, who had ruled the region since the sixteenth century.[5] Evidence of the Salin *Thugaung* families as creditors has been found in the Pyi, Sale, Sagu, and Kyaukpadan regions, indicating their widespread influence on both sides of the Ayeyarwady River.

Form of debt-slave contracts

As seen in Table 3.2, there were distinctive features in the regional distribution of debt-slave contracts. They were concentrated in such areas as the royal capital, Mandalay, urban Shwebo, and Amarapura,[6] or in rice-producing areas with large irrigation networks, and especially in areas where there existed powerful local families who amassed vast land and human resources through their money-lending operations (Salin, Sale, rural Shwebo, and Meiktila, etc.). In stark contrast, debt contracts with farmland mortgages are found widely throughout the central plains.

First, let us consider how debt-slave contracts were written with reference to two examples. The first is a contract from Salin, the rice-producing region, served by the large river-based irrigation on the west bank of the Ayeyarwady River, and the second is a contract written in the royal capital, Mandalay, in 1881.

(1) In M.E. (Myanmar Era) 1194, on 2 *lazan Wagaung* (July 29, 1832), Nga Lay and his wife Mi Hnin, in order to repay a loan to *Thugaung-ma* Me Hnin,[7] asked Minzeya-shwedaung-kyaw and his wife, 'Please buy me, Nga Lay, for 35 *kyat*s under the condition of *shin-pwa, thei hsoun*', whereupon the husband and wife accepted the offer and bought Nga Lay. The witnesses were the *Taik-soe*[8] Maung Tha Yit and Maung Soe Gale, the money was weighed and assayed and the contract drawn up by Nga Myat Toe, and the scribe was Maung Tu Pyu.[9]

(2) In M.E. 1242, on 4 *lapyegyaw Pyatho* (18 January 1881), Ko Aing, a resident of Meikgagiri quarter, composed a contract that included the words, 'I need money. Please order my wife, Mi Yut to cross large rivers, go down rivers, and go anywhere throughout the rainy season and the dry season on the condition of *thei ma hsoun, shin ma pwa*.' 'Please use her (to climb) tall trees. Please treat her harshly,' and he said to Maung Maung Gyi and his wife, 'Please buy her and use her for 100 *kyat*s in silver coins. After five months have

76   Chapter 3

passed, I will repay the money and redeem Mi Yut. In the event that I should desire her redemption before five months have passed, I will add money in accordance with the customs of towns and villages and redeem her.' Maung Maung Gyi and his wife agreed and drew up a contract with the conditions that they would employ Ko Aing's wife as a slave on terms that *thei mahsoun, shin ma pwa*, would use her to cross large rivers, go down rivers, and go anywhere, would use her to climb tall trees and low trees, and would treat her harshly, and they paid 100 *kyats* in silver coins, which was exceptional for a female debt-slave, and bought her. In the future, if Mi Yut would abscond, or be drafted for public duties, or in cases if there might be interference by a former patron, or any law suits would arise, Ko Aing and his wife Mi Yut will repay all the costs spent together with the price for Mi Yut recorded in this contract. Ko Aing promised that if he were unable to repay the money, my guarantor U Shwe Tun, his wife Mi Nyun, and U Bo Te would repay all the costs spent, together with the price for Mi Yut, and so Maung Maung Gyi and his wife paid 100 *kyats* in silver coins and bought Ko Aing's wife Mi Yut. The witness was U Soe, the drafter was the creditor, and it was written down by Maung Tu Po.[10]

As can be seen in the above two examples, these contracts followed a set format, starting with the date and including the debtor's name and place of residence, the name of the person about to become a debt-slave, the amount of money borrowed (and the name and purity of the currency, in the case of contracts written before 1865), the creditor's name, collateral conditions, and the names of witnesses, weighers, and assayers of the money, drafters of the contract, and scribes. These contracts can be broadly divided into two types; namely, contracts written in a succinct style like (1) and lengthy contracts like (2), from the royal capital Mandalay, which list many collateral conditions. It was a common style of contract writing to begin with the request for a loan by a person in need of money, followed by the creditor's consent to the request, repeating the same sentences about the conditions to ensure that there was no discrepancy in the content of the contract. As far as debt-slave contracts were concerned, instances of the succinct style (1) were fewer in number because the collateral was a human who had his or her own will, and the creditor wanted to avoid, in

Human-mortgage Contracts in the Eighteenth and Nineteenth Centuries 77

advance, possible future risks, such as the debt-slave absconding or the possibility of illness or death of the person mortgaged.

A point that needs to be noted regarding the terminology used in the contracts is that, in spite of being debt-slave contracts, the word 'sell' (*yaun-de*) was used instead of 'mortgage' (*paun-de*). The above two contracts were not exceptional in this regard, and almost all human-mortgage contracts referred to the buying or selling of a person. But it seems that in the case of real slave trading, a contract was almost never drawn up, since we have not been able to discover a single human-sales contract among several thousand written contracts. It can be confirmed from other sources that the slave trade existed in eighteenth- to nineteenth-century Burma,[11] and it is likely that, as in the case of goods, even in the case of the sale of a person, when payment was completed at the time of the transaction, there was no need to draw up a contract.

When farmland was used as security, however, a sharp distinction was made between mortgaging and selling, and there was no confusion whatsoever to be seen in the terminology. Apart from certain districts, there were still strong constraints, both institutional and customary, on the sale of farmland. Not only were there laws prohibiting the disposal of monastic lands and appanage lands,[12] but the custom and notion that farmland was linked in perpetuity to the person who had originally cleared the land and to his descendants remained deep-seated and acted as a brake on the selling of farmland. Even in districts where farmland was bought and sold, not only were the words 'sell' and 'buy' used when selling farmland, but solemn adverbial expressions were invariably added to indicate that the land was being sold 'in perpetuity down to the remotest descendants' or 'so as to build a pagoda or monastery'.[13] It is to be surmised that such wording was considered necessary because the sale of farmland often resulted in litigation in later generations.

In contrast, the slave trade has a long history, as can be seen in frequent references to the trading of slaves and the prices of slaves in inscriptions from the Pagan dynasty founded in the eleventh century, and there existed no provisions in royal ordinances or customary laws banning the slave trade. It is thus true that there was, from early times, no taboo against the buying and selling of people, but, even so, there remains the question of why, even in human-mortgage contracts, the words 'sell' and 'buy' were so readily used and the words 'mortgage', 'pledge', or 'pawn' were not used.

78   Chapter 3

It would seem that, unlike in the case of farmland, the absence of any socially prevalent notion or customary law preventing either the selling or pawning of people was one factor that led to this imprecise usage.

Covenants in the form of fixed phrases

The above two contracts include stereotypical parallel phrases demanding submission, and the contract drawn up in Mandalay, in particular, includes many such phrases. All of these phrases are now completely extinct, and some of them remain unclear as to the meaning in which they were used in those days.[14]

Couplets relating to the death of a debt-slave and a child born to a debt-slave

The most important couplets which are invariably found in slave contracts of the Konbaung period are *shin pwa, thei hsoun* and *thei ma hsoun, shin ma pwa*. *Shin* means 'to live' and *thei* 'to die', while *pwa* means 'to increase' and *hsoun* 'to lose', and the particle *ma* preceding a verb signifies negation. Therefore, *shin pwa, thei hsoun* means literally 'lives and increases, dies and loses', while *thei ma hsoun, shin ma pwa* means 'dies and does not lose, lives and does not increase'.[15]

Regarding the interpretation of these phrases, Daw Ohn Kyi wrote in an article published in 1982 that *shin ma pwa* had two meanings: first, it meant that interest would not be added to the debt while the slave was alive and, second, that a child born to a parent working as a slave would not become a debt-slave.[16] But in 1991 she narrowed the meaning down to the former meaning; namely, that interest would not be added to the debt while the slave was alive.[17]

I would like to argue that the former phrase stated that if a debt-slave died during the period of service, the debt he or she owed was cancelled (*thei hsoun*), but if the slave in service bore a child, the child should become the master's slave (*shin pwa*) and, conversely, the latter phrase meant that if the debt-slave died while serving the creditor, that the heirs of the debt-slave should take over the debt (*thei ma hsoun*), but that the birth of a child to a debt-slave would not automatically make that child a slave (*shin ma pwa*). I discuss this in more detail in the next chapter with examples as to why this is interpreted in this way.

In the case of the Salin region, from 1829 to 1836, these two conditions coexisted, but from 1837 to 1885 only the condition of *thei ma hsoun, shin ma pwa* was written in all human-mortgage contracts. This trend was the same in other regions, and with the passage of time, more emphasis was placed on getting the money back from the offspring rather than on securing the born children as slaves.

Demand for obedient service

Contracts (1) and (2) above include stereotypical parallel phrases demanding submission, and contracts drawn up in Mandalay, in particular, include many such couplets. Phrases such as 'cross large rivers, go down rivers' and 'tall trees and low trees', and (although not found in the above two contracts) 'near journey, far journey' were used when demanding obedience to difficult orders or even contradictory orders without complaint.

The most widely used customary law text in those days, the Manugye Dhammathat, says in regard to debt-slaves, 'They shall not be made to cross the great river, or to go down the river, or to climb a tree or a shrub in their services. If you do so, let them go.'[18] As the Manugye Dhammathat was 'not really a code, nor a legal synopsis, but rather an encyclopedic record of the prevailing customs and practices of the time, together with the rules of governance laid down in earlier Dhammathats',[19] even if there were instances that were clearly contrary to the norms set forth by the Dhammathat, it was not possible to invalidate the contracts. Rather, if the customs were widely practiced in society, that reality should take precedence. Even so, it is noteworthy that the norm shown in the customary law text was clearly negative for the extreme abuse of debt-slaves.

The phrase translated as 'please treat her harshly' uses a verb that in modern Burmese means to contravene, overcome, or suppress. Since this phrase was used only when a woman became a debt-slave, it was probably a tacit understanding that the creditor could request sexual services from the woman about to become a debt-slave, as Daw Ohn Kyi presumed.[20]

According to the customs of the towns and villages

The phrase 'in accordance with the customs of towns and villages' seen in the contract from Mandalay meant that an extra payment, in addition to the money borrowed, would be necessary if the debt-slave was redeemed with the intention of moving to another household. This phrase was also

80   Chapter 3

often used in contracts of Salin *Thugaung* families, although not found in example (1) above.

Immunity from liability for negligence

All of the above conditions were intended to protect the interests of creditors. Were there any conditions, then, that would protect the debt-slaves? The only one that seems to fall into this category is the phrase 'in case the tray or bowl is broken', which meant if a slave broke furniture or a utensil while working, the master would not demand the slave to pay for it. However, there are only a few examples of this phrase in the contracts, and it was not used in isolation, but was accompanied by such phrases as 'across the large river and down the river', or 'low tree, high tree', which demanded the obedience of debt-slaves.[21]

Guarantees in case of escape and so on

These clauses were not phrased in any particular way, but some words were often written for the contingency of being unable to use a debt-slave and to make compensation for a creditor. The contingencies envisaged were the escape of the slave, drafting by the government, the intervention of the former master or other persons concerned, or law suits. In such cases, a guarantor who signed the contracts should reimburse all costs incurred, including the total amount borrowed and the price of unfulfilled labor, or the cost of litigation. For example, in one contract, where a mother borrowed money by mortgaging her divorced daughter, the name of two guarantors and the following words were added: 'In the event of the daughter's escape, or her former husband or son should attempt to take her back and cause a dispute, the money borrowed and all expenses incurred should be repaid by the two guarantors herein named.'[22] There were cases in which the guarantors were actually forced to repay their debts, most often in cases of escape, but I have not yet found a single case in which compensation was demanded from guarantors because of the drafting of the debt-slave by the royal government.

As for a law suit relating to debt-slaves, there is one case in Mandalay in 1862 in which parents made an accusation against a village head, saying that they mortgaged their daughter in order to borrow money from the head, but the headman sold their daughter to an official from Mandalay, without informing her parents.[23]

Restrictions on redemptions

Being a debt-slave was not a status but a temporary situation; once the debt was repaid, the debt-slave returned to being a free person. However, some contracts limited the time when they could repay their debts. This was not a fixed phrase, but was written down as a specific number of years after which the debt-slave could repay the debt and redeem freedom. In the case of the Mandalay contract mentioned above, the period was five months, but in the case of the Salin and Sale regions, the period was extended to between one and three years. In a contract written in the Pyobwe region in 1882, a promise was made to repay the debt with interest of 5% per month if the mortgaged person was redeemed before a set time.[24] The number of contracts with this redemption limitation was not large, and not a few contracts included words that the mortgaged person could be redeemed at any time of the day or night if the debt was cleared.

Among these covenants, a form of fixed phrases, '*thei hsoun shin pwa*' or '*thei ma hsoun shin ma pwa*', and the clause on guarantees in case of escape were often written down as important rules, regardless of the region. In the vicinity of the royal capital, there was a tendency to write stricter and more detailed clauses, as exemplified by the above-quoted contract from Mandalay. In Salin *Thugaung* contracts, no formulaic clauses were written to encourage obedience to service, and it seems that the guarantor in case of escape was only specified if the fear of escape could be perceived in the slightest in advance. In the 51 debt-slave contracts of Salin *Thugaung*, only six contracts were provided with a guarantor.[25] This may be due to the fact that the creditors, the Salin *Thugaung* families, were well aware of the situation in the provinces and could judge whether there was a possibility of escape or not. On the other hand, in all the contracts in the Meiktila region, where the governor of the Three Towns of Indaw and his wife were the creditors, a guarantor was nominated in all the contracts. In debt-slave contracts in Mandalay, both contracts with guarantors and without guarantors coexisted. Whether or not a guarantor was considered mandatory seems to be more a difference in the mindset of individual creditors and methods of slave management than a difference between the royal city and the provinces.

Regional characteristics of debt-slave contracts

Royal capital

The people who lent money and held debt-slaves in urban areas such as the royal capital were mainly royalty such as queens, princesses, and princes, as well as eminent military personnel, ministers, and high-ranking officials. Among military personnel who were creditors in debt-slave contracts, there were especially commanders of the royal cavalry, the navy, and infantry. Wealthy people in the private sector, known as donors of pagodas and monasteries, were also included in the list of creditors in debt-slave contracts. Among the royalty, some people engaged in the money-lending business on a large scale. The Princess of North Ladies' Palace, Princess Pinthay Kaung Tin; Min-maha-min-tin-yaza, the elder brother of the Zabwe-daung Queen; Prince Tigwin and his sister; and Prince Sain Pyun were often seen in money-lending contracts in Mandalay. In Amarapura, the governor of Myedu Myo, called by the title of Min-nei-myo-si-yan-aung, often appeared as a money-lender, and among the high-ranking officials, the name of Min-gyi-maha-min-gaung, the provincial governor sent from the center to the Shwebo region, also appeared frequently. In addition to the current high-ranking officials, retired officials such as a former official in charge of propagation also appeared in the contracts.

The people who became debt-slaves were commoners, represented only by the names of their villages and their own name in the debt-slave contracts. In the vicinity of the royal capital, there was a document in which an *ahmudan* called *ahsaun kain* (namely, an attendant who accompanied the king with arms) and his wife worked as debt-slaves at Min-maha-min-tin-yaza's residence, but there were very few cases where *ahmudan*s became debt-slaves.[26] In the capital area, the proportion of *ahmudan* population tended to be high, but the number of cases in the debt-slave contracts in the capital area in which the *ahmudan*s offered themselves as debt-slaves was unexpectedly small, except the example above. The village chiefs, who were often hereditary officials in localities, were also included in the *ahmudan* group, as they had received the land and recognition letter from the king. I have not yet found any examples in which village chiefs or their family members became debt-slaves in the capital area.[27]

Cases of mass runaways

The escape of debt-slaves occurred across the regions, but there were also examples of escape unique to the royal capital. For those who had to pledge family members as debt-slaves, it was very difficult for them to repay their debts and regain their freedom. Because labor, while they were used as debt-slaves, was considered as interest on the borrowed money, no matter how long they worked, the initial debt principal would never be reduced. In the meantime, in order for their families to survive, they tended to pile up debts one after another on the initial amount of debt, and it is likely that many ended up in debt-slavery for the rest of their lives, carrying the accumulated large amount of debt on their shoulders. Many of the debt-slave contracts from the Salin region, which are discussed in detail in the next chapter, illustrate such an outcome.

It is not hard to imagine that people in such circumstances were tempted to take up an emergency measure, namely absconding. However, the consequences for those around them if they resorted to the last measure of escaping were immeasurable. Often, another family member was offered as a debt-slave for compensation. In some cases, the guarantor was charged with the sum of the debt and the labor price of the runaway slave, and when he was unable to pay it, the guarantor's wife or daughter was taken in the place of the escapee.[28]

It is also questionable whether runaway debt-slaves were able to escape successfully. A circular was delivered at once, and the guarantors and witnesses were called immediately in order to dispatch a search party. In the Manugye Dhammathat, the customary law text in which a surprisingly large number of pages are devoted to how to deal with runaway slaves, it is noted that those who gave fugitive slaves overnight lodging or shelter would be subject to fines or alternative labor. It shows the strictness with which the escape of debt-slaves was treated.

Despite this, there were numerous examples of debt-slaves escaping. The following case happened in the residence of Min-maha-min-tin-yaza, the General of the Royal Navy, who lived in Mandalay. It is noteworthy in its scale and deliberate planning.

> (1) In 1861, having become a debt-slave of a queen living in the lady's quarters of the palace, Nga Tei and his wife Mi Ngwe, three sons, a daughter and her husband, a family of seven in all, proposed to Min-

84   Chapter 3

maha-min-tin-yaza and his wife that they wished to change their patron from the queen and asked to redeem them and buy them as debt-slaves. This proposal was accepted, and the family, having become debt-slaves of the couple, each applied one after another for additional loans, and as far as the evidence is known, they added loans of 170 *kyat*s in total on 22 occasions.[29] In the meantime, they succeeded in having their son and daughter, who were debt-slaves of another family, changing to the couple's residence,[30] and in the end the family, nine in total, worked for the couple. However, Nga Tei's entire family ran away in 1863, and a document calling for cooperation in the search was dispatched to people concerned.[31]

This was a tough way of life and took full advantage of the laxity of control on the part of the master, making a bold move to get the whole family back to freedom.[32]

The following cases also happened in the residence of Min-maha-min-tin-yaza.

(2) Nga Tei and his wife Mi Sa U and their son and daughter, a family of four, with total loans 266 *kyat* 5 *mu*, ran away, in 1863.[33]

(3) Nga Chit Pwe and his wife Mi Lei transferred from another master in 1862 and, after they piled up their loan as much as possible, ran away in 1863.[34]

(4) Nga Kyu and his wife Mi Kyaw and their children, a family of four, ran away in 1865.[35]

In each case, the debt-slaves moved from their previous creditor to Min-maha-min-tin-yaza, whereupon they gathered the remaining family members at the residence of Min-maha-min-tin-yaza and, after having made additional loans, they all ran away. The reason that four instances of escape by debt-slaves occurred one after another in a few years may have been that they made clever use of loose supervision by a high-ranking patron who left such matters to stewards, or a broker who helped them run away might have been involved. But it is not known whether these four families were able to escape from their pursuers and succeeded in making a living as free people.

Such a case of an entire family escaping together was not common in rural communities. It was not unusual for a single debt-slave to escape

Human-mortgage Contracts in the Eighteenth and Nineteenth Centuries   85

from a creditor, but rarely did an entire family abscond. Most of those who escaped alone were traced and found, but it was almost impossible for a large group of people to escape in a rural society. It seems that factors such as the concentration of the population in the capital, the urban anonymity of the city, and the loose management of debt-slaves by a master of extremely high status made mass absconding possible in Mandalay.

It was not uncommon for debt-slaves to change masters. When their old masters demanded repayment of their debts and they were unable to do so, they often moved on to influential big money-lenders who could lend them larger sums of money. Thus, debt-slaves also tended to be concentrated from small and medium-sized money-lenders to powerful money-lenders with large financial resources, as well as farmland. These offers were usually accepted, and it made sense for the royalty and high officials to have and use a large number of debt-slaves.

Among the 21 debt-slave contracts of Min-maha-min-tin-yaza written during four years (1860–63), 16 were related to the change of patrons from other creditors to Min-maha-min-tin-yaza,[36] and only five were new debt-slave contracts.[37] Because of the high status of a patron with many slaves working in the residence, they could expect relatively light labor and loose control over the slaves. The phrase 'As I was not happy under my old master', which was written in a contract when a person wished to change masters, was a fixed phrase and did not mention the specific circumstances.

However, as land became the most secured collateral for loans from the latter part of the eighteenth century, not only in agricultural regions but also in the capital area, creditors were eager to get farmland, especially irrigated paddy fields, as mortgage. The mortgaged land was cultivated either by share-cropping tenants or by household slaves, as well as debt-slaves. In the case of Min-maha-min-tin-yaza, there were 20 contracts of land mortgage or purchase written in the period 1854–76,[38] and it is worth noting that the size of the land pledged or purchased was very large. For example, in 1862, he bought 54 plots of paddy field in Ava from a royal family,[39] and in 1866 he took paddy fields as a mortgage for 500 *kyats*, which were large enough to plant 4,750 bundles of rice seedlings. In 1875, he took a group of paddy fields that produced 1,200 baskets of paddy as a mortgage for 1,000 *kyats*,[40] and later he added 400 *kyats* and purchased the paddy fields at the price of 1,400 *kyats*.[41] The money spent on pledging or purchasing the land amounted to 3,648 *kyats*, without counting seven contracts in which amounts of money were missing due to loss of letters. The purchased paddy fields and orchards were spread over several regions, including the irrigated rice fields of Madaya, Mekkaya, and Ava.[42] The management of agricultural land was thought to have been another major source of accumulating fortune.

Royalty, high-ranking court officers, or military personnel who accumulated debt-slaves and land through their money-lending businesses sent managers to supervise the cultivation of the land acquired and the sale of products to the market. In the case of paddy, they also lent it out widely (the interest on paddy loans was estimated to exceed 100% in ten months), and although the risk of recovery was higher than with cash loans, they were extremely profitable.

Debt-slaves in agrarian regions

Unlike debt-slave contracts in the capital area, people who appeared as creditors in debt-slave contracts in rural regions were hereditary rulers of local administrative units, such as *myo*, *taik*, and *ywa*, and people called *daga* (donor), who were benefactors of religious or public utilities. In some cases, people in charge of managing irrigation channels, such as canals, weirs, and water allocation, appeared as creditors in debt-slave contracts, but the number was limited. Brokers who mediated various transactions also acted as creditors. The governors of *myo* sent from the royal government, and assistant governors called *sit-ke*s,[43] also appeared, but less frequently. On the other hand, the people who were indebted and enslaved did not differ from those in the urban areas, and were common people who were not associated with any position or office, and were described only by their personal names. Land mortgage *thet-kayit*s reveal village chiefs who mortgaged village land in times of social disruption in order to pay taxes on the village, but it was very rare that village chiefs or their family members became debt-slaves.

Debt-slave contracts in Meiktila

The Meiktila region is located right in the middle of the semi-arid region, at the midpoint of the traffic route between Mandalay and Pagan. The area is widely used for rice cultivation supported by the huge tank irrigation system fed from Meiktila Lake, which is believed to have been built during the Pyu period. Nearly 1,000 land-mortgage contracts have already been collected from the area, but there are very few debt-slave contracts; only 18 contracts written in 1873–85 are included in the DMSEH database.[44]

Most creditors in the debt-slave contracts were hereditary local rulers, and 12 contracts were related to the local ruler, known as Thon Myo Ok (the ruler of three *myos*) in Indaw. The creditors of two other debt-slave contracts were a man called Ko Bo Tu and his wife. As the witnesses and draft scribes in their contracts were the same people used by Thon Myo Ok, it is possible that this couple were close relatives of Thon Myo Ok.

The condition *thei ma hsoun, shin ma pwa* (i.e., if the debt-slave died, the debt would be owed to his descendants, but a child born to the mother while working as a debt-slave would not become a slave) was included in 13 contracts. There was not a single instance of a *thei hsoun, shin pwa*. As already mentioned, this condition had disappeared completely since the late 1830s in Salin and the surrounding region, and emphasis was moving from securing the children as slaves to the debt collection from the family members of deceased debt-slaves.

The conditions of 'cross large rivers, go down rivers' and 'climb high trees and low trees' were seen in nine contracts, as were two instances of the condition 'please treat harshly'. Only one contract included the phrase 'even if plates and bowls are broken' and, in contrast, compensation in the case of escape was specified in 13 contracts. However, in four cases, the father (the contractor of the certificate) was the guarantor and, in two cases, a party to the contract other than the parent was the guarantor, which was a somewhat simpler form of guarantor than a third party. In the case of fugitive slaves, the amount that had to be repaid was the total amount of debt piled on the slave, the price of labor not performed, and all costs incurred in the event of incidental litigation and so on, which was a common practice in both urban and local areas. When the amount of debt was high, the number of guarantors tended to increase, and in the three cases where the amount of debt exceeded 100 *kyats*, more than one guarantor was nominated.

There were two contracts in which the guarantor was made to promise not only to repay the total amount owed but also to repay the debt with interest at 1% or 5% per month until the debt could be repaid. This was rather an exceptional promise, which I have not yet found in contracts in other regions:

88   Chapter 3

M. E.1242, 5 *lazan Wagaung* (A.D. 1880), Mi Po, a villager of Kanbya said that we need money, please buy my daughter Mi Ma Ma as a debt-slave, with the condition of <u>*thei ma hsoun, shin ma pwa*</u>, to Indaw Thon Myo Ok and his wife. Indaw Thon Myo Ok and his wife agreed to buy Mi Po's daughter Mi Ma Ma with the conditions that <u>*thei ma hsoun*</u>, <u>*shin ma pwa*</u>, <u>climb tall trees and low trees</u>, <u>cross large rivers</u>, <u>go down rivers</u> and paid 115 *kyat*s. The guarantors are Ko Tha of Indaw Thon Myo, and Ko Kyaw Toe of Kanbya village. In case Mi Ma Ma won't work and escape, they should repay all the money with the interest of 5% a month. Witnesses are the donor of a rest house, U Po Thei, Judge U Hmon and U Pan Kyaun, Ko Thugyi, and the scribe is Ko Chin Po.[45]

As for the change of masters, the only one case which I found was that of a mother and her three children, each a debt-slave in a separate house, who were transferred together to Thon Myo Ok's house for the price of 438 *kyat*s. It seems that the number of influential families who were wealthy enough to hold many debt-slaves was limited in Meiktila.

The two contracts of the chief of Natsun Hmo village reveal the escape of a debt-slave who was a young girl called Mi Mi Hkin. She became a debt-slave of the village chief in the summer of 1885, escaped five months later, and had not been found after a month's search. The guarantor of Mi Mi Hkin was then asked to offer his own daughter Mi Bay as a debt-slave in exchange for the escapee.[46]

Debt-slave contracts in Kyaukpadan, Sale, and Pyi

Kyaukpadan is a region slightly northeast of Salin on the east bank across the Ayeyarwady River. Sale is also on the east bank and closer to the riverbank than Kyaukpadan. Pyi is located at the midpoint between Upper and Lower Burma, and has developed as a major transit point for commodities. Pyi is also known as the hub of the fortified city-state of the ancient Pyu State, Sriksetra. Pyi money-lending contracts collected in the Museum Library in Pyi include 22 debt-slave contracts, of which up to nine overlap with the debt-slave contracts of Kyaukpadan and Sale. As it was a custom to make multiple copies of contracts for the creditor, the debtor, and the witnesses or guarantors, copies of the same contracts are often found at different places. Of the remaining 13 copies, eight were of Salin *Thugaung*

Human-mortgage Contracts in the Eighteenth and Nineteenth Centuries   89

families as creditors, and only a few were considered to be from the Pyi region.

The creditors in Kyaukpadan's 12 debt-slave contracts[47] were the donor of the monastery and his wife, a chief of the irrigation canals, another donor of the monastery, and the Salin *Thugaung*s on the opposite bank. Creditors in Salin were Ma Hkaing and Ma Hkaing's daughter, Me Kyi Nyo, who was called the donor of the Ngazin monastery. There were four contracts in which Me Kyi Nyo was a creditor. On the other hand, the people who appeared as debtors were all common people who were called only by their personal names. In four cases, the parents or one of the parents made their daughters debt-slaves, in three cases sons were pawned, in one case a son-in-law was pawned, in another case a husband mortgaged his wife, and one case was a contract in which a man mortgaged himself. The other two were contracts to put additional loans on the debt-slaves. Nearly half of the creditors in Kyaukpadan contracts were Salin *Thugaung*s and, perhaps because of their influence, in all debt-slave contracts in Kyaukpadan, the distinction between the body price of the slave[48] and the additional debt on the slave was written separately. The body price fell within the range of 24 to 60 *kyat*s, and additional loans varied widely.

Furthermore, there were no fixed phrases such as 'cross large rivers, go down small rivers' or 'please treat harshly' (to demand the submission of the debt-slaves) written in the contracts. It was very important for creditors in the capital area to set up guarantors in case of escape, but in Kyaukpadan only two contracts included the names of guarantors; in one instance, a neighbor was appointed, while in the other, the father, the contractor who had sent his son into slavery, was a simple guarantor. There was only one contract with the phrase *thei ma hsoun, shin ma pwa* (meaning that if the debt-slave died, the debt should be repaid by the guarantor or slave's relatives, but if a slave gave birth to a baby, the child wouldn't become a debt-slave). In another contract, the phrase *ngwe ma hsoun, lu ma hsoun* was found, which, in literal translation, means 'not losing money, not losing human', but, as already mentioned, the implications of this term have not yet been grasped.[49]

There are two examples of family members who became debt-slaves to replace a family member who had been in debt-slavery: the first was a case of a daughter becoming a debt-slave in place of her mother, who was in poor health. The mother owed her body price, 30 *kyat*s, and an additional

90   Chapter 3

loan of 90 *kyats* (in total, 120 *kyats*). The daughter owed the debt of 120 *kyats* on the mother and an additional 80 *kyats* (in total 200 *kyats*) on herself and become a debt-slave.[50] Another example was a contract in which a father and his son were both debt-slaves to Me Kyi Nyo of Salin *Thugaungs*, but it was agreed to make a new contract in which the father alone would take all the debt (which included his body price and debts and the son's body price and debts, and the price of borrowed paddy, etc.), which amounted in total to 168 *kyats* 1 *pe*, and would become a debt-slave of Me Kyi Nyo.[51]

There is also an example in Salin *Thugaung* contracts where a father signed a contract to become a debt-slave for 30 *kyats* and, at the same time, the two sons were made to promise to take turns working in his place if the father was unable to work because of his age or because of his bad health.[52]

Because Kyaukpadan is a smaller region compared to Meiktila, the human relation seemed to be closer compared to big regions or urban areas, and the contracts written in Kyaukpadan lacked the fixed phrases to demand submission of debt-slaves. Being under the influence of the Salin *Thugaungs*, who also lent money widely in Kyaukpadan, the style of the contract was succinct and responded well to the specific circumstances of both the creditor and the debtor. These were characteristics of the contracts found in Kyaukpadan and the neighboring areas.

Only two debt-slave contracts were found from Sale, south of Kyaukpadan. The creditors were the donors of a monastery and the chief of a village and his wife. These contracts were written in 1883 and 1884 (i.e., near to the end of the dynasty). In one, the husband made his wife a debt-slave, and in the other the father made his son a debt-slave; in both cases it was stated that they were to be used as domestic slaves and, in the latter case, the chief of another village was made a guarantor to compensate the creditor in case of escape. In this contract, the fixed expression 'in accordance with the customs of towns and villages' was written to ensure that any change of masters should be done with the payment of additional money to the total amount of debt owed.

From Wundwin, north of Meiktila, two human-mortgage contracts were found in a monastery in the village of Pan-kyain,[53] both of which were attributed to the same creditors, Mr. and Mrs. Maung Kaung Mya, who were engaging in a brokerage business (*pwe-sa*); one was dated 1795, and the other was partly broken and the date lost. In one case, a couple was unable to pay the legal fees owed to Maung Kaung Mya and his wife, so they pawned their daughter instead. The other is that of Nga Hla Bin, a cavalry captain who had borrowed the cost of his horse and soldier's expenses for the campaign against Siam from Maung Kaung Mya and his wife, but was unable to repay it, so had to pawn his own son to the creditors. This is one of the few instances of a cavalry captain, a mid-level *ahmudan*, taking his family into debt-slavery.

Among Pyi contracts, one, written in 1850, shows how the death of a debt-slave would be dealt with if he or she died in service under the terms of *thei ma hsoun, shin ma pwa*.[54] Maung Pe, a resident of a village called Min-ywa, had pawned his two sons as debt-slaves to the donors of a monastery, Mr. and Mrs. U Pu, for 170 *kyats* in 25% silver alloy. However, both sons died for unknown reasons. Mr. and Mrs. U Pu demanded repayment of the 170 *kyats* from their father, who was the principal of the contracts and also guarantor, but he was unable to pay and had to pledge his farmland, for the time being, to Mr. and Mrs. U Pu in place of his dead sons. The father promised to pay the creditors 170 *kyats* with 5% interest per month if he failed to repay the loan by the due date, and that he would reimburse the creditors for any costs and damages if the creditors could not use the field because co-heirs intervened[55] or if they filed a complaint against him to the village chief. Thus, he signed a new contract to that effect in the presence of two villagers as witnesses. From the creditors' point of view, this was the strict enforcement of the condition in the contract, *thei ma hsoun, shin ma pwa*, but it reveals the harsh situation in which the father was placed: he had lost two sons, pawned his farmland, and the debt he owed was still intact.

Various contracts in the form of human mortgage

Some human-mortgage contracts, while entered into as debt-slave contracts, actually allowed debtors to pay debts in other forms, rather than being subjected to service as debt-slaves. The number of such contracts is limited, and I found only four cases as follows: (1) a contract written in 1861, collected in Pyi; (2) a contract written in 1867, collected in Kyaukpadan; (3) a contract written in 1869, collected in Salin; and (4) a contract written in 1884, collected in Salin. However, if we look at the creditors, the creditor of the first and the second contracts was Ma Hkaing

92 Chapter 3

of Salin *Thugaung*s, and the creditor of the third and fourth contracts was none other than Me Kyi Nyo, the daughter of Ma Hkaing (the donor of the Ngazin monastery). In other words, the creditors of all four contracts were Salin *Thugaung*s.

(1) Mi...[letters missing], who lives in [letter missing] village, said to Ma Hkaing, the mother of the governor of Salin Myo, 'As I have to repay a debt to Ma Nu Tha, the donor of the monastery, I would like to ask you to buy my son Nga Kun as a slave for 20 *kyat*s. Then I will deliver to your residence 15 baskets of paddy per year, like a share-cropping tenancy, until the price of his body will be repaid.' Ma Hkaing paid 20 *kyat*s by 2 *kyat* 8 *mu* alloy, measured with a *hinda* weight,[56] and bought Nga Kun under the conditions of 15 baskets of paddy delivered to her place per year.[57]

(2) Shin Ako, a resident of Paungbin-ze area, said, 'Please buy my daughter Mi Pyo for 30 silver coins as the body price on the terms of *shin ma pwa thei ma hsoun*. However, please not take her into your residence, but I will deliver 15 baskets of paddy per month to your place, until I will repay the debt.' Ma Hkaing agreed and bought Mi Pyo under the above conditions and made a contract.[58]

(3) Nga Hmon, a resident of Thein Chan village, once signed a debt-slave contract with the donor of the Ngazin monastery at the body price of 30 *kyat*s with additional loan of 35 *kyat*s, in total 65 *kyat*s by silver-copper currencies of 60% silver purity, which is equivalent to 50 *kyat*s in silver coins. However, instead of working as a slave in the creditor's residence, Nga Hmon promised that he would repay the debt by working as farm labor for both the rainy and dry seasons for six years and repay 17 *kyat*s in each year in silver-copper currencies. He had already paid for three years. But there remained 51 *kyat*s for three other years farm labor, his son Nga Kya Yaw's body price of 30 *kyat*s, and additional loan on him of 35 *kyat*s, in total 65 *kyat*s, equivalent to 50 *kyat*s in pure silver coin, and if the price of paddy loan is also counted he owes 168 *kyat*s 1*pe* in pure silver coin. Nga Hmon asked the creditor to take him as a debt-slave, at the total sum of his debt, and to annul the contracts both of himself

and his son. The donor of Ngazin monastery agreed, and made a new contract.[59]

(4) Maung Myat Twa and his wife, Mi Daw, who live in an orchard in Paing-yin area, said, 'We need to repay our debts to others, so please buy our daughter, Mi Ya Pyu, as a domestic slave under the terms of *shin ma pwa, thei ma hsoun*, at 25 *kyat*s in silver and copper alloy currency which is equivalent to 24 silver coins as a body price and additional loan of 76 *kyat*s. Please do not make her work in your residence, until we can repay the money, as we will deliver 15 baskets of paddy per month to your residence.' Then the mother of the *myo-thugyi*, the donor of the Ngazin monastery, agreed and prepared a contract.[60]

In the above contracts (2) and (4), the parents borrowed money by pawning their daughters as debt-slaves, but in both cases the parents asked for their daughters not to be taken to the creditor's residence; instead, they promised to deliver 15 baskets of paddy per month to the creditor until they could repay the debt. Similarly, in contract (1), a mother offered her son as a debt-slave to Ma Hkaing, the creditor, but she asked Ma Hkaing not to take him as a house-slave and, instead, let him deliver 15 baskets of paddy per year to the creditor's residence.[61] Her request was admitted by the creditor. In case (3), separate debt-slave contracts of a father and son were canceled and a new contract was made, in which the father would owe all the debt of his own, as well as his son's. It is noteworthy that there was a time when the father had repaid his debt by working in the creditor's paddy fields, and his labor contribution was counted at 17 *kyat*s per year. These documents show us that there were cases in which people could repay their debt by labor or paddy, like in the case of unsecured loans, even under the debt-slave contracts.

People who entered into debt-slave contracts were the most vulnerable and poorest in society, those who had no way of earning a living other than to send a family member into debt-slavery. In the four cases given here, they had no other choice but to pledge themselves in order to borrow money, but at the same time there seems to have been a pressing need for fathers, sons, or daughters not to be taken into custody by their creditors' households. It seems that the creditors Ma Hkaing and Me Kyi

94　Chapter 3

Nyo allowed them to repay the debt in the form of labor or paddy, in consideration of their circumstances. However, if the debtors failed to repay their debts, the creditor could demand service as a debt-slave, as seen in the third contract.

Although we can sense consideration on the part of the creditor, it would be difficult to assert that these contracts express generosity of the creditors as patrons. This is because, for example, in cases (2) and (4), when calculating the interest charged on the debt, while the monthly interest rate on the unsecured debt was 5%, the interest rate charged in these contracts was more than twice as high as the rate of unsecured debt. The high rate of interest might be demanded as compensation for not using the daughter as a domestic servant. On the other hand, in case (1), the interest is quite low, and in case (3), it is only slightly higher than the interest on unsecured debt. The small number of sources and the wide variation in interest make it impossible to draw a unified conclusion, but it shows that debt-slavery contracts were not always entered into on certain terms, and that different terms were sometimes applied depending on the circumstances of debtors.

Lastly, I would like to consider the relation of human-mortgage contracts and human trafficking. In the case of farmland mortgages, if additional borrowing on the same land was repeated many times, it often resulted in the sale of the mortgaged land. In such a case, a land-selling contract was made without fail. How about human mortgage? Repeated heavy borrowings on the same mortgage were common phenomena, both in the case of land mortgage and human mortgage. However, among the 309 debt-slave contracts which I could see, there is only one contract, written in Kyaukpadan in 1878, in which a daughter of one family was a debt-slave, but was finally sold to the creditor, as seen in the following contract.

> Maung Kain, a resident of Kyaukpon village, and his wife asked Mr. and Mrs. Ko Taw, the chief of the irrigation systems of Paukma village, to buy their daughter Mi Tun ultimately under the term of *thei hsoun shin pwa*, at 50 pieces of silver coins.
>
> Then, Ko Taw and his wife bought Mi Htun ultimately under the term of *thei hsoun, shin pwa*.[62]

The words 'ultimately buy' were expressed in Burmese as *ahsoun apain we-de* and means, in the literal sense, finally (*ahsoun*) buy with ownership (*apain we-de*). In an ordinary debt-slave contract, the term *thei hsoun, shin pwa* had already fallen into disuse at this time, but the use of this phrase in the above contract indicates that the daughter was owned by the creditor and became a slave to be passed down from generation to generation. In other words, if she would give birth to a child, the child would also be owned by her creditors as a slave.

As in the case of land, piled-up additional debts on the same mortgage were quite common in the case of human mortgage. In the runaway cases that happened in Mandalay, mentioned earlier, they also put additional loans on each family member as much as possible. So, what was the merit for the creditors of lending these additional loans so many times? Did it make sense to the creditor to give additional loans to the debt-slaves already under a creditor's control? The answer to these questions seems to be that, for the wealthy money-lenders who owned vast farmland, it was necessary to keep labor for agriculture and for domestic use in perpetuity. And another inducement would have been that if the debt-slave was unable to repay the total amount of debt swelled by additional loans, other members of the debt-slave's family would become debt-slaves one after another, and the creditor could expect the pool of labor to expand. In case the creditor was not wealthy enough to lend additional loans, debt-slaves often sought other creditors who could provide the loans they needed.

However, in the middle to late Konbaung period, debt-slave contracts accounted for less than 10% of all money-lending contracts, while the number of land-mortgage contracts increased rapidly. As time passed, various types of land-mortgage contracts developed, while, on the other hand, human-mortgage contracts went into a gradual decline.

Debt-slavery in the context of history

In the above, we have examined the actual conditions of debt-slaves that appeared in human-mortgage contracts in eighteenth- to nineteenth-century Burma. The next issue to examine is the characteristics and significance of the debt-slaves during this period in the historical context. In addition, it is necessary to overview structural changes in the economy as a background factor for the declining position of debt-slaves.

96   Chapter 3

The most important work to be referred in this regard is V. Lieberman's landmark study,[63] which shows us the significance of the debt-slave as a historical actor from the late sixteenth to the early eighteenth centuries in Burma.

Framework of Lieberman's argument

Lieberman noted that slaves owned by private individuals and organizations were a lost population to the Crown, as they were not subject to labor levies or taxation, and in the period of the kingdom's decline (i.e., when levies and tax burdens would fall on a limited population), lots of *ahmudan*s made themselves debt-slaves of powerful families in order to avoid the excessive claims of the king.[64] As a result, the population available to the royal power became increasingly narrow and that often caused the collapse of dynasties.

For example, after the death of the founder of the first Taungoo dynasty, King Bayin-naung (r. 1551–81), who had built a large empire through military success, his successor, King Nanda-bayin (r. 1581–99), recruited large numbers of men from the delta region to suppress rebellions by Thai tribes and tributary states. However, repeated expeditions against these rebellions failed to yield any results and only exhausted the men and resources. The conscriptions and taxation imposed on the population became increasingly severe, and many people sold themselves as debt-slaves to escape the king's claims. Then, the king used harsh measures to compensate for the shortage of personnel, such as forcibly transferring young *ahmudan*s who had escaped and hidden themselves in the army, or compelled the return of young monks to secular life. These measures did not succeed, but the result was the further decrease in the population, the shortage of paddy production, and the skyrocketing price of the crop. Thus, the decline of the dynasty was accelerated.

In the second Taungoo period (1597–1752), the first three kings (Nyaung Yang, Anauk-hpetlun, and Thalun) initiated administrative reforms to control the countryside and restructure the *ahmudan* population to maximize the labor force under the monarchy, with some success accomplished. However, in the midst of this, royalty, ministers, and all rank officials and local chiefs were in a constant race to control taxes and people beyond their own sphere of authority in order to increase their control over resources and political influence. Officials were given rights to receive 7–10% of tax collected as commission and judicial court fees under their jurisdiction, but they had no fixed salaries. They attempted to deprive the people under their jurisdiction as much as possible and, as a result, many people went into debt-slavery. King Thalun took preventive measures, such as the expansion of arable land through irrigation, and issued an edict to cut off the limbs of tax collectors who collected more tax than the prescribed amount.

After King Thalun's death, successive kings took measures to prevent enslavement of *ahmudan*s, but the situation deteriorated, and from the mid-seventeenth century onwards, the kingdom entered a prolonged period of decline over a century. During the period of 1664–98, an unprecedented number of edicts related to debt-slavery were issued to restrict the enslavement of *ahmudan*. In 1728, King Taninga-nwei issued an edict that forbade lower class *ahmudan* from becoming slaves or monks, and took emergency measures, such as ordering soldiers who were enslaved to take up arms and return to the original force.

This is the gist of Lieberman's argument that the struggle between the central and local elites for human resources drove the cycle from rise to decline and final collapse of kingdoms, and that debt-slavery was a significant channel through which the most important resource, the *ahmudan* population, was diverted from the central power to the private sector.

The kings of the Taungoo period indeed repeatedly issued edicts forbidding the conversion of *ahmudan* into debt-slaves, and we can read the kings' impatience with the outflow of the population from under the kingship. These arguments by Lieberman are still the most convincing argument for explaining the rise and fall of ruling power in the first and restored Taungoo periods.

Debt-slavery in the Konbaung era

If we look at the founding period of the Konbaung dynasty, we can certainly see a similar phenomena to what Lieberman describes in his book about the Taungoo period. Alaunghpaya, the founder of the Konbaung period, tried to prevent the flow of the *ahmudan* population into debt-slavery, as he needed a large fighting force in his war efforts against the Mon kingdom in Pegu and other neighboring countries. In 1752, he ruled that prisoners and exiles could not be converted to private slaves, but instead should receive provisions and residence sites so as to be incorporated into

98   Chapter 3

the *ahmudan* groups.[65] At Pegu, he issued a decree freeing all *ahmudan*s and other people captured in Upper Burma and sold into debt-slavery in Pegu.[66]

The successive kings of the early Konbaung period, who had also devoted their energies to foreign wars, were generally successful in their war efforts and brought a large number of war captives to Burma, which contributed to the economy of the kingdom, as well as to strengthening *ahmudan* groups. In other words, the early days of the Konbaung dynasty can be regarded as an era in which they succeeded in gathering sufficient troops and labor force under the royal authority.

With the exception of one of two such edicts issued during the founding period of the Konbaung dynasty, no such edicts were seen during the Konbaung period. Whereas the royal orders of Burma include 11 edicts from 1636 to 1692 that imposed restrictions on *ahmudan* becoming debt-slaves, there was not a single such edict from the Konbaung period.

Coinciding with the fact that such interdictory edicts were no longer issued during the Konbaung period, the 309 debt-slaves that I have been able to examine include very few contracts in which someone belonging to the *ahmudan* class made himself or a family member a debt-slave. I have found only the following three examples.

(1) Around the late 1790s, a cavalry commander in the Wundwin region offered his son to a broker as a debt-slave. This was because he had borrowed a horse and campaign expenses from this broker, but had been unable to repay him.[67] (2) In 1862, an *ahmudan* belonging to the *ahsaun-kain* group (namely, a bodyguard for the king) and his wife became debt-slaves of Min-maha-min-tin-yaza and his wife.[68] (3) In 1875, a village headman's son in Salin who was a debt-slave ran away, so the father, the village headman, and a guarantor wrote a pledge in which they promised to repay the son's total debt and the money for the labor that the son had not provided.[69]

Of course, we cannot assert that it was entirely impossible that *ahmudan* slipped among the people who appeared in debt-slave contracts by name alone, but it seems that the frequency of such happenings was extremely low. As people had no surnames, there were often a number of people with the same name in the same village if the name was commonplace, and it would serve the purpose of identifying the individuals in the contract to write down any sign of honor, office, or status, if there was one.

From the above, we can conclude that in the Konbaung period, debt enslavement of *ahmudan* rarely happened, and there was no large-scale exodus of the population from the royal sector to the private sector to the extent of shaking the foundation of the royal government, as was the case in the Taungoo period.

In light of the above investigation, it is certain that during the Konbaung period, not only was there a sharp decline in the debt-servitude of *ahmudan*, but debt-servitude of all people, including commoners (*athi*) who became debt-slaves, was also in decline. During this period, farmland became the main type of security for loans, and the demand for debt-slaves existed only in a concentrated fashion among the royal family, high-ranking officials, and powerful families in irrigated rice-producing areas who had accumulated vast amounts of farmland. Those who became debt-slaves were the weakest in society; namely, people who had almost no land to cultivate and were constantly exposed to difficulties in making a living. Even though they may have been on an equal footing with the creditor in the sense that they themselves concluded the contract and became debt-slaves, in reality it became increasingly difficult for the remaining family to make a living once one of its members was engaged in restrictive labor for a creditor, and there are many examples of people going down a path in which the family took out more and more loans and other family members became debt-slaves one after another.

Even during the Konbaung era, the demand for debt-slaves was not completely lost, and there were some influential people who accepted debt-slaves as agricultural labor or as domestic labor. However, as socioeconomic conditions were fostered in which taking agricultural land as collateral was far more advantageous in terms of collecting loans and profitability than taking debt-slaves, it can be said that debt-slaves were rapidly losing their role as an actor of history.

The kings of the Konbaung period seem to have been surprisingly laissez-faire when it came to the exchange of these resources through money in the private sector, as money power, rather than the number of people under their control, determined their power directly. Members of the royalty themselves appear to have been actively engaged in attempts to control resources through their own financial power, and were turning toward securing financial revenues through the introduction and expansion of the royal monopoly system and a system of competitive bidding for resources under royal control. With regard to human mortgages, as well as farmland pledges, the royal power tacitly acknowledged them and did not seek to intervene in contracts between private individuals. The significance of private contracts in the allocation of resources was expanding, and along with direct control and mobilization by the royal power, or patron–client relations between the powerful and the weak, at the center, as well as in the provinces, contracts made by equals were emerging as a system of resource allocation.

For people who had no access to land and were constantly exposed to difficulties in making a living, the option of becoming a debt-slave functioned as a means to ensure their survival, because it guaranteed food and shelter, even if they were tied to bonded labor as long as they did not repay their debt.

Compared to debt-slaves in the Taungoo period, the debt-slaves of the Konbaung period gradually lost their importance as historical actors. It was a time when the need for bonded labor in society slowly declined and the emphasis shifted from the restrictive control of people to the procurement of resources by monetary means.

Chapter 4

Human-mortgage Contracts in the Salin Region[1]

It is well known that in Southeast Asia, before European colonization, there was quite a large population of people who fell into servitude as a result of debt. In an era when free labor was not abundant, the existence of non-free labor was also an important and indispensable means of mobilizing a labor force for the society. Those who were enslaved to their creditors and subjected to their service at will while they were unable to repay their debts, commonly referred to as debt-slaves, were more universal and widespread in Southeast Asian societies from the fifteenth to sixteenth centuries onwards than those who were captives of war or plunder, or hereditary slaves donated to religious institutions.[2]

Debt-slaves were peoples who were able to return to the free peoples by repaying their debts, and were therefore not slaves as a status but, rather, as a temporary condition of servitude. The existence of debt-slaves in Southeast Asia was often documented by European travelers from the seventeenth century onwards, who described them as people who voluntarily sold themselves into slavery, and noted also that since they were treated so generously by their masters, the term 'slaves' was not fit for them. However, there are very few studies that rely on the historical records of Southeast Asian societies to clarify how these people were born and what social roles they played. In 1983, the fruits of a joint study of fifteen researchers of Southeast Asian history were published under the title, *Slavery, Bondage and Dependency in Southeast Asia*, edited by A. Reid, which is notable for its attempt to place a large number of people in a subordinate position in the history of Southeast Asian societies prior to colonial rule.

102   Chapter 4

M. Aung-Thwin, who contributed a chapter on Burma to the book, puts forward several distinctive views as follows, while making it clear that his research was still at an early stage.[3]

(1) The Burmese word *kyun*, translated as slave, has a meaning similar to that of a subject or servant.[4]

(2) There were two types of *kyun*s: hereditary and voluntary. Debt-slaves, religious slaves, and those who became a *kyun* of an influential person in order to avoid claims of the royal authority were voluntary *kyun*s. These *kyun*s could be understood in the context of patron–client relations rather than slavery.

(3) In human trafficking, in many cases, the *kyun* was itself the principal of the contract, and it was more like an employment contract between employee and employer than a slave–master relationship.

(4) The basic framework of social institutions of the Burmese dynasty did not change from the Pagan dynasty onwards until the Konbaung dynasty. As most of the fertile irrigated farmland was owned by the royal authority and the Buddhist monasteries, a private large landowner class had not yet emerged.

(5) Throughout Burmese history, there was never a situation in which slaves played an important economic role in the literal sense of the word.

With regard to point (4) of these arguments, the controversy between Aung-Thwin and V. Lieberman and the development of the study of Burmese history based on the primary sources from the Pagan period onwards has made it clear that Aung-Thwin's argument that the social composition and basic institutions did not change from the eleventh century until the nineteenth century is difficult to sustain.[5] As for argument (3), as we will discuss later, the customary use of the words 'sell or buy a person' in human-mortgage contracts suggests that Aung-Thwin might have misinterpreted the human mortgage as trafficking in persons. On the other hand, his view that *kyun* was not a slave is widely accepted as common knowledge in

Burmese history. In his view, the *kyuns*, as they were called, were embedded as part of a vertical patron–client relationship that stretched throughout the dynastic society, with little recognition of the unique historical significance of their existence. It seems to me that this aspect needs to be reexamined once again, now that the situation concerning the availability of the relevant materials has changed significantly.

This chapter examines the situation of debt-slavery with the help of debt-slave contracts in nineteenth-century Burma that have survived collectively in one family, the Taungzin family (one of the Salin *Thugaung* families), who had ruled the Salin region as *myo-thugyi*s since the sixteenth century. We can use 104 human-mortgage documents written in *para-baik*s for 57 years from 1829 to 1885; namely, from the reign of King Sagaing to the year of the fall of the kingdom after the defeat in the Third Anglo-Burmese War. These documents show us the actual situation of the debt-slaves, as well as the character of debt-slave contracts in early modern Burmese society.

Salin and the Salin *Thugaung* families

The Salin region, located in central Burma on the west bank of the Ayeyarwady, stretches over the valley plains of the Salin River, which slopes gently from west to east from the Arakan Mountains towards this great river. Many canals drawn from both banks of the Salin River irrigated the vast paddy fields on the plain. Salin is located in the northern part of the Minbu district, which had become the second-largest rice producing area of the kingdom after Kyaukse since the eleventh century, and has developed the most elaborate irrigation networks in Minbu. At the same time, it was a key point of defense as a route to the periphery of the kingdom, Chin, Naga, and Arakan, and during the Arakan expedition of King Bodawhpaya (r. 1782–1819), many officers and soldiers from Salin also served in the war.[6]

In the mid to late nineteenth century, the Salin region was the area bordering the Ayeyarwady River in the east, Legaing Myo in the south, the Naga hills in the west, Laung-shay Myo in the northwest, and the Ayeyarwady River in the northeast, and was the administrative center of the region. In addition to Salin Myo, there were four other *myo*s, namely,

104   Chapter 4

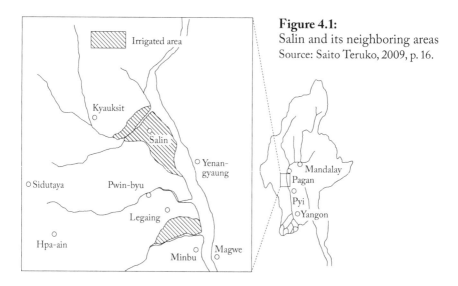

Figure 4.1:
Salin and its neighboring areas
Source: Saito Teruko, 2009, p. 16.

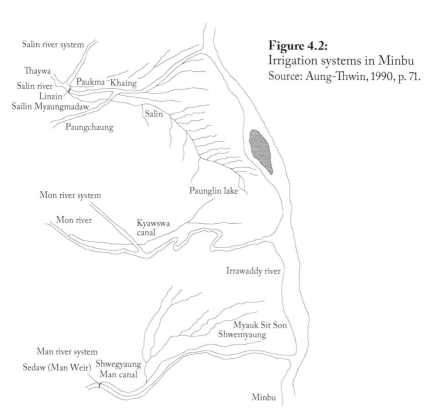

Figure 4.2:
Irrigation systems in Minbu
Source: Aung-Thwin, 1990, p. 71.

Human-mortgage Contracts in the Salin Region 105

Photo 4.1: Irrigation system in Salin
(**above**) Linzin Weir. The word 'Linzin' means Vientiane in Burmese. It is said that people of Vientiane who were taken as prisoners of war were settled in this land and assigned weir maintenance labour. .
(**below**) Midstream Canal. As the irrigation canals were excavated along contour lines, they created a landscape that looks like it has natural rivers.

Photo 4.2: The mansion of Salin *Thugaung*
The mansion was built during the colonial period with materials imported from Britain, including balconies and window. It has not been inhabited by the owners for a long time, but has one caretaker.

Hpa-ain, Kyauksit, Sidutaya, and Kyabin.[7] The inhabitants consisted mainly of Burmese and Chins, with a few Chinese and Indians in addition.

During the Konbaung era, the region was ruled by the powerful local families, commonly known as the Salin *Thugaung*, which had four main lineages: Poza, Taungzin, Kainza, and Maha-thaman. The extent of each family lineage was not clearly divided, but could be united or separated, depending on the political factors, such as the repeated intermarriages within the families and their relationship with the central royal authority.

The Taungzin lineage, which has left the historical record that is the basis of this paper, is thought to have ruled the Sidutaya Myo and the Chin provinces of Taungzin Hkayain[8] in the early days of the Konbaung period, while the Poza lineage ruled Salin Myo, the heart of the Salin region. However, the two families were closely linked through intermarriage, and by the middle to late Konbaung period, the two families had almost completely merged. On the other hand, the Maha-thaman family, which is thought to have governed the villages on the left bank of the Mon River and the Hpa-ain Myo region, was strongly linked to the Kainza family, and competed with the Poza family for the position of the ruler of Salin Myo.[9]

However, in November 1786, King Bodawhpaya attempted to organize the local administration by issuing an edict, which stipulated that there should be one ruler in one *myo* in principle.[10] In the *sit-tan* of 1802, only one person, U To of the Poza lineage, submitted a *sit-tan* from the Salin region that might be a reflection of this.[11] Subsequently, throughout the late Konbaung period, there was a fierce struggle between the Maha-thaman and Poza families over the status of the *myo-thugyi* of Salin. Both sides sued each other for the recognition of their status by the Crown, and the status of the *myo-thugyi* was transferred several times between these two families. One of the creditors mentioned in this study, who was also a party to this status dispute, married a Taungzin lineage woman and exercised a great power over all of the Salin region.[12]

The *thugaung* families were also known for their accumulation of land, mainly in the irrigated areas of the Salin region. How much land the creditors appearing in this study owned at the time cannot be detailed, but in a report of land settlement work first carried out in the Minbu region in 1893–97 after Burma was finally annexed by the British, 13 individuals and co-owners, such as husband and wife or brothers and sisters, of the *thugaung* families are listed as large landowners with more than 100 acres of land. Their landholdings ranged from a minimum of 124.23 acres (about 50.3 ha) to a maximum of 1,170.03 acres (about 473.5 ha),[13] when the average landholding per household was around five acres.

Among the money-lending contracts of *thugaung* manuscripts in the eighteenth to nineteenth centuries, land-mortgage contracts were the largest in number. This indicates that they made widespread loans, taking agricultural land as collateral, to the people in Salin and the neighboring provinces and accumulated farmland through mortgages and purchases.[14]

Human-mortgage contracts in Salin

The human-mortgage contracts used in this chapter are 104 deeds from Volume 10 of the Salin *Thugaung* Manuscripts collection (STM-KT), which was preserved by the Myanmar Historical Commission's office in the Department of History at the University of Yangon. The breakdown of the 104 items is shown in Table 4.1. The reason why the total number of items is larger than the number of contracts is that there are a few examples of two contracts in succession, a personal-mortgage contract and an additional debt contract, which are counted as separate contracts in what appears at first glance to be a single sheet of contracts.

108   Chapter 4

Table 4.1: Breakdown of contracts (Salin *Thugaung* debt-slave contracts)

Human-mortgage contract	51
Additional loan contract	46
Certificate of repayment	4
Letter of commitment (pledge)	3
Agreement on abrogation of contract	1
Testimony on child born to slave mother	3
Total (nos.)	108

Source: Salin *Thugaung* Manuscripts, Vol. 10, *Ko-nei Thet-kayit* (Human-mortgage contracts (STM-KT).

What we classify here as a human-mortgage contract refers to an original contract made between the creditor and the person who borrowed money and became a debt-slave to the creditor. An additional loan contract is a deed written when a debt-slave needed more money and borrowed additional money from the creditor, as seen in the following example (2).

(1) Mortgage of Nga Ni, the son of Mi Pu in Segan village, for 25 *kyat*s. M.E. 1191, *Thadingyut lazou'* 4 (October 16, 1829), Mi Pu, and Maung Nga Hmwe of Segan village said to *Myo Thugyi*, Zeya-shwe-daun-kyaw and his wife, 'We need money to pay tax, please buy Mi Pu's son Nga Ni at the price of 25 *kyat*s, in terms of '*Shin ma pwa, Thei ma hsoun*,' whereupon Zeya-shwe-daun-kyaw and his wife accepted the offer and bought Nga Ni, paying 25 *kyat*s by *Ngwe-mwe Ywet-ni, hman-baw* 1 *kyat* 6 *mu* alloy,[15] weighed by *hinda* weight.[16] In case Nga Ni would hate being a slave and run away, Nga Po, the chief of the Kanny-taung village, promised to take responsibility for his actions and made a written testimony. The witness was Maung Myat Ei, the assayer; Maung Taw Da, a broker living in the marketplace, the drafter; Maung Myat Tu, the scribe; Maung Tu Pyu.[17]

(2) Additional debt on Nga Ni, 15 *kyat*s. M.E. 1191, *Thadingyut lazou'* 4 (October 16, 1829), Mi Pu and Maung Nga Hmwe, residents of Segan village, told Mr. and Mrs. Zeya-shwe-daun-kyaw that the body price of Nga Ni was not enough for them, and asked to lend them additional money without interest, which they would repay with the body price of Nga Ni. Mr.

and Mrs. Zeya-shwe-daun-kyaw agreed to their request and handed over *ngwe-mwe ywet-ni hman baw* 15 *kyat*s by 1 *kyat* 6 *mu* alloy, weighed by the *hinda* weight, free of blemishes or chips. The witness was Maung Myat Ei who lives in the marketplace, the assayer; Maung Taw Da, broker and the drafter; Maung Myat Tu, the scribe; Maung Thu Pyu.[18]

The second contract was made on the same day as the first contract, and names of the witness, assayer, drafter, and scribe were the same in both contracts. There was an approximate standard of body price for a debt-slave, and if the debtor needed more money than the body price, that amount was added to the body price. This practice of making a human-mortgage contract and an additional loan contract as separate contracts was a practice found in Salin *Thugaung* contracts and those of the neighboring provinces, while in other provinces, the total amount of the body price and the additional loan were often written in a single contract.

The number of repayment certificates was very small, with only four cases.[19] None of them were for the full repayment of the body price and additional debts, but were for partial repayment of the debt, specifying the amount repaid and the date when the remaining amount would be paid. As with the land-mortgage contract, it was common to discard the original note when the debt was paid in full, and a partial repayment note might have been prepared only when there was a balance remaining.

The three letters of commitment[20] were all specific promises of how the guarantor would compensate the creditor when faced with the escape of a debt-slave. In a pledge written in 1861,[21] a debt-slave named Nga Thet Shay escaped, and a couple in the house where he had gone into hiding was forced to make a pledge to Ma Hkaing, the master of Nga Thet Shay, that 'we admonish Thet Shay and make him promise to work, and if he should escape again, we will repay his debts'. These pledges were also made with witnesses, as well as with the parties concerned.

The Salin debt-slave document No. 77, which contained an agreement to annul the contract, and No. 31–33, which recorded the testimony regarding the ownership of the slave child, are considered separately later.

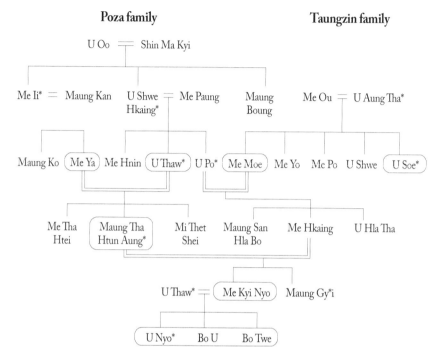

Figure 4.3: Poza and Taungzin families and marriage relations
Sources: Kyaw Hmu Aung, 1992, pp. 9–21; Ohn Kyi, 1987, additional chart.
Note: ◯ The creditors appear in money-lending *thet-kayit*s in this chapter.
*Those who worked as *myo-thugyi*s.

People who appeared in the debt-slave contracts

Creditors

Figure 4.3 shows the genealogy of the people belonging to the Taungzin and Poza lineages. The people who actually appeared in the debt-slave contracts were Mr. and Mrs. U Soe, Me Moe (U Soe's sister), Me Ya, and U Thaw of the Poza lineage, Ma Hkaing (Me Moe's daughter) and her husband Maung Ta Htun Aung (son of U Thaw), and their daughter Me Kyi Nyo and her three sons. Table 4.2 shows the dates in which each person appeared as a creditor, the number of contracts, and the designations in the contracts.

As shown in the table, the main creditors were Mr. and Mrs. U Soe, Ma Hkaing, Maung Tha Tun Aung, and Me Kyi Nyo, but in terms of individuals, Ma Hkaing and Me Kyi Nyo were the most prominent creditors.

Human-mortgage Contracts in the Salin Region   111

Table 4.2: Creditors in debt-slave contracts

	Name	Designation in the contracts	Years	Number of contracts
1	Mr. & Mrs. U Soe	Zeya-shwe-daun-kyaw and wife	1829–36	22
2	Me Moe	*Thugaung-ma* Me Moe	1834	1
3	Me Ya & U Thaw	Maha Patta Yaza Myothugyi & Kadaw	1832	2
4	Ma Hkaing & Maung Tha Htun Aung	Zeya Pattaya Maha Myothugyi & Kadaw	1838–45	17
	Ma Hkaing	*Thugaung-ma* Me Hkaing Mother of Myothugyi	1839–68	27
5	Me Kyi Nyo & U Kyi	Sister of Myothugyi Myothugyi	1865~67	5
	Me Kyi Nyo	Daughter of Myothugyi Sister of Myothugyi Donor of Ngazin Temple	1864–85	16
	Me Kyi Nyo & eldest son (U Nyo) Second son (Maung U) Third son (Maung Twe)	Mother of Myothugyi Myothugyi Bo U Bo Twe	1876–85	12
6	Others			2
	Total			104

Source: prepared by the author from Salin *Thugaung* Manuscripts, *Ko-nei Thet-kayit* (STM-KT), No. 1–104.

Notes: *Bo* refers to a military officer. The eldest son of Me Kyi Nyo is identified as *Myothugyi*, and the second and third sons are military officers. The coronary titles *Me* and *Ma* were put before a woman's name. *Me* was often given to the older woman, but they were interchangeable and *Ma* Hkaing was sometimes written as *Me* Hkaing.

In the contracts, creditors were often referred to by titles and status designations rather than by their personal names. In the Salin region, the principal creditors were those who belonged to the most influential families of the local community, and therefore titles and status designations appeared frequently. One of the earliest people mentioned in the contracts was U Soe, who served in the Arakan campaign during the reign of King Bodawhpaya and was given the title of Zeya-shwe-daun-kyaw, and he was always designated in contracts by this title.[22] Ma Hkaing's husband, Maung Ta Htun Aung, also appeared as Zeya Pattaya Maha, a title given by the king. Which title took precedence over the other titles reflected the hierarchy of authority at that time, so the titles given by the king came first, next came *myo-thugyi*, the highest administrative position in local

112   Chapter 4

society, and the *daga*, an expression of social and religious honor, was the third in rank.

The word *thugaung* is also said to be an ancient title conferred by kings on a particular family or group of people, but in this group of contracts we see that its power did not match titles conferred by the king of the time, or the status of *myo-thugyi*. Not everyone born into the *thugaung* families was called *thugaung*, and only the most prominent members of the *thugaung* families were awarded *Thugaung* before their own names. *Thugaung-ma* (the female *thugaung*) was used to refer to Me Moe and Ma Hkaing, and after their passing, they were referred to in later contracts as *Thugaung-ma-gyi* (the Great *Thugaun-ma*).

Debt-slave contracts were the same as land-mortgage contracts in that a contract listed the names of the weigher, assayer, witness, drafter, scribe, and so on. The weighing and appraisal of coins was an essential part of the transaction in an era when various types of metal coins cast by private individuals were in circulation.

Both debt-slave contracts and land-mortgage contracts were completed as transactions between private individuals and did not require notification or authentication by the royal authority or local authority. As the presence of witnesses was thought to be extremely important as a guarantee of the effectiveness of contracts, influential persons in the local society were asked to be present at the time when the contracts were prepared. In the 104 examples of debt-slave contracts used in this chapter, there were always one to four witnesses before the time of Me Kyi Nyo, and they included donors of pagodas and temples, *sit-ke*,[23] the cavalry commander, *taik-so*,[24] the deputy of a *myo-thugyi*, the broker, and the manager of the irrigation system, and so on.

However, after 1878 (i.e., during the reign of King Thibaw, the last king of the Konbaung dynasty), only three of the 21 contracts contained the names of the witnesses. This might be due to some ongoing changes in the environment surrounding debt-slave contracts, rather than the change in the style of creditors in making contracts. This is because, as discussed below, the tendency in Salin to fix the body price was going in the direction of rationalization and simplification, and the need for witnesses was diminishing during this period.

Debtors

In debt-slave contracts, it often happened that the contractor and the one who became a debt-slave were different. In the case of land mortgage, the one who owned land was the contractor who borrowed money by pledging his land. In some debt-slave contracts, the contractor pledged himself as a debt-slave, but there were many cases where parents pledged their children or husbands pledged their wives as slaves. It also often required the presence of a guarantor other than the contracting parties, since, unlike land, a person could attempt to abscond.

If we look at the debtors and those offered as debt-slaves, they were clearly different from the creditors, who were usually the most powerful people in the region in terms of wealth and social status. There was only one contract in which the debtor was a man who worked in trial advocacy, who turned a young man of a relative's lineage into a debt-slave in order to get him to repay his own debts.[25]

In all other contracts, debtors, as well as people offered as debt-slaves, were represented only by their names and places of domicile. There was no mention of the ethnicity of the debtor at all in any of the contracts, but almost all names can be read as ordinary Burmese names. There were a few names such as Mi Shan (Miss Shan) and Ko Tayo (Mr. Chinese), but it did not mean that these names suggest the person was an ethnic Shan or a Chinese.[26]

If we look at the relationship between the contracting person and the person offered as a debt-slave, the largest number of cases (23 cases) involved parents offering their children as debt-slaves. Among them, 11 cases involved daughters as debt-slaves, nine cases involved sons, one case involved a daughter and her husband, and two cases involved a son-in-law, but none involved a daughter-in-law as a debt-slave. The cases in which the contractor himself became a debt-slave were 11 in number, of which seven were contracted alone, and in the other contracts, the names of the wife, son, and son-in-law were listed as joint contractors. There are seven cases where the contractor and the debt-slave were siblings, and in four cases among these, the brothers-in-law (i.e., a sister's husband) were offered as debt-slaves.

There were four cases in which the husband was the contractor and the wife was the debt-slave (in two of these cases, the husband himself had already been a debt-slave), and there was no contract in which the wife was the contractor and the husband was the debt-slave.

The relationship between the contractor and the debt-slave indicates an increase or decrease in age or position within the kinship or marriage relationship, and there were many cases of parents making their children debt-slaves, but not vice versa, and husbands placed wives in debt-slavery, but not vice versa. However, the relationship between the contractor and the would-be debt-slave was not only about these hierarchical relationships, but also seemed to indicate the smallest economic unit that jointly owed the debt and was responsible for its repayment.

One contract written in 1834 was unusual in that it stated that the younger brothers made a contract with the creditor to make their elder brother and his family debt-slaves, but it can be read, in fact, as an aid offered by the two brothers to their elder brother's family.[27] In the contract, they asked *Thugaung* U Soe and his wife to buy their elder brother and his family, who had been debt-slaves to the chief of another village, and U Soe and his wife accepted this request. This contract was followed by another contract of an additional loan, saying that the total amount of the body price of the elder brother's family was insufficient to repay the debt they owed to the former master.[28] The contractors of the debtor's side in the second contract were the elder brother and two younger brothers, altogether three in number. It was common practice that the debt-slave himself became a contractor, but the fact that the two brothers were named as contractors suggests that the creditor or the elder brother's family requested them to take responsibility jointly for the debt, as the amount of debt was too large, and the younger brothers accepted their request.

The relationship between the contractor and the would-be debt-slave was, as we have seen above, limited to those who were related to each other, or to those who were related by marriage, and in the Salin *Thugaung* documents used here, there was no contractual document in which the debt-slave master sold the debt-slave with the deed to a third party. In the case of land-mortgage deeds, the deeds were not only inherited but sometimes sold to third parties, and, as a result, the collateral land could be transferred to other people. But in the case of debt-slaves, as we have seen in the previous chapter, debt-slaves changed masters voluntarily and became the contractual subject of the newly created deeds.

The third point of Aung-Thwin's argument ('In human trafficking, in many cases, the *kyun* was itself the principal of the contract, and it was more like an employment contract between employee and employer than a slave–master relationship') may be an assertion based on a misreading of these human-mortgage contracts as human trafficking. As we saw earlier, the widespread use in debt-slave contracts of the words 'buy' and 'sell' makes such a misreading more likely to occur. In the case of human trafficking, the contractors of the transaction were the original master of the slave and the new buyer, and the slave being bought and sold could never be a contractor of the transaction.[29]

Characteristics of human-mortgage contracts

Factors behind the birth of debt-slaves

In many debt-slave contracts, people wrote a few words about their reasons for borrowing money by mortgaging oneself or family members, as follows:

- difficulties in repaying debts (23 cases)
- difficulties in repaying the paddy bought on deferred payment (eight cases)
- to redeem the debt-slave from the former creditor and shift to another creditor (seven cases)
- to pay judicial costs (four cases)
- forced to pay rent in paddy (four cases)
- to pay various levies (two cases)
- poverty stricken (two cases).

Although the reasons were expressed in different words, it is clear that all cases related to economic hardship. Except for the law suits and levies, the other reasons were directly related to poverty.

The frequently cited reasons for being forced to repay debts or to pay for rice were often overlapping, as it often happened that people bought paddy from the granaries of *thugaung* families in deferred payment and accumulated the amount without paying the price. Not a few people became debt-slaves of the *thugaung* families in this way. These debts were

116   Chapter 4

not always debts of their own, but were often inherited debts from their parents. For example, in a contract dated May 3, 1850, it was stated that a father-in-law, a debt-slave, died without repaying his debt and the son-in-law was demanded to repay his father-in-law's debt, but he could not repay it, and made himself a debt-slave of the creditor.[30] In another case, a father mortgaged his two daughters one after the other as debt-slaves because of the combined debt for his mother's body price, for the price of the borrowed paddy, and for the unpaid rent to a landowner.[31]

There were also examples of taxation and recruitment for military campaigns or labor services by the royal government, which became a trigger for making debt-slaves. In one contract made in 1829, the debtor stated that the reason for offering his son as a debt-slave was the payment of public taxes and dues.[32] In another contract made in 1838, a man borrowed 35 *kyat*s and offered his wife as a debt-slave in order to make money to hire someone to be sent for the military campaign.[33] Those who could not or did not want to be recruited for the military campaigns could pay a fixed amount of money instead, or hire someone to be sent in his place. These examples show that in the Konbaung period, people had a way of settling money even for royal claims, such as military service, rather than by making themselves the debt-slaves of powerful men, as seen in the Taungoo period.

Let us turn to examine the matter of a change of masters: a contract dated April 30, 1830, states that a man called Nga Shwe asked U Soe and his wife to buy his brother-in-law Nga Kyaw as a debt-slave, because Nga Kyaw, a debt-slave of a certain group of *ahmudan*, was obliged to move to the capital with the group, but he did not want to move. U Soe and his wife agreed and bought Nga Kyaw, paying 30 *kyat*s as a price on his body.[34]

Also, in a contract dated June 3, 1834, we find the following statement:

On the 12th day of *lazou*, the month of Nayon, 1196 B.E. (June 3, 1834 A.D.) Nga Thu, a resident of Kanna village said to Zeya-shwe-daun-kyaw and his wife, 'I was working as a debt-slave at Me Sun's place, but as Me Sun died, I was confiscated by the provincial governor, as a property of the king. I need money to redeem myself. Please buy me at the price of 35 *kyat*s on the term of *shin pwa, thei hsoun*.' Mr. and Mrs. Zeya-shwe-daun-kyaw accepted his offer and bought Nga Thu at his body price of 35 *kyat*s.[35]

It was the custom when the master of a debt-slave died that the slave should be inherited by the heir of the master, but if there were no heirs, the debt-slave would be confiscated by the provincial governor appointed by the king. In the above case, Nga Tun did not want to be confiscated by the governor sent from the capital, but preferred to become the debt-slave of the *myo-thugyi*, the local ruler who belonged to the *thugaung* family.

There were some other contracts in which the debtor asked to become a debt-slave of the *thugaung* family, saying that he or she was not happy under the former master. These contracts might be understood in the context of the patron–client relationship, as they were seeking protection under the *thugaung* families in order to avoid being cut off from their native place, or because they expected better treatment and additional loans.

Thus, in the range of issues discussed in this paper, poverty was undoubtedly the most important factor attributable to debt-slavery: roughly two-thirds of those who entered into debt-slavery were suffering economic deprivation. Debt-slave contracts with the local powerful families were the ultimate survival guarantee for those in need. However, if we understand debt enslavement in those days only in the context of the patron–client relationship, we may overlook the strict character of the debt-slave contracts.

Contents of the debt-slavery contract

A debt-slave contract itself explained very little about the nature of the debt-slave's work or the conditions of work. This means that once the debt-slave contract was signed, the debt-slave was subjected to any service the master ordered him or her to perform. In addition to agricultural work in the creditor's paddy fields, they were required to perform miscellaneous labor, such as wood gathering, water drawing, night watch, repairing the residence, and other domestic works, but in the case of young women, they were sometimes obliged to perform sexual service to their master, if the term *cho nin ba-ze* (Treat her harshly) was written in the original contracts. Debt-slaves could be provided a hut in the creditor's compound, or they could live in the servant quarters of the mansion, but there were a few debt-slaves who did not move to the creditor's residence, and instead worked for the master from their own dwellings.

No consideration was paid for any labor performed until the debt was completely cleared, nor was the amount of the debt reduced by the length

118   Chapter 4

of time subjected to service. This is because, as in the case of land pledges, the usufruct was transferred to the creditor, and the labor of the debt-slave was considered as payment of interest. If the needs of the debtor could not be met by the body price, additional debts were piled on the body price. Although no interest was charged on the additional debt, the total amount of debt to be repaid increased and made it more difficult for the debt-slave to get out of servitude.

In some contracts, there was a clause prohibiting the redemption of debt-slaves for a certain period in order to secure their labor. In one contract, redemption was prohibited for two years, while in seven other contracts the prohibition of redemption was three years. Most of these clauses were concentrated in 1884 and 1885, the last years of the Konbaung period, when Me Kyi Nyo was the creditor of these contracts. It was a time of social unrest and high mobility of people, when many people left Upper Burma and went to the delta in search of jobs.

There were six contracts in which rules were stipulated for the case of debt-slaves absconding. According to these rules, the guarantors should take responsibility when the debt-slaves absconded, and the way of taking responsibility was to compensate for the burden of the slave labor and to repay the body price, and additional loans on the debt-slave, if any.[36] Nevertheless, it often happened that the guarantors could not bear the burden of repayment when the debt-slave actually absconded, and in a certificate dated May 27, 1885, the guarantor settled the matter by offering the son of the escaped debt-slave as a debt-slave in his place and became a guarantor for him.[37]

Most of the clauses written in the contracts were intended to protect the interests of the creditor, but, in turn, were there any covenants that intended to protect the party entering into debt-slavery? Although there are very few examples, one contract was an agreement that the daughter would be offered as a domestic slave and receive the body price, but, in reality, she should pay a certain amount of paddy every month in exchange for living in the creditor's mansion.[38] Although the debtor needed money very much, the parents' wish was not to let her go and work at the creditor's residence and the creditor agreed. Other than this example, there were no other contracts in the documents relating to Salin *Thugaung* that specified the protection of debt-slaves, but it is true that there was no mention of phrases such as 'You may use the debt-slave in any way you wish' or

Human-mortgage Contracts in the Salin Region   119

'You may flog me as you wish', which were sometimes found in debt-slave contracts from other regions.[39] These facts provide some basis for the assessment that the treatment of debt-slaves by Salin *Thugaung* families was generous, compared to the creditors in other regions.[40]

Shin pwa, thei hsoun and *shin ma pwa, thei ma hsoun* again

As we saw in the previous chapter, there were special phrases written in almost all human-mortgage contracts, namely *shin pwa, thei hsoun* and *shin ma pwa, thei ma hsoun*. In the documents used here, there were eight cases of *shin pwa, thei hsoun* and 36 cases of *shin ma pwa, thei ma hsoun*. Regarding the meaning of these phrases, which use two opposing sets of words—*shin* (alive) and *thei* (dead), and *pwa* (increasing) and *hsoun* (losing)—Daw Ohn Kyi offered two interpretations of the meaning of this couplet in 1991, stating that *hsin ma pwa* means that no interest is paid on the debt during the slave's lifetime. Her earlier paper, in 1987, suggested a double meaning, that there is no interest on the principal of the debt and that the children born during the period when their parents worked as slaves would not become slaves.

I suggested in the previous chapter that *shin pwa, thei hsoun* means that a child born while the mother worked as a debt-slave automatically became a slave, and when the debt-slave died, the debt was cancelled, whereas *shin ma pwa, thei ma hsoun* means that a child born to the debt-slave mother was not enslaved, but when the slave died, the debt was passed to the debt-slave's descendants. In other words, these couplets were irrelevant to the issue of interest and were a covenant about the attribution of the children born to the debt-slave and the disposition of the debt upon the debt-slave's death.

In the case of debt-slave contracts, however, the labor provided by the debt-slaves represents the interest on the loan, so it is obvious that interest in cash was not paid on the loan. That being the case, how should we interpret these phrases? A clue for interpreting their meaning can be found in the following document written in Salin in 1841.

The question of Mi U's attribution

B.E. 11th *lazou, Tazaungmon*, 1203 (November 8, 1841), the answer of Mi Kyan Tha.

120   Chapter 4

Regarding my sister Mi U, I remember that she was born after my father and mother had been bought on the condition of *shin pwa, thei hsoun* by *Zayat Daga-ma-gyi* (Great Donor of the Rest House) as debt-slaves. I have not heard whether or not my mother was pregnant before they became debt-slaves. Together with Mi U, her elder sister Mi Kyan Tha deposed the above in the presence of the town clerk Maung Kya Yit, the cavalry commander Maung Maw, Maung Pe Ta Lu, and Nga Chin Ok. The document was written by Maung Pein.[41]

Mi U's husband Nga Zi's answer
On the same day (November 8, 1841 A.D.), Nga Zi answered.

'My wife Mi U was born during the time when my father-in-law was being used as a debt-slave at the house of *Zayat daga-ma-gyi*. I have heard that, before she died, my mother-in-law told Mi Thei that when she became a debt-slave of the female donor of the rest house, she was four months pregnant with my wife Mi U. If Mi Thei will make a deposition, the matter will become clear.'[42]

According to these documents, in order to determine the affiliation of a woman called Mi U, Mi U herself, her elder sister, and her husband were questioned and the point at issue was whether or not Mi U had been born during the time when her parents, in particular her mother, were being used as debt-slaves. The contract drawn up when her parents had become debt-slaves included the condition *shin pwa, thei hsoun*, and it is clear from the above replies that the phrase *shin pwa* is unrelated to interest on the loan. It means that under the condition of *shin pwa*, a child born, while the mother is a debt-slave, automatically becomes a slave, while *shin ma pwa*, with the negative particle *ma*, can be taken to mean that a child born while the mother is a debt-slave will not be made a slave.

Another contract dated March 5, 1843, shows that although a child had been born to a couple who had been debt-slaves to their former creditor (Me Moe) during the period of their service, this fact had been concealed and neglected. But as the fact was disclosed, the people concerned wrote a letter of commitment to Ma Hkaing, the daughter of Me Moe, promising that they would put the child and the mother under their supervision and prevent them from absconding.[43]

Thus, the condition of *shin pwa* had a tendency to make the child who was born to be a slave as a status. However, the condition of *shin pwa, thei hsoun* appears only in the period of U Soe and Me Moe until 1836. During this period, both conditions were used interchangeably, with eight cases of *shin pwa, thei hsoun* and seven cases of *shin ma pwa, thei ma hsoun*. After that, the condition of *shin pwa, thei hsoun* disappeared completely from the Salin *Thugaung* debt-slave contracts, as did the *shin ma pwa, thei ma hsoun* condition. However, if the condition in the original contract was *shin pwa, thei hsoun*, both the creditor and the debtor should keep the term even after a long time.

Body price of a debt-slave

Next, let us look at the body price of a debt-slave. When a human-mortgage contract was first made, the price of each person was determined as the body price of the person. In the deed, first of all, the debtor made an offer to buy him (her) at a certain price, as it was a format of making human-mortgage contracts, but in reality, the creditor was supposed to offer a price based on the person's sex, age, and physical ability. If the debtor's needs could not be met by that amount, another contract of an additional loan was made on the spot, which had to be repaid when the body price was repaid.

The money used in debt-slavery contracts was all privately cast metal currencies up to 1864. The one with the highest percentage of silver was the 7 *mu* alloy (i.e., alloy containing 93% silver), and the one of the poorest quality was the 30 *kyat* alloy (i.e., alloy containing 70% silver). The body price of men was from 25 *kyats* to 40 *kyats* and for women from 15 *kyats* to 35 *kyats* during this period. The difference of the body price is thought to have reflected the quality of money used and also the fitness of the person for the required work and service.

The first minted coin appeared in Salin *Thugaung* debt-slave contracts in December 1864, almost a year before the monetary reform by King Mindon, and should have been the British Indian rupee circulated in British Lower Burma. After the monetary reform, the new minted coins were very quickly circulated, and both body price and additional loans were paid in these minted coins. Accordingly, assayers, weighers, and authorized weights for weighing currencies disappeared quickly from the money-lending contracts. Instead, the name of the person who counted

122   Chapter 4

the coins was sometimes mentioned for a while. From 1864 until 1885, the period when Me Kyi Nyo and her sons appeared as creditors, the body price of debt-slaves tended to be standardized. From 1878 onwards, without exception, the body price was fixed at 29 *kyat*s per man and 24 *kyat*s per woman. The standardization of coinage eliminated the complications of appraising and weighing coins of varying quality, but it also seems to have played a role in promoting uniformity in prices for debt-slaves.

In the late Konbaung period, the gap between the body price of debt-slaves and the total amount of their debts increased rapidly: from 1829 to 1863, except for one case in which 33 *kyat*s 3 *mu*s were added to the body price of 25 *kyat*s,[44] the sum of an additional loan did not surpass the body price. After 1865, the total amount of debts tended to increase, especially after 1878, the period of King Thibaw's reign, as shown in Table 4.3.

As seen in Table 4.3, it often happened that the original debt-slave contracts and additional debt contracts were made on the same day during this period. The sum of the additional debts was four to seven times as large as the body price. The body price paid to each slave had hardly risen for half a century and remained low, while the amount of money required on the part of the debtor increased rapidly. Even in Salin, where agricultural production was stable owing to the irrigation networks, the people in the lower strata of society were living in poverty and their dependence on debt was increasing rapidly. A quarter of a century had passed since Lower Burma came under British rule and the development of the delta was in full swing, and some people from Upper Burma began to move southward in search of employment and land in British Lower Burma.

The cycle of accumulated debts and debt-slavery

Some documents used in this chapter include individuals and families whose names appear frequently. These contracts offer a glimpse into the history of the family and the difficulties they encountered in their lives and how they coped with them. Let us take a look at some of these examples.

The name of Nga Shwe Pe appeared for the first time in the contracts on June 3, 1838. On this day he offered his wife, Mi Hmo U, as a debt-slave to Ma Hkaing and Maung Tha Tun Aung, her husband, for 20 *kyat*s by 20 *kyat* alloy.[45] Whether Nga Shwe Pe himself was already in the situation of a debt-slave was not stated in the contract, but it seems quite possible

Human-mortgage Contracts in the Salin Region   123

Table 4.3: Body price and added debt (1878–1885)

Date of deed	Debt-slave	A Body price	B Additional loan	C Total debt	A/C (%)
March 3, 1878	Nga Pyo	29 *k*			
ditto			141 *k*		
May 14, 1884			50 *k*	220 *k*	13.2
September 29, 1882	Nga Thet U	29 *k*			
ditto			124 *k* 5 *m*	153 *k* 5 *m*	18.9
March 30, 1884	Nga Thet Kyi	29 *k*			
ditto			171 *k*	200 *k*	14.5
April 1, 1884	Nga Shwe Myan	29 *k*			
ditto			171 *k*	200 *k*	14.5
April 22, 1883	Mi Hcoun	24 *k*			
ditto			126 *k*	150 *k*	19.3
March 4, 1885	Nga San Yin	29 *k*			
ditto			181 *k*		
May 3, 1885			40 *k*	221 *k*	11.6
April 5, 1885	Mi Chan	24 *k*			
ditto			156 *k*	180 *k*	13.3
May 13, 1885	Nga Kya	29 *k*			
ditto			171 *k*	200 *k*	14.5

Source: Salin *Thugaung* Manuscripts, Vol. 10. *Ko-nei Thet-kayit* (STM-KT), No. 84~103.
Note: *k* = *kyat*, *m* = *mu*, 1*k* = 10 *mu*.

that he was also a debt-slave of Ma Hkaing. On the same day, he asked an additional loan of 15 *kyat*s because his wife's body price was not enough to cover their necessity, and they made an additional debt contract on the same day.

Three years later, on April 16, 1841, the couple failed to pay 2 *kyat*s for the paddy and corn borrowed from the creditor's granary, and they added this to the wife's debt. On 14 August, Nga Shwe and Mi Hmo U failed again to pay for the paddy they had bought from Ma Hkaing on several occasions, and the total amount of 7 *kyat*s 8 *mu*s and 4 *ywet*s was added to the debt of Mi Hmo U. On the same day, he offered one of his daughters, Mi Tun Aung, to Ma Hkaing as a debt-slave for 20 *kyat*s.

Two years later, on July 20, 1843, the couple again borrowed 22 baskets of paddy from the creditor's granary when they ran out of food, and added

124   Chapter 4

the price of 13 *kyat*s 2 *mu*s to the wife's debts. On March 14, 1845, they offered their second daughter, Mi Tha Shun, as a debt-slave in order to pay for paddy and various other debts, and borrowed 30 *kyat*s from Ma Hkaing. On September 26, 1847, they again borrowed 7 *kyat*s and 1 *mat*, which was added to the elder daughter's debts, and on July 28, 1850, they borrowed another 2 *kyat*s to add to the younger daughter's debts.[46] This is the last surviving record of this family, and it is unclear whether they were ever able to repay this enormous debt and get out of debt-slavery.

There are many examples of families like that of Nga Shwe Pe. When one member of a family became a debt-slave, it would become increasingly difficult for the other members to maintain their livelihood and they would become debt-slaves one after another. There occurred a chain reaction in which first the father would become a debt-slave, then the mother, and then the sons and daughters. In such circumstances, the total debts would grow enormously, and the path for the family to return to freedom would grow ever narrower.

As the creditor, the *thugaung* families, responded to requests of additional loans and deferred payments of food crops without refusal, it can be said that the existence of the *thugaung* families was a lifeline for those people living on the edge of survival. However, it often happened that whole family members fell into debt-slavery one after another, and worked for *thugaung* families.

Nga Shwe and his family

Nga Shwe's name appeared for the first time as a contractor in the document dated April 30, 1830, which we saw earlier (i.e., a contract to take his brother-in-law Nga Kyaw from the *ahmudan* group for 40 *kyat*s and place him as a debt-slave under Mr. and Mrs. U Soe). In addition to the body price on Nga Kyaw, an additional debt of 20 *kyat*s was added. On May 27, 1831, Nga Shwe himself was made a debt-slave of Mr. and Mrs. U Soe for 25 *kyat*s, claiming that he needed money for a lawsuit over cattle. Again, as the body price was not enough to pay for the lawsuit cost, an additional debt of 25 *kyat*s was put on Nga Shwe.

On May 15, 1833, to repay the debt borrowed from another creditor, his wife Mi Oo also became the debt-slave of the same couple for 16 *kyat*s. For some time afterwards, the name of this family does not appear in the contracts, but suddenly Nga Shwe's name was restored in a contract of 30 March, 1876, but as a dead person. The creditors had already been replaced by Me Kyi Nyo, the granddaughter of the former creditor, and her sons. Nga Shwe had continued to serve under the new creditor, but 'as he died while a debt-slave', the creditors demanded repayment of Nga Shwe's debts by his son, Nga Hnaun, and his son-in-law, Nga Shwe Hlaw. The total amount of the debt amounted to 187 *kyat*s 5 *mu*s at this time. The details of the debt were recorded in the contract, as summarized in Table 4.4.[47]

Although being forced to repay the large debts Nga Shwe had accumulated, the son, Nga Hnaun, and his son-in-law, Nga Shwe Hlaw were unable to pay them. They split this debt, each owing 29 *kyat*s for the body price and 64 *kyat*s 7 *mu*s 1 *pe* as additional debts (in total 93 *kyat*s 7 *mu*s 1 *pe*), and became the debt-slaves of Me Kyi Nyo and her sons. A new contract was drawn up for the two men and a promise was made to destroy the old contract for Nga Shwe.

Thereafter, three contracts of additional debts were written for Nga Shwe Hlaw.[48] Taken together, his debts were as large as 175 *kyat*s 7 *mu*s 1 *pe*, suggesting that this son-in-law would also have had extreme difficulty in escaping the circumstances of a debt-slave.[49]

Thus, the debt of a deceased debt-slave passed to his children, who were his heirs, because Nga Shwe's first debt-slave contract had the condition of *shin ma pwa, thei ma hsoun*. The contract made in 1831 between U Soe and Nga Shwe when he became a debt-slave included this condition.

The way towards liberation from debt-slavery

Those who were put into debt-slavery by human-mortgage contracts could be released from the bonded labor once the debt was paid off. As for the repayment of debts, as we have seen, there were cases where this could be done anytime, and cases where the debt could only be repaid after a certain period of service. The certificates of repayment were rarely written; only four cases were found, which were all partial repayment rather than proof of full repayment. It was the custom to abrogate all the loan contracts when the debt was completely paid off. Although material we can use here is limited to partial repayment certificates, let us follow the path out of the situation of debt-slavery.

126   Chapter 4

Table 4.4: Nga Shwe's debt history

B.E.	A.D.	Reason	Debt amount
1204	1842	to pay the rent	28 *k*
		to pay the price of 20 baskets of paddy	16 *k*
1209	1847	cost for a lawsuit on cattle	5 *k*
1214	1852	to pay borrowed paddy from the granary	4 *k*
1221	1859	to compensate for missing things	30 *k*
1224	1862	borrowed paddy from the granary	
1226	1864	borrowed paddy from the granary	19 *k* 5 *m*
1227	1865	borrowed paddy from the granary	
1227	1865	to repay debts from others	20 *k*
1229	1867	to pay borrowed paddy from the granary	10 *k*
1231	1869	to repay the debt of the son-in-law	30 *k*
1232	1870	to pay the price of paddy	7 *k* 5 *m*
ditto		to repay the borrowed paddy from the granary	17 *k* 5 *m*
Total amount of debts			187 *k* 5 *m*

Source: compiled by the author from Salin *Thugaung* Manuscripts, Vol. 10, *Ko-nei Thet-kayits*, No. 78, 79, 80, 81.
Note: *k* = *kyat*, *m* = *mu*.

Example of the couple Nga San and Mi Dei Ba

On March 3, 1843, Nga San was offered as a debt-slave to Ma Hkaing by his brother Nga Tha for 27 *kyat*s for his body price.[50] Two years later, on May 2, 1845, 10 *kyat*s for 30 baskets of paddy borrowed by his brother were added to Nga San's body price.[51]

Nga San's wife, Mi Dei Ba, who was also a debt-slave, once attempted to escape. Then, a written agreement dated March 26, 1848, was made in the joint names of her husband, Nga San, and her two brothers, Nga Pain and Nga Pwa, with the creditor Ma Hkaing, as follows:

> When Mi Dei Ba, Nga San's wife escaped, we found her and detained her and demanded that she should repay her body price and the 300 baskets of rice she had consumed. Then her brothers asked to release her from confinement and said that if their sister Mi Dei Ba and brother-in-law Nga San could not repay the 300 baskets of rice, they would

reimburse her body price and the price of paddy. So, we made this written testimony.[52]

In May of the same year, Nga San again made a promissory letter for Ma Hkaing by himself:

The total amount of the unpaid tenancy rent, and paddy borrowed from various granaries amounted to 470 baskets. I will settle this sum on the 15th of the month of Tazaungmon when the rice market is opened in the town of Sidutaya.[53] In case I could not repay the price of paddy, please take my wife, son, and daughter as debt-slaves at the price of 470 baskets paddy.[54]

Judging from the text, it seems difficult to anticipate his emancipation from debt-slavery; rather, it might cause new family enslavement. The promised month of Tazaungmon was not met, but in February 1850, Nga San repaid 17 *kyat*s and, in March of the same year, Mi Dei Ba and his uncles repaid 83 *kyat*s 1 *mat* to the creditor Ma Hkaing, at the rate of 1 *kyat* per four baskets of paddy.[55] With the total amount of 100 *kyat*s 1 *mat*, the price of 400 baskets of paddy was settled and only 70 baskets of paddy and the price of Nga San's body were left unpaid. The couple then promised to pay off the remaining amount in the month of Tagu.[56] In fact, there is no more documentation left about Nga San and Mi Dei Ba, but it is clear that the couple was in the process of escaping the situation of debt-slavery with the great help of the wife's relatives.

Annulment of debt-slave contract of Nga Pwa

There is an interesting piece of testimony, dated April 9, 1873, entitled 'Annulment of the body price of Nga Pwa'.[57] After the death of a man called Nga Pwa, who had been put out as a debt-slave by his parents 12 years earlier, the creditors (Me Kyi Nyo and her sons) demanded the repayment of the sum of 80 *kyat*s from his parents. However, U Ba Zi and U Pyaun said that his price as a debt-slave had already been met and the contract should be annulled, and then the contract was annulled in the presence of Nga Pwa's wife, uncle, father-in-law, father, sisters, and their husbands, and this was recorded.

We do not know who U Ba Zi and U Pyaun were, but they might have been the witnesses at the time of the contract when Nga Pwa became a debt-slave. In any case, it seems likely that some influential local elders intervened and mediated with both debtors and creditors to ensure that the remaining family members, especially aged parents, were not overburdened. This is the only example of such mediation which I could see, but it shows that in some circumstances social and moral interventions served to break the chains of debt-slavery.

I have consistently used the term 'debt-slave' throughout the discussion in this book because it still seems to me that it is the most appropriate term to describe the circumstances in which people were placed as a result of the human-mortgage contracts. The basic form of being placed in a condition of bonded labor by taking on a debt, and restoring freedom by repaying the debt, is more accurately described by the term 'debt-slave' than by the various other terms that describe subordinate conditions. Substituting terms such as 'subordinate' or 'servant' does not seem to be effective in understanding the specific daily lives of those who lived in these circumstances, but only blurs the contours.

One important feature in human-mortgage contracts was that the debt-slave was often a party to the contract. Also, as noted earlier, there was no evidence in this material that the debt-slave's master (the creditor) sold the debt-slave to another person as a debt-slave without his or her consent, and a change of master was done at the wish of debt-slaves themselves. These points show well that debt-slaves were in temporary circumstances for as long as they were indebted, and that there were no status boundaries with free people.

However, it is also true that, depending on the terms of the contract, a debt-slave might automatically become a slave when born as a child of a debt-slave, and thus a debt-slave, which was supposed to be a temporary circumstance, could effectively become a status. This practice, expressed in the term *shin pwa, thei hsoun*, disappeared over time. Under the terms that became dominant instead, on the death of a debt-slave, the descendants would be required to repay the total debt left to them, and if this could not be repaid, the descendants would have no choice but to become debt-slaves, and here, too, the result was that the condition of debt-slavery was passed down from one generation to another.

There is a well-established reputation for the *thugaung* families in Salin for their warm and generous treatment of peasants and debt-slaves. Indeed, even from the scope of the material used in this study, it is clear that the *thugaung* families widely allowed the needy to buy paddy from the granaries they placed in many villages, and they repeatedly responded to requests for additional loans from debt-slaves. The presence of the *thugaung* families played an important role in the survival of the poorest members of the rural communities, and in this sense it could be argued that the *thugaung* families were indeed the greatest patrons of the rural community in Salin.

At the same time, however, these deferred payments and additional loans were accurately documented and their repayment was strictly required. In many cases, as was often the case in the contracts, when repayment was not possible, sons, daughters, and sons-in-laws were offered one after another as debt-slaves.

The fact that slaves often asked to change their masters from other creditors to *thugaung*s proves that the treatment of debt-slaves of *thugaung*s was better compared to other creditors. On the other hand, however, there were often cases of escape from *thugaung* households and, in such cases, as well as the search for the fugitive slave, several people concerned were called in to draw up a written agreement, and the person to be cosigned was identified and held liable for compensation.

In the Taungoo period, as Lieberman argued, entering debt-slavery under an influential person was a way for *ahmudan* people who owed hereditary services to the kingship to escape from the royal claims when these burdens became too strenuous. In the Konbaung period, no such figure emerges, at least not from the sources used. In the Taungoo period, not only the poor and needy, but also people of a high status, were said to have become debt-slaves, but there were no such cases and, in most cases, the poor living a precarious life with a shortage of food became debt-slaves as a means of survival.

The *thugaung* debt-slaves were mainly engaged in agricultural labor on land accumulated by *thugaung* families. The large local landowners of other regions who emerged during the middle to late Konbaung dynasty held not only land but also many debt-slaves. The importance of having a large number of debt-slaves for the economy of these provincial powerful families seems to have been still undiminished.

In sum, it seems that the relationship of debt-slave and master that emerges from human-mortgage contracts in Salin should first be clarified as a special contractual relation between money and people, rather than summarized as a form of patron–client relationship.

In the sight of Ma Hkaing and Me Kyi Nyo, who signed deeds and demanded strict performance of the agreements made therein as a matter of course, it is not necessarily wrong to see a competent administrator in pursuit of economic wellbeing rather than a warm-hearted patron.

In so far as the debt-slave was also a party and subject to the contract, it was a contract made by equal persons and was fair and binding on both sides. The creditors pursued the fulfillment of promises with confidence, and the debtors accepted that it was only natural for them to meet their obligations, even as they reduced their families to a succession of bonded labor conditions. It was still a long way off until a sense of value and awareness emerged that such contracts were a problem to the society.

Part III

Land as Collateral for Debt

5

Chapter

Land-mortgage Contracts in Byangya Village

Land-mortgage *thet-kayit*s occupied a large portion of the money-lending *thet-kayit*s during the Konbaung period. The 61 *thet-kayit*s related to the land mortgages written during the period from 1776 to 1843 in one village called Byangya show us the factors behind the land alienation, as well as its consequences on the lives of people and on the land system established by the royal government.[1]

*Thet-kayit*s in Byangya village

Byangya is a village in Dibeyin Township, Shwebo District, located in the center of the rice-farming plain irrigated by Ye-U canal, which takes water from the west bank of the Mu River. Shwebo, known in the Konbaung period as Mokhsobo, was the native place of Alaunghpaya, the founder of the Konbaung dynasty, and was the capital of the Konbaung dynasty during the period 1752–64. After that, the capital moved from one place to another between Ava, Amarapura, and Mandalay, but the irrigated plains of the Shwebo area, along with Kyaukse and Minbu, remained as the central granary of the kingdom, and also played an important political role.[2] The Ye-U canal that feeds the present-day rice fields of Byangya was constructed during the British period (1911–18) and did not exist in the eighteenth and nineteenth centuries.[3] However, judging from the fact that all the farmland in the village used as collateral for debts were paddy fields, it is evident that rice was being cultivated with irrigation facilities. The canals and small rivers in the vast plain along the Mu River valley are often silted because the plain is very flat, gently sloping from the north to

133

134   Chapter 5

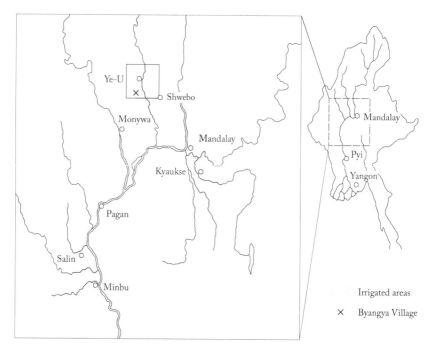

Figure 5.1: The location of Byangya village
Sources: Teruko Saito, 1994, p. 177. Williamson, 1963, Map No. 2.

the south. The old canals in the Konbaung period had been almost filled with sediment before the British colonization.[4]

From Byangya village, 61 *thet-kayit*s written in the period from 1776 to 1843 were found and collected, most of them being related to land mortgages and sales. Let us take the first and last of them as examples of the form of money-lending *thet-kayit*s secured by paddy fields.

1) On the 6th *lazou Nayon*, M.E. 1138 (June 6, 1776 A.D.), Nga Aung and his wife, the residents of Taung-legyi Village, and donors of Pagoda said to Nga Po Aing and his wife, the residents of Magyi-zauk Village, and donors of Pagoda, 'As we cannot make our living, we want to borrow money by mortgaging one of our four paddy fields called *Thet-kya-laun-mye*, a field sown with 25 baskets of seeds.[5] Please lend us 15 *kyat*s in 50% alloy and 15 *kyat*s in *ngwe zou* in total 30 *kyat*s. Nga Po Aing and his wife accepted their offer and lent them 15 *kyat*s in 50% alloy, and 15 *kyat*s in *ngwe zou*, and took the

paddy fields as collateral, on the 6th day, *lazou, Nayon* in 1138. The witness was Nga Pu, the weigher of money was Nga Tha U, the donor of the monastery, the scribe was Min-nga-aye-thwin, and the land inspection was omitted.[6]

2) On the 11th *lazan Wagaun*, M.E. 1205 (August 6, 1843 A.D.), Maung Yin, who lives in Hsin-hnamaung village, said to Min-kyaw-tin-sithu-naw-yata of Byangya, 'I need money and would like to pledge the paddy field called Pauk Yin, which is sown with one basket of seeds and also nursery fields sown with three baskets of seeds to borrow 33 *kyat*s 2 *mat*s in *gwe-mwe-ywet-ni*.[7] These fields situated in the south of Ko'-ko'-zu, the monastery land of Shin-mati Pagoda in Pagan, for *ngwe-mwe ywet-ni* 33 *kyat*s 2 *mat*s.' Min-kyaw-tin-sithu-naw-yata and his wife accepted this offer and lent 33 *kyat*s 2 *mat*s of *ngwe mwe ywet-ni* and took the paddy field sown with 1 basket of seeds, and nurseries sown with 3 baskets of seeds. Witness was Maung U Ngwe, Maung Yan Hmu assayed the money and also he was the scribe.[8]

It is noteworthy that the wording of the above two land-mortgage *thet-kayit*s is almost identical, although written 67 years apart. It seems that the form of the land-mortgage *thet-kayit*s was standardized as early as 1776, in the early part of the Konbaung period. Starting with a date, the contract is written in the form of a request for a loan from a party in need of money, the name and village of the party, the location and name of the paddy field to be pledged as collateral, and the size of the field expressed in terms of the amount of seed for sowing, cattle, or human labor. The amount of the debt comes next, and since there were various weights and qualities of private metal coins in circulation, the type and weight of the coins are specified. Then, it is stated that the creditor accepts the offer and lends the money and takes the paddy fields as collateral. Finally, it ends by stating the names of the witnesses and assayer and weigher.

Looking at the debtors and creditors in the contracts, both the borrower and the lender in the 1776 contract are described as the donors of a pagoda. The borrower, Nga Aung and his wife, had once been rich enough to build a pagoda, but faced economic difficulties at the time of making this contract. The paddy field they pledged as collateral was not

136   Chapter 5

very small, but about 6~7 hectares,[9] and they still owned a considerable amount of paddy fields.

On the other hand, in the contract written in 1843, the borrower, Maung Yin, had no honorific title and he pledged a small paddy field of 0.4 hectares with nurseries. The creditor who lent money and took the paddy field as collateral was known by the very long title of *Min-kyaw-tin-sithu-naw-yata*, and as we will see later, his occupation was *ahsaun-daw-mye*, which means a chamberlain of the king. Here, the economic status of the debtor and the creditor seems to be far apart.

People who appeared in the *thet-kayit*s

The people who appeared in the *thet-kayit*s of Byangya village were the king's courtiers, other officials, village chiefs, *ahmudan*s belonging to the cavalry, *athi* (free people, commoner), pagoda slaves,[10] and so on, covering most of the social strata of the time, but the majority of them were farmers cultivating paddy in the irrigated land, and these people were mentioned in the contracts only by their residential villages and names. However, since a *thet-kayit* does not always specify the status of the person in question, there might be cases in which the people were referred to only by name, including not only *athi*, but also subordinate *ahmudan*. However, if the debtor was an *ahmudan*, the name of the group the debtor belonged to was mentioned for the purpose of identification. In the case of *ahmudan* of high position, the position was always stated before the name; for example, *Min gaung* (cavalry commander) or *Thwet Tauk-kyi* (infantry commander). In the case of village chiefs and other officials, the title was written in front of the name, like *ywa-thugyi* U Taw (chief of village, U Taw). Some people were described not by their names but only by their *bwe* (honorary titles), which were bestowed by the king. These titles could be used only when they were serving under the king. On the other hand, there was another title of honor to praise the behavior of people who donated for the promotion of Buddhism or public welfare. These donors were called *daga* (donor), and this title was prefixed to the personal name, like *paya daga* U Po (U Po, donor of Pagoda) or *kan daga-ma* Mi Nan Daw (Mi Nan Daw, female donor of pond). These donors of Buddhist institutions or public facilities were highly respected in the Buddhist community and the word *daga* or *daga-ma* was prefixed to their names without fail, even in money-lending contracts.

Table 5.1: Assayers and weighers of currencies (Byangya)

Thet-kayit no.	Assayer & weigher	Thet-kayit no.	Assayer & weigher
1	Nga Tha U	23	Maung Ywe
3	Maung Thu Hla	24	Nga Ywe
4	Maung Oo	25	Maung Chin
5	Maung Taik	26	Maung Hmaing
7	Kaung Min	28	Maung Kyaw
9	Nagan-daw Min	29	Maung Kin
11	Maung In	30	Maung Saw
12	Nga Byan Hmu	33	Maung Yan Bye
13	Nga Pyo	38	Maung Shwe Ye
14	Maung Tha Tun	44	U YanBye
15	Maung Shuwan	47	Maung Yan Bye
16	Maung Myat Tha	50	Thu-yin-shwe-daun Thiha Yaza
17	Maung Waing	51	Min Kyaw Tin
19	Maung Shwe Mi	53	Maung Hmwe
20	Maung San Shuyin	58	Maung Yan Bye
21	Maung Kyaw Zaya	61	Maung Yan Hmu
22	Maung Gyi		

Source: *Thet-kayit*s of Byangya village, in Toe Hla, 'Konbaung Hkit Leya Thetkayit pa Luhmu Sibwaye Thamaing' (unpublished typescript), 1981 (KLT). UCL *para-baik* No. 151107, 151113.

Note: in many areas, different people served as assayers and weighers of metal coins, but in the *thet-kayit*s of Byangya, only the name of one person appeared in one contract as an assayer or a weigher. It seems that in Byangya, the appraisal and weighing were carried out by one person at the same time.

As the presence of witnesses was very important for the contract to be effective, people who were respected and influential in the community were asked to sit and watch the conclusion of money-lending contracts. Nearly half of the witnesses who appeared in Byangya *thet-kayit*s were village chiefs, *ahmudan*s of high rank, and donors of Buddhist or public facilities.

In contrast, assayers and weighers of money were mostly common people without any honorary titles, as shown in Table 5.1. It is somewhat surprising that so many different people appeared as assayers and weighers in different contracts in Byangya *thet-kayit*s. Considering the complicated monetary situation when alloys of various qualities were circulating simultaneously, it seems that a high level of skill was required to assay

138   Chapter 5

Table 5.2: Land-related *thet-kayit*s in Byangya village (1776–1812)

No.	Date	Creditor	Honorary title etc.	Abode
1	1776.6.6	Nga Po Aing and wife	donor of pagoda	Magyizauk
2	1780.6.6	U Myat and wife	donor of monastery	Magyizaukkon
3	1782.2.19	Thiri Kyaw Tin and wife*		Byangya
4	1783.5.5	Maung Tha U and wife	donor of monastery	Byangya
5	1786.5.29	ditto	ditto	Byangya
6	1786.8.16	ditto	ditto	Byangya
7	1787.10.12	ditto	ditto	Byangya
8	1787.11.19	ditto	ditto	Byangya
9	1788.5.15	ditto	ditto	Byangya
10	1791.8.12	Maung Tha Nyunt	*Htidaw Mo-gaung*	unknown
11	1791.9.6	Mi Dun and Son	donor of monastery	Byangya
12	1792.9.3	ditto	donor of monastery	Byangya
13	1794.6.19	Mi Mye Shu		unknown
14	1796.6.7	Maung Ko Naw and wife		Byangya
15	1797.6.14	Maung Tha Myat and wife	donor of pagoda	unknown
16	1804.5.28	Maung Po Lwin and wife	*Taung-daw-U-Mitta*	unknown
17	1804.6.5	Maung Shin Gyi and sister		Byangya
18	1805.5.14	Maung Po Lwin and wife	*Bo thugyi*	unknown
19	1805.6.27	Maung Myat Thu and wife	donor of pagoda	Hsinla-maung
20	1805.6.15	Maung Naw and wife	donor of pagoda	Magyizaukkon
21	1806.7.8	Mi Nan Daw	donor of pond	Byangya
22	1808.8.3	Maung Bye and wife	donor of resthouse	Byangya
23	1809.6.5	ditto	donor of resthouse	Byangya
24	1809.7.15	Maung Thi and wife	donor of monastery	Byangya
25	1809.7.18	Maung Tha Yan and wife		Byangya
26	1810.8.16	Mi Nan Daw	donor of pond	Byangya
27	1810.10.7	Maung Shwe Ain		Byangya
28	1810.11.14	Maung Shin Gyi and sister		Byangya
29	1812.10.12	Maung Ye and wife		Nga Baing

Source: UCL *para-baik* No. 151107, 151113, transcribed by U Toe Hla, KLT, 1981, pp. 195–244.
Note: the full title of the creditor in contract no. 3 is Min-nanda-thiri-kyaw-tin-nawyatha.

the coins, although weighing was not difficult. Was it that the quality of the currencies circulated in the region was standardized to the extent to make assaying work not so difficult? But this assumption dose not seem to be valid, since the varieties of currencies that appeared in the contracts were so wide in Byangya. Different people also appeared in the contracts as drafters and scribes, but this is not surprising, as Burma has been a society with a relatively high literacy rate owing to the widespread literacy education in Buddhist monasteries.

Debtor	Abode	Remark
Nga Aun and wife*	Taung-le-gyi	paddy field pledge
Nga Tun Byi	Kanni	paddy field pledge
Mi Talaing, Shin Ka Yin	Kya-hkat	paddy field pledge
Shin U Ma, Maung Kya Yok	ditto	paddy field pledge
Maung Kyain and wife	Kanni	paddy field pledge
Ama Talaing, Mi Ka Yin	Kya-hkat	additional loan
Mi Kywe Ma	Pagan mye	paddy land pledge lokhpet
Maung San Pyu	Tozin	paddy land pledge lokhpet
Nga Kaung and son	Padwin	paddy field pledge
Nga Tha Pe	Maletha	paddy field pledge
Mi Kywe Ma	Pagan mye	paddy field pledge
Maung Ne	unknown	paddy land pledge lokhpet
Nga Kala and family	unknown	redemption of monastry land
Nga Ba Lu and brother	Hsinhna-maungkon	monastery land pledge
Maung The and wife	unknown	additional loan
U Myat Kan	Au'tin	additional loan
Maung Hmi and wife	Hsinla-maung	change of creditor
Maung Tha Ywe and wife	Hsinla-maung	paddy field pledge
Maung Shwe New	Taung-Chaung-yo	paddy field pledge
U San Kyin and son*	Hsinla-maung	monastery land pledge
Mi Nan Zu and son	Hsinla maung	paddy field pledge
Maung Tayet	Byangya	paddy field pledge
Maung Wain	Hcyauk-einzu	paddy field pledge
Nga Tu Yin	Mingyi-zaukmye	monastery land pledge
Maung Myet Yin	Hsinhna-maungkon	monastery land pledge
Mi Min Ywe	Hcyaung-lo	paddy field pledge
Maung Kan Pyu	Kyi	monastery land pledge
Nga Shwe Yit	Hsinhna-maungkon	paddy field selling
Mi Nan	Byangya	paddy field selling

Some debtors (*) hold honorary titles such as donor of pagoda or monastery, which denotes they were once wealthy enough to donate such Buddhist institutions.

Contents of the *thet-kayit*s

Table 5.2 and Table 5.3 show a summary of the contents of 61 *thet-kayit*s related to Byangya village, divided into the early and the late Konbaung period in chronological order. Table 5.4 shows the number of *thet-kayit*s counted by contractual content.

In all land-mortgage contracts found in Byangya, paddy fields were used as collateral, and we have not yet found a case where dry fields or orchards were used as collateral. There were 34 paddy field mortgage con-

140   Chapter 5

Table 5.3: Land-related *thet-kayit*s in Byangya village (1827–43)

No.	Date	Creditor	Title, official status etc.	Abode
30	1827.1.31	Min Kyaw Tin	Asaung-daw-mye	Byangya
31	1827.2.3	Maung Shin Gyi		Byangya
32	1827.10.21	Min Shwe Sanda Thu		unknown
33	1828.6.2	Min Kyaw Tin	Asaung-daw-mye	Byangya
34	1829.2.11	Maung Naw and son		unknown
35	1829.5.21	Min Kyaw Tin	Asaung-daw-mye	Byangya
36	1829.9.29	Min Kyaw Tin	Asaung-daw-mye	ditto
37	1830.2.14	Maung by		Paya-htwet
38	1830.6.5	Maung Bye and wife	Asaung-daw-mye	Byangya
39	1831.4.13	Min Kyaw Tin	ditto	ditto
40	1832.8.30	Min Kyaw Tin	ditto	ditto
41	1834.4.4	Court decision for a dispute over paddy fields		
42	1834.9.9	Min Kyaw Tin	ditto	ditto
43	1835.2.19	mostly broken, unreadable		
44	1837.9.8	Min Kyaw Tin	ditto	ditto
45	1837.10.29	Min Kyaw Tin	ditto	ditto
46	1838.9.24	Min Kyaw Tin	ditto	ditto
47	1840.8.27	Maung Shin Gyi		ditto
48	1840.10.29	Min Kyaw Tin	ditto	ditto
49	1840.11.14	Min Kyaw Tin	ditto	ditto
50	1841.6.4	Min Kyaw Tin	ditto	ditto
51	1841.6.4	Min Kyaw Tin	ditto	ditto
52	1841.7.26	Min Kyaw Tin	ditto	ditto
53	1842.5.28	Min Kyaw Tin	ditto	ditto
54	1842.5.30	Min Kyaw Tin	ditto	ditto
55	1842.6.2	Min Kyaw Tin	ditto	ditto
56	1842.6.6	Min Kyaw Tin	ditto	ditto
57	1842.6.19	Min Kyaw Tin	ditto	ditto
58	1842.6.26	Min Kyaw Tin	ditto	ditto
59	1842.7.2	Min Kyaw Tin	ditto	ditto
60	1842.7.26	Min Kyaw Tin	ditto	ditto
61	1843.8.6	Min Kyaw Tin	ditto	ditto

Notes: the full title of the creditor Min Kyaw Tin was Min Kyaw Tin Sithu Naw-yatha.
He was an *Ahsaun-daw-mye* (royal court official). The borrower of contract No. 34 was
a village head of Kyi. The borrower Min Pyo, who appears in contracts No. 40 and 44, was

tracts, three additional loan contracts, one redemption certificate, and ten
contracts of changing creditors. There were also three contracts of selling
paddy fields, and in four cases the contracts were sold to a third person.

Among the 34 deeds of paddy field mortgage contracts, paddy fields
were pledged in 31 deeds, where usufruct rights were transferred to the

Borrower	Abode	Remarks
Maung Byaung		
Maung Byaung	Ok-tin	paddy field pledge
Nga Yan Hmu	unknown	ditto
Maung Ta Naw and son	Shin La Maung	change of creditor
Thamanda Zeya Kyaw	Kyi	paddy field pledge
Mi Ok Le	Shan	change of creditor
Nga Shwe	Magyi zauk	monastry land pledge
Min Pyo	Byangya	paddy field pledge
Maung Baik	unknown	paddy field pledge
U Shwe Twet	unknown	borrowing paddy
Min Pyo	Byangya	change of creditor
Shin Gwe Mon	Hsin Nahtaung	change of creditor
Min Pyo	Byangya	monastry land pledge
Maung U Ka	Shinhna maung gon	ditto
Maung Po and wife	unknown	change of creditor
Maung Twet	Paya htwet	monastry land pledge
Nga Shwe Za	unknown	paddy field pledge
Shin Hmo U	Royal capital	sale of thet-kayit
Maung Shwe U	Ye-htwet	monastry land pledge
Maung Shwe U	ditto	paddy field pledge
Maung Shwe Taw	Paya htwet	borrowing paddy
Maung Myat Kyaw	unknown	sale of thet-kayit
Maung Yan Bye and son-in-law	unknown	change of creditor
Maung Meik	Hnabe-hla	repayment of paddy
Maung Tin	Byangya	sale of thet-kayit
Maung Ye and son	Ngabaing	sale of paddy field
Mi Dok and son	unknown	sale of thet-kayit
Maung Nyunt	Kountha	borrowing paddy
Maung Ye	Tha-hkwat	change of creditor
Maung Yin	Hsinhna-maung	paddy field pledge

a younger brother of Min Kyaw Tin. It was not unusual to make a money-lending contract even between family members.

creditors. In other words, the creditor cultivated the paddy fields either by himself or by hiring someone to cultivate them, and then reaped the harvest as his own, or rented out the paddy fields to a third party and collected the land rent.

In other areas, land-mortgage contracts often included a condition to restrict the period when the debtor could repay the debt and redeem the

142   Chapter 5

Table 5.4: The contents of *thet-kayit*s of Byangya village

Types of *thet-kayit*		Nos.
1) Land (paddy field) mortgage contracts		34
Type of paddy field	Privately owned (*bo-ba bain*)	25
	Monastery land	9
Form of collateral		
Pledging (usufructuary rights are transferred to the creditor)		31
Mortgage (the debtor continues to cultivate the paddy field, but the creditor takes 50% of the harvest as interest)		3
2) Additional loan (i.e., a debt overlaid on pledged paddy fields)		3
3) Repayment certificate		1
4) Change of creditors		10
5) Buy and sell contracts of paddy fields		3
6) Buy and sell contracts of *thet-kayit*s		4
7) Paddy-borrowing contracts		4
8) Litigation on paddy field		1
9) Others (illegible due to damage)		1

land, as the creditors usually wanted to secure the harvest for a certain period. For example, if a phrase such as *thon hni thon thi* (three years three harvests) was specified, it meant that the paddy field could not be redeemed for three years. In Byangya contracts, we have not yet found any such limitation of the period, meaning, theoretically, that the debtors could redeem their paddy fields whenever they wanted to.

The remaining three contracts were what they called *lo'hpet* contracts, in which the debtor continued to cultivate his or her paddy field and paid half of the harvest to the creditor as interest on the money borrowed. In the document, this arrangement was expressed as 'the money should be lent on the terms of *lo'hpet*'.[11]

A repayment certificate was exchanged between the parties to the land-mortgage contract in front of the witnesses to confirm that the debt was repaid and the land was redeemed, in order to avoid future disputes. Usually, people did not make this type of certificate, but just disposed of the original land-mortgage *thet-kayit*s. The only example, written in 1794, shows that there was a special reason to make a repayment certificate; namely, the pledged field was originally the monastery land, which was forbidden to be pledged or sold. Moreover, the person who was repaying the debt was not the person who had borrowed money, but the chief of the monastery cultivators.[12]

There were ten contracts relating to the change of creditors, which means that such cases happened quite frequently in this area. When the creditor asked for the loan to be repaid and the debtor could not repay, the debtor often sought a bigger money-lender who could lend enough money to repay the debt, and, if possible, could provide an additional loan. If a new creditor appeared, the mortgaged paddy field was transferred to the new creditor. Let us look at one example:

> On the 4th *lazo Nayon* 1191 (May 21, 1829), a resident of Shan village, Mi Ou' Le, had offered a paddy field sown by 2.5 baskets of seeds, called Tauk-Sha-Yin, located to the south of Ko Ko Zu as a collateral for a large quantity of paddy borrowed from U San Bye, a resident of Paya-twet village. However, she said to *Ahsaun-daw-mye*,[13] that she wanted to take back the paddy field and mortgage it to *Ahsaun-daw-mye* and to borrow 60 *kyat*s in 2 *mat* alloy, which was equivalent to the price of paddy in the market. *Ahsaun-daw-mye* accepted her offer and lent her 60 *kyat*s in 2 *mat* alloy, i.e., the market value of 100 baskets of paddy and took her paddy fields as collateral. The witness was Maung Kya Shun, a resident of Shan village, and the drafter was Shwe-daun-ya, a resident of Byangya village.[14]

It seems that U San Bye asked to repay the price of paddy, but because Mi Ou' Le was unable to do so, she borrowed money from *Ahsaun-daw-mye*, and as a result, the collateral (i.e., paddy field) was transferred from U San Bye to the new creditor, *Ahsaun-daw-mye*. We can see in this example, a path of accumulation of paddy fields from small and medium-sized money-lenders to wealthier money-lenders.

There are three sale and purchase contracts of paddy fields found in Byangya *thet-kayit*s. In most cases, the debtors repeated additional borrowings on the mortgaged paddy fields and when they could no longer afford to repay the accumulated debts, they sold the mortgaged paddy fields to their creditors at the price equivalent to the total amount of debts. For example:

144   Chapter 5

On the 4th *lazo Tazaungmon* 1172 (May 21, 1829), Nga Shwe Ei, the resident of Shin-hna-maun-gon village who was the son of the donor of pond, and other co-heirs asked to Maung Shin Gyi, the son of Mi Nan Daw in Byangya village and his siblings, that they wanted to sell three paddy fields called Le-bein, sown with two baskets of seeds, for good and all. Nga Shwe Ei said, 'As the price of paddy field sown with 1 basket seeds is now 24 *kyat*s in *ywet-ni*, we want to sell our paddy fields sown with 2 baskets of seeds at 48 *kyat*s to you for good and all.' Maung Shin Gyi and his siblings accepted this offer and bought the 2 paddy fields called Le-bein paying 48 *kyat*s in *ywet-ni*, for good and all, up to the generation of their children and grand-grandchildren. The witness was Maung Tha Bo, Maung Kyaw assayed and weighed the money, Maung Tha Lu drafted and scribed the contract.[15]

As shown in this example, when it came to the buying and selling of paddy fields, instead of using the simple words to buy (*we-de*) and to sell (*yaun-de*), such solemn phrases as 'sell for good and all' or 'buy the final ownership which will be handed to posterity' were used in paddy field transactions. In land-sale contracts in other regions, a phrase to sell paddy fields 'like building a pagoda or a temple' is often found. It was an idiom which implied that a Buddhist's promise to donate the most important Buddhist facilities would not be broken and must be solemnly kept forever. Using this idiom, they showed that in the case of a land transaction, the promise made in the contracts should be kept forever. As discussed later, there remained a deep-rooted conception that paddy fields were not a commodity that passed from hand to hand through sales, but were, rather, forever and strongly linked to the person who reclaimed and cultivated the land and his descendants who inherited and continued to cultivate it. That would be the reason they needed special wording in land-sale contracts.

Sometimes a *thet-kayit* itself became the object of transaction. I found four *thet-kayit*s in which *thet-kayit*s were sold to a third person. The sale of a *thet-kayit* brought the same result as a change of creditor, but in the case of a change of creditor, the debtor was one party to the contract, whereas when a *thet-kayit* itself was bought and sold, the creditor selling the *thet-kayit* directly to a third party and the debtor were no longer a party of the contract. The selling and buying of *thet-kayit*s often happened when a long time had passed since the original *thet-kayit* was made, but the original owner did not redeem the mortgaged paddy fields. However, the sale of a *thet-kayit* without the consent of the original owner could be a remote cause of litigation, as we will see in Chapters 7 and 8.

Here is an example of a sale of a *thet-kayit*:

On the 14th *lazo Nayon*, 1204 (June 6, 1842), Maung Tin, a resident of Byangya village, said to *Min-kyaw-tin-thiri-naw-yata* of the same village as follows. 'As I need money, I want to sell the land-mortgage contract of a paddy field named Magyi-in-gale, which had been pledged to us by someone else, for a sum of 14 *kyat*s in *ngwe-mwe-ywet-ni*. If the original owner would appear and want to redeem his paddy field in future, please let him redeem the paddy field.' *Min-kyaw-tin-thiri-naw-yata* and his wife accepted the offer and paid the money and bought the original contract. The witness was U Maw, a resident of Magyi-zauk village, the drafter and scribe was Maung Pyo.[16]

When people borrowed paddy, the interest was paid in paddy or paid by pledging paddy fields to the creditor. Two paddy-loan contracts found in Byangya stated that the borrowed paddy should be repaid six or ten months later with 50% interest in paddy, and in one contract a promise was made to pledge the paddy field as collateral if the paddy could not be repaid until the fixed date. In another two paddy-borrowing *thet-kayit*s, paddy was borrowed by pledging paddy fields from the very first.

On the 9th *lazan Wagaung*, 1203 (July 26, 1841), Maung Shwe Thu and Maung Ta Bo, residents of Paya-htwet village, said to *Min-kyaw-tin-thiri-naw-yata* and his wife, 'We need paddy to eat. Please lend us 110 baskets of paddy. We will repay the paddy loan with 50% interest by the full moon day of the month of Pyatho.[17] If we cannot repay the loan, we will pledge 7 paddy fields sown with 5 baskets of seeds, owned by Shwe Thu, located in the east of Shinzaw Pagoda in Chin village, in exchange for 165 baskets of paddy, as the principal and interest of the loan.' *Min-kyaw-tin-thiri-naw-yata* and his wife accepted the request and lent 110 baskets of paddy to them. The witness was Maung Shwe Ket, a resident of Chin village, the drafter and scribe was the lender, *Ahsaun-daw mye*.[18]

146   Chapter 5

Process of land alienation
Transfer of farmland to influential people

A comparison of Tables 5.2 and 5.3 reveals that the loans secured by the paddy fields developed in various forms over time. Up to 1810, the simple form of the land-mortgage contracts occupied about 80% of all the contracts, and among the rest there were three additional-loan contracts and one contract of changing the creditor. The contract of selling paddy fields first appeared in 1810 and next in 1812.

As for the period from 1813 to 1826, I have not yet found any *thet-kayit*s and, as a result, could not trace what was going on during these 13 years. However, the subsequent 32 *thet-kayit*s written during the period 1827–43 describe an extremely diverse range of transactions. The paddy fields mortgage contracts were still the largest in number, with a total number of 12, including cases where monastery paddy fields were mortgaged, but there were eight contracts of changing creditors, four contracts of selling contracts, and four contracts of borrowing paddy, one of which (No. 59) was an agreement to borrow paddy and money from Min-kyaw-tin-sithu-naw-yata by offering a paddy field as collateral.

Similarly, if we compare the period covered by Table 5.2 and the period covered by Table 5.3, there was a significant change in the hierarchy of people lending money to people in Byangya and neighboring villages. Table 5.2 shows that there were many people who lent money by taking paddy fields as collateral, and their statuses were diverse. The most common were the donors of Buddhist institutions and public facilities, who were considered to be the wealthy segment of the free commoners.

In contrast, from 1827 onwards, an extremely influential money-lender appeared on the scene, lending money and paddy to a wide range of people in the neighboring villages and accumulating vast land. He was an *ahsaun-daw-mye*, a courtier of the king's chamberlain, and held a very long honorary title, *Min-kyaw-tin-sithu-naw-yata*, bestowed by the king. The fact that some of the small and medium-sized money-lenders who once could afford to lend money to others had to transfer their paddy fields to borrow money from this influential person is well illustrated by the cases of change of creditors and sale of contracts.

As seen in the table, during the 17 years from 1827 to 1843, the *Ahsaun-daw-mye* accumulated paddy fields sown with 43.1 baskets of seeds, five paddy fields of unknown size and four nurseries through money-lending activities. In total, it is estimated that he accumulated paddy fields and nurseries sown with about 50 baskets of seeds, which is equivalent to 13~14 hectares.

The following contract clearly shows how the paddy fields were passed between a succession of people:

On the 14th *lazan Thadingyut* 1170 (August 3, 1808), Maung Ta Yet, a resident of Byangya village, said to Maung Bye, a donor of the rest house of the same village, and his wife, 'I am in need of money to buy paddy. Please lend me money and take my paddy fields called Le-gyan-kondaw and Zyi-byu-yin located in Kyi village and sown with one and one-eighth baskets of seeds as collateral.' Maung Bye and his wife accepted the offer and lent 23 *kyat*s 3 *mu*s in 15-*kyat* alloy, and took the paddy fields as collateral.

Maung Yan Tha and wife asked *Ahsaun-daw-mye* and his wife to take this *thet-kayit* of land-mortgage in which Maung Ta Yet pledged his *Zyi-byu-yin* paddy fields to the donor of the rest house, Maung Bye, at the price of 19 *kyat*s calculated in terms of the present paddy price. *Ahsaun-daw-mye* agreed and bought the *thet-kayit*s.

The witness is the donor of pagoda, Maung Shwe Ti. The drafter and script is Maung Yan Tha.[19]

The undated latter part of the *thet-kayit* was added years later to the first part. This *thet-kayit* tells us that the right over the paddy field called Zyi-byu-yin was transferred one person after another from Maung Ta Yet to Maung Bye and then to Maung Yan Tha and finally to *Ahsaun-daw-mye*. This was not at all an extreme or rare case in Byangya *thet-kayit*s in the period of Table 5.3. I found many cases where *thet-kayit*s were sold or lands already mortgaged were transferred to other money-lenders. More than half of the lands held by *Ahsaun-daw-mye* as mortgages from 1827 to 1843 were lands already pledged to other money-lenders. As there was no practice of double mortgage in Byangya *thet-kayit*s, mortgagers of lands redeemed their lands with the money borrowed from new money-lenders and pledged it again.

These facts tell us that the dependency on debt among villagers was such that from the 1820s onward they were not able to redeem their

148   Chapter 5

lands and had to seek another money source to clear the old debts. This naturally accelerated the speed of the transfer of lands. According to the custom of the day, the original reclaimer and his descendants could always redeem the lands, no matter how many years had passed or how many hands of mortgagees they had gone through. However, it is certain that the tie between the original reclaimer and the land reclaimed became more and more obscure as land was transferred from hand to hand. In such land circulations, no distinct differentiation between the private lands and monastery lands was made, and the original land distinction gradually disappeared as the land-mortgaging custom became more and more widespread.

Monastery lands under mortgage

It is particularly worth noting that some *thet-kayit*s in Byangya mortgaged monastery lands of a famous pagoda in Pagan as collateral for debts. Among the 34 original land-mortgage *thet-kayit*s, there were nine cases where the mortgaged lands were monastery lands.

The outline of the land tenure system from the early to middle period of the Konbaung era can be drawn as follows, based on customary codes,[20] royal decrees, U Tin's *Myanmar Min Ok-chok-pon Sadan*,[21] and J. S. Furnivall's classic text, *An Introduction to the Political Economy of Burma*:[22]

- royal land (*Aya-daw*)
  - king's property: royal paddy fields and garden cultivated by lamaings[23]
  - official land: land given to the *ahmudan*s; they had only usufruct right on the land; no taxation on the land, but they owed hereditary services to the king

- monastery land (*Wut mye*): donated lands by kings, other royalties or very rich persons, to support Buddhist edifices;[24] cultivated by *paya-kyun* (people who donated to a pagoda or monastery); they had only usufruct right; tax exempted

- private land:
  - reclaimed land (*Dama-u-kya-mye*) and the land cultivated by three successive generations from the reclaimer, which was called *Bo-ba-baing-mye* (ancestral land)

> – purchased land: both usufruct and disposal rights; tax in the form of tithe (in crop or in cash).

The monastery land was the land donated by the royal family or the wealthy for the maintenance of pagodas and temples, and once the land became monastery land, it remained monastery estate permanently, and was exempt from taxation. However, Byangya *thet-kayit*s raise a big question as to whether this institutional framework was actually maintained or not in the period of our study.

Let us look at a *thet-kayit* in which monastery land was mortgaged for the first time in our Byangya *thet-kayit*s:

> On the 7th lazo Nayon 1156 (June 19, 1794) two paddy fields sown with 1.25 baskets of seeds, called Nyaun-yin, and belonging to *Pagan-mye*[25] had been mortgaged to Mi Mye Shu by the family of Nga Kala, the donor of the pagoda. As the lands were under their charge, *Le-gaung* Maung Nyunt and his wife redeemed them and paid 38 *kyat*s 3 *mat*s in 2 *mat* alloy, for Mi Mye Shu's *thet-kayit*.[26]

In this *thet-kayit*, the *le-gaung* redeemed the paddy fields on behalf of the debtor. As the word *le-gaung* meant a chief of pagoda slaves or tenants who cultivated monastery lands, it seems that this *le-gaung*, Maung Nyunt, felt some responsibility or necessity to restore the order to this portion of monastery land.

However, this was the only instance in which *le-gaung* appeared and redeemed the mortgaged monastery estate, and I have not found any such restoration by a *le-gaung* or anyone else in the later *thet-kayit*s that deal with monastery lands. The temple estate was not private land but land conceived as permanently belonging to the pagoda or temple, although cultivators of those lands in Byangya *thet-kayit*s did not hesitate to refer to it as 'my paddy field'. The large number of money-lending *thet-kayit*s secured by such monastery lands indicates that this had become the accepted norm in the local community, as these *thet-kayit*s were written openly in the presence of many people, such as witnesses, assayers and weighers, drafters, and scribes.

In 1785, the royal government of Bodawhpaya attempted to confiscate at least those monastery lands where pagodas and monasteries had long since collapsed. However, the king's attempt was thwarted by his archpriest,

150   Chapter 5

who argued that monastery lands should remain as they were for good and if the original pagodas and monasteries were ruined, then the monastery lands should be handed over to the nearest religious establishments.[27] What this episode tells us is that many of the pagodas and monasteries constructed centuries ago had collapsed and the cultivators of monastery lands, donated to these pagodas and monasteries, gradually began to treat these lands as their own properties. Although the Buddhist organization had been reluctant to relinquish land once it was recorded as monastery estates, as time passed, the Buddhist organization's rule over the monastery lands was in an irreversible decline from the early sixteenth century onwards, as Lieberman explained:

> Amidst the disorders of the early 1500s, Shans expropriated some religious lands, while numerous lithic dedicatory markers disappeared. At the same time, many Burman monks abandoned their properties to move to Toungoo and other southern locales; the Forest Dweller sect virtually disappeared. Extensive glebe lands thus shifted, illegally but in effect permanently, from religious to lay ownership. As they established their authority over the north in the seventeenth century, restored Toungoo kings severely restricted landed donations by laymen other than themselves.[28]

Some reports written by British officials after the final annexation of Upper Burma in 1885 described the situation of monastery lands in Upper Burma during the first several years after the annexation. According to *The Gazetteer of Upper Burma and the Shan States* (GUBSS), there were two types of monastery estates, one still cultivated by pagoda slaves and exempted from taxation, and the other cultivated by ordinary people and taxed tithes.[29] It had been a custom since the Pagan period to inscribe the names of donor and the size of donated lands in steles, but in the last years of the nineteenth century, the British officials found that the size of monastery lands inscribed in steles was very different and much larger than the area actually cultivated by the pagoda slaves. In Kyaukse and Mingyan districts, the large portion of monastery lands were alienated and never redeemed.[30]

From these references, we can trace the privatization of monastery lands for centuries. It started as early as the beginning of the sixteenth century and the process accelerated during the collapse of dynasties and resultant social confusion. However, as the number of *thet-kayit*s I have read became larger, I realized that the situation in Byangya was an example of the most advanced trends in land alienation, and that the regional deviations were quite large, as we will see in the next chapter.

For example, Thu Nandar's study based on the 364 *thet-kayit*s related to land-mortgage contracts collected in Meiktila revealed that she could not find land-selling contracts at all.[31] Pledging of irrigated paddy fields also occurred frequently in Meiktila, but it did not result in the sale of the land, and instead there were a number of legal documents relating to pledged agricultural land. In Meiktila and its neighboring areas, the norms of the customary codes which strongly bound agricultural land to the reclaimers and their descendants were more in play, contrasting with areas such as Byangya, where traditional norms had broken down and the power of the money economy had come to prevail. It is reasonable to assume that a variety of local realities existed in between these two extremes. As we will see in the next chapter, there were also waves of times when the number of debt contracts secured by agricultural land rose sharply in some periods and not in others. During the latter part of King Bodawhpaya's reign and after the defeat of the First and the Second Anglo-Burmese Wars, the number of land-mortgage and selling *thet-kayit*s increased rapidly.

With regard to the pledging of monastery lands in the vicinity of Byangya village, only in the first instance, written in 1794, had the chief of cultivators (*le-gaung*) redeemed the monastery lands mortgaged by one of the cultivators under him. It seems that in this case the land had still been cultivated by pagoda slaves and the traditional monastery land system had been maintained by a narrow margin. The other cases seem to be examples of monastery lands that had already been substantially privatized. But the fact that those lands were, or had been, donated to a famous pagoda in Pagan was commonly recognized in the community, and even when these lands were offered as security, they were clearly identified in the deeds, as they had been once monastery lands to a pagoda.

Transfer of official lands

Then, how were the royal lands treated in the spread of debts secured by the paddy fields? Did not the same thing happen to the lands granted to officials and *ahmudan*s? These granted lands were usually located in the

152   Chapter 5

best irrigated areas and it often happened that newly organized *ahmudan* groups, mainly of war captives from Manipur, Assam, Vientiane, and Siam, were settled. Since the *ahmudan* groups were of vital importance to the monarchy, providing military power and special skills or essential goods for the maintenance of the monarchy, many of them were bestowed lands in the most productive rice-growing belts in the central plain. Granted lands were included in the category of royal lands (*aya-daw*) and were not supposed to be disposed to others. However, the most common and preferred security for debt was irrigated paddy fields so far as we know.

It was not until 1861, during the reign of King Mindon, that the system of granting land to *ahmudan*s was abolished and the remuneration of all *ahmudan*, from ministers to village chiefs, and from generals to soldiers, was changed to a fixed monthly salary system. Initially, the monthly wage for the ministers was fixed at 1,000 *kyat*s and, for the lowest-ranking soldiers and *ahmudan*s, at 6–7 *kyat*s, but the transition was not always smooth and there were delays, shortages, and payments in kind in the form of paddy.[32] However, even before this change, the land granted to *ahmudan*s might have been used as collateral for loans. Byangya is located in Dibeyin, which had a large *ahmudan* population due to its irrigated paddy fields fed by the Mu River. If almost half of the population was *ahmudan*,[33] there is a strong possibility that some of the land pledged in *thet-kayit*s of Byangya might be lands granted to *ahmudan*s.

Among Byangya *thet-kayit*s, I found two examples in which it is clear that lands granted to *ahmudan* were used as collateral for debt:

On the 2nd *lazo Tawthalin* 1154 (September 3, 1792), Maung Nay, a cavalry commander and *Ywa-za*[34] of Magyi-zauk village said, 'I need money to send men on an expedition to *Yo-daya* (Siam). Lend me money on the security of two plots of paddy fields. These lands were granted to me for being the chief of a cavalry unit; they are located below the tank in the north of the village.' When it was stated, Mi Dun, the donor of Byangya village monastery and her son Nga Myat Thu lent a loan of 1 *viss* 70 *kyat*s 6 *mu*s of which 66 *kyat*s were in flowered silver for the price of paddy, and 1 *viss* 4 *kyat*s 6 *mu*s were in 2 *mat-ke* silver.[35] These lands were rented to the mortgager to work as a share-cropper at his expense, by paying the land revenue and cost of cultivation. The assayer and weigher was Nga Pya Hmwe, the donor of a pagoda, and the scribe was Nga Hpyu, a novice.[36]

In this contract, written in 1792, the cavalry commander, Maung Nay, stated that the paddy fields were *sa-mye* (land for eating) granted to him by the royal government. Granted lands to *ahmudan*s were given as a set of land for cultivation (*lok-mye*), housing land (*ein-mye*), and *sa-mye*, and, among them, only *sa-mye* could be leased out to others for rents. This suggests that *sa-mye* might have been the easiest to transfer among the granted lands. However, the official land system did not, of course, envisage that the land would be given to a third party as collateral for a loan.

Maung Nay said that the reason to borrow a large amount of money was to send soldiers for the Siam expedition, which indicates that Maung Nay was ordered to lead the cavalry to the repeated counterattacks against Siam after the heavy defeat of King Bodawhpaya's campaign against Siam in 1785. The defeat and frequent battles against Siam not only sapped the troops but also reduced agricultural production and devastated many agricultural villages. The population also began to decline, especially in the north and northwestern regions of the kingdom, where Byangya village was located. In the period from 1783 to 1802, the number of households in the north and northwest regions declined by 38%,[37] of which *ahmudan* households declined by 39%.[38] It seems that this was a time of extreme hardship for the people. The reason why the cavalry commander borrowed a large sum of money to pay for rice was probably because the cavalry men under him were unable to prepare their own foods. It was customary for the unit commanders to provide rations, horses, and weapons for soldiers who were unable to prepare these necessities by themselves. In this *thet-kayit*, the usufruct of the collateral paddy field was not transferred, but was left to the debtor Maung Nay, who was to lead his troops on the expedition. It can be presumed that the paddy field was cultivated by his family members, or lent out to any other cultivators, on the condition that half of the harvest should be sent to the creditors as interest.

Another *thet-kayit* said:

On the 5th *lazo Kason*, 1171 (June 3, 1809), Nga San Hla, a resident of Magyi-Zauk village and the *myo-sayei*[39] said, 'There is no paddy to consume in the house, and the funeral expenses are also to be paid. Five

154 Chapter 5

baskets of paddy have already been consumed, for which I have to pay 25 *kyat*s of silver. All these loans, totaling 47 *kyat*s 6 *mu*s, are to be paid to Maung Thu, the donor of a monastery and his wife. I cannot afford to settle these debts now. I have a paddy field sown with 3 baskets of seed, known as Pauk-yin, located in the Kanni land; I acquired it through mortgage from the head man of Kanni horse village. Please take this land and work on it until I have liquidated all debts.' Then, Maung Myat Thu and his wife lent Nga San Hla, the *myo-sayei*, 25 *kyat*s for paddy, and 22 *kyat*s 6 *mu*s in 20 *kyat-ke* silver, totaling 47 *kyat*s 6 *mu*s. The witness was Maung Kaung; the drafter, Maung San Hla; the writer, Nga Hmu.[40]

In these *thet-kayit*s we see that *ahmudan*s and a cavalry captain (the headman of a cavalry village) pledged their lands. The paddy field Nga San Hla offered as collateral was the one he once took as collateral when he lent money to the cavalry captain of the Kanni village. It is not clear from this contract when this happened, but, like Maung Nay, the Kanni village cavalry captain also faced economic difficulties and had to borrow money from Nga San Hla. But Nga San Hla, the creditor who had lent money to the cavalry captain and held an official post as the *myo-sayei*, also became impoverished in 1809 and had to write a money-borrowing *thet-kayit* offering as collateral the paddy fields which he had taken as collateral from the cavalry captain.

Maung Nay stated clearly that the land used as collateral for borrowing money was granted land. But as for the paddy fields which the cavalry captain offered as collateral to Nga San Hla, there was no mention about the identification of the land. It is highly possible these paddy fields were granted land, as the village itself was granted to the cavalry unit by the king.

There is some evidence in which local chiefs, especially village headmen, pledged their lands. According to one striking *thet-kayit* in Taun-dwin-gyi district, a village headman pledged not only his lands but also the royal order of his appointment as a village headman:

On the 10th *lazan*, month of *Tazaungmon*, 1154 (November 5, 1791), the headman of Inn village, Nga Bin said, 'I am deeply indebted to settle the village obligations and desperately in need of money. I will pledge my lands and the royal appointment letter at 60 *kyat*s in 10 *kyat-ke* silver. Please take the charge of my village. If I, my son, or my grandson can redeem them in future, we shall pay not only the sum noted in this *thet-kayit*, but also the money you will spend to settle the village obligations.' When this was said, Mintha Maung Hmon of Neimyo district lent Nga Bin of Inn village 450 *kyat*s for paddy, 6 (*viss*) in 2 *mat-ke* silver, and 610 *kyat*s in 3 *mu-ke* totaling 1,660 *kyat*s and held the village under mortgage. Witnesses were the chief of Myin-hkaing village, Maung Ok, and Maung Shwe Aung. The assayer was Maung Nyo and the weigher Maung Tha Ya. Maung Nyein, the headman of Thegon village, drafted and Maung Min wrote the *thet-kayit*. The commission fee for the broker (*pwe-sa*) 12 *kyat*s 2 *mat*s, was paid by Maung Hmon.[41]

Although the lands allotted to village headmen were official lands exempted from taxation, it was not rare for a village headman to have to pledge land in order to pay taxes on behalf of villagers when they could not bear the burden. However, in this case, the headman Nga Bin had to pledge his whole village to the money lender. If the headmen could not manage to lessen the villagers' hardship in economically disastrous years, many villagers deserted their villages.

Emergence of large landholders

Salin *Thugaung*s

The trend seen in Byangya was not a phenomenon peculiar to that area. Similar situations arose in many districts in Upper Burma, especially in the well-irrigated agricultural centers where the transactions and accumulation of lands, as well as debt-slaves, seem to have been particularly prevalent. There emerged several very powerful families who much exceeded *Ahsaun-daw-mye* of Byangya village in the scale of their land accumulation. The most famous families were Salin *Thugaung*s, who I introduced in the previous chapter as the creditors of debt-slave contracts.

During the eighteenth~nineteenth centuries, the Salin irrigation system had about 25 canals fed by the Salin River and irrigated about 22,000 acres (approximately 8,800 hectares) of paddy fields.[42] All four families called Salin *Thugaung*s engaged in money-lending widely in the area, and

156   Chapter 5

through this operation acquired vast irrigated paddy fields amounting to some 11,500 acres (approximately 4,600 hectares) in the latter half of the Konbaung period.[43] The largest landholder among the families at that time was Me Kyi Nyo, who held 618 hectares of paddy fields, and altogether 4,680 hectares of paddy fields were held by 21 *thugaungs*.[44] These paddy fields were cultivated by peasants who had become the debt-slaves of *thugaungs* or by share-cropping tenants.

The power and wealth of the *thugaungs* were well illustrated on an occasion when they made an appeal to King Bodawhpaya, offering 3,600 baskets of paddy as an annual payment if the king would exempt them from the irrigation tax, labor contribution, and personal service to officials sent from the capital. Their appeal was granted, and 3,600 baskets of paddy were annually collected and forwarded to the capital.[45] This appeal was made not only for their own benefit, but also in order to protect peasants of the area from various forms of corvee labor.

However, under the reign of King Mindon, the *thugaungs* had to pay 5,000 *kyat*s every year in cash instead of paddy, which was much more expensive than payment in paddy, so the *myo-thugyi* of the time, one of the *thugaungs*, had to pawn his gold and diamonds in Mandalay to raise this amount of money.[46]

The *thugaungs* also built magnificent pagodas and monasteries in and around Salin and reinvested considerable portions of their fortune in merit-making.

Other powerful families

According to Toe Hla, there were several other families who accumulated vast amounts of land and debt-slaves. Some examples were the *Sayei-daw-gyi* (Great Clerk) in Wunbye village, the Poppa *Wun-dauk* (Deputy Minister) family, and the Le-zin family in Monywa.

The case of the *Sayei-daw-gyi* family in Wunbye was a typical example of how to acquire wealth, high status in the central administration, and social respect in the local community. In Wunbye village in Min-mu district, there was a wealthy *athi* couple who made a fortune by money-lending and land accumulation in the 1830s. They were well known in the locality as donors of a golden umbrella, a script chest, and a pagoda. Their daughter married U Yauk, who came to the village as a bailiff. U Yauk gradually rose to higher positions under the patronage of kings and queens, and finally was appointed as a great clerk (*Sayei-daw-gyi*) and a royal financial steward (*ban-da-zo*). While serving as a court official, he succeeded the money-lending business of his parents-in-law. His sons and grandsons began their careers as royal pages and rose to higher positions while also engaging in money-lending. The family owned several hundred acres of lands, orchards, toddy palm groves, and debt-slaves.[47]

U Hmon, later called Poppa *Wun-dauk* (Deputy Minister), was the son of a junior officer and money-lender. During the 1830s he was enrolled in the royal service as a junior naval officer. In 1840, he was appointed as a herald (*than-daw-shin*) and, in 1842, he became a deputy minister (*wun-dauk*) and a *myo-sa* of Poppa Myo, adjoining Pagan, the old capital of the Pagan dynasty. He engaged in not only money-lending and land transactions, but also in trade in crops and clothing, and making advance payments for crops to some village headmen and peasants. Being a man of undoubted ability, as Henry Yule described him,[48] he shipped imported clothes that could not sell at a high price in the royal city to the Shan state for sale. It is said that this deputy minister was harsher than other creditors in collecting loans from the peasants who were unable to repay their debts, by filing lawsuits and imprisoning them. He accumulated vast lands in Madaya, Yin-daw, Nyaunyan, and Meiktila, and lent these lands to tenants.

Under the reign of King Bodawhpaya, naval officers were permitted to monopolize the trade of certain goods along the Ayeyarwady River, the most important route for trade, so it would appear that the commercial activities of U Hmon owed much to his career, which started from the position of junior naval officer.

Le-zin village was a large village in Monywa, which was designated as one of the ten cavalry villages in 1318 and remained a horse soldier's village right up to the First Anglo-Burmese War in 1824–26. In the later Konbaung period, it was reorganized into a village of palace guards. It is reported that most of the land of the village belonged to the headman's family and two other families closely connected by blood and marriage ties to his family. In the 50 years from 1800 to 1850, more than 100 people in and around the village mortgaged or sold their lands to these families. It is estimated that the families owned more than 1,000 acres of paddy fields and dry fields and many debt-slaves.[49]

158   Chapter 5

The fact that the village of Le-zin was allocated to a single cavalry unit suggests that most of the arable lands in the village were originally official lands granted to the cavalry *ahmudan*s. However, if the Le-zin headmen family and relatives could accumulate most of the lands in the village, this fact suggests that most of the cavalry and royal guard *ahmudan*s gave up their agricultural lands in order to borrow money or paddy to eat.

These examples show us that during the middle and later Konbaung period, there emerged several very powerful families in various districts in Upper Burma who could dominate the economic foundation of the area. The common factor in the making of their fortunes was money-lending, dated from the early Konbaung period. Some displayed their entrepreneurial abilities by investing their money in other commercial activities, but others chose to reinvest large parts of their properties in merit-making for the after-life. Their origins were different from each other, some being of a local hereditary chief lineage, while some were the sons of petty money-lenders or junior officials. But when they climbed their career ladders in the world, they enjoyed not only wealth but also high status and social prestige.

Generally speaking, wealth enabled a person to readily attain high status in the central administration by way of gifts or even bribes, and in turn the status provided them more opportunity to obtain wealth. At the same time, the fact that they contributed much to religion and social welfare, as donors of pagodas, monasteries, tanks, reservoirs, wells, bridges, and rest houses, won them widespread popular respect. The trinity of wealth, status, and prestige made them true patrons of the rural people, even though they siphoned off the meagre assets of the rural majority and amassed their own fortunes. Although the number of such big families was limited, there were countless money-lenders, and it is said that there was always one in every village.

Implications of changes

It is difficult to determine exactly how far the monetary economy had penetrated to the level of rural villagers, which constituted the majority of the population during the eighteenth and nineteenth centuries. Most of the *thet-kayit*s of Byangya contained only 'because we need money' as a reason for borrowing money, but did not say why it was necessary. A few of the reasons that were given were to buy rice, to pay taxes, to repay debts, to pay for lawsuits, and so on. Therefore, the most common reasons were food shortage, tax burden, and war expenses. Every time there was a war, the household which could not send one man as a soldier (not only from *ahmudan*, but also from the free commoners) was levied 3 to 12.5 *kyat* per person; some people could not pay this amount and had to borrow money by pledging their paddy fields or themselves as collateral. As for the tax, peasants were, as a rule, obliged to pay one-tenth of their production plus various fees as the main tax; for these purposes, payment in silver was also admitted. Fishermen, those who engaged in slash-and-burn agriculture, ethnic Karens, and miners paid silver rather than in kind. Tolls, transaction taxes, and judicial fees were also paid in metal coins. Lieberman estimates the extent to which the royal government collected taxes in cash from the provinces to have been 42% by 1600–1752, before the Konbaung dynasty, and 70% by 1752–1802.[50]

*Thet-kayit*s listed the prices of a wide variety of goods, starting with lands, rice paddy, onions, sorghum, betel nut, pepper, tobacco, palm sugar, sesame seeds, beans, cooking oil, salt, tea, silk, loincloths (*longyi*), blankets, cattle, buffaloes, horses, and oxen. These goods were sold in the permanent markets in the cities and at local fairs held every five or 15 days. Chinese traders frequented Upper Burma, and peddlers from the Shan Plateau traveled all over the country to sell wares such as paper and pickled tea leaves. Local festivals and pagoda festivals were also lively trading places. The existence of villages of artisans specializing in certain occupations, the origins of which are thought to have been partly due to the *ahmudan* system, was another factor in the development of trade. Necessities such as water jars, ox carts, farming tools made of iron, salt, pickled tea, crude oil, and fish sauce were obtained through trade.

As money became an integral part of rural life, people of all classes who were forced into debt for various reasons borrowed money from wealthy and influential people, regardless of their class, using their land as collateral. As this process progressed, the distinctions of lands became obscure. In other words, we can say that the movement to privatize all kinds of land began to progress gradually but intensively.

Such a trend must have been in conflict with the fundamentals of the royal monopolistic system of resource mobilization established during the second Taungoo period and inherited by the Konbaung royal government.

The *ahmudan* system was a system to procure human resources not only for military purposes but also to procure production of various important goods, skills, and labor for the maintenance of the royal governance and, in exchange, the kings granted good lands with irrigation facilities. The trend of privatization of all kinds of land diminished the meaning of the grant of land clothed in the garments of the king's favor. The children of the *ahmudan* were entitled to inherit the land by succeeding to their parents' duties, but after several generations of inheritance, the sense that the land was granted by the king must have diminished. In addition, the beginning of the alienation of land due to the spread of the monetary economy seems to have diluted the original meaning of land as a reward for the services rendered by the *ahmudan* class. This was a situation that could have affected the loyalty of the *ahmudan* class to the king. In this sense, the measures taken by King Mindon's government in 1861, when it abolished the grant of land to *ahmudan* and introduced the salary system, did not represent a new institutional reform but, rather, an attempt to adapt the system to the conditions already prevailing in wide regions in the kingdom.

Land-related *thet-kayit*s of Byangya village from 1776 to 1843 clearly show that the alienation of farmland through debt in this area was intense from the early years of the Konbaung period. Those who took farmland as collateral for loans were diverse in the early years, but as the time passed, it was concentrated in the hands of one powerful man, *ahsaun-daw-mye*. This is an example of the process of formation of a powerful family with status and wealth, which was found in several other regions, where vast tracts of farmland were accumulated.

The types of farmland pledged included not only the ancestral private lands known as *bo-ba-baing*, but also the granted lands to the *ahmudan*s and the monastery lands; that is to say, all the lands were treated as private properties.

Were these situations occurring simultaneously in other parts of the kingdom? What was the position of the village of Byangya within the whole kingdom? We will find out in the next chapter.

Chapter 6

Land-mortgage Contracts in the Central Plains

The *thet-kayit*s of Byangya village revealed that the irrigated paddy fields were used as collateral for debts, regardless of their origins, whether they were private lands or monastery lands or royal lands granted by the king. Since the agricultural land system to divide land into these three categories was maintained up to 1861, theoretically, the cultivators of granted lands and monastery lands did not have the right to pledge or sell lands which they cultivated. However, among 59 *thet-kayit*s of Byangya village related to paddy field transactions, I found eight *thet-kayit*s of pledged monastery lands and two *thet-kayit*s of pledged lands which had been granted to the cavalry *ahmudan*s. The privatization of monastery lands seems to have been widespread, and that of granted lands was also advancing, but at a slower pace.

I also found that in Byangya and its vicinity, various forms of land transaction had developed from the original simple land-mortgage *thet-kayit*s, such as contracts of changing creditors, where the mortgaged land was transferred to a new creditor, or contracts of final selling of the mortgaged lands, or the selling of a land-mortgage *thet-kayit* itself. As a result, many paddy fields were transferred from one hand to another, and former small or middle-scale money-lenders gave away their secured lands in order to borrow money from one powerful money-lender. The deteriorated economic situation since 1785, brought about by the defeats in foreign wars, and the drought and famine in the early nineteenth century, accelerated the process of economic deprivation of the middle class of the village societies, and many people had to pledge their paddy fields, with the result that one powerful family accumulated lots of lands through money-lending operations.

162   Chapter 6

As this is an observation based on the land-mortgage *thet-kayit*s found in one village, it may not be enough to assert that a similar phenomenon was going on in other parts of the kingdom. Therefore, we should broaden our observation to the whole central lowland plains and examine whether similar trends of land alienation were going on simultaneously or not.

Another issue to be discussed is the difference between land sales and land mortgages in the Konbaung period. According to V. Lieberman, land sales, once practiced only by the upper echelons of society residing in the royal capital, became overwhelmingly regional during the Konbaung period and were practiced by the various social classes.[1] I agree with his point of view, but would like to add a few points in this chapter, by making it clear that land mortgages were widespread, but farmland sales were rather concentrated in specific areas. It seems that during the Konbaung period, the strong brakes were still working in many areas to avoid the sale of farmland. The brakes were not in the form of official prohibition, but rooted in the customary norms and consciousness of people regarding the relationship between people and the lands they reclaimed and cultivated.

Lastly, I discuss how to interpret the 'mortgage tenancy' in J. S. Furnivall's classical text, the special form of tenancy observed in the central plains during the 1930s.[2] As there had been the same form of mortgage tenancy in nineteenth-century Burma, it is often misunderstood that both mortgage tenancies were the same in character and purpose. The cautious observation will make it clear that the backgrounds and contents of these two mortgage tenancy were quite different.

Increasing land-mortgage *thet-kayit*s during the eighteenth–nineteenth centuries

The oldest land-mortgage *thet-kayit* which I could find was one written on February 7, 1752, just before the establishment of the Konbaung dynasty. It says, 'Maung Kun and his wife pledged paddy fields planted with 500 bundles of seedlings to Maung Hmwe and his wife, the donors of Pagoda in the royal capital, for 50 *kyat*s silver and 10 baskets of paddy at a price of *ywet-ni* 7 *kyat*s.'[3]

It was only ten days before Alaunghpaya's accession to the throne as the first king of the Konbaung dynasty. As the construction of the new royal capital began in July in Shwebo,[4] the creditor Maung Hmwe, the donor of a pagoda, was probably living in Ava, the last royal capital of the second Taungoo dynasty.

This is the only land-mortgage *thet-kayit* that was written prior to the Konbaung period, but the main reason for the lack of old *thet-kayit*s is the nondurable nature of *para-baik*s, so that the origin of the land-mortgage *thet-kayit*s is likely to be sought at an earlier date. However, it is presumed that it was not too much earlier that land-mortgage *thet-kayit*s extended to ordinary villagers in a wide range of areas. To confirm this point, Table 6.1, Table 6.2, and Figure 6.1 show the proportion of land-mortgage *thet-kayit*s in all money-lending *thet-kayit*s and the chronological trends among the various types of debts in the Konbaung period. The data are from KUMF and DMSEH, which cover most regions of the central plains, the core area of Konbaung Burma, and contain all types of debt documents. The other databases used in this study are not appropriate to present a comprehensive picture of the debt documents, as *thet-kayit*s in these data were selected at the time of collection for specific research targets.

The proportion of land-mortgage *thet-kayit*s during the Konbaung period is much higher than expected. Table 6.1 shows the breakdown of money-lending *thet-kayit*s contained in the 12 reels of the microfilm in the KUMF database.[5] Table 6.2 also shows a breakdown of the money-lending *thet-kayit*s in the 11 volumes of DMSEH and their regional distribution.

As shown in Table 6.1, the number of land-mortgage *thet-kayit*s is 403 (58.4%), compared to 188 (27.2%) for money-lending with interest, and 99 (14.3%) for debt-slave *thet-kayit*s in KUMF.[6] In DMSEH, the number of money-lending contracts with interest is 995 (33.7%), 185 for debt-slave contracts (6.6%), and 1,639 for land-mortgage contracts (58.1%). The result indicates that land-mortgaging was the most frequent method of borrowing money. The second most common method of debt (i.e., borrowing money with interest) accounted for about 30% of the total money-lending contracts, while debt-slave contracts accounted for only a little more than 10%.

If we compare the money borrowing to the paddy borrowing (which is thought to have been as widely practiced in the eighteenth to nineteenth centuries as money borrowing) found in KUMF, in the same 12 volumes, there are a total of 192 paddy-borrowing (*zaba-hkyi*) *thet-kayit*s, in which the principal and interest were paid in paddy. The number is slightly more than the 188 money-borrowing *thet-kayit*s, but this is far short of the

164   Chapter 6

Table 6.1: Breakdown of money-lending *thet-kayit*s in KUMF (nos.)

Reel No.	Loan with interest	Land-mortgage			Debt-slave		Location
		Paddy field	Others	Related*	Original	Related	
52	27	38	0	15	1	0	Shwebo
53	69	9	0	0	4	0	Shwebo
54	29	1	0	0	0	0	Shwebo
55	3	1	0	0	0	0	Shwebo
60	14	150	11	37	0	0	Ye-U
61	4	19	1	11	0	0	Ye-U
62	0	1	0	0	0	0	Ye-U
63	2	1	0	0	0	0	Ye-U
67	15	7	1	6	7	0	Magwe Sagu
68	0	0	0	0	0	0	
82	13	15	3	1	14	69	National Library
84	12	38	1	36	2	2	National Library
Total	188	280	17	106	28	71	

Land-mortgage & related contract   Debt-slave contract
Grand total 403   Grand total 99

Note: *Original *thet-kayit*s and related *thet-kayit*s are counted separately. Some of the related *thet-kayit*s include additional loan *thet-kayit*s, certificates of redemption, and changing-creditor *thet-kayit*s.

**Other items of farmland include dry fields, *kaing* land (alluvial land), and orchards.
Source: prepared by the author from the 12 reels of the Microfilm of Myanmar History of Kagoshima University (KUMF).

number of debts secured by farmland. Only 12 *thet-kayit*s were found in the method known as *zaba-pe*, where money was borrowed and principal and interest were paid back in paddy.

On the other hand, 92 *thet-kayit*s of *zaba-hkyi* and *zaba-pe* are found in the 11 volumes of DMSEH, but the number is extremely small when compared to the number of unsecured money borrowing (995) or the land-mortgage loans (1,639). During the colonial period, especially after the 1920s, when the downfall of the delta farmers was going on, it was often pointed out by British officials that the main reason for the small farmers' impoverishment was the bad custom of *zaba-pe* which had originated from the custom in the Konbaung period. However, it seems that both *zaba-pe* and *zaba-hkyi* had been very limited practices in the Konbaung period.

Figure 6.1 shows the chronological distribution of the three forms of money-lending *thet-kayit*s: land-mortgage, debt-slave, and unsecured debt with interest. First of all, we noticed that the debt secured by agricultural

Land-mortgage Contracts in the Central Plains 165

Table 6.2: Breakdown of money-lending *thet-kayit*s in DMSEH

Volume	With interest	Land-mortgage	Debt-slave	Location
1	164	237	6	Mandalay, Monywa
2	6	1	11	Mandalay
3	67	111	66	Salin, Meiktila, Mandalay
4	82	149	21	Salin
5	277	291	34	Salin, Prome, Takkonshwe, Mawbin, Meiktila, Wundwin, Malain, Dawe
6	62	249	21	Meiktila, Wundwin, Malain, Hsinbyushin
7	46	119	0	Meiktila, Malain
8	5	40	0	Wundwin, Takkon, Malain, Tazi, Kyaukpadan
9	164	191	16	Sale, Malain, Tazi, Madaya, Yaw, Kyaukpadan, Salin, Sagu, Inle, Kanni, Mandalay, Tada-U, Minbu, Meiktila
10	14	55	2	Mandalay, Pyobwe
11	108	196	8	Wundwin, Amarapura, Pyobwe, Mandalay
Total	995	1639	185*	

Source: DMSEH, Vols. 1–11.
Note: *there are nine duplicate *thet-kayit*s, so the actual number is 176. In this table, only original land-mortgage *thet-kayit*s are counted, and redemption certificates, additional loan *thet-kayit*s, and changing creditor *thet-kayit*s, etc. are not included.

land had increased rapidly after 1785, at the beginning of the period of crisis in the Konbaung era, when the kingdom suffered a major defeat to the war against Siam. For the next 90 years, until 1875, with the sole exception of the early 1840s, debts secured by agricultural land accounted for the largest portion of all debts. However, under the reign of Thibaw, the last king of the Konbaung dynasty (1878–85), debt with interest increased rapidly and began to surpass the debt secured by agricultural land. The massive exodus of people to British Burma (i.e., Lower Burma) and repeated armed rebellions in the Shan region against the weakened royal government of Burma showed that this period of political and economic turmoil was also marked by a change in the form of debt. There are several possible reasons for this change, such as that stable agriculture had been eroded, or that the amount of farmland already pledged as collateral became so large that new farmland available for collateral should have decreased.

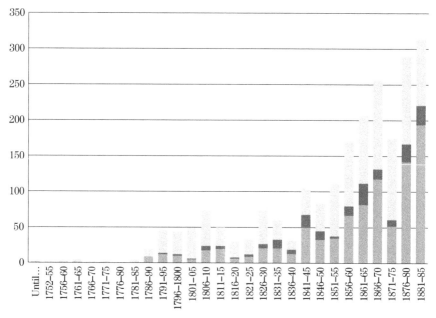

Figure 6.1. Distribution of three forms of debt (1752–1885) (nos.)
Note: from top to bottom: land-mortgage contracts, debt-slave contracts, and debt with interest. Source: author's compilation of 2,242 items from the DMSEH and KUMF debt contracts data, excluding duplicates and documents illegible in date portions. The date portion appears at the beginning of the documents, and was easily corrupted or disappeared. This is the main reason why there are differences between the total numbers in Tables 6.1 and 6.2 and the numbers used in this graph.

There might have been exceptions, but, in general, the successive royal governments in the Konbaung period seem to have been noninterfering in the movement of agricultural land. However, one study noted that King Thibaw issued an imperial decree in 1883 that prohibited the pledging and selling of all lands regardless of the location and the owner's status.[7] However, this decree is not included in the largest collection of Royal Orders of Burma (ROB) which covers the period from 1598 to 1885. It is not possible to confirm its existence for the moment because the source of the edict of King Thibaw was not given in that book.

From the middle of the Konbaung era onwards, land was most commonly used as collateral for debt, and the most important collateral was none other than the paddy field. Table 6.1 shows that agricultural lands used as collateral were overwhelmingly dominated by paddy fields, with 280 money-lending contracts in the KUMF data secured by paddy fields and 17 secured by other lands. The DMSEH data in Table 6.3 also show that paddy field mortgages accounted for 1,387 (84.6%) of the total 1,639 land-mortgage deeds. If we add the 52 cases where paddy fields and dry fields were mortgaged as collateral together, paddy field mortgages account for 87.8% of the debts secured by agricultural lands, which indicates that paddy fields were preferred as the safest and most advantageous collateral by the creditors. Whether the collateralized paddy fields were irrigated or rain-fed fields was not always specified in the individual *thet-kayit*s, but since the majority of the *thet-kayit*s were found and collected from the semi-arid areas of the kingdom (i.e., areas where rain-fed paddy cultivation was very difficult without irrigation facilities), we can safely assume that the majority of the paddy fields mortgaged in the *thet-kayit*s were irrigated either by canals or reservoirs.

Although the number of dry fields as collateral was less than that of paddy fields, Table 6.2 and Table 6.3 show that there were 182 cases where only dry fields were mortgaged and 52 cases where dry fields were mortgaged with paddy fields, resulting in a total of 234 cases, which exceeded the number of humans as collateral. Therefore, although there was a large difference in terms of value between paddy fields and dry fields, dry fields were the second most important collateral after paddy fields. Cotton, sesamum, and peanuts, cultivated in the semi-arid plains or on the slopes, were important as both subsistence crops and cash crops, and the fields where these crops could be cultivated were also treated as good collateral.

On the other hand, it is also noteworthy that there was very little collateral for alluvial land (*kaing*), the sandbars created in or near the banks of rivers, which was suitable for cultivating new crops coming from the New Continent, such as tomatoes, eggplants, and tobacco. There was also very little collateral for sugar palm or mango orchards. Although both *kaing* land and orchard could produce highly profitable vegetables and fruits, nonetheless these lands were rarely pledged as collateral. There was only one case in Salin *Thugaung thet-kayit*s in DMSEH where an orchard was pledged as collateral. It was noted that a man called Maung Shwe Maung and his brother Maung Pyu pledged all the sugar palm trees and mango trees planted in their orchard, in 1835.[8] Generally speaking, these fruit trees could be used as collateral, and people often pledged only trees, not orchards. For example, in one *thet-kayit* written in 1865, a man named

Table 6.3: Types of agricultural land pledged (DMSEH) (nos.)

Volume	Paddy	Dry field	Paddy +Dry field	Orchard	Unknown	Total
1	232	5	0	0	0	237
2	1	0	0	0	0	1
3	101	9	0	0	1	111
4	147	0	0	0	2	149
5	249	29	7	0	6	291
6	182	39	21	0	7	249
7	70	31	17	0	1	119
8	19	18	2	0	1	40
9	188	3	0	0	0	191
10	29	22	4	0	0	55
11	169	26	1	0	0	196
Total	1387	182	52	0	18	1639
	84.6%	11.1%	3.2%	0%	1.1%	100%

Source: DMSEH, Vols. 1–11.

Maung San Min pledged his mango tree in order to borrow 20 *kyat*s in silver coins from a man in a neighboring village on the condition of 'three years, three harvests'; in other words, the borrower could not repay his debt for three years and the creditor could harvest mango fruits for at least three years.[9] The fact that the fruit trees could be used as collateral seems to be the main reason why orchards were rarely mortgaged.

As for the *kaing* land, I found three *thet-kayit*s of *kaing* land mortgaging in KUMF. The reason for this very small number is that *kaing* lands comprised alluvial deposits that were submerged in the rainy season and reappeared in the dry season, so *kaing* land not only changed in shape and area each year, but, in some cases, was washed away and lost. One *thet-kayit* written in Ye-U district in 1849 states, 'Ko Tar San pledged the *kaing* land located in the northwest point of the village to Mr. and Mrs. U Tha Thwe, the donors of pagoda.'[10] Another *thet-kayit* from Ye-U district, dated 1861, states, 'Maung Ma pledged the *kaing* land, called Kyibin, to Maung Shwe Hkon and his wife for 20 *kyat* in silver under the condition of "three years and three harvests".'[11] The *kaing* lands pledged in these contracts should have been fairly stable and should have appeared every year during the dry season. *Kaing* lands were fertile due to the sediment carried annually by the water from upstream, and were suitable for growing tobacco, tomatoes, eggplants, and other new cash crops of the time. Some villages made rules for the use of *kaing* lands, but, as seen in the above example, there were cases where the exclusive private utilization of *kaing* land was established.

In the central plains, the economic importance of paddy fields for the production of the staple food, and also the limited supply of land suitable for wet rice cultivation, made paddy fields the most important agricultural land and the best collateral preferred in money-lending contracts.

Regional distribution of land-mortgage *thet-kayit*s

If we look at the regional distribution of land-mortgage *thet-kayit*s in terms of the original location in which each *thet-kayit* was made, we find that the documents kept in monasteries have close ties to the local community, whereas the collections of the local historians, universities, and individuals tend to be somewhat less connected to the community and include documents from other areas. The historical materials collected in national libraries, museums, and so on are the product of national collecting activities and purchases of collections, and cover documents from various regions.

Of the 12 volumes of KUMF microfilms, volumes 52, 53, 54, and 55 contain manuscripts collected primarily from monasteries in the Shwebo region; volumes 60, 61, and 62 contain manuscripts collected from monasteries or collected by local historians in the Ye-U region adjacent to Shwebo; volumes 67 and 68 contain manuscripts collected in Sagu and Magwe in central Burma. Volumes 82 and 84 contain manuscripts from the National Library and the Ministry of Culture in Yangon, including some manuscripts that can be identified as having been written in Shwebo or Mandalay, and some documents in which we cannot identify the place where they were made. In general, the *thet-kayit*s in KUMF were mostly from Shwebo and the Ayeyarwady riverside regions of the central plains, such as Magwe and Sagu, and Mandalay, and the rest were from various regions that were collected and preserved by the state institutions.

Thus, the distribution of loan documents in KUMF is regionally skewed in the vicinity of Shwebo and Ye-U, plus Mandalay and the Ayeyarwady riverside regions of central Burma. Byangya village, discussed in the previous chapter, is also located in the Dibeyin region near Ye-U.

DMSEH documents, as seen in Table 6.2, cover much wider areas, going beyond the core area of the kingdom, including Inle in the Shan

Plateau and Yaw on the west bank of the Ayeyarwady. In addition, there is material from Pyi, which lies on the border dividing Upper and Lower Burma, Dawei on the coast of the Gulf of Martaban, and Mawbin in the heart of the Lower Burma Delta. However, the Pyi manuscripts deposited in the Pyu Museum Library do not necessarily represent documents of the Pyi region, but contain a large number of *thet-kayit*s from the central region along the Ayeyarwady River, mainly in the Salin region. Several manuscripts deposited in Dawei Museum, located in the area facing the Gulf of Martaban, are related to unsecured debts with interest, and not to land mortgages.[12] The manuscripts from Mawbin, located in the delta region of Lower Burma, also relate to unsecured debts with interest written during the 1890s after the annexation of Lower Burma by Britain.[13]

From these facts, we can see that the land-mortgage *thet-kayit*s were written in a wide area of the central plains that extended from the royal capital to the plateau at the foot of the mountainous region. As for Lower Burma, with a relatively small population and covered with jungle in the downstream, it is presumed that few land-mortgage *thet-kayit*s were written during the dynastic period. Until the British occupied the whole Lower Burma and encouraged rain-fed paddy cultivation for export, the population density had been very low. Some Karen people engaged in slash-and-burn shifting cultivation in the tropical rainforests, but there was no momentum that land would become a scarce commodity. One of the characteristics of premodern Southeast Asian societies, 'abundant land and small population', was a situation that was applicable to Lower Burma until the middle of the nineteenth century.

Factors determining land mortgages and land sales

During the Konbaung period, land-mortgage *thet-kayit*s seem to have occupied the largest portion of all the money-lending *thet-kayit*s. In addition, the land-mortgage *thet-kayit*s have been collected from various areas which covered most districts in the vast central plains of Upper Burma. Then, how about the frequency of agricultural land sales and their regional distribution?

V. Lieberman, who has led the study of premodern Burmese history by his work on the Taungoo period, described in his magnum opus, which covers the Eurasian continent, land sales in the Konbaung period as follows:

whereas early inscriptions involved capital elites with easy access to bullion, Kon-baung commercial actors were socially diverse and overwhelmingly rural. Land sale documents show finally that by comparison with the 15th century, when land transfers were encumbered by *athi* communal rights vested in local headmen, by the Kon-baung period such restrictions had lessened dramatically. Nor apparently did royal claims prevent de facto alienation of *ahmu-dan* land. In other words, a limited system of private, marketable land, with individual rights to ownership and alienation enforceable by contract (*thet-kayit*), had emerged.[14]

I agree with his observation, but would like to point to something Lieberman did not mention here: there is no doubt that during the Konbaung period, private land transfers were tacitly tolerated by both the king's government and local rulers without any restrictions. It is important to note, however, that another force put strong restraints on the sale and purchase of agricultural land. It was the notion, contained in the customary law books[15] and widely shared by the people, that agricultural land belonged to the reclaimers and their heirs forever, and although this notion worked little as a deterrent against the use of land as security for debt, it provided a powerful check on the sale and purchase of land. Let's examine the number of land-selling contracts, their regional distribution, and special wording used in the farmland-selling *thet-kayit*s. One reason for the outbreak of conflicts over farmland, as discussed in the next chapter, is the contradiction between the economic factors that drove land transfer and the customs and ideas that discouraged land alienation.

First, let us look at the frequency of agricultural land sales and the areas in which they occurred: in the 13 reels of the KUMF, we count 61 examples of agricultural land being sold, mostly in paddy fields. The number of farmland-mortgage *thet-kayit*s, excluding the related certificates such as additional contracts, is 297, so the number of farmland sales represents 17% of the total number of farmland transactions, including sales and mortgages. Although it is not enough to say that farmland was frequently bought and sold, it is clear that there was more than a negligible amount of farmland transfer through sales. However, the regional distribution of these agricultural land sales shows that 35 of them were in Shwebo and Ye-U regions and 12 in Mandalay, thus the total for these three regions accounted for 77% of the number of land sales, while the remaining 14

172   Chapter 6

Table 6.4: Regional distribution of farmland-selling *thet-kayit*s in DMSEH (nos.)

Region	Paddy field	Paddy + dry field	Dry field	Kaing land	Orchard	Total
Mandalay	15			1		16
Monywa	2	1	2			5
Salin	64	5			2	71
Malain	3		1			4
Mawbin	1					1
Meiktila	4	2				6
Legaing*	0		2			2
Wundwin	1					1
Kyaukpadan	60					60
Minbu	3					3
Thazi	1					1
Laungshe	1					1
Sagu	1					1
Kanni	1					1
Pyi**	3					3
Unknown	2					2
Total	162	8	5	1	2	178

Source: compiled by the author from DMSEH, Volumes 1–11.

Notes: *the document of Legaing is included in the table because it is described as a farmland sale document, but its content shows that it was a sale of the right to use a field with a housing estate for a limited period of time, so it can hardly be called a sale of property rights.

**Thet-kayit*s of Pyi region come from the museum and, exactly speaking, were written in other regions, mainly in Salin.

were scattered in other regions. This indicates that farmland sales were concentrated in specific regions.

On the other hand, within DMSEH, 178 farmland-selling *thet-kayit*s were found, as shown in Table 6.4. Compared with the 1,639 land-mortgage *thet-kayit*s, the number of land-selling *thet-kayit*s is very small, accounting for only 9.8% of the total number of farmland transactions. Furthermore, two regions, namely Salin and Kyaukpadan, were dominant in the number of farmland-selling contracts (71 for Salin and 60 for Kyaukpadan), and the total for these two regions comprised 73.6% of the total number of farmland sales. Mandalay came next, with 16 contracts, accounting for 9.0% of the total number of farmland sales contracts. This, together with the data from KUMF, shows that the areas where agricultural land was traded to some extent were the Shwebo and Ye-U regions, Salin, Kyaukpadan, and urban Mandalay.

Going a little deeper into the content of these farmland-sale documents, most of the farmland sales in Mandalay were examples of farmland purchased by the royalty and high officials who were active in acquiring farmland after the reign of King Mindon. Sales of land in Kyaukpadan were found to be contracts where the people of Kyaukpadan were selling their paddy fields to Salin *Thugaung*s after borrowing a large amount of money from them. Salin *Thugaung*s were also very active in financing and accumulating agricultural land in Kyaukpadan, located on the opposite side of the Ayeyarwady. The Shwebo and Ye-U areas had an ancient history of agricultural land transaction, as it was known that irrigated paddy fields were often purchased by the royal family and donated to pagodas and monasteries since the Pagan period. This might have reduced people's psychological resistance to farmland transactions as compared to other regions. As mentioned above, agricultural land sales were different from pledges in that they were concentrated in a specific area and were not as frequent as pledges.

When did the sales of agricultural land become a somewhat more visible phenomenon? Table 6.5, which summarizes the farmland-selling *thet-kayit*s of the two databases, shows that the number of farmland-selling contracts had started increasing rapidly from the mid-Konbaung period onward. Despite the fact that the newer documents were more likely to be preserved due to the fragile nature of the writing material, the greatest number of farmland-selling contracts were written in the middle period of the Konbaung, namely in the reigns of Bodawhpaya and Bagyidaw, as seen in the Table 6.5. Both land-selling contracts and mortgage contracts had increased from the middle of the Konbaung era, but it is noteworthy that, in the case of farmland selling, the number of contracts per year decreased after the middle ages. On the other hand, the number of land-mortgage contracts increased rapidly during the reigns of King Mindon and King Thibaw, the last two kings of the Konbaung period. The frequency and geographical and chronological distributions of farmland mortgaging and farmland selling differ greatly, and it cannot be said that both mortgaging and selling farmland proceeded simultaneously.

It should also be noted that terms used in land-selling contracts were very special and never used in any other land-related contracts; for example, to sell 'for good and all', 'for good with complete ownership', ' to hand down to your posterity', 'like building a pagoda or a temple', and 'by cutting off

174   Chapter 6

Table 6.5: Distribution of farmland-selling *thet-kayit*s by period (nos.)

Before Konbaung era		KUMF	DMSEH	Total	Nos./year
		1	0	1	
Alaunghpaya	1752–60	0	0	0	0
Naungdawgyi	1760–63	2	0	2	0.7
Hsinbyushin	1763–76	2	1	3	1
Singu	1776–82	0	3	3	0.5
Bodawhpaya	1782–1819	3	83	86	2.3
Bagyidaw	1819–37	18	31	49	2.7
Tharawadi	1837–46	8	2	10	1.1
Pagan	1846–53	1	2	3	0.4
Mindon	1853–78	15	25	40	1.6
Thibaw	1878–85	2	9	11	1.6
British era	1886–	3	12	15	
Date unknown		6	11	17	
Total		61	179	240	

Source: extracted from KUMF, DMSEH.

the lineage' (*yo-pyat*). These phrases were used before the verbs 'sell' or 'buy', which denoted that the selling of agricultural land was something very special and different from the ordinary sales of commodities. By using these phrases, the seller of the land had to promise that the land would not be inherited by the descendants of the original owner. The reason for the special wording in the land-selling *thet-kayit*s was the shared concept among people that the relationship between the land and its reclaimer and his descendants would not be lost even after the sale of the land. The lien repurchase right of the original owners and their descendants was also clearly stated in the Manugye Dhammathat and the more ancient Wagaru Dhammathat.[16] Dhammathat is not a law in the strict sense of the word, and sometimes the norm described in it does not fit the reality of the changing society. However, as the cases of lawsuits over pledged land will show us in Chapter 8, the pledged land, no matter how much time had passed, was promised back to the cultivator and his heirs or descendants in priority, or the creditor could not resell the land to a third party without the consent of the former owners, even if the debt was unsettled. Because the right of the original owner was recognized and respected widely, it was necessary to write special phrases in the land-selling *thet-kayit*s to prevent loss for those who would buy the land.

The use of such phrases was not only a practice in the Ye-U and Shwebo regions, where the village of Byangya is located, but also in other regions. For example, in one *thet-kayit* from the Salin region in 1855, it was written as follows.

> Maung Kyu and his sister Shin Min Be, the former head of Naungdaw village, combined the initial debts of the paddy fields pawned by their grandparents, with the additional debts and finally sold the paddy fields like 'building a pagoda and a monastery' to Me Kyi Nyo, daughter of Ma Hkain of *Thugaung*.[17]

As seen in the above example, in the most common land sale scenario, the total amount of debt became the same as, or higher than, the value of the land pledged, and the debtor had to sell the land to the creditor in exchange for the total debt. Nevertheless, the sale of farmland was avoided as much as possible, and if it was impossible to repay the debt, the first step was to find someone who could lend them more money and to change the creditor. In this way, those families rich in financial resources were able to accumulate a large amount of pledged farmland.

There are a few instances where it is presumed that the sale of agricultural lands suddenly took place, rather than after the accumulation of debts through the writing of a number of additional-debt *thet-kayit*s. In the *para-baik*s of the couple of *Min-maha-min-tin-yaza* and their niece, Princess *Pin-thei-kaung-thin*, paddy fields were bought on a large scale from many royal families, and there were several cases where it seemed that they bought paddy fields at once without giving a series of loans. For example, in 1863, they bought 54 paddy fields from the son of Prince Pyinzi (a famous author of Thai-style songs) for *ywet-ni* 398 *kyat*s, 'like building a pagoda and building a monastery',[18] and as no debt or additional-loan contract was found before this land-selling *thet-kayit*, it gives the impression that it was a direct sale of paddy fields. In reality, however, the family had been in debt to many people since Prince Pyinzi's generation, and although his son inherited many paddy fields, most had already been pledged, and the son had to sell paddy fields to the *Min-maha-min-tin-yaza* family in order to repay the debts inherited from his father.

Some *thet-kayit*s of *Min-maha-min-tin-yaza* show that he took paddy fields pledged to a third party as securities for the new loan he gave, and if the borrower could not repay it, he bought the lands. In this way, he and his family accumulated agricultural lands. In these cases, the lands were sold by the former owner after piling up debts on the land, which he could not repay. Most land selling was a result of piled-up debts secured by lands.

Another reason for disposing of a field was due to the custom of an equitable inheritance among all the children, regardless of age and gender. If, as a result of the equal distribution, the land of one's share would become too small to cultivate, one heir might sell his or her small plot to another heir, or heirs might unite to sell their paddy fields to other persons.

In one *thet-kayit* written in Meiktila in 1836, a heir purchased paddy fields from all the other heirs,[19] and in another *thet-kayit* from Salin written in 1810, a number of heirs joined together to sell paddy fields with ownership to *Thugaung-ma* Me Ya and Maung Ko, the donors of the monastery.[20]

As we have seen above, pledging and selling of agricultural land did not proceed simultaneously during the Konbaung era. While pledging lands spread to wide areas and increased in number, overwhelming other forms of borrowing, sales of farmland were concentrated in rather limited areas around the royal capital and regions like Shwebo, Ye-U, Salin, and Kyaukpadan, where influential people with both wealth and status actively engaged in the money-lending business and gathered agricultural lands. Even in those areas, the number of land sales was much lower than that of land mortgaging. It is possible that a similar phenomenon might have occurred in Kyaukse, which was a granary with finer irrigation networks than any other irrigated areas in the kingdom, but, unfortunately, the collection of *thet-kayit*s was difficult in Kyaukse, where many temples were destroyed and burned down during the Second World War. There are reports that in the early years of colonial rule, much of the monastery land in Kyaukse had already been privatized and sold off during the dynastic period, but it is unclear when and how this movement began in Kyaukse.[21]

In other parts of the country, the sale of farmland was the exception rather than the rule, with only a few examples. This was because, even as money permeated all levels of society, there was a widely held view of farmland as something special, something that could not be reduced to a mere commodity and was strongly tied to the reclaimers and their descendants.

Issues in the interpretation of land-mortgage documents

There was no word for agriculture in eighteenth- to nineteenth-century Burma; that is, there was no conception to group together paddy cultivation, vegetable cultivation, and slash-and-burn cultivation into one economic activity as agriculture. Therefore, paddy fields (*le*), dry fields (*ya*), slash-and-burn fields (*taung-ya*), and alluvial lands (*kaing*) were not grouped together as agricultural lands. Sometimes I use the words 'agricultural land' in this study for the sake of convenience, but in those days each category of land was referred to in land-mortgage *thet-kayit*s as 'paddy field mortgage' or 'dry field mortgage' separately.

In the land-related *thet-kayit*s, there were four categories; namely, the original *thet-kayit*, the repayment certificate, the additional-loan *thet-kayit*, and the *thet-kayit* of changing creditors. In addition, although the number is very small, there were selling contracts of the *thet-kayit* itself and land-selling *thet-kayit*s. Selling or purchasing land-mortgage *thet-kayit*s was something entirely different from ordinary goods transactions that were settled at once without the need for making contracts, but when it came to the sale and purchase of land-mortgage *thet-kayit*s, various problems could arise in the future. In fact, there were only four examples of selling contracts of land-mortgage *thet-kayit*s in KUMF;[22] in all four cases, the person who bought land-mortgage *thet-kayit*s between 1842 and 1845 was none other than the *Ahsaun-daw-mye* in Byangya village. This means that the speed of alienation of farmland in Byangya village, seen in the previous chapter, was one of the most advanced phenomena in Konbaung Burma. There were not a few examples of *thet-kayit*s changing the creditors from other parts of the country, but as far as I know, there were no examples of sales of *thet-kayit*s themselves outside Byangya and its vicinity.

There were two types of *thet-kayit*s for changing creditors: one was an offer from the initial creditor to the new creditor, and the other was an offer by the debtor to the new creditors:

178 Chapter 6

(1) On 10th lazan Wagaung, 1222 (July 27, 1860), Maung Pyu said to Thamanta Yan Aung, the chief of Kywetalin village, 'I have a dry field mortgaged by Maung Kyu and his associates, located behind the Talingon village for 15 *kyat*s by 10 *kyat*s *ke* alloy. Please take the field at 15 *kyat*s by 10 *kyat*s *ke*.' Kywetalin village headman agreed and took the mortgaged field. The witnesses were Hmo Gaung Maung Yauk and Ko Tha Dhu. Kywetalin headman was the draft.[23]

(2) On 13 lazo Tagu 1227 (April 23, 1865), Maung A', the chief of the village of Pandwin and his son Maung Aye, told Mr. and Mrs. Ko Mat Kyi, 'U Kyaw Ya and Maung Kye have pledged 13 paddy fields of our family to U Wun Tha and Nga Mon for *ywet-ni* 28 *kyat*s 6 *mu*s. These paddy fields take water from In-ma-bin Weir and are bordered by the Taung nga-zin canal to the south, by the paddy fields of Ko Khaw Ya to the west, by the village hedge to the north, and by the paddy fields of U Pan Gaung to the east. Should any other heirs interfere and prevent us from using these fields, we will reimburse you.' Then, Mr. and Mrs. Ko Mat Kyi lent another 20 *kyat*s, and also paid 28 *kyat*s 6 *mu*s in *ywet-ni* for the old *thet-kayit* and took it as a collateral. The *thet-kayit* was drafted by Maung Kho of Zyi-kyaw-bin village, and scribed by the creditor's son-in-law Maung Kyaw. The witnesses were Maung Nyut. U Mat Kyi paid brokerage fee of 5 *mu*s each to both parties.[24]

These two *thet-kayit*s were both collected from Meiktila. In example (1), a new *thet-kayit* was made as a contract between the old creditor and the new creditor, whereas in the second example, the contract was made between the debtor who had pledged the paddy fields and the new creditor. It is supposed that the situation was such that not only was the debtor unable to borrow an additional loan from the old creditor, but also he was under pressure to repay his debt. They were trying to overcome their immediate financial difficulties by paying off their debts to their old creditors, using 20 *kyat*s they borrowed from the new creditor.

The creditors, if they were in want of money, often demanded the repayment of the loan and, if not repaid, it was natural to seek a new person who would be willing to pay money in exchange for the *thet-kayit*, but if the new *thet-kayit* would be signed without the consent of the original owner of the paddy field, there could be trouble in future. Given the customary norm of the time that the cultivator and his descendants had the right to repurchase the land forever, the overlapping of credit transfers gradually blurred the relationship between people and farmland, and this was a cause of some litigations over farmland. The existence of other heirs mentioned in the second example was also a major cause of farmland litigation.

The sale and purchase of land-mortgage *thet-kayit*s, in which the claim itself was the object of sale and purchase, was based on the premise that there should have been a certain degree of alienation and commercialization of farmland.

Judging from the large number of additional loan *thet-kayit*s, the practice of piling debts on the same collateral was widespread throughout the central plains.[25] This was also the case with debt-slaves, and it often happened that the total amount of debt owed by a debt-slave grew over the years. These additional-loan *thet-kayit*s were mostly done without any new or additional collateral. This was possible because, unlike other goods, both human and land created new value as long as their use was possible.

Additional-loan *thet-kayit*s seem to be very common and easy to understand. However, there is a problem quite difficult to interpret. The following three *thet-kayit*s are one paddy field mortgage *thet-kayit* and two additional-loan *thet-kayit*s written between 1864 and 1887. How can we interpret these *thet-kayit*s?

(1) On 10th lazo Wazo 1225 (March 1, 1864), Maung Shwe Myo, a resident of Ywa-thit village and his brother Maung Kye said to U Lu and his wife of Ainda village, donors of pagoda, 'Please take our paddy fields which we inherited from our ancestors, drawing water from the Yon Pond, i.e., paddy fields sown with three baskets of seed, and another one with three-quarter baskets of seeds in the north of the stone pile, the paddy field sown with three-quarter baskets of seeds, and the paddy fields sown with three-quarter baskets of seeds underneath the stone pile, for a total, paddy fields sown with five baskets and a quarter of seeds.' U Lu and his wife accepted this offer, [missing words] and took the paddy fields as mortgage and pay 40 *kyat*s in silver coin. Witnesses were Ko Me, Ko Myat Ywe, Drafter was the owner of the paddy fields.[26]

180   Chapter 6

Table 6.6: Paddy field mortgage and additional loan on the same field

Year	Remarks	Owner of paddy field	Creditor	Money borrowed
1864	Pledge paddy field	Maung Shwe Myo Maung Kye	U Lu and his wife (donors of pagoda)	40 *kyat*s
1879	Additional loan	Maung Kye	Me Zat (donor of pagoda)	20 *kyat*s
1887	Additional loan	Maung Pya	Ma Ae	20 *kyat*s

(2) On 12th lazan Tabaung 1231 (March 13, 1870) Maung Kye, the owner of the paddy field of the Yon Pond, said, 'I need money. Please lend me 20 *kyat*s on my paddy field which has been already mortgaged.' The donor of the pagoda, Me Zat[27] gave him 20 *kyat*s in silver coins. The witness was Ko Me, the scribe was the owner of the paddy field.[28]

(3) On 9th lazan Tagu 1249 (April 1, 1887), Maung Pya, the son of U Shwe Myo, the owner of the paddy field of the Yon Pond, asked Ma Ae to lend him 20 *kyat*s on the paddy field of the Yon Pond, which his father had mortgaged earlier, because he needed money. Ma Ae accepted his request and lent 20 *kyat*s. The witness was Ko Po.[29]

Table 6.6 is a summary of the above three *thet-kayit*s.

Maung Shwe Myo and Maung Kye were brothers and inherited from their parents the land known as the paddy fields of the Yon Pond. Since equal inheritance to all siblings was the dominant practice, it was very common to have more than one heir to the same farmland. Shwe Myo and Kye pledged the paddy fields in exchange for 40 *kyat*s to Mr. and Mrs. U Lu, the donors of pagoda. Six years later, the younger brother Kye borrowed 20 *kyat*s on the same collateral, and 17 years later, Shwe Myo's son, Pya, borrowed 20 *kyat*s on the same paddy fields. In the meantime, the creditors seem to have been replaced; U Lu and his wife Me Zat were gone and replaced by their daughter Ma Ae. It appears to be just like that. However, the interpretation of these *thet-kayit*s should be open to debate, and it is possible that they could be considered as a simple money-lending or, in fact, a mortgage tenancy, which Furnivall pointed out in his classic work as having been practiced in Upper Burma since the dynastic period. This point should be discussed next.

Money-lending contracts, or tenancy contracts?

In his famous book, Furnivall explained what he called mortgage tenancy, one of the forms of tenancy practiced in the early twentieth century in Upper Burma, as follows.

> *Mortgage Tenancies* are tenancies in which the landowner mortgages his land to the tenant. These are noteworthy for several reasons. Ordinarily one thinks of the mortgagee, the man who lends money, as a wealthy man, and the mortgagor, the man who borrows money, as a poor man. But in a mortgage tenancy the man who lends money is usually the poorer and the wealthy man is usually the man who borrows it, the landlord. Another noteworthy character of this mode of tenancy is that it lends itself to the exploitation of the tenant by rack-renting and is exceptionally difficult to regulate by law. If Mg. Gale agrees to pay U Chantha 200 baskets as his rent for one year, he will probably object to pay 210 baskets in the following year. But if he lends Rs. 100 to U Chantha one year, it seems a comparatively small matter to lend him another Rs. 5 next year. Thus, as land values gradually rise the landlord can easily exact the whole of the increment, while if land values should fall the tenant might not be able to recover the whole of the mortgage money from his landlord. Before the introduction of co-operative credit into Upper Burma money was very scarce and land worth little. The formation of a co-operative credit society in a village brought money into the village, the value of land rose and it became possible for landlords to demand much larger sums of money from people who wished to cultivate land on mortgage. Thus, in some villages where this mode of tenancy prevailed, the sole effect of establishing a co-operative credit society was to hand over large sums of money to the landowners; the cultivators remained as badly off as ever. Still the system of mortgage tenancies has certain advantages, chiefly in discouraging the subdivision of holdings, as it is easier to divide up money raised by the mortgage of an inheritance than to divide up the estate.[30]

What Furnivall discussed here was the situation in Upper Burma during the British period. It is based on the first-hand knowledge gained from his assignment to Burma as a young Indian Civil Officer in the early twentieth century, working as an Assistant Commissioner and settlement officer,

182   Chapter 6

and especially on his experiences in the 1930s when the need for 'peasant protection first' came to the attention of the colonial administration. It should be no surprise that the background and meaning of the mortgage tenancies during the British colonial period and those practiced during the Burmese dynasty before 1885 cannot be the same. However, Furnivall himself believed that the land system and the tenancy he saw in the early twentieth century in Upper Burma had its origins in the dynastic period and had evolved over a long period of time. However, it was sometimes misunderstood that the mortgage tenancies which Furnivall saw in the 1920s and 1930s in Upper Burma were the same as those practiced in nineteenth-century Upper Burma. I think that both mortgage tenancies are similar only in their forms, namely money-lending secured by land, but quite different in terms of their objectives.

In order to understand the mortgage tenancy in the context of nineteenth-century land-mortgage contracts, let's examine a few *thet-kayits*. The following contracts related to paddy fields in Meiktila are good examples.

(1) On 3rd lazan Tabodwe 1231 (February 3, 1870), Bo Nyein, the father said, 'I need money, so lend me money.' When this was said, son-in-law Ko Maung Tha and his wife lent 5 *kyat*s in one *kyat* coin and took the paddy field by the Indian elm tree.[31]

(2) On 14th lazo Tagu 1232 (April 29, 1870), Bo Nyein of Se-gon village said to his son-in-law Ko Maung Tha and his wife, 'I am in need of money so lend me money and take the paddy field by the Ko Ko tree as mortgage.' Then, Ko Maung Tha and his wife lent their father five pieces of one-*kyat* silver coins. The witnesses were Ko [missing letters] and Ko Myat Thin. The creditor paid 5 *mu*s for brokerage.[32]

In the above *thet-kayit*s, the father pledged his two paddy fields to his daughter and her husband one after another in a short period of time and borrowed a total of 10 *kyat*s from them. The amount of money lent by the daughter and her husband was quite small, as in those days 10 *kyat*s could buy only 10~20 baskets of paddy.[33] If the father tried to borrow money from other people, he could borrow much more money, even if he offered one paddy field as collateral. Was it because of the daughter and her husband's character, which was too stingy?

However, considering the circumstances of this case, the most reasonable presumption is that the father asked his daughter and son-in-law to cultivate his paddy fields because he could no longer cultivate them by himself and that he was taking the rent for the land. Therefore, it is more likely that it was not a contract of debt, but a contract of tenancy, or, as Furnivall called it, a mortgage tenancy.

Let's see another case of a cotton field in Meiktila. Six *thet-kayit*s were written between 1867 and 1875:

(1) On April 5, 1864, Maung Yan Hnin of Gwe-gon Village said to Maung Meik, 'I am in want of money. Please lend me money, and take my cotton field called Wa-gyi-tat which was mortgaged to other person.' Maung Meik accepted his offer and lent 9 *kyat*s 8 *mu*s in *ywet-ni* and took the mortgage with the right to use for three years. The witness was Maung Ye, and Maung Meik was the assayer, weigher and scribe.[34]

(2) On April 8, 1867, U Lu of Lekpan-daw village below the Meiktila Lake, said, 'Please lend me money again on the previous *thet-kayit*.' According to his request, Maung Meik lent again 5 *kyat*s in silver coins. Maung Kyaw was the draftsman and Maung Tha Tun was the scribe.[35] On March 12, 1869, U Lu, the cotton field owner said to Maung Meik, 'Please lend me money again on the previous Wa-gyi-tat cotton field *thet-kayit*.' According to U Lu's request, Maung Meik lent 5 *kyat*s and took the mortgage again with the right to use for three years. Maung Pyo was the draft and scribe.[36]

(4) On May 15, 1870, U Lu of Kan-bauk village said, 'I am in need of money. Please lend me money again on previous Wa-gyi-tat cotton field mortgage.' According to his request, Maung Meik of Tcbin-te village lent 24 *kyat*s for a bull and took again the cotton field as mortgage. Maung Ya was the witness. Maung Meik, the bull owner was the scribe.[37]

(5) On April 9, 1875, U Lu said to Ko Kyaw Pe and wife, 'I am in want of money. Please lend me 12 *kyat*s again on the mortgage which was redeemed from Ko Meik by Ko Kyaw Pe and his wife.' According

184   Chapter 6

> to U Lu's request, Ko Kyaw Pe and his wife lent again 12 *kyat*s and took the mortgage. Ko Kyaw Lay was the witness. Maung Kho was the draft and scribe.[38]

(6) On April 20, 1875, U Lu said to Maung Meik, 'I am in want of money. Please lend me money again on the previous cotton field mortgage. If you cannot use the land because of other heirs' interference, I will pay the loss.' According to his request, Maung Meik lent 16 *kyat*s and took the mortgage with the right to use three years. U Kho and Ko Kyaw from Tebin-te village were witnesses. Maung Chit Pin was the draft and scribe.[39]

According to the contents of the six contracts about this cotton field called Wa-gyi-tat, written during 11 years from 1864 to 1975, the cotton field was owned by Maung Yan Hnin and U Lu jointly, which means that they were related to each other as co-heirs. Both had chosen to use it as collateral to get money rather than to cultivate the field themselves. On the other hand, the people who took the cotton field as a mortgage were an unnamed third party; Maung Meik, who had redeemed the cotton field back from this person in order to work on it; then Ko Kyaw Pe and his wife, who received part or all of the field back from Maung Meik; and, lastly, Maung Meik took the field back again. From 1867 to 1870, Maung Meik gave 5 *kyat*s to U Lu; by 1875, the amount of money given to U Lu by Ko Kyaw Pe and Maung Meik was much higher. Looking at these records, it is quite possible to understand the amount of money paid here as a fee for the use of the cotton fields, rather than a random amount of money borrowed for the necessities of life; in 1875, the payment leaped as cotton cultivation became more profitable. This example may also fit what Furnivall called the mortgage tenancy.

Then, how can we interpret the example of the paddy fields mortgaged by the brothers Maung Shwe Myo and Maung Kye seen in the previous section? Should it be considered as a case of mortgage tenancy, or just an ordinary mortgaging and additional loan on the paddy fields? In this example, as the creditors, U Lu and his wife, were the donors of a pagoda (an indicator of wealth and prestige in the community), it is clear that this was not the situation that Furnivall described as mortgage tenancy in the colonial period (that the one lending money is poor and the one borrowing money is rich). Also, four paddy fields sown with a total of 5.25 baskets of seeds cannot be said to be too small to be divided among brothers and sisters. Then, it seems to be a case of common money-lending and additional-loan *thet-kayit*s. But it is not impossible to suppose that there were several owners of the same paddy fields, and that they were getting cash by renting out the entire paddy fields and distributing the rent. No definite conclusion can be drawn from these three *thet-kayit*s, and we can only say that either interpretation is possible.

There were many instances in which additional-borrowing *thet-kayit*s were repeatedly made on the same pledged land, and the total amount of money borrowed became enormous, and the debtor had to sell the mortgaged land finally, but in such cases it is difficult to consider them as a mortgage tenancy. This is because if the landowner is offering his farmland to a tenant under the guise of security for a loan, it is unlikely that he would eventually sell it off. Most additional-borrowing *thet-kayit*s could be read as indicative of the severe situation that not a few people had to offer their farmlands to borrow money because of hardship in making their living, and most of them could not redeem their lands but piled up additional loans.

However, it must be true that the mortgage tenancy that Furnivall observed in Upper Burma in the first half of the twentieth century had its roots in the dynastic society. The question, then, arises as to how such a contract, which was actually a tenancy contract, had to take the form of a money-lending contract in eighteenth- and nineteenth-century Burma.

I suppose that the situation in Upper Burma during the Konbaung period, when the practice of fixed-rent tenancy had not yet been developed, prompted this somewhat strange practice of using money-lending contracts as fixed-rent tenancy. In British Lower Burma, fixed-rent tenancy had been widely introduced and became the dominant form of agricultural land tenancy, although most of the fixed rent was paid in paddy. However, in Konbaung Burma, fixed rent paid in cash had hardly developed. Those who accumulated land on a large scale used debt-slaves to cultivate the land, or they divided the land accumulated in various areas into small plots and lent it out under the share-cropping called *lo'hpet*. In those days, there was no word for tenant in Upper Burma, but they used *lo'-hpet*, or *hpet-sat*, meaning the people working together.[40] In the case of *lo' hpet*, the landowner provided the land, livestock, seeds, and water use,

186 Chapter 6

and those who cultivated the land provided labor, and they shared the harvest equally.

The aged parents and the sick and infirm who had already withdrawn from production, or those who owned small pieces of land that were too small to be cultivated as a result of the equitable inheritance system, could earn some money by renting out their lands. It often happened that co-heirs gathered each small piece of land together and rented them out to others and took the land rent annually or every three years. Thus, in eighteenth- and nineteenth-century Upper Burma, where the practice of fixed-rent tenancy had not yet been established, some people devised a method equivalent to fixed-rent tenancy by borrowing from existing forms of money-lending *thet-kayit*s.

In the below example, we see that the paddy field inherited by Maung Aye was mortgaged to his uncle for 15 *kyat*s. The money given to Maung Aye should be considered as a land rent rather than a loan if additional borrowing contracts were written regularly every year or every two~ five years.

> On 11th lazan Thadingyut, 1204 (October 15, 1842), Maung Aye in Tha-byo village said to his uncle U Yauk, 'Please take my share of the inherited paddy field called Sein-pan-zin as collateral, and lend me some money, as I am in need of money.' Then U Yauk lent him 15 *kyat*s in *ywet-ni*, and took the paddy field of Maung Aye's share as mortgage. The witnesses were the Burmese medicine doctor, U Myat and U Shei Yauk. Maung Kala, the donor of the scripture chest, was the draft. The scribe was Maung San Pyo. The brokerage fee was 3 *mus*.[41]

When additional-loan *thet-kayit*s were written repeatedly after an original land-mortgage *thet-kayit*, it might actually represent a contract of a different character. There were two cases in such repeated additional loans, one in which the borrower pledged his farmland for cash, because of his further destitution, and he was obliged to borrow money again and again. In another case, the additional loan was not a debt but the payment of land rent. The newly arising demand to borrow land for the cultivation of profitable crops was met by using the established form of money-lending *thet-kayit*s. The reality of the active and the passive or the powerful and the weak in human relations that appeared in the *thet-kayit*s can be hidden sometimes, if we cannot read the background and the situation of the *thet-kayit*s.

One aspect of mortgage tenancies that Furnivall observed during the British period (i.e., contrary to common sense, the money-lenders were poorer than the borrowers) cannot be applied to the Konbaung period. In order to accumulate agricultural land, the rich and influential people in the Konbaung period resorted to money-lending secured by land, or buying up land, but they never entered into mortgage tenancies themselves. Those who were rich enough to lend money in wide areas could accumulate vast lands as land became the best collateral for loans in the Konbaung period.

The background of the transfer of cultivation rights by means of money-lending contracts has several reasons, such as the case of the aged father who could not cultivate his paddy field any more, or the case of land inherited by many co-heirs which became too small to cultivate.

In the British era, landowners in Upper Burma adopted the method of mortgage tenancies, trying to raise the land rent easily, and also to evade the legal protection of tenant farmers. As there was no such form of fixed-rent tenancy in the Konbaung period, it is most probable that the mortgage tenancy of the Konbaung era came to be practiced as a way of obtaining cash by offering farmland to another person, by using the old form of money-lending *thet-kayit*s. The 'reversal of the rich–poor phenomenon', as Furnivall put it, with money-lenders being poor and borrowers being wealthy, also cannot be applied at all to the Konbaung period.

The land-related *thet-kayit*s in Byangya village clearly show that the alienation of farmland through debt had proceeded uncontrollably since the late eighteenth century. Not only ancestral private lands, but also official lands and monastery lands that were not allowed to be pledged or sold, were caught in this vortex. Land was being alienated to such an extent that it rendered the land system of the dynastic society practically meaningless.

One purpose of this chapter has been to expand our gaze to the entire central plains and examine how widely these phenomena were spreading. From the middle of the eighteenth century to the late nineteenth century, debt secured by land became the dominant form of debt, accounting for nearly 60% of the total number of debt contracts. Agricultural land pledging was also confirmed to be widespread throughout the central plains of Upper Burma. However, the sale of farmland was concentrated in certain areas, such as Shwebo, where Byangya village is located, Salin, Kyaukpadan, and Mandalay, while in other regions, land-selling *thet-kayit*s were very few. The fact that the wording used for the sale of agricultural land was not the simple words 'to sell' or 'to buy', but were expressed with heavy adverbs, such as 'to build a pagoda and to build a monastery' or 'to hand down to your posterity', also shows that the sale of agricultural land was a different act from the sale of ordinary goods.

People were driven to sell their farmland primarily when they were unable to repay their piled-up debts, but in many rural areas strong brakes existed to hold back the sale of the land. This was because there was a notion, backed by customary law, which strongly tied farmland to the reclaimer of land and their descendants who continued to cultivate it.

Finally, this chapter has discussed the issue of mortgage tenancy. The practice corresponding to a tenancy contract in the form of a money-lending contract, which Furnivall observed in Upper Burma during the colonial period, had already appeared in the Konbaung period, but its meaning at that time was quite different: 'mortgage tenancy' in the eighteenth to nineteenth centuries meant that, as a result of old age or the fragmentation of arable land, some people could not cultivate their lands. They tried to secure money by using the traditional form of money-lending by land security, a device used when the practice of fixed-rent tenancy had not yet been established. Even though the form was similar, the background and purpose of the mortgage tenancy in the Konbaung period and that of the colonial period were quite different from each other.

Part IV

How to Characterize Early Modern Burma?

Chapter 7

Early Modern Burma as a Contractual Society

To call any precolonial Southeast Asian society a contractual society might sound irrelevant. Perhaps this is because contracts have long been understood in the context of a modern Western nation-state, where promises made between individuals, with certain formalities, are placed under the legal protection of the nation-state.[1] The use of the term 'contractual society' in reference to Southeast Asia in the period long before the introduction of Western-style administrative and legal systems might be difficult to apply. When I first became interested in the rural society of the Konbaung period, the word 'contract' hardly existed in my mind, as it seemed to have no connection to such a concept at first. However, after reading through many varieties of *thet-kayit*s, I realized that the formation of contractual relationships between private individuals has played a very important role in this society.

Recent historical studies have increasingly revealed that in different civilizations and distant eras around the world, contracts between private individuals have gained recognition within the society and have been protected by some kind of system of that society. The accumulation of research works on contracts in the Islamic world and in China is a prime example of this.[2] Terada Hiroaki writes about the Ming and Qing societies in China as follows:

> Through the study of contractual documents over the past hundred years and the study of civil lawsuits over the past thirty years, the common image of Chinese society, consisting of a fixed geographical and blood-related community and a state that was detached from it, has been broken down, and China's early modern society has become a society

191

192   Chapter 7

filled with the formation of relationships based on the mutual consent of private individuals (contracts in the broadest sense of the word). It has become clear that the state was actively involved in resolving disputes and generally working to protect and realize their private agreements.[3]

The words above, referring to China's Ming and Qing societies, have a lot of curious resonances when we think of the Burmese Konbaung society in the eighteenth and nineteenth centuries, located on the western edge of Southeast Asia. However, it is not the main purpose of this paper to point out that there was an aspect of contractual society in Konbaung Burmese society. Studies on precolonial Southeast Asian societies have focused on the formation of personal relationships, such as the web of two-party relationships based on familiarity and the patron–client relationship, which was formed by seeking the patronage of influential people, as a principle of social organization, whereas the contractual relationship for economic resources was rarely mentioned. Therefore, the importance of introducing a contractual perspective to early modern societies in Southeast Asia should be emphasized. In this chapter, we will also explore the social system and the notion shared by people which supported the money-lending *thet-kayit*s to be accepted as a legitimate contract. By doing so, I would like to connect this study to the larger issue of reconsidering the nature of early modern Burmese society.

The social system that guaranteed the validity of *thet-kayit*s

In the style of money-lending *thet-kayit*s, the borrower made a request to the lender using a simple salutation, 'please lend me', and the owner of the money complied with the request, which always implied a nuance of favor. However, this does not deny the fact that the agreement was formed as a voluntary act of both parties involved; in the Burmese society of the Konbaung era, both the creditor and the debtor were the actors who made a contract and were obligated to fulfill the promises made, and received the consequences of the contract. It seems to have been accepted as natural and self-evident. Even in the case of a debt slave who engaged in servile labor in exchange for debt, he or she could be one of the subjects of a new

Early Modern Burma as a Contractual Society   193

contract, such as an additional-loan contract or a contract to send one's family members into debt slavery, as a contracting party.

But it would not be possible to call it a contract, simply because there is a voluntary consensus between private parties and the contents of the agreement are put into writing as a certificate. In order to make the agreed promise effective, there must be not only a mutual promise between the parties, but also a power in the society to enforce its performance in some way, if either party should fail to perform the promise. This is because, unless there is a force of mental pressure, not to say physical force of restraint or arrest, strong enough to make the society believe that the obligation of performance cannot be avoided, the agreement of the parties cannot be considered to be a contract by itself.

The entity that recognizes and protects the agreement as legitimate might be, in other societies, the commonly believed God and his agents in this life, or the governing power in some cases. However, in the *thet-kayit*s of the Konbaung Burmese society, the god was absent, and neither the central royal government nor the local rulers exerted influence.

Then, what kind of power and relationships supported the early modern Burmese contractual documents to maintain their effectiveness?

The presence of witnesses

The money-lending contract in the Konbaung period was drafted and scribed between the parties in the presence of multiple observers such as numismatists, weighers and assayers of money, witnesses, drafters, and scribes, and, among them, the most important observers were witnesses. Not only simple, unsecured money-lending with interest, but also the human-mortgage (debt-slave) contracts or land-mortgage contracts, did not require copies of the contracts to be submitted to the village chiefs or to the chiefs of the broader local administrative units, such as *myo* or *taik*, nor was it necessary to obtain the seal or signature of these administrative officials.

The most important key factor to the formation of the contract was to have not only the parties, but also many witnesses, present to observe the making of the contracts. The most important of these observers was the witness, called in Burmese 'one who witnesses, sees, hears, and understands',[4] and it was common to list the names of multiple witnesses

194   Chapter 7

in the important contract documents. What kind of person, then, was selected by both parties as a witness?

If we look at the people who appeared in *thet-kayit*s as witnesses, we notice that many of them were the donors of facilities and equipment related to Buddhism, or public utilities such as ponds, wells, bridges, and rest houses. The village heads and captains of the cavalry and the infantry also appeared in contracts as witnesses, but not so often. Also, managers of irrigation systems, such as chiefs of canal and weirs, were asked to sit as witnesses in some contracts. However, people who did not hold any titles and were called only by their personal names appeared more often than these captains or chiefs of irrigation systems.[5]

It is important to note that when people in governing administrative positions appeared as witnesses, they did not necessarily represent the governing structure or organization, but only stood as influential persons on both sides of the case. The fact that the majority of the debt contracts did not have any witnesses of these administrative officials indicates that the presence of people in administrative positions was not a prerequisite for concluding contracts. Even if the village chief appeared as a witness, it was unexpectedly rare that this person was the head of either or both parties or the village in which they both resided. It also indicates that they were not chosen as witnesses in terms of their administrative position. What was desired for a witness was a person whose opinions and actions were respected by both parties to the contract and who had a spiritual influence upon both parties, as well as in the local community. The fact many witnesses were the donors of Buddhist institutions or public utilities also indicates that the criteria for selecting witnesses was different from the governing power and status hierarchy. The formation of an agreement in the presence of people who were influential on both sides, as people whose ideas and comments were important to both parties, may have made them more aware of the crucial obligation they had to carry out their agreements in order to live in the community, more so than the promises made by the parties themselves.

Legal validity of *thet-kayit*s

Although it was very important to have reliable and respectable people as witnesses in making *thet-kayit*s, what seems to be more important was that *thet-kayit*s were treated as the most important evidence for the resolution of disputes in the courts at all levels from village to the royal capital. If the promises made in a *thet-kayit* were not fulfilled by either side, or if, after a long time, there was a discrepancy in the understanding of its contents that led to disputes, people often resorted to litigation. In some *thet-kayit*s, the reason for borrowing money was written as follows: 'we need money because we have to pay the judicial costs'. This is a good indication that private litigation was not an uncommon occurrence.[6]

Courts to adjudicate disputes were established at various levels, from the village level to the level of the Privy Council (*Hlut-taw*), which was hosted by the crown prince.[7] However, in all these courts, the most important evidence for the resolution of disputes was the *thet-kayit*, which, without fail, the judges asked to be submitted to the court. The court heard the case on the basis of what was recorded in *thet-kayit*s and handed down the judgment. For this reason, a *thet-kayit* was passed down and preserved from generation to generation as an extremely important document, and was the most reliable evidence in case of a dispute.

In that sense, the *thet-kayit* was recognized and sanctioned as a legally binding document in Burmese society during the Konbaung era, at all levels from the village to the capital. In this way, Burmese society as a whole at that time seems to have given legal validity to the agreements between private individuals compiled in the form of *thet-kayit*s, giving them a character as a contract that went beyond mere promises.

Private contracts and royal or local authorities

It is true that *thet-kayit*s did not require notification or authentication of the central or local governing authorities at the time of their creation, but was there ever any regulation or intervention by the central or local administrative power in the outcome of such transactions? If so, to what extent and in what cases did the interventions take place? As we have seen, money-lending with security took humans and farmland as collateral, and also, during the Konbaung era, the collateral for debt was rapidly shifting from humans to farmland. These free movements of vital resources in the private sector might have undermined the economic foundations of the royal and local governments. How did the administrative authorities of the Konbaung dynasty respond to this resource transfer?

196   Chapter 7

The answer to this question is rather simple; neither the kingship nor local authorities in Konbaung Burma showed any willingness to take an active role in controlling the movement of resources among private people. Broadly speaking, in terms of the transfer of resources through financing, both royal and local authorities seem to have been players in their own right, acting as both creditors and debtors, trying to accumulate wealth or avoiding the unexpected financial failures and bankruptcy of their estates.

Certainly, as already mentioned, from the Taungoo period to the founding period of Konbaung, the kings were anxious about the enslavement of people though debt-slave contracts, especially those of the *ahmudan* class, because *ahmudan*s were the foundation of the king's power. Therefore, the kings of the second Taungoo period repeatedly issued edicts preventing or prohibiting the conversion of *ahmudan*s and their children into debt-slaves. During the Konbaung period, however, no measure was taken to prevent debt-slavery in particular, and for the new and rapidly developing land pledges, both royal and local authorities sat back as onlookers and gave silent approval.

Possibility of land confiscation by the king

Strictly speaking, the fear that the king might attempt to intervene in the transfer of land was at least partly maintained throughout the Konbaung era. This is shown by a few, if not very few, land mortgage *thet-kayit*s in which the words suggest the possibility of royal intervention.

In general, creditors wished to write a clause in *thet-kayit*s which would enable them to avoid any loss arising from the pledged land if there was the slightest possibility that the land might become unusable for any reason after they took the land as collateral. Contemplated cases in which the land might become unusable were 'by the interference of some other person', or 'by the intervention of a relative', 'by the interference of another heir', 'by the intervention of the original owner', and so on. Similarly, in a very few examples, a clause, 'if [the land] is confiscated by the king in future', was included to protect the creditor's right, as seen in the following two examples:

(1) On 12th lazo Tabaung, 1217 (April 1, 1856), Yei-hla-yan-nain and his heir Maung Pu said to U Hla and his wife, donor of monastery, living in Ywa Thit village, 'We need money. Please take our 2 paddy

fields as mortgage and lend us some money. If you could not use the paddy fields because the other heirs would interfere, or the king or *thugyi*s would forbid, or a dispute over irrigation water would arise, we will recompensate it.' In response to this request, U Hla and his wife, the donors of monastery, gave 13 *kyat*s in *ywet-ni* and took the paddy fields as a pledge for three years and three harvests. The monk's father, U Lau was the witness, Maung Hmon was the drafter and Ye-hla-yan-naing, the owner of the paddy fields was the script.[8]

(2) On 8th lazan Thadingyut 1235 (September 29, 1873), Prince Maung Hcyin, his grand-daughter Mi Mi Hkin, and Maung Shwe Loun, the chief of paddy fields, living in Magyi-bin-sauk village said, 'We need money. We have 5 paddy fields which they call Hna-seik-bon, located in the south of the village, a private property reclaimed by our ancestors. Please take these paddy fields as pledges and lend us 80 pieces of 1 *kyat* silver coins.' Minister of Home Affairs, Mr. and Mrs. Maha-mingyi-min-gaung, who were known for their academic achievements and were the *Myo-sa* of Saw Myo, accepted this offer and took the paddy fields as pledges for three year and three harvests, and lent 80 *kyat*s in silver coins. If it should happen that the paddy fields to be confiscated by the king, or if the previous owner should appear and the creditors could not use the fields, the creditors have the right to claim the amount of rice that could be taken from the land, and the amount of money written in this contract. The witnesses were Kon U Meik, Leze-daw-da-laik Maung Po, and Maung Tun Hla, the Grand Chamberlain. The drafter was Maung Than Daing.[9]

Example (1) is a land-mortgage *thet-kayit* from Meiktila region written in 1856. In this *thet-kayit*, the creditors, Mr. and Mrs. U Hla, included many provisions concerning the compensation for any possibility that the pledged land might become unusable. Judging from the honorary title of the debtor, Yei-hla-yan-nain should have been an *ahmudan* of the upper-middle class. Since the contract was written in 1856, when administrative reforms by King Mindon had not yet been introduced, *ahmudan*s were not paid their salary in cash but in land granted by the king for their services. *Ahmudan*s had only the usufruct right of the land, but they had no right to dispose of the land granted.

198   Chapter 7

From the many provisions to protect the creditors' interest in this *thet-kayit*, it is quite possible that the pledged land was granted land. However, as we have already seen, pledging of granted land was often practiced from an earlier time, and there was no case found, as far as I know, in which it was prohibited or punished by the royal or local rulers. Nevertheless, it seems that the possibility of the intervention of kings and *thugyi*s had not yet been dispelled from the consciousness of the people, regardless of the official land system being in a state of disrepair.

Example (2) is a *thet-kayit* from Mandalay in 1873, at the end of the reign of King Mindon. Already the *ahmudan*s were being paid a monthly salary in cash instead of a grant of land, and taxes in cash were levied on the *ahmudan* class.[10] In this period, there was no longer any basis for the prohibition or punishment of disposing of land belonged to the royal family or the *ahmudan* class. The *thet-kayit* also states that the paddy fields pledged had been cultivated by the ancestors, and if true (as ancestral land (*bo-ba-baing* land) could be pledged, even sold, freely[11]), there should have been no need to consider the situation of confiscation by the king. The words 'confiscation by the king' seem to have been written in the contract for another reason.

According to U Tin, who served as a bureaucrat in the courts of the last two kings of the Konbaung era, Mindon and Thibaw, and also served the British colonial government, the confiscation of land by the Konbaung kings was limited to cases of death without leaving an heir, or a grave crime against the king, such as treason, committed by the owner of land, and not to the case of self-disposal of the granted land.[12] Moreover, in the former case, if a legitimate heir appeared within ten years, the land was readily returned, and even in the latter case, if the land of the guilty party had been pledged to a third person, the creditor was sometimes paid for it.

It seems that the reason why the phrase 'if the land is confiscated by the king' is written in the above *thet-kayit* is because the representative of the group of pledgers was a prince of the king. King Mindon himself had rebelled against his brother, King Pagan, and took the throne. And later on, King Mindon had to face a rebellion by his son, Prince Mingun, and his sympathizers, with the result that his brother, Prince Kanawun, who was supposed to be his successor, was killed. The rebellion of Prince Mingun and his sympathizers failed, and the estates of those who had rebelled against the king, including those of Prince Pathein, who also rebelled against the king, were confiscated. It seems that the fact a prince and his family members were mortgaging their paddy fields was a source of anxiety to creditors, since rebellions over the succession to the throne had been referred to as an incurable disease for the royal lineage of the Konbaung dynasty. This clause may therefore have been necessary to relieve the creditors.

Compared to the clause 'if the land is confiscated by the king', which hardly happened, other clauses such as 'if the other heirs should interfere' or 'if the former owner of the land would appear' were based on real threats for the creditor. I found lots of these clauses in the land-mortgage *thet-kayit*s such as the following:

On 9th lazan Nayon 1238 (May 31, 1876), Ko Shwe Nge, a resident of Tha-hkwa-gon village said, 'As I need money, please take 3 paddy fields called Pauk-bin watered by the Bonzi-kwa South Canal under Lake Meiktila, sown with 1.5 basket of seeds, under the condition of three years and three harvests. If the other heirs would interfere and get into a lawsuit, we will pay for the cost. In response to the offer, U Tha Kyaw of Pauk-bin-tha village lent 18 *kyat*s 8 *mu*s 8 *pe*s and took the paddy fields as collaterals for three years.[13]

In Burmese society, where, as a rule, all children, male and female, received equal shares of inheritance, it was very common to find joint heirs on a piece of land too small to divide, and, in these cases, the joint heirs took their turn to use the land once every few years or left it to one of the co-heirs to cultivate and others would take small amounts of land rent. If one of the joint heirs was in need of money and pawned the land without permission of the other heirs and was unable to return the land to them for a number of years, there would be a great likelihood of disputes and even lawsuits among the heirs. Or, if the creditor who took the land as collateral sold the written contract to someone else without an agreement between the original owner of the land and the new creditor, this also caused disputes over the terms of redemption and other conditions. In fact, documents related to disputes and lawsuits over pledged land show that such situations occurred frequently.

There were many judicial cases raised by creditors who could not use the pledged land because of 'other heirs' intervention' or 'the original

200   Chapter 7

owner's interference'. On the other hand, I have not yet seen any lawsuits raised as a result of 'the confiscation by the king'. It seems that confiscation of land by the king rarely happened in the Konbaung period, with the exception of land owned by the rebels against the king.

Private financial activities and the royal government

Generally speaking, the Konbaung kings did not interfere in the transfer of resources through private financial activities. However, I found royal edicts on this subject issued three times, the first by Alaunghpaya, the founder of the dynasty, the second by Bodawhpaya, the sixth king, and lastly by Mindon, the tenth king.

King Alaunghpaya, while he led the army against Ayuttaya on January 1, 1760, issued the following orders.

- Stop all lawsuits for repayment of the loans on any member of the families belonging to men in the fighting forces against Ayuttaya.

- Postpone all such lawsuits for loans, until the said campaign is over.

- For other loans, a demand for repayment is prohibited until a period of ten months is over.[14]

It was a time of warfare when the number of impoverished people was increasing amidst repeated expeditions, even after the establishment of the dynasty, and families that had to send soldiers to the long expedition were likely to have run out of ways to repay the accumulated debts. The main purpose of the edict was to prevent soldiers at the front from becoming upset by the plight of their families and from fleeing from the expedition.

The decree issued on March 6, 1783, the year after Bodawhpaya's seizure of power, was issued in the midst of the construction of the new royal capital at Amarapura. The decree stated that all those involved in the construction work must not be summoned by any lawsuits, and also that the creditors of loans should not employ brokers to realize payment of debts, but they should do it by themselves.[15] Presumably, the collection of debts by brokers used to be much harsher and made the conscripted workers in Amarapura feel uneasy about it.

In 1855, the third year after King Mindon's accession to the throne, he issued three edicts related to debt problems. One decree, issued on April

Early Modern Burma as a Contractual Society 201

20, stated that as many local rulers and chieftains owed large amounts of debt in order to carry out their official duties, the lawsuits and petitions for the collection of their debts were to be judged by the king's own court.[16] Then, on June 1, another decree was issued calling for a six-month postponement of the payment of debts by the musketeers and artillerymen and other *ahmudan* troops.[17] This was followed by another decree on June 16, which applied the same measure to free commoners (*athi*) as well, which was advised by the chief ministers.[18] The urgent task of securing financial resources, bureaucracy, and military organization was pressing the new king and there was a widespread feeling among these public servants that debt was hampering their ability to perform their duties.

Although no hasty conclusions can be drawn because of the small number of edicts dealing with the debt issue, the above examples show that the heavy debts which had spread to all social strata from the founding period to the end of the Konbaung dynasty became a serious social problem when the royal government needed to recruit a large number of people for foreign expeditions or for the construction of a new capital. The measures taken by the kings in such critical times were similar, indicating that the position of the royal government on the debt problem had basically not changed. The king did not intend to regulate or interfere in private money-lending business, and took it for granted that the creditors' claims should be protected. When an emergency situation arose, in which the local chiefs, *ahmudan*s, and soldiers were impoverished by the heavy debt to the extent that they could not perform the tasks assigned to them, limited interventions were made, such as asking creditors to postpone the repayment date or prohibiting them from summoning debtors on official services for litigation.

The fact that the intervention of the royal government was always partial and did not undermine the creditors' claims means, in other words, that the rights of the creditors were basically respected and indirectly protected by the king's government. This stance of the government can also be considered to have created the conditions for the money-lending *thet-kayit*s of this period to stand as contracts.

Kings as creditors

In fact, the successive kings were themselves financiers and holders of large amounts of claims. Although the loans extended by the kings were made

202 Chapter 7

without a clear division between the state treasury and the king's personal property,[19] they were extended by the kings to the local chiefs, officials, the *ahmudan* leaders, and the common people. This is well illustrated by the following edict issued by King Bodawhpaya in 1782, when he ascended the throne:

> My father King Alaunghpaya gave loans from the royal treasury, to Chieftains of Shan (*so-bwa*), *Myo-za*s, *Thugyi*s, *Kalan*s,[20] other officials and ordinary people in accordance with the laws of the Sangha. A substantial part of these loans has not yet been repaid. Some of the loans made by my brother, the King,[21] and Hsinbyushin,[22] have also not yet been repaid. On my accession to the throne, in the interest of the prosperity of my kingdom and Buddhism, and in order to realize the eight sacred virtues of a king, I have removed Singu *Myoza*[23] and other sinful persons. They were executed for bringing mischief to the country. Their real and personal properties were confiscated, and the goods obtained from them are now available for use. The kings tried to collect their debts, but no matter how much pressure the collectors put on the debtors to repay their debts, the money was never collected in the royal treasury, but rather the debtors tried to squeeze the money out of the people in general, that is, their subjects. If this were to be repeated in my reign, it would be an unbearable situation for all people. I have therefore resolved that I will not collect the loans of the previous kings. In the interest of the well-being of my subjects and of my virtue in reincarnation, I renounce the claims to my subjects in the sum of over 23,000 *beita*s of silver and 10 *beita*s of gold.[24] All debts of people to the successive kings will be cancelled on the 3rd lazo Kason 1144 (April 14, 1782), in front of the Privy Council, at the sound of a drum.[25]

According to the decree, the amount of uncollected loans from the state treasury during the 30 years from 1752–1782 amounted to 2.3 million *kyat*s in silver alone. It indicates that the kings themselves were the largest money-lenders in the kingdom. Unlike the decrees of the Kamakura and Muromachi Bakufu (government) in Japan, called Tokusei-rei, which ordered private money-lenders to abandon their claims as a countermeasure to the impoverishment of the vassals of the Shogunate, Bodawhpaya's decree did not mention the private financial activities, but

Early Modern Burma as a Contractual Society   203

declared that only the claims of the king would be waived. It is possible to understand this decree as a staging by the king, who himself usurped the throne by force, to present himself as a righteous king in accordance with the Buddhist law.

In such loans of the kings, sometimes interest was charged and sometimes not, and in cases when the borrower was struggling to raise money for the expenses of administration, it is said that the loans were made without interest, but only at the discretion of the king or his government. In loans to the Shan rulers (*so-bwa*), four kings, from Alaunghpaya to Singu and, the last, Thibaw, lent money with interest, while Bodawhpaya, Pagan, and Mindon gave loans without interest.[26] In the vicinage of the king, there were wealthy people, whom Thant Myint-U called the king's bankers,[27] through whom the king would lend money to more people, or conversely, the royal family would receive loans from the wealthy men. There are also a number of *thet-kayit*s in which not only the king but also the members of the royal family appeared as creditors, and loans by the queens or their relatives were particularly prominent. Many queens, princes, and princesses were given a right to receive a portion of tax revenues from a *myo* or a village, and those who received *myo*s or villages which had special products or popular commodities took their portion of taxes in these commodities and sold them at markets. For example, tea leaves produced in the Shan Plateau had become popular during the Konbaung period, and those who were given the right to take a portion of the tax from the tea-producing villages gained an enormous profit. Each member of the leading royalty had a trusted treasurer (*bandar-zo*) who controlled the commodity trade and financial activities.

During the reign of King Mindon, the most active financial player was the queen, who had the right to take a portion of the tax from Zabwe-daun Taik, her daughter, Princess Pin-htei-hkaung-tin, and the queen's brother, Min-maha-min-tin-yaza, who served as a king's great messenger, the magistrate of king's estate, and captain of the royal navy. They accumulated a great number of people and lands.

In a *thet-kayit* dated December 1878, an officer of the army, who had borrowed 111 *kyat*s from the queen and her relatives for the tobacco trade, was unable to repay the loan due to a loss caused by the collapse in the price of tobacco. It is said that he offered his wife as a debt-slave and to move his family to the residence of his creditor, which was accepted.[28]

204   Chapter 7

While the royalty with financial resources were actively engaged in financial business, some of them had to live in considerable hardship, and mortgaged their inherited fields and accumulated debts. As already mentioned, Prince Pyinzi, who was famous for writing Thai-style songs, also seems to have been in financial distress, and we know that he and his son wrote many *thet-kayit*s to borrow money, offering a large amount of farmland, including paddy fields and *kaing* lands as securities.[29]

Handling disputes over debt

Another point of contact between the king's government and private financial activities was seen when lawsuits over debts could not be settled in the local courts and were appealed to the Privy Council. If a civil case could not be settled at the local level for a long period of time, adjudication could be sought by the Privy Council, and the basic position of the royal government on private debt contracts was well illustrated in the judgments and rulings of the king's government in 1758, when the dispute between the *So-bwa*[30] of Yauk-sauk in the Shan states and his debt-slave Hla Chit was brought to the Privy Council.

The Lord of the Yauk-sauk claimed that Hla Chit was a born slave, while Hla Chit refuted that he was a debt-slave and had worked long enough to cover his debts and should be freed, and both sides sought the decision of the Privy Council, which suggested the following three points: (1) study similar cases carefully in the law books; (2) avoid hasty or biased decisions; and (3) take at least one to six weeks to make a decision.[31] That is to say, it did not settle and deliver a decision on which side was right in the dispute, but only set out the principles of how to solve the dispute. This was the basic form of adjudication when a civil lawsuit was brought before the Privy Council without being settled in the local courts. In many cases, the Privy Council did not give a final verdict on the case, but sent the case back to the local courts, only providing a road map for resolution and guidance. If the Privy Council decided that there was a suitable magistrate in the royal capital, it could conclude the dispute under it,[32] but the Privy Council itself avoided, as far as possible, the settling of private disputes.

In 1782, shortly after his accession to the throne, King Bodawhpaya outlined a wide range of administrative policies and, with regard to the solution of debt problems, an edict suggested taking 'the way in which widows handle the difficult tasks'; that is to say, begin with the easy tasks and solve the problem gradually. Also, the edict showed the principle in money-lending, using the phrase 'the branch of the tree does not exceed its trunk', meaning that the interest should not exceed the principal. The basic position of the king's government on the issue of heavy debts among people was limited to the suggestion of guidelines or principles for the solution.[33]

As we have seen above, the king's government had never imposed restrictions on private financial activities, and when serious social problems arose (for example, a number of *ahmudan*s had been summoned to court by lawsuits for repayment of debts and, as a result, this hindered the performance of their official duties), the king only intervened in a limited way, postponing repayment requests for a certain period. It is also noteworthy that the king himself was a player in financial activities, lending money at the same interest rate as the general public.

In the eighteenth and nineteenth centuries, the royal governments avoided direct intervention in private financial activities compared to the Taungoo and the second Taungoo (Nyaung Yang) governments during the sixteenth to the eighteenth centuries. The kings of the Taungoo and Nyaung Yang dynasties worried about the transfer of the population from the monarchy to powerful private individuals through money-lending. Not a few *ahmudan*s became debt-slaves who were beyond the reach of the monarchy in order to avoid the unbearable burden that the king imposed on them. The loss of the *ahmudan*s was an issue of vital importance to the kings, so they forbade the debt-slave contracts of *ahmudan*s and punished both debtors and creditors. During the Konbaung era, besides humans, farmland emerged as the most important collateral for debt, and debt-slave contracts decreased in number rapidly. As for the transfer of humans and farmland, the royal government did not take any specific action to prevent it. Although in some of the *thet-kayit*s, people wrote words suggesting that the king might confiscate the pledged land, there were no examples of such an invocation of royal power, and the attitude of the king's government was one of tacit approval and indirect involvement in disputes by providing guidelines for their resolution.

206   Chapter 7

Local rulers and debt contracts
Farmland price assessed by village elders

Then, what kind of relationship did local rulers, such as village chiefs and *myo-thugyi*s, who were in close contact with the residents on a daily basis, have with the private financial activities and the resulting transfer of important resources? Even if the transfer of farmland or the enslavement of humans occurred as a result of the financial activities within or across the boundaries of a village or a *myo*, the parties involved were not obliged to report the transaction to *myo-thugyi*s, nor to the village chiefs. I have not yet found any evidence that the local chiefs had exercised any control over the contracts between private citizens.

However, some land-sale *thet-kayit*s from the early Konbaung period show that the village chiefs and elders were involved in land inspection and valuation before the transaction was concluded, indicating that the final transfer of land ownership sometimes required the judgment of influential people in the community. For example, in one land-sale contract written in 1776, a person sold a large tract of land, including fields, irrigation canals, and hills in a mango grove, to a donor of the pagoda, but the elders who stood between them inspected the land and estimated the price at one-third of the official price[34] (namely, 240 *kyat*s in *ngwe-wunbwe*[35]) and the land selling was concluded in the house of one of the elders.[36]

In a *thet-kayit* written on a *pe-sa* (writing material made of dried palm leaf) in 1811 from Lezin village in Monywa, a man in the position of a royal herald pledged his two paddy fields planted with 600 bunches of seedlings as collateral for a loan, which he was unable to repay, so he signed an agreement to sell the paddy fields to his creditors for 120 *kyat*s in *ywet-ni*, the sum of his debt. It was recorded that the transaction was made in accordance with the decision of the chiefs of the village of Ywa-pale.[37]

Furthermore, one *thet-kayit* written in 1814 from Nwa-thein village in Monywa states:

> On the 14th lazo Tabodwe 1175 (February 24, 1814), Mi Win, Mi Lun Du, the son Maung Ta Htut offered to Maung Shwe Tha, the village chief of Shwe-yin-mar village, to buy a large dry field that they owned, and Maung Shwe Tha said he would buy the field after the assessment by elders, so Maung Nu, the donor of the temple, and Maung San Pu, a donor of Pagoda and Maung Nyin of Leppan village, also a donor of

Pagoda, valued the field at 270 *kyat*s in 2 *mat* alloy.[38] The village head, Maung Shwe Tha, bought the field at the price of 270 *kyat*s…[39]

Thus, in Monywa and some other regions from the mid-eighteenth century until the first decade of the nineteenth century, village elders inspected the land and assessed the purchase price of arable land. In the absence of a land market that could give a standard price for farmland, the parties involved in the sale of farmland accepted the price that was determined to be reasonable by influential people in the local community. The elders who assessed the price of the land in the above *thet-kayit* were all donors of pagodas or monasteries, and it reminds us that many witnesses who appeared in money-lending *thet-kayit*s were also donors of Buddhist institutions or public facilities. To be a donor showed not only their economic abilities, but also respect and trust from other villagers.

In the above examples, the sale of farmland was approved by the influential people and the price was set by them at a reasonable level. It might have been necessary where land sales rarely occurred, and people wanted the help of village elders to decide the appropriate price and admit the land sale transaction itself. However, such inspections and appraisals by the village elders were rarely conducted in land-sale *thet-kayit*s of other regions. In Byangya village, for example, some paddy field-selling *thet-kayit*s were written during the period between 1810 and 1812, but in these cases, there was no appraisal by elders on the land at all, which suggests that this was a phenomenon limited to a specific area such as Monywa and a specific period.

On the other hand, we have so far not seen any example of a *myo-thugyi*, the hereditary chief of a *myo*, conducting similar inspections, or assessing prices in private land sales.

Local ruler as creditor or debtor

It was not unusual for the *myo-thugyi* families, many of whom were the hereditary rulers of *myo*, to be on the side of the money-lenders. The most prominent families, who had accumulated enormous wealth through their extensive financial operations, were the Salin *Thugaung*s, already mentioned on several occasions. The Salin *Thugaung* families produced many *myo-thugyi*s in the region over the years and had been deeply involved in the governance of the region, and they had accumulated a large number

208   Chapter 7

of debt-slaves and vast farmlands through money-lending, and kept the *thet-kayit*s carefully, passing them down from generation to generation.

In cases where *myo-thugyi*s appeared as creditors, it was often the wife of the *myo-thugyi* who actually ran the money-lending business. The creditors were often listed as husband and wife on the loan documents, but in many cases the wives dealt with the loan business alone. Ma Hkain, known as the great female *thugaung* of the Salin region,[40] virtually took charge of all money-lending businesses of the family.

On the other hand, there were times when a person in the position of a *myo-thugyi* had to borrow money in connection with the management of the *myo*, as well as for their personal requirements. *Myo-thugyi*s were allowed to keep for themselves about 10% of the taxes on products raised from the territory, as well as half of the transaction taxes, tolls, and court fees, and were in a far stronger economic position than the villagers who cultivated land and made a living from their own labor. In peacetime and in areas where the productive base was relatively solid, such as irrigated areas for paddy cultivation or the cotton belt during the middle of the nineteenth century, this provided great economic power for the *myo-thugyi*. This was probably the reason why Ma Hkain's husband in Salin won the position of *thugyi* after a fierce battle for it with a rival.

At times of crisis when *myo-thugyi*s were required by the royal government to pay additional taxes, besides the usual tax payments for large construction projects or military campaigns, some of them were not able to bear such a burden and had to mortgage their *myo* or village in order to borrow money. According to Ito Toshikatsu, there were some cases of mortgaging and selling of *myo* or villages by the *myo-thugyi* or the village headman.[41]

In 1794, the hereditary *thugyi* of one small *myo* called Aka-yein finally sold his *myo*, which had already been mortgaged for years as a result of heavy debts, in order to perform various duties imposed on the *myo* by the royal government. Two years after the foreclosure of Aka-yein *myo*, a lawsuit was filed by the purchasers of Aka-yein *myo* against the former *myo-thugyi* and his wife. The former *thugyi* had sold the pond in the *myo* to a third party, and the couple who bought the *myo* sought an injunction against the use of the pond. A court judged that the sale of the pond was invalid, and the former *thugyi* and his wife were forced to borrow money again to repay the money earned by the sale of the pond.

The second case was related to the gold-producing villages in the Katha region, where some village headmen who could not pay tax in gold and additional revenue to the government mortgaged their villages and finally sold out villages to the gold officer in charge of other gold-producing areas. The gold officer who had supervised these four villages brought the case to the Privy Council in 1802, and the Privy Council ruled that the chiefs of four villages had no right to mortgage or to sell their villages, and that they should be punished and the villages should be redeemed. The gold officer of the other areas who had bought the villages agreed to return the village accordingly, but his right to take land rent from these villages was admitted until the money used for the purchase of these villages was redeemed.[42]

These two cases illustrate how the courts of the royal government, as well as the local courts, dealt with unexpected new situations that arose in *myo*s and villages, namely, the sale of *myo*s and villages by the *thugyi*s, the headmen. The legitimacy of the *thugyi* as the ruler of a *myo* or village was recognized by the royal edict, and the *thugyi* title itself could not be freely transferred by private transaction. However, in these cases, the rights of the person who bought a *myo* or village were recognized as legitimate until the *myo* or village was redeemed. In other words, even in such irregular transactions, the ownership rights of those who bought a *myo* or village were protected by the royal government.

From these cases, the royal government in Konbaung Burma can be seen as unwavering in protecting creditors' claims and purchasers' property rights. Unlike the farmland mortgage or human mortgage, mortgaging or selling *myo*s or villages might have been very irregular and unexpected problems by the government, so the Privy Council ordered the *thugyi*s who sold their *myo*s or villages to repurchase them, while the purchasers were allowed to collect land rent and other profits from the domains until the money used for purchasing was redeemed. These examples also show that the king's government in the Konbaung period had a consistent policy of protecting private claims and property rights and kept a non-intervention policy towards them.

210   Chapter 7

During the Konbaung period, private transactions related to humans and farmland were made by people of all social strata and played an important role in the transfer of resources. These transactions were written in a fixed format and the documents were called *thet-kayit*s, and these *thet-kayit*s were always treated as valid contracts in the Konbaung society. Behind this was the notion that private claims and ownership rights were socially recognized as something very certain that could not be threatened even by the kings. In addition, not only the kings but also the local chiefs acted as players in the transactions, acting on the same principle as a creditor or a debtor, rather than restricting or interfering in such transactions.

The presence of multiple congregations, mainly witnesses who were respected in the community, when preparing the *thet-kayit*s, and recognition by the judicial courts at all levels of the legal validity of the contracts written in the form of *thet-kayit*s, were the first factors to make *thet-kayit*s real contracts. In addition, the notion of respect for private claims and property rights prevailed in the society, and the actions based on this notion permeated from the royal government to the local rulers. These factors made the *thet-kayit*s suitable to be called legitimate contracts.

Chapter 8

Mediation of Disputes over Pledged Land

The frequency of documents related to lawsuits in the *para-baik*s is quite high, indicating that lawsuits were not uncommon in Burmese society during the Konbaung period. One reason for the relatively frequent occurrence of lawsuits in Burmese society may be attributable to the state of the judicial system in this period. The judicial system for civil matters did not exist as a solid system, but as a flexible, irregular, and soft system, and the barriers to the courts were very low for ordinary people living in rural areas. In fact, court deliberations at the local level were held at the residence or the yard of the person acting as a judge, and the judges included not only local rulers, village chiefs, and officials dispatched by the central government, but also the donors of pagodas and temples, traditional doctors, and monks. According to a royal decree, the persons who could be judges were the persons appointed by the king, the king himself, the ruler of a *myo* and village, a preceptor, a Brahmin, or a person chosen by the consent of both litigants.[1] In addition, *Myanmar Min Ok-chok-pon Sadan* (MMOS) written by U Tin, lists five qualifications for judges; namely, having great faith, being a guardian of the true law, being a man of wisdom, speaking comforting words, and knowing how to decide a case. In some cases, he added authority, good family background, and knowledge of the law to this qualification list.[2]

In this way, except for authority and family background, the qualifications of a judge were not external qualifications but personal qualities. In particular, the practice of appointing judges to whom both litigants agreed seems to have lowered the boundary between appealing to the court and asking elders to arbitrate disputes.

The major causes of conflicts over pledged farmland were also deeply rooted in Burmese society in the Konbaung era. One cause was the fact that the relation between farmland and people continued to be a close one that could not be easily replaced by money. Those who had reclaimed the land and continued to cultivate it were considered to have full ownership of the land, and even if they pledged the land for money, they and their descendants had the right to redeem the land forever from the money-lender. It was not only written in the customary law texts but observed in practice. With the penetration of the monetary economy to every corner of the society, pledging farmland as collateral for debt had become widespread. On the other hand, the customary notion that tied land to the reclaimer and his descendants had remained strong. It can be said that the result of the contradiction between economic needs and the traditional notion was conflict over farmland. A typical example of this type of conflict occurred when the parties who signed the original land-mortgage contract had passed away long time ago, and when their grandchildren or great-grandchildren noticed, or sometimes assumed, that the pledged land had been their inherited land and tried to redeem it.

Another cause of farmland dispute was the practice of the equal inheritance system. It was widely practiced that all children, regardless of gender, should inherit property equally, and in many households where farmland was the main asset, the farmland became extremely fragmented as the generations passed. In the plains of central Burma, it was not uncommon for a single paddy field to have dozens of owners, and a variety of complex practices developed, such as rotational land use or the use of a paddy field by one person with the promise of paying a certain percentage of the harvest to other co-heirs. In such a situation, there was always the possibility of conflicts of interest among co-heirs who had rights to the same paddy field over how to share the cost of cultivation, as well as harvests, and particularly in the case of pledging the paddy field by one heir without the consents of other co-heirs. In these cases, the battle would be fought between the co-heirs (i.e., between brothers, sisters, and other relatives).

Other types of disputes over farmland also happened frequently, but these two types of disputes were very common in the cases related to mortgaged farmland. Let us examine in the following conflicts how they occurred and how they were resolved. From the statement of claimants, defendants, and witnesses, and decisions given by the judges, the atmo-

Mediation of Disputes over Pledged Land 213

sphere of the rural courts in eighteenth-nineteenth century Burma might be replicated.

The first case is a dispute over the paddy field between two people in 1848 in Dibeyin region in Sagaing District.[3] The land in dispute was a paddy field called Leik-kya-daw, and the claimant was Nga Yan and the defendant was Nga Yin. The original source of the documents is the *parabaik* in the Universities Central Library in Yangon, but here I use the copy in the manuscripts collected by U Toe Hla.[4] Nga Yin, the defendant, was a resident of Byangya village in the Shwebo district and Nga Yan's village was not mentioned but he was said to be a resident of the same area, so he might be also a resident of Byangya or a neighboring village.

Litigation over the paddy field called Leik-kya–daw

Complaint by Nga Yan, the claimant (April 23, 1848)

Nga Yin, a resident of Byangya village, and his father Nga Hmu have been secretly pledging the paddy field called Leik-kya-daw in Magyi Zauk village within the jurisdiction of Dibeyin Myo, which is my ancestral land. When I complained that it was unjust for them to pledge my paddy field in my absence, Nga Yin refuted my claim by saying that my father had pawned it to Nga Myat Tu, Nga Yin's grandfather, before his death, and that he also had a *thet-kayit* of the mortgaging of the paddy field. We had once pledged the paddy field called Kyaw-bin-gon-daw to Nei-myo-kyaw-thu-yaza, who was a father-in-law of Nga Hmu, and Nei-myo-kyaw-thu-yaza seemed to have transferred the claim to Nga Yin and his father, Nga Hmu. The paddy field, Leik-kya-daw had been pledged by us to Mi Yin, so we have a right to redeem it. My parents never pledged Leik-kya-daw paddy field to Nga Myat Tu, Nga Yin's grandfather, and it is unfair that Nga Yin pledged this paddy field to someone else.

Nga Yan accused Nga Yin and his father of pledging the paddy field which Nga Yan had inherited from his ancestors to a third party without any right to do so. Nga Yin's response to this accusation was as follows:

Nga Yin's rebuttal[5] (on the same day)

The paddy field called Leik-kya-daw in Magyi-Zauk village is a piece of

214   Chapter 8

land that I inherited from my grandparents and that my father and I have pledged to a third person. Nga Yan has never, at any time, intervened, claiming that it is his ancestral land. Nga Yan's father, Nga Mit, pledged two paddy fields sown with 5 baskets of seeds[6] called Kyaw-bin-gon and the other sown with 3 baskets seeds called Leik-kya-daw to my grandfather, borrowing 1 *beita* 2 *mu*s 1 *pe* in silver. Out of the total of 8 baskets of seeds sown paddy fields, 5 baskets of seeds sown fields were redeemed by Nei-myo-kyaw-thu-yaza[7] a relative of Nga Yan, paying 50 *kyat*s to my father, Nga Hmu. So my father and I pledged the paddy field sown with 3 baskets of seeds to a third person at the amount of unpaid debt. The disputed paddy fields had been pledged for a long time, but now Nga Yan came out to sue us.[8]

Nga Yin claimed that the paddy field in question, Leik-kya-daw, along with other paddy fields, had been pledged to his grandfather by Nga Yan's father and that, as the Leik-kya-daw paddy field had not been redeemed, Nga Yin and his father pledged the Leik-kya-daw field to others.

A month later, on May 22, the court issued the following judgment to settle the dispute between the two parties. The judge was the deputy governor of Dibeyin Myo, who was called by the long title of Min-nemyo-thiri-yaza-kyaw, who was sent to Dibeyin from the royal government.

Decision on the 5th lazo Nayon 1210 (May 22, 1848)[9]
In the case of Nga Yin vs. Nga Yan over the paddy fields, *thet-kayit* was submitted by Nga Yin for examination and according to the *thet-kayit* two paddy fields, Kyaw-bin-gon, sown with 5 baskets of seeds, and Leik-kya-daw, sown with 3 baskets of seeds, were pledged for 1 *beita* 2 *mu*s 1 *pe* in silver. A relative of Nga Yan, Nei-myo-kyaw-thu-yaza, redeemed Kyaw-bin-gon paddy fields from Nga Hmu, paying 50 *kyat*s of silver. The name of Leik-kya-daw paddy field was also recorded in the *thet-kayit* for the remaining 50 *kyat*s of silver, so the matter can be settled if the people related make an oath and be questioned. Once the matter is settled, there should be no further dispute. Have Nga Yan redeem the Leik-kya-daw paddy field, paying 50 baskets of paddy to Nga Wu to whom Nga Yin and Nga Hmu pledged the said paddy field. The *thet-kayit* held by Nga Yin should also be entrusted to Nga Yan. As for the various court fees, both parties should pay the fees accordingly.

Nga Yan should be the one to withdraw the lawsuit from the Privy Council. From now on, Nga Yin and Nga Yan should not claim that the dispute over the paddy field has not yet been settled, but should let it go and live in peace. Both Nga Yan and Nga Yin agreed, and pickled tea leaves were exchanged and eaten.[10] The tea was served by Nei-myo-Kyaw-zwa.[11]

From the above records, we come to know that the description of *thet-kayit* submitted by Nga Yin to the court confirmed that the paddy field called Leik-kya-daw had been pledged to Nga Yin's grandfather, as Nga Yin had claimed. The court's decision to allow Nga Yan to redeem the land was in accordance with the customary codes, which states that farmland should belong to those who reclaimed it and his descendants, and they had the right to reclaim the pledged land no matter how much time has passed. Therefore, although Nga Yin's statement was accepted, it was not a defeat for Nga Yan, who had sued, and the paddy field could be redeemed by Nga Yan after paying the pledged price. In general, it was customary for the losing party to pay the court fees, but due to the circumstances described above, each party was required to share the court fees according to how much they had spent. Since both Nga Yan and Nga Yin agreed to the judgment, they exchanged the pickled tea leaves and ate, which means that the case was concluded. Nga Yan's determination to get his ancestral paddy field back seems to have been firm, and we also learn that he was in the process of filing an appeal to the Privy Council in case the dispute should not be settled at the Dibeyin Myo court. It was also written in the judgment that the appeal to the Privy Council should have been withdrawn by Nga Yan since it had been settled in the Dibeyin court.

This case is a dispute that arose because the people who had made the land-mortgaging *thet-kayit* had long since passed away, and the descendants of both parties had lost accurate memories over the land. Nga Yin, the accused, had believed that the land was his ancestral land which he had inherited from his father and continued its cultivation, while Nga Yan, the accuser, whose memory over the land had also been lost for a long time, for some reason came to know that the land had been owned by his ancestors, which impelled him to recapture it at any cost. This was the most common pattern of agricultural land disputes, where the descendants

216   Chapter 8

of the two parties claim that it was the ancestral land of their fathers and grandfathers.

Litigation over the paddy fields called Pauk-yin-daw

The next case is an example of a similar process that led to a lawsuit. The paddy fields in dispute were located in the village of Kanni, southwest of Dibeyin, and the person accused was the same Nga Yin who appeared in the previous case. The *para-baik* in which this case was recorded is a separate volume from the manuscript in the previous case,[12] but it seems to have been owned by the same Nga Yin. The person who sued Nga Yin was Nga Kyauk Ke, and the case was fought from May 1856 to July 1857, changing from one court to another. Some parts of the record seem to be missing, but still it gives us an understanding of the reality of litigation in the various courts of the time.

The first record began with the statement of Nga Kyauk Ke. The judge was the donor of pagoda in the Maungtan village.

Statement of Nga Kyaw Ke, the Claimant, 13th lazou Tagu 1218 (May 2, 1856)

As my grandparents and parents both passed away when I was very young, I had no recollection of the paddy fields owned by them, and when I made a research, I found out that there were paddy fields in Kanni village called Pauk-yin-daw, sown with a little over five baskets of seeds, and that it was used and harvested by Nga Yin of Byangya village. I had tried to sue Nga Yin, but when my parents died, I was too young to investigate and interrogate them, so their lawless behavior continued. When I became able to investigate, I found out that the paddy fields called Pauk-yin-daw, sown with 5 baskets of seeds, were the legitimate property of my great-grandparents. When we tried to stop Nga Yin from using the paddy fields, we had to file a lawsuit against him because he was a person who did not say the truth, did not follow the law, and continued to cultivate the paddy fields aggressively.[13]

Nga Yin's rebuttal (on the same day)

After my mother passed away, I have cultivated and harvested the paddy fields as my own, since we had cultivated the paddy fields for many generations. During my father's and grandfather's lifetime, Nga Kyauk Ke's parents did not prevent or sue my father or grandfather. Nga Kyauk Ke suddenly interfered and sued me for using and harvesting the paddy fields called Pauk-yin-daw.

When Nga Kyauk Ke's father was alive, we used and harvested the same paddy fields as we do now. After my grandfather's death, my parents continued to cultivate and harvest land. Since I am a descendant, an heir, I have been cultivating and harvesting in the same way, but the lawless Nga Kyauk Ke, relying on the power of money, has been looking for my faults and talking about me as if I were a bad person. I cultivate and harvest only the paddy fields that rightfully belonged to my grandparents and parents. I did not know about and have not harvested any of the paddy fields sown with 5 baskets seeds and called Pauk-yin-daw that belonged to Nga Kyauk Ke's grandparents and parents.[14]

Both sides claimed that the paddy fields under dispute were ancestral land that they inherited from their grandparents and parents. The stage was set in the court of the Maungtan village and the judge was Maung Min Maung, the donor of the pagoda, and a resident of Maungtan village. Judge Maung Min Maung summarized the arguments of the two parties and then gave the following judgment.

Summary and judgment by the donor of the Pagoda, in Maungtan village, 13th lazan Kason, 1218 (May 7, 1856)

The main points of Nga Kyauk Ke's statement were as follows. The defendant, Nga Yin used and harvested the paddy fields called Pauk-yin-daw, sown with 5 baskets of seeds, which Nga Kyauk Ke inherited from his grandparents. When he found out that Nga Yin was using and harvesting the paddy fields, he filed a complaint. Whether this Nga Kyauk Ke's argument was correct or not must have been examined and clarified since Nga Yin has refused to stop his use and harvest of the said paddy fields.

Nga Kyauk Ke should have to present three witnesses to the court. If the testimonies of the witnesses matched the above summary, Nga Kyauk Ke should get the paddy fields. If not, Nga Kyauk Ke should not get the paddy fields. The loser should pay the fees of the trial. When Maung Min Maung, a resident of Maungtan Village and the donor of

Pagoda, delivered the verdict on the 13th lazan the month of Kason, 1218, Nga Kyauk Ke and Nga Yin agreed to eat pickled tea together. The tea was served by Nga Ka.[15]

By eating the pickled tea leaves, Nga Kyauk Ke and Nga Yin showed their agreement to this ruling, rather than a verdict, which set the course for a solution that required the witnesses and revealed the winner based on their testimony. About two months later, two witnesses for Nga Kyauk Ke appeared, but the courtroom had already been moved from the house of the donor of pagoda to that of the captain of 50 infantry soldiers.[16] The reason for the change of court is unclear, but even if the case was tried in the court of the infantry captain, it does not mean that both or either the claimant and defendant belonged to this unit. This is because litigants could choose the judge who would adjudicate their dispute, and the first criterion was that the person would be someone both parties could put their trust in.

Statement of witness, Nga Yaung: 4th *lazan Wazo* 1218 (July 5, 1856)
The judge put the affidavit in the hands of the witness, Nga Yaung, sixty years old, read it to him three times, explained the two merits in this life and in reincarnation, and then asked him if he was sure that the paddy fields used by Nga Yin, which were sown with 5 baskets of seeds, were the paddy fields that Nga Kyauk Ke had inherited from his grandfather and father.

The witness replied that he knew about the land-mortgage *thet-kayit* that Nga Kyauk Ke's father, U Bo, pledged the paddy fields called Pauk-yin-daw to my father-in-law, Nga Yan Bye and Nga Shwe Mya, but he did not know about the paddy fields itself.[17]

Statement of witness, Nga Myat Hmo: 4th *lazan Wazo* 1218 (July 5, 1856)
The judge put the affidavit in the hands of the witness, Nga Myat Hmo, 70 years old, read the oath three times, explained the two merits in this life and in reincarnation, and then asked him if he was sure that the paddy fields used by Nga Yin, which were sown with 5 baskets of seeds, were the paddy fields that Nga Kyauk Ke had inherited from his grandfather and father.

Nga Myat Hmo replied that he did not know anything about it.[18]

Nga Kyauk Ke called only two witnesses instead of three, and the testimony of one of them seems to be of little use because he said he did not know anything about it. Since none of the testimonies clearly supported Nga Kyauk Ke's argument, the infantry captain delivered the following judgment on the same day.

Judgment by the captain of the infantry 6th *lazan Wazo*, 1218 (July 5, 1856)

In the dispute between Nga Kyauk Ke and Nga Yin over the paddy fields called Pauk-yin-daw in Kanni village, Nga Yin rejected Nga Kyauk Ke's arguments and the case was brought to the court of Maungtan village. The court ruled that Nga Kyauk Ke should call three witnesses to make it clear that the paddy fields in question are the paddy fields that Nga Kyauk Ke inherited from his grandfather and father, and if the testimony of the witnesses matches the claim, Nga Kyauk Ke must acquire the Pauk-yin-daw paddy fields, and if not, Nga Yin should acquire the paddy fields. In accordance with the decision, the witnesses Nga Myat Hmo and Nga Yaung were asked about it after making an oath, but their statement did not agree (with Nga Kyauk Ke's claim). Let Nga Yin acquire the paddy fields called Pauk-yin-daw in accordance with the judgment to which both parties agreed by eating pickled tea given by Nga Min Maung at the Maungtan village court. Nga Kyauk Ke should pay for the expenses incurred by Nga Yin and admit fault. The pickled tea served was not eaten.[19]

The most noteworthy part of this record is the end, 'The pickled tea served was not eaten.' If either the claimants or the defendants were dissatisfied with the judgment, they could express their dissatisfaction by not eating the pickled tea and reject the judgment. In this case, of course, the claimant Nga Kyauk Ke, who lost the case, should have been dissatisfied. If one of the litigants who was dissatisfied with the court decision could deny it, how could they settle the dispute by the courts?

The following record shows that the two parties in the dispute broke the impasse by making the following promise.

220 Chapter 8

Agreement between the two parties, 12th lazan Wazo,
1218 (July 13, 1856)

We have not been able to reach an agreement on the court decision in Ein-oo[20] regarding the lawsuit over the paddy fields called Pauk-yin-daw, and have not been able to resolve the issue. Since different courts and judges make different decisions, we both agreed to go to the court of a person whom both of us regard as appropriate to settle the matter. If Nga Kyauk Ke would not accept the result of the court's decision and continued to fight, he would lose the disputed paddy fields and admit the defeat in court. If Nga Yin would not accept the result and fight further, Nga Yin would transfer the paddy fields to Nga Kyauk Ke, and admit his defeat. The two parties made the agreement and exchanged pickled tea and ate it. The tea was served by Nga Aung.[21]

In other words, a promise was made that both parties would choose a court with a judge whom they could agree with and accept the conclusions reached there, and if either party refused to accept the decision and continued the dispute, he would lose the disputed paddy fields.

Unfortunately, the rest of the story is lost in the records, and the next record is one from five months later in December, when the dispute was brought to the Eastern Court of Justice in the Royal Palace.[22] The judge in the Eastern Court was the *Myo-sa* of Natmauk Myo, and he ordered the collection of related documents from the former courts[23] and then summoned the captain of the infantry, the former judge, and the litigants, Nga Kyauk Ke and Nga Yin, for questioning. He then gave them a written order to hand over to the chief of the Eastern Palace Guard, who was the provincial governor of Dibeyin at that time.[24]

The record of this trial at the Eastern Court in the Royal Palace was very brief, as shown above, and although we do not know the details, it seems that the trial was more about preparing the documentary evidence and giving instructions to the provincial governor concerned, rather than going into the substance of the dispute itself and passing judgment.

A new dispute in the court of Mu-dha village

There is another gap of about six months in the record, and the next record began on June 25, 1857. It seems that there were several court cases during this period, and it had already been made clear that the paddy fields in question were Nga Kyauk Ke's ancestral lands, and that he paid the price settled by a judge and redeemed the paddy fields called Pauk-yin-daw. However, according to the court records of June 1857, Nga Kyauk Ke filed a new lawsuit against a man named Nga Yaung, claiming that the area of paddy he had redeemed was insufficient. Nga Yaung was the grandson of the creditor who first took the Pauk-yin-daw paddy fields as a security and his grandparents pledged the fields to Nga Yin's father. The court that adjudicated the case was the Mu-dha Village Court, but the name of the judge was not mentioned.

Statement of the defendant, Nga Yaung, 5th lazan Wazo 1219 (June 25, 1857)

The four paddy fields of Pauk-yin-daw, which is the ancestral land of Nga Kyauk Ke, had been pledged by my grandparents to Nga Yin's grandfather when my grandparents were in want of money. As it was made clear by the court judgment that the paddy fields were Nga Kyauk Ke's ancestral land, he filed a suit for taking back these paddy fields. According to the court decision, I redeemed the paddy fields from Nga Yin and Nga Kyauk Ke paid for it. When I returned the paddy fields and the land-mortgage *thet-kayit* to Nga Kyauk Ke, he sued me, claiming that the paddy fields returned were not of the same size written in the original land-mortgage *thet-kayit*. It is not that we have used or harvested the four paddy fields written in the first land-mortgage *thet-kayit*. Nga Myat Tu and his grandson Nga Yin, to whom my grandfather pledged the paddy fields have been using and harvesting the paddy fields for a long time, so only Nga Kyauk Ke and Nga Yin can tell if the area of the paddy fields have decreased or not. I have no idea.[25]

From this statement, we come to know that the paddy fields called Pauk-yin-daw, like the ones called Leik-kya-daw in the first case, had been transferred from hand to hand to new creditors. The person who was sued was the grandson of the first creditor. It is clear that not only the passage of time but also the change of creditors in the meantime made the situation even more complicated. Following Nga Yaung, Nga Yin was also questioned and testified as follows.

222   Chapter 8

Interrogation of Nga Yin and his answers on the same day

We all agreed and ate pickled tea leaves with the previous court decision, which ruled that Nga Yaung should give the paddy fields to Nga Kyauk Ke at 15 *kyat*s, after reducing half of the amount which Nga Kyauk Ke's father had borrowed by pledging the paddy fields to Nga Yaung's grandfather.

Nga San Hla, Nga Yaung's grandfather, pledged the paddy fields to my grandfather Nga Myat Tu and borrowed 47 *kyat*s 6 *mu*s. The court ordered me to hand over the paddy fields to Nga Yaung for 37 *kyat*s 6 *mu*s after reducing 10 *kyat*s. Therefore, I handed over the paddy fields with the *thet-kayit* to Nga Yaung for 37 *kyat*s 6 *mu*s, with a reduction of 10 *kyat*s.[26]

On the same day, the judge ordered Nga Yin to submit the judgments of several earlier courts, and ordered Nga Kyauk Ke to submit the land-mortgage *thet-kayit* made between his father and Nga Yaung's grandfather, saying that he would examine them and make a judgment. The judgment in the court of Mu-hda village was delivered on July 9, 1857. The judge first summarized the arguments of each side, and then delivered his judgment with the following admonition.

Judgement at Mu-hda Village Court (July 9, 1857)

Nga Kyauk Ke complained that the paddy fields that Nga Yaung handed over to him were smaller than the original paddy fields. Nga Yaung said that he gave him the paddy fields as described in the *thet-kayit*, but the first *thet-kayit* exchanged between Nga Kyauk Ke's father and his grandfather had been damaged and lost, so a new *thet-kayit* was made in the generation of their fathers. There were witnesses for the new *thet-kayit*, the headman of Byangya village and Nga Yan We. I will interrogate the two witnesses to see if the new *thet-kayit* is genuine or not. And if the new *thet-kayit* is confirmed by them, Nga Kyauk Ke should accept the paddy fields given by Nga Yaung, according to the legal principle that the agreed problem should not arise again in his son's generation, and he should not complain that it should be more spacious. Let it go. If the witness does not make such a statement, then Nga Yaung should compensate Nga Kyauk Ke until the above mentioned four paddy fields called Pauk-yin-daw become four baskets

Mediation of Disputes over Pledged Land   223

of seeds sown. The cost of the trial shall be paid by the loser. Nga Yin should not sue any further for the paddy fields of Pauk-yin-daw. Give it up. Nga Kyauk Ke, Nga Yaung, Nga Yin, all three agreed to this decision and ate the pickled tea.[27]

If the area of the paddy fields written in the new *thet-kayit* would match the area of the paddy fields that Nga Yaung handed over to Nga Kyauk Ke, then the case would be concluded. The record of the disputes over Pauk-yin-daw paddy fields ends here, so it is not clear whether or not the case was finally settled. However, it does reveal the circumstances of the dispute over the paddy fields and shows that the situation made some progress toward reaching a consensus among the parties involved. And it shows us also that a *thet-kayit* was always treated as the most important evidence in the courts of all levels from village to the Privy Council.

In the case of the Pauk-yin-daw paddy fields, the record spans two years and various courts appeared during that time. There were four courtrooms that were known, and several more courts that must have been used during the period of interruption. The judges included Maung Min Maung, the donor of the pagoda, the captain of the infantry called by the title of Thi-za-kyaw-tin, and the magistrate of the Eastern Palace, called as Min-gyi-maha-min-kyaw-tin. The litigants expressed their disagreement with the infantry captain's decision by not eating pickled tea leaves, and the claimant and the defendant agreed to settle the case by selecting a new courtroom agreeable to both of them. The changes in courts are summarized in Table 8.1.

The record of the lawsuit over Pauk-yin-daw paddy fields, where the judges were either the donor of the pagoda (who held no administrative position and was not considered an expert in customary law) or the judge chosen by the consensus of the litigants, shows a different reality from the former Burmese historical narrative that administrative, judicial, and police powers were all concentrated in the hands of the hereditary *myo* rulers, *Myo-thgyis*, in precolonial local society.[28] Were these cases in the Shwebo area only anomalies to the general rule? Shwebo was the birthplace of the Konbaung dynasty and a center of rebellions and uprisings over the throne throughout the eighteenth and nineteenth centuries. It was a politically important region, as it had a relatively large percentage of the *ahmudan* population organized into cavalry, infantry, and other military units

224   Chapter 8

Table 8.1: Court changes in the case of the paddy fields called Pauk-yin-daw

	Location of court	Judge	Judgment
May 1856	Maungtan Village	Donor of the pagoda	Agreed by both parties
July 1856	Thegon Village	Captain of the infantry	Disagreed
Record interruption period			
December 1856	Eastern Court of the Royal Palace	Eastern Palace Magistrate	Agreed
Record interruption period			
June 1857	Mu-hda Village	Unknown	Agreed

directly under the royal control. Against this backdrop, one might think that the local population enjoyed exceptionally great judicial freedom, but the many legal records that remain in various parts of the country show that this was not an exception or deviation at all. According to Thu Nandar, among the 16 judges in the lawsuits related to farmland in Meiktila, there were two village headmen, one *Myo-wun*, three *Myo-thugyi*s, three village elders, four donors of Buddhist institutions, one monk, one relative of a litigant, and one Burmese traditional doctor.[29] In other words, among these judges, the total number of people in charge of local administration and governance was only six, and the other ten people were donors of religious facilities, village elders, a monk, a traditional doctor, and a relative of a litigant.

As we have seen earlier, the behavior of the litigants in these two cases was well within the rules of eighteenth- to nineteenth-century Burmese society, judging from both the codes of customary law and the decrees of the royal government.

Disputes among co-heirs

Another major cause of conflicts over farmland was the presence of many co-heirs on the same land. In the central plains in the nineteenth century, the subdivision of farmland by the equal inheritance system seems to have been quite common. Furnivall, who had served as a land settlement offer in Mingyan District in the early twentieth century, wrote that it was not uncommon for a single farm to have 100 or more co-heirs and that this was probably the case in other provinces as well.[30] The higher the economic value of the land, the more co-heirs crowded onto it, especially in paddy fields with irrigation facilities. In Lower Burma, where the population was small and rice cultivation depended on monsoon rainfall, it was easy to expand cultivated land extensively, but in Upper Burma, where the suitable areas for wet rice cultivation were defined by water catchment and the population was relatively dense, it was not easy to open new paddy fields. As a result, a situation was created in which a large number of heirs had rights to a limited number of paddy fields, and the number of joint heirs tended to increase as the generations passed. When many heirs have rights on the same piece of land, there is a high probability that various disputes will arise.

For this reason, in the case of inheritance of agricultural land, it was often the case that the heirs prepared a document of distribution of the estate according to the form of *thet-kayit*, as shown in the following example, and exchanged pickled tea in front of the witnesses to form an agreement.

> On the 8th lazan, month of Nayon, 1233 (May 26, 1871), the five heirs of Ko Ta Yo, together with their witnesses, gathered in the presence of U Nanda-ma-lar, the monk from Magyi Zauk village, and drew up an agreement in front of him. Mya Pyu and Mya Mwe will inherit the paddy fields in Kongan and Ke-tow, Pyat will inherit the paddy field below the pond in Kongan, and Mya Hla and Mya Lu will inherit the paddy fields in Tan-Bin-Kyun and Chin-ya-chaun.[31]

In the case of joint inheritance of paddy fields that had already been mortgaged, the heirs would often agree in advance on the cost of redemption of the paddy fields and other burdens to be borne by the heirs, and made the agreement in writing.

> The heirs of Bo Aung Ke and Me Hmat San, U Po Tha Yauk, U Shwe Pyi, and U Chit, the donor of a bodhi tree, and Ko Tha Gaung, agreed to the following matters.
>
> 'We will pay equally the redemption price of the paddy fields pledged by our grandparents. In case there are some other debts of our grandparents we will pay equal sum of money to repay the debts. And

226   Chapter 8

if lawsuits may arise we will also bear the judicial fee equally. If any one of us would break this promise, he should pay 60 *kyat*s.' Everyone ate pickled tea leaves and agreed, and the contract was made. U Shwe Min drew up the text. Ko Tan Hsoun wrote it down. Lu Pe served the tea.[32]

We do not know how common it was to make such certificates among the co-heirs. However, as well shown in the example above, where the inherited paddy fields had been pledged to a third person, it was not a custom limited to wealthy families with considerable assets. It is surprising that so many *thet-kayit*s were made by ordinary people, but even if the inherited farmland was only a fraction of a paddy field, they could pledge their rights and borrow money, as shown in the following *thet-kayit*.

On the 6th *lazan*, the month of *Kason*, 1233 (April 24, 1871), Maung Shin and Maung Kyan Bet of Kontaung village asked for an additional loan over our share of the paddy fields in Lepan-gan. Then, Maung Kain lent 12 *kyat*s in silver coins.[33]

Most of the disputes over paddy fields among joint heirs started with a complaint that the inherited share was occupied by other heirs and could not be used. In the background of such disputes, there was often a problem of cost sharing related to the inherited farmland, as shown in the following *thet-kayit*.

On 12th *lazo Thadingyut*, 1227 (October 16, 1865), a dispute arose over the paddy fields called Kanbwe-kandwin and Hinyoke-binai, between Nga Tun Aung and his wife Mi Min Yan on one side and Nga Chit, Nga Shwe Pyi, Nga Shwe Min, and Nga Shwe U the other side. Nga Tun Aung and Mi Min Yan complained that they could not use these paddy fields even though they had paid the costs of the lawsuit regarding the paddy fields, and Nga Chit, Nga Shwe Pyi, Nga Shwe Min and Nga Shwe U claimed that they had an agreement that the couple would pay three-fifths of the total cost of the lawsuit of 15 *kyat*s, and the other four would pay the remaining two-fifths. After hearing their arguments, U Kala, the donor of the monastery of Kyauk-taing village, gave the following ruling. 'The couple should pay two-fifths, and the other four should pay three-fifths. Thus, you should share the cost equally according to the rule of inheritance. Do not make any further complaint. There should be no disputes in the future.'

All agreed and ate pickled tea leaves together. U Kala wrote the draft and Maung Kan Ya from Lei-daung-gan village was a writer.[34]

In the above case, a disagreement over the cost of litigation related to the paddy fields led to a dispute among the heirs, and some refused to allow the use of the paddy fields to other heirs. Similar cases arose in other families.

On the 4th *lazan Tabaung* 1211 (February 14, 1850), Maung Pyu claimed his share of the paddy fields in Youn-gan owned by his grandparents and fought with Maung Shwe Maung, Maung Hmo, Maung Bilu, and Maung Pu. Maung Bilu said, 'Our father told us while he was alive, that if Maung Pyu would want to inherit his share, he should pay 30 *kyat*s spent on the lawsuit regarding irrigation water. So if you will pay the money, I will add you to the list of heirs.' Maung Pyu disagreed and insisted that there was no reason to pay the money and that he should be given his share. The elders of the village of Ainda gathered and gave the following decision. 'A long time has been spent in litigation. There should be no more disputes. Maung Pyu should pay 13 *kyat*s 5 *mu*s out of the 30 *kyat*s to Maung Bilu and the other heirs, and cultivate and harvest the land equally. The heirs all agreed to this decision. The witnesses were U Chit, Maung Tha Min, the village chief, Maung Htwa, the donor of the ordination platform, Maung Tha Be, the donor of pagoda, Maung Shwe Taung, Maung Chit Thu, Maung Hpaw Gyi, and Maung Shwe Maung.[35]

Here again, the dispute arises from a difference of opinion on the sharing of judicial fees in a lawsuit over the irrigation water of inherited paddy fields. It was the principle that both good and bad inherited properties should be borne equally among the heirs, and this practice seems to have been widely accepted. In the above example, one of the heirs, Maung Pyu, claimed that he would not share the burden but would receive his share of the property, while the other heirs contested that he would not be allowed to inherit the paddy field without paying the cost. The dispute could not be resolved among the co-heirs, but was settled by the ruling of several elders in the village, and Maung Pyu also accepted their decision.

228   Chapter 8

In these disputes among co-heirs, the memories of the parties involved were clearer than in the lawsuits between the descendants of the original debtors and creditors. There was a high probability that a *thet-kayit*, if any, was preserved, and the kinship between the parties made it easier for them to talk to each other. I have not yet found any cases where lawsuits among co-heirs were fought for several years, changing the courtroom many times. Such disputes were settled by simple trials and mediation in the homes of elders, monks, village chiefs, donors of pagodas or monasteries, and other respected figures within the local communities.

Economic aspects of a litigation

In the judgments of lawsuits, we often find a phrase, 'If you continue to fight, you will exhaust your time and money.' In a lawsuit in Meiktila held in 1859, an elder who served as a judge said, 'If you two continue to fight each other, in search of justice with more and more details and words, you will spend a lot of money and become exhausted. Stop fighting.' The case was a complicated conflict in which both sides were sued by the other, and many people were involved, including the village headman, the deputy headman, and several other people.[36] The judge of the trial came to a reasonable conclusion for both sides and, at the same time, gave a kind of admonition.

In addition, there are many money-borrowing *thet-kayit*s that state 'I must pay the cost of litigation' as the reason for borrowing money. In the local society, judicial decisions were friendly to the people because anyone could serve as a judge if they were deemed worthy of respect, and even if the court decision was not acceptable to one of the litigants, he could refuse it by not eating pickled tea leaves. However, if litigation should be accompanied by a high cost burden, it must have been an unaffordable solution for the poor.

Nga Yin, who fought as a defendant in two lawsuits over the paddy fields named Leik-kya-daw and Pauk-yin-daw, wrote a memo that listed the detailed expenditure in these lawsuits in a *para-baik* that belonged to him. It shows us how much and what kind of costs were incurred in the litigation. This note, which showed the costs of the Leik-kya-daw paddy fields lawsuit, was dated April 2, 1848, which predates the dispute in the *myo*-level court that started on April 23 and was introduced as the first

Mediation of Disputes over Pledged Land   229

Table 8.2: Nga Yin's expenses in the Leik-kya-daw paddy fields lawsuit, April 2, 1848

Cost breakdown	Amount
1. Payment to *Myo* (court)	2 *kyat* 5 *mu*
To clerk	1 *kyat* 6 *mu*
For making of the covenant	5 *mu*
To the village (court)	7 *mu* 1 *pe*
Cost of court summons	2 *mu* 1 *pe*
Payment to *Saya* Kyaw	5 *mu*
Money given as food expenses	2 *mu* 1 *pe*
Subtotal	6 *kyat* 3 *mu* 1 *pe*
2. *Myo*'s court costs	1 *kyat* 5 *mu*
To the minister's clerk	5 *mu*
To the guarantor Maung Yan Lin	5 *mu*
Lawyers' transportation fee	2 *kyat* 2 *mu* 1 *pe*
To Maung Bo, Manuscript Writer	2 *mu* 1*pe*
To Me Yei for meals	2 *mu* 1*pe*
Weight reduction compensation	8 *mu* 1*pe*
Subtotal	6 *kyat* 1 *mu*
3. To appeal to the Privy Council, the transportation fee for royal attorney	3 *kyat*
Payment to Maung Nga Le	3 *kyat*
Maung Yan Min's meal payment	1 *kyat* 5 *mu*
Pay again to Maung Nga Le	1 *kyat* 5 *mu*
Payment for tea	2 *mu* 1 *pe*
Pay the tea server, U Soe	2 *mu* 1 *pe*
Payment to Maung Yan Shin	1 *kyat* 2 *mu* 1 *pe*
Payment to U Yei	1 *kyat*
Food cost	3 *kyat* 3 *mu*
Weight reduction compensation	8 *mu*
Payment of brokerage for pledging paddy fields	2 *mu* 1 *pe*
Subtotal	16 *kyat* 1*mu*

Source: Toe Hla (ed.), *Konbaung Hkit Leya Thet-kayit pa Luhmu Sibwaye Thamaing* (KLT), Vol. 1, pp. 82–83. Universities Central Library, *para-baik* No. 151107.

Note in original source: money borrowed form Maung Meik, first 10 *kyat*s 1 *ma* 1 *pe* of *ywet-ni*, and again borrowed 2 *kyat*s in 10 *kyat* alloy, and 14 *kyat*s 1 *mat* of 1 *kyat* 3 *mat*s alloy, in total 26 *kyat*s 1 *mat*. 2 *kyat*s for minting coins. Total of 28 *kyat*s 2 *mat* 1 *pe*.

Notes: 1 *kyat* = 4 *mat*s = 10 *mu*s = 20 *pe*s. 'Weight reduction compensation' is thought to have been the compensation for the detrition of metal currencies.

230   Chapter 8

Table 8.3: Nga Yin's expenses in the Pauk-yin-daw paddy fields lawsuit (date unknown, c. December 1856)

Cost details	Amount
Payment to unit commander	1 *mat* (= 2*mu* 1*pe*)
Payment to the government	1 *kyat* 7 *mu* 1 *pe*
Subtotal	2 *kyat*
Payment to the court	7 *mu* 1 *pe*
Payment to court servant	2 *mu* 1 *pe*
Payment for scribe of decision	2 *mu* 1 *pe*
Payment for scribe of oath	2 *mu* 1 *pe*
Subtotal	1 *kyat* 5 *mu*
Gratuity for the wisdom on appeal	5 *mu*
Payment for scribe of decision	2 *mu* 1 *pe*
Copying of decision	2 *mu* 1 *pe*
Payment for tea	2 *mu* 1 *pe*
Subtotal	1 *kyat* 2 *mu* 1 *pe*
Gratuity for the wisdom on appeal for the Mu-hda Village court	5 *mu*
Payment for the scribe of decision	2 *mu* 1 *pe*
Payment for tea	2 *mu* 1 *pe*
Subtotal	1 *kyat*

Source: Toe Hla (ed.), *Konbaung Hkit Leya Thet-kayit pa Luhmu Sibwaye Thamaing* (KLT), Vol. 1, pp. 82–83. Universities Central Library, *para-baik* No. 151107, p. 95.

case in this chapter. Nga Yin had been involved in previous lawsuits at the village and *myo* levels regarding the paddy fields, and had also arranged for an appeal to the Privy Council, for which he had already paid a total of 28 *kyat*s 2 *mat*s 1 *pe*. According to a memo written above the list of expenditure, Nga Yin borrowed the money from a man named Maung Meik. The cost of the subsequent trial must have been similar, for it was written in another *thet-kayit* that Nga Yin and his father Nga Myat Hmo borrowed 14 *kyat*s 1 *mat* from Maung Meik and his wife and pledged two paddy fields on June 6, 1848. In total, Nga Yin had to borrow 42 *kyat*s 3 *mat*s 1 *pe* in order to pay for the judicial case over the Pauk-yin-daw paddy fields.[37] It is difficult to estimate how heavy this amount was for a farmer, but if we compare it to the paddy prices at that time, the highest price per

100 baskets of paddy in 1847 was 50 *kyat*s, and the average was 43 *kyat*s 6 *mu*s 5 *pe*s, and the highest price in 1849 was also 50 *kyat*s.[38] The weight of 100 baskets of paddy was estimated to be about two tons, which was equivalent to the annual yield of a farm household with paddy fields of a medium size. The cost of the lawsuits which Nga Yin paid should have been fairly high.

In addition, as seen in Table 8.3, Nga Yin also left a small list on his expenses in the lawsuit on the Pauk-yin-daw paddy fields. It is unclear what period of time the list covered, but the expenses related to the lawsuits must have been extremely large for Nga Yin, who was sued in both cases and continued to fight against them.

What is more, the two tables show that he had to pay a lot of people related to the lawsuits, such as the judges, courtroom servants, the scribers of documents, lawyers, servers of tea, brokers, advisors, and women who served meals, and so on. Cash payments were made to almost everyone involved in the litigation process for their services, large and small, inflating the cost of the case. In the underdeveloped market, the distance between supply and demand was bridged by real people, and this seems to have been one of the ways in which the circulation of money permeated the society.

On the other hand, as was the case with most lawsuits between joint heirs, it is unlikely that a single lawsuit in a local community would have cost as much as Nga Yin's did. However, even in a village-level court case, it was still necessary to pay fees to the judge, to the scribe, and to the tea server, and other expenses. The fact that the phrase 'I need money to pay for litigation' is often found in the money-lending *thet-kayit*s shows the frequency of lawsuits, as well as the high cost of litigation for people in eighteenth- and nineteenth-century Burma.

The Burmese local courts as a system were extremely flexible, as typified by the fact that any influential and respected person could become a judge. It was a system that people could use without anxiety because it was based on mediation. However, from an economic point of view, apart from the social effect of distributing the fee income to a large number of people, it was not so easy for litigants to use the system because it entailed a huge burden,

232   Chapter 8

sometimes to the extent of giving up their paddy fields. Nevertheless, once a dispute over such an important source of livelihood as paddy fields arose, people would turn to the courts to resolve disputes, fought their cases, and left it to the judges, who were regarded as men of both authority and virtue. The courts of the local community were fully effective in resolving such disputes.

Conclusion

One of the greatest difficulties for those who are studying the precolonial history of Southeast Asia is the availability of relevant documents. This is particularly true for the area of social history. Of course, we can make use of the documents of traders and tourists from the outside world written in Chinese, Indo-European, and Middle Eastern languages. These records provide important clues to understanding the diverse perspectives of Southeast Asia as seen by people from different cultures. Records written in local language have also been preserved in the form of royal chronicles, collections of imperial decrees, and customary law. We have also a variety of documents written by the successive kings, the great generals, high priests, and outstanding court poets and entertainers in various fields. However, the question remains as to whether or not there is such a thing as an archive of the daily lives and activities of ordinary people. For those wishing to portray a history that reaches into the daily lives, behaviors, and minds of ordinary people of Southeast Asia, the past records are far from sufficient.

It was exciting to learn that the common people in early modern Burma wrote down some important matters of their daily life, such as transactions, law suits, inheritance agreements, indigenous medicines, and so on, in *para-baik*s, which were used widely among commoners in the eighteenth and nineteenth centuries. Such records are also found in *pe-sa*s, dried palm leaves, but not so frequently as in *para-baik*s.

The *thet-kayit* documents used as the main source for this book are part of the records of many people who have never appeared under their own names in history, and they contain many important promises that directly relate to their daily lives. I highly appreciate the fortune of having been able to access these documents, since it has been a hidden ambition of this book to unveil a new, hitherto unwritten, history of early modern Burma.

As mentioned in the introduction, two main issues are discussed in this book.

(1) Based on the analysis of the money-lending contracts, which were the most numerous among the contracts exchanged between private individuals, I have tried to identify the socioeconomic changes observed in

every corner of the society during the eighteenth and nineteenth centuries, and to articulate their historical significance.

(2) In early modern Burma, where it was still an official principle that all the resources of the kingdom belonged to the king, the private individuals wrote contracts in which they freely pledged land and people, the kingdom's most important resources, as collateral for debts. Nonetheless, this type of contractual document was widely accepted in the society, and there appears to have been no hindrance in the parties to the contract complying with its contents. It was neither necessary to submit the deeds to the central government, or the local rulers, nor to obtain their approval. Then, why was it that the promises made between private individuals were socially recognized as a contract, when they were compiled in the form of a *thet-kayit*, and both parties were encouraged to fulfill their obligations in the contract? By what system and force was it possible to guarantee the fruits of the contract?

The second issue was also an attempt to be free of the shortsighted viewpoint to which economic historians are easily subjected. The tendency to project modernity into the past, and to look to the past as the source of economic development or social problems, has prevented us seeing and accepting the past as it was. Or is it that the desire to emphasize Southeast Asia's contemporariness with the rest of the world—in order to counter the colonialism and Orientalism that have made the whole of Southeast Asia a lagging economic and social entity—has ultimately clouded our view of the region? After retirement from the university, I could spare more time to spend reading the manuscripts, as well as books on the methods of historiography. As a result, I became more interested in characterizing the society through careful dialogue with such a period and society under study: 'Going back through historical time is not about projecting the past onto the present and tracing its genesis, but it is about seeing the past as a different culture.'[1] Also, we learn from the view that 'the shared social perceptions of the people of that time are what make a society—the social order that binds and sustains us is the product of their joint subjectivity.'[2]

Arguments and summaries have already been presented at the end of each chapter, so I will not repeat them here, but would like to review some of the issues in this book that might bring some insights to our conventional historical knowledge about early modern Burma.

Conclusion   235

In the first part, given the fact that in Burma in the eighteenth and nineteenth centuries, money-lending contracts were written extensively in almost all areas of the central plains, involving people of all social strata, and that the debt secured by farmland played a major role among them, we assume the basic factors that led to the emergence of this situation are firstly the 'climate'.[3] The word 'climate' implies the nature transformed by human effort over a long period of time in contrast to the original nature. This concept of climate is one of the keys to show the change taking place in the arid central plains, where the production of paddy, the staple crop for the people, was not possible before the construction of large-scale irrigation networks. After the completion of irrigation networks, the arid central plains became the grain-basket for the kingdom.

These irrigation networks had been constructed and maintained by the successive kings' governments from ancient times. However, there was an upper limit to the supply of agricultural land that could be watered by irrigation, which created the conditions for land to become a scarce commodity. In other words, irrigation systems created disparity in terms of land productivity, thus land value. In addition, these irrigation networks could not prevent food shortages or famine during extreme droughts. The great famine that struck in the second decade of the nineteenth century quickly increased the number of debt contracts and provided the backdrop for the widespread emergence of debt secured by farmland mortgage.

The next background reason for the major socioeconomic change in this period can be found in foreign relations and their upheaval. It is not exaggerating to say that the kings of the early Konbaung period spent much of their time in foreign warfare, advancing their armies to the west against Manipur, Cachar, and Assam, and to the east against Vientiane, Chiang Mai, and Ayutthaya, taking thousands of prisoners of war from these areas. A large number of those war captives were organized into the *ahmudan* groups and given irrigated farmland to encourage their settlement. However, after the first major defeat in the war against Siam in 1785, the road to the east was closed, and after the First Anglo-Burmese War, the kingdom not only lost two coastal provinces of Arakan and Tenasserim, but also the suzerainty over Manipur, Cachar, and Assam in northeast India. And in the Second Anglo-Burmese War, the kingdom lost the whole of Lower Burma and became landlocked. These results not only made it impossible to supplement the population in the form of prisoners of war, but also disrupted the economic cycle of interregional trade within the kingdom and destroyed the system of self-sufficiency in necessities. As a result, even in Burma, where there was relatively little necessity to seek trade with other countries, except for modern weapons, arms, and ammunition, trade with other countries became indispensable to the economy. This change in Burma's position in foreign warfare and foreign trade was a key factor in the penetration of the money economy into every corner of local society.

However, the currency situation in the Konbaung era was extremely complex, with coins of different qualities and weights in circulation at the same time. The fact that several currencies of different qualities were in use within a single money-lending contract did not pose a significant hindrance, as there were numerous assayers and weighers all the way down to the village level who mediated the circulation of the different currencies. Reforms aimed at unifying the currency were carried out twice during the Konbaung era, with the 1797 reform being a failure and the 1865 reform being a success. The reason why those two reforms achieved opposite results is often attributed to the king's personal qualities and character in conventional studies. This book argues that the failure of the reforms at the end of the eighteenth century is attributed to the quiet resistance to the king's coins by assayers and weighers, as well as private coin minters. It would not be a surprise that they refused the acceptance of the king's coins at marketplaces and thus tried to stop the circulation of the standardized coins.

The success of the monetary reform by King Mindon's government is attributed to the difficult political and economic situation after the defeat of the Second Anglo-Burmese War, which interrupted the interregional circulation of resources within the kingdom. The royal government was forced to purchase rice and other necessities from Lower Burma in severe competition with foreign traders and merchants. The success in the monetary reform was achieved, ironically, by facilitating trade by issuing a currency that was almost identical in purity and weight to the British India rupee coin.

In Parts II and III, devoted to the analysis of the money-lending documents, several arguments are made based on the findings from the documents. First, it was found that less than 10% of all the money-lending documents in the Konbaung period contained debt-slave contracts, and that these contracts remained only in the areas around the royal capital and in the main irrigated rice-producing areas where the powerful local ruling families had accumulated vast lands through the money-lending business. In the first and the second Taungoo periods, lots of *ahmudan* people became debt-slaves of influential people in order to escape the excessive claims of the king (service, conscription, and taxation) when the fate of the dynasty was declining. Such phenomena almost disappeared in the Konbaung period, and it was more common to see people who had borrowed too much money and rice to repay and became debt-slaves as a last resort. The number of debt-slaves declined during the Konbaung period, and their importance in history was also diminishing. However, the demand for debt-slaves still existed among influential people in the vicinity of the capital or the wealthy families in the agricultural center, and for those who lacked food and a livelihood, debt-slavery was an option to guarantee food and shelter, even if they were bound by the constraints of labor.

Next, an analysis of pledged farmland that became the mainstay of collateral on behalf of humans reveals that in certain localities, intense liquidation of farmland, mostly of paddy fields, was underway through the medium of debt. In Byangya, a village in the Shwebo region, between 1776 and 1843, not only the ancestral private land known as *bo-ba-baing*, but also the granted land to the *ahmudan* people, and even monastery land, was used as collateral for loans, and virtually all the land was treated as private land. Moreover, it was not unusual to see the final sale of farmland after the resale of money-lending contracts or the accumulation of heavy debts. However, if we look at the central plains as a whole, the progression from pawning to the final sale of farmland, seen in Byangya, was a phenomenon found in a limited area, and even if debt was accumulated on the same farmland, it often did not lead to the sale of the land. In most areas, the number of land-selling contracts is very small, and the final sale of farmland was avoided as much as possible because of the perception that farmland was tied forever to those who reclaimed the land and their descendants. This perception remained strong in society up to the Konbaung period and customary law texts used in those days also supported this perception as a fundamental code which regulated the relation between cultivators and land.

238 Money-lending Contracts in Konbaung Burma

In Part IV, on the basis of the fact that in Konbaung Burma the relations through contractual transactions over economic resources permeated all social strata, our study examines how a certificate written in the form of a *thet-kayit* could function as a binding contract in society. First, we paid attention to the fact that many people other than the parties to the contract were listed in the testimonies. Among them, assayers, weighers, drafters, and scribes were indispensable for the conclusion of the transaction from a technical and professional standpoint. However, the most important people present at the transaction were thought to be witnesses, who played a certain role in binding contracting parties to fulfill the contract. The most popular people asked to stand as witnesses were donors of public property, such as Buddhist institutions, pilgrim lodgings, ponds, and wells, known by the honorific title of *daga*, whose number far exceeded that of local chiefs and officials. Witnesses required were those who were influential to the extent that the parties to the contract felt obliged to obey their words, and whose words and deeds were respected by the community. Their power was something different from the administrative authority, status hierarchy, or mere economic power.

Looking at the way in which the dispute resolution system worked when disputes arose between contracting parties, it was confirmed that the most important evidence required to be submitted to the courts at all levels, from the village to the royal capital, was the *thet-kayit*, and the courts heard cases on the basis of the contents of *thet-kayit* documents. The tribunal had thus given legal validity to the agreement between private parties compiled in the form of a *thet-kayit*, giving it the character of a contract that went beyond mere promises.

The royal government, which seemed to claim ultimate ownership over all the resources of the kingdom, was, in fact, unlikely to intervene or place restrictions on the financial activities of these private individuals, even on transactions of pledging people or land. There were instances of limited interventions, such as the temporary postponement of claims for repayment by creditors for a certain period of time in cases such as wartime, where the accumulated debt problem had developed into a serious social problem (e.g., a problem that interfered with the ability of *ahmudan*s to carry out their duties). There were no instances where the Crown denied creditors' claims or banned the transactions themselves. Rather, both the

Conclusion 239

king and the local rulers were considered to be creditors or debtors, acting under the same rules.

Furthermore, specific examples of lawsuits over farmland revealed the unique method of resolving civil lawsuits at that time. One of the causes of farmland disputes was the contradiction between the traditional concept of linking farmland to those who reclaimed the land and their descendants and the flow of farmland brought about by the rapid increase in debt secured by farmland. The customary law texts clearly stated that if a landowner pledged his *bo-ba-baing* land (ancestral land) for money, the privilege of repossession of the land was permanently in place for the former owner and his descendants. It was typical of this type of dispute that both parties to the original contract had long since passed away, and lawsuits arose in the generation of grandchildren or even of great-grandchildren, with the descendants of one party claiming that the land was their ancestral land and the descendants of the other claiming that the land was pledged by their ancestors, and thus they had rights to redeem it. Another cause of farmland disputes was the practice of equal share inheritance, whereby all children, male and female, inherited property in equal shares over the generations, which led to extreme fragmentation of farmland to the point where it could not be cultivated. Complex practices developed, such as the rotation of heirs to use the land in turn, or the cultivation of the land by one person and the distribution of a certain percentage of the harvest to the other heirs, but there was always the possibility of conflicts of interest between co-heirs over the use of the land or mortgaging the land.

The specific examples of how these lawsuits over farmland were resolved reveal the unique nature of the Burmese civil courts in the Konbaung period. The judicial system at that time, which dealt with disputes between people, was flexible and amorphous. One of the most striking features of the system was that anyone could be the judge of the court if both litigants agreed. Another striking point was that if either party disagreed with the judgment handed down by the court, the court would not be able to make a decision.[4] Disagreement could be shown in the form of not eating the pickled tea leaves served after judgment, as shown in one case introduced in the previous chapter in which the person who lost the case did not eat the pickled tea leaves. As a result, both litigants began to exchange ideas and came to an agreement in which the case was retried under a new judge. The way in which these trials were conducted shows that they were

240 Money-lending Contracts in Konbaung Burma

based on the principles and procedures completely different from those introduced in the colonial period.

A *thet-kayit* was required to be presented in all law courts as the most important evidence, but sometimes it had been lost over the years. In such case, courts at all levels usually mobilized the available documents, such as the testimony of the parties involved, previous court records, and so on, and let both plaintiffs and defendants fully state their own claims, encouraged them to reach a consensus that both sides could agree on, and then reached a decision in the form of mediation to settle the case. If either party did not eat the pickled tea leaves, the judgment became meaningless, so this kind of approach seems to have been essential. In this way, what made a *thet-kayit* a contract was the traditional Burmese law texts, which were also a collection of customs, and the ideas based on them, as well as the nature of the courts, which were nurtured in a culture and customs that differed from what we call 'modernity'.[5]

This is the conclusion of this book, and by recovering some of the perspectives that were missing from the previous studies, including my own, I hope that we can set forth a new vision on the early modern period of Southeast Asia.

I have not discussed the definition of the early modern period, although it is in the subtitle of this book, 'Another interpretation of an early modern society in Southeast Asia'. This is simply because I do not have my own theory of modernity, and 'the early modern period' is used as a synonym for the earlier part of the broad framework of modernity. No matter what region or kingdom we study, I share the same view with leading scholars that the changes of the early modern period can only be grasped in the context of world history, not in the confines of a single region or country.

Therefore, I do not propose any new arguments on the issue of periodization, but have consciously attempted in this book to shift the perspective of the early modern era as a time of the emergence of the phenomena that characterize modernity, the integration of the nation-state sphere, and the penetration of the monetary economy into every corner of society. The early modern era was not simply a time to prepare for the modern era, but an era in which the culture, in the broadest sense of the word, that had been nurtured by each region, including its own climate and customs, encompassed new changes, translated them, and moved them in a way that society could accommodate. It is from this perspective that

I refer to the Konbaung period (1752–1885) as the early modern period of Burma in this book.

These customs and cultures do not always become obsolete and disappear in the midst of change, but sometimes they could be sustained by retaining their vitality and becoming a feature of a society. I spent two years in Burma in the mid-1970s during the so-called Burmese Way to Socialism era, and could not help but marvel at the ubiquity of *pwe-sa*s, or intermediaries, who were everywhere, linking supply and demand, through the stagnation and confusion of the official distribution network of goods and services. Despite the failure of the new system designed by modern socialist ideology, the old system of connecting people to people and things to things was active in every corner of society. Although this may be a small personal observation, I believe that observing the customs and culture that permeate people's behavior and consciousness will help us to improve our understanding of the societies of Southeast Asia as they exist today.

Notes

Introduction

1. Toe Hla, 'Money-lending and contractual "thet-kayit": A socio-economic pattern of the later Kon-baung period, 1819–1885', PhD dissertation submitted to Northern Illinois University, 1987, p. 5.

2. In Burma, as in many other Asian countries, the date is written from top to bottom, year–month–day.

3. Some *para-baik*s are said to have been made of gold, silver, copper, brass, and other metals, or even leather, without paper as a raw material. U Tin, who served as a minister in the Konbaung dynasty, said that he had seen gold and silver *para-baik*s made as treasures for pagodas but had never seen brass and leather *para-baik*s. U Tin, *The Royal Administration of Burma*, translated by Euan Bagshawe, Bangkok: Ava Publishing House, 2001, p. 624.

4. U Thaw Kaung, 'Myanmar traditional manuscripts and their preservation and conservation', *Myanmar Historical Research Journal*, No. 1, November 1995, pp. 241–273. U Thaw Kaung, 'Unearthed story of Myanmar history: Preserve palm-leaves in digital format', lecture given at Fukuoka Public Forum, September 17, 2005.

5. A *sit-tan* was a kind of revenue inquest, which local or regimental rulers had to submit to the royal government and which contained the ruler's name, territories or groups under their jurisdiction, amounts of royal revenue, etc.

6. However, in Meiktila, a few land-mortgage *thet-kayit*s written in the 1920s and 1930s were found. They remained valid as contracts for a long period of time even under British rule. In Lower Burma, the forefront of the colonial export-led economy, Burmese cultivators who mortgaged their reclaimed land borrowed money mostly from members of the Indian money-lending caste, Chettiar, who migrated from the east coast of India. They used the official paper for money-lending contracts, but it is surprising that the format of making contracts was very similar to that of *thet-kayit*s.

7. Toe Hla, *Konbaung Hkit Kye-let Luhmu Sibwa Bawa (1762–1885)*, Yangon: Myanmar Historical Commission, 2004, p. 13. As for Burmese villages today, based on his extensive field surveys, Takahashi Akio pointed out that there is no longer such a close relationship between the villagers and monasteries. Villagers choose monasteries to attend individually, and the notion of the village monastery itself has almost disappeared. Takahashi Akio, *Myanmar, The Nation and the People*, Akashi Shoten, 2012.

8. Toe Hla, '*BI-DA-KAT-TAIKS*: A brief survey', in Saito Teruko & U Thaw Kaung (eds.), *Enriching the Past, Preservation, Conservation and Study of Myanmar Manuscripts*, Tokyo University of Foreign Studies, CEO Project, 2006, pp. 88–89.

9. Famous individual *bidakat-taik* include the *bidakat-taik* of Kinwun Mingyi, who was a minister during the reign of King Mindon and King Thibaw, and the *bidakat-taik* of U Tin, the author of *Governance of Myanmar Kings* (Yangon: Ministry of Culture, 1962 reprint), who served as a clerk in the palace during the reign of the aforementioned kings.

10. As for the information of archives related to *para-baik* and *pe-sa*, see Saito Teruko, 'A brief history of the Burmese archives: From *bidakat-taik* to the archives', *Journal of Historical Studies*, No. 789, June 2004, pp. 13–23.

11. For other examples, see Ito Toshikatsu, 'Sale of mortgaged local domain–cases of small and medium *thugyis* in the early Konbaung period', *Journal of Oriental Studies* (Toyo Gakuhou), Vol. 82, No. 2, 2000, pp. 97–129.

12. The supervisor of the irrigation system (*Myaung Gaung*) was given the right to collect water rates charged to the beneficiary farmers of the canal and to obtain fees from it as his income. The custodian of the pier was also given the right to collect duties and tolls, and could take a commission from these.

13. A *myo-sa* is one who has been granted the right by the king to receive a certain amount of tax from the said *myo*. *Myo-sa* is sometimes translated as lord, but he has no authority over the governance of that *myo*.

14. Toe Hla, 'Konbaung Hkit Leya Thet-kayit pa Luhmu Sibwaye Thamaing: Pyin-nya-ye Tekkato Thamain Htana i Thutei Thana Siman-ken (1978–81) atwe Tin-thwin-tho Kyan', typescript, 1978 (hereafter, KLT).

15. KLT, Vol. 1, 1977–78, Vol. 2, 1978–79.

16. Ohno Toru, 'Financial forms of rural Burma in the 18th and 19th centuries', *Ajia-Keizai*, Vol. 16, No. 5, 1975, pp. 69–77.

17. Toe Hla, 1987.

18. This trend is not only due to the academic style of prominent historians such as Dr. Than Tun and Dr. Yi Yi, who received their degrees in the United Kingdom and led Burmese historiography in the post-independence period, but also to the political interventions in the disciplines that followed during the Burmese Socialism Period of 1962–88, especially in history. There was certainly an aspect of scholarship that was forced to defend itself with the claim that it was 'objective fact' rather than the historian's interpretation under the censorship of the military government.

19. John Nisbet, *Burma under British Rule and Before*, 2 vols, Westminster: Archibald Constable & Co. Ltd, 1901.

20. H. Fielding Hall, *The Soul of a People*, London: Macmillan & Co. Ltd, 1899, p. 116.

21. V. Lieberman, *Burmese Administrative Cycles: Anarchy and Conquest, c. 1580–1760*, Princeton: Princeton University Press, 1984, pp. 92–96.

Notes   245

22. Thu Nandar, 'Characteristics of land-mortgage contracts in the 18th–19th century Myanmar society: An analysis based on *thet-kayit* manuscript', PhD dissertation submitted to Tokyo University of Foreign Studies, 2008.

23. Kinshichi Norio was very instructive for me in recognizing the shortcomings of historians who are inclined to look back at the past with their modern viewpoint. In our high school days, Henrique the Navigator was introduced in textbooks of world history as a pioneer who opened the Age of Discovery, embodying the spirit of modernity. But in reality, he fought against Islam in the spirit of crusade and was driven into foreign lands, unintentionally opening a door to the 'modern' era. Moreover, as early as the 1930s, the legends created about him and his deification had been explicitly rejected by Portuguese historians. Kinshichi Norio, *Prince Henrique, the Navigator, the Pioneer of the Age of Discovery*, Tosui Shobo, 2004.

Chapter 1

1. Karl Polanyi, *Great Transformation: Formation of Market Society and Its Collapse*, translated by Yoshizawa Hidenari et al., Toyo Keizai, 1975, pp. 68–69.

2. Tsubouchi Yoshihiro, *Tonan Ajia Jinko-Minzoku-shi*, Keiso Shobo, 1986.

3. B. R. Mitchell, *International Historical Statistics* (3rd ed.), Macmillan, 1998.

4. Saito Teruko, *Rural Societies in Southeast Asia* (in Japanese), Yamakawa Shuppan, 2008, pp. 23–24.

5. The dynasty was built by Prince Nyaung Yang, son of the third king of the Taungoo dynasty, Bain Naung. He chose Ava in Upper Burma as the royal capital. The new dynasty is also called the Second Taungoo Dynasty or Restored Taungoo Dynasty.

6. A few *thet-kayit*s were found in the Yaw region, located at the foot of the Arakan Mountains, and in Taungyi in the Shan Plateau.

7. In the Museum of Pyi, located on the border of Upper Burma and Lower Burma, some land-mortgage *thet-kayit*s were found, but these contracts were written in the Salin region. No contracts were written in Pyi, nor in southern downstream regions.

8. J. S. Furnivall and W. S. Morrison, *Burma Gazetteer, Syriam District*, Rangoon: Superintendent, Govt. Printing and Stationery, 1963 (reprint), p. 71.

9. Given the presence of Pyu remains and numerous Pyu inscriptions in the Kyaukse region, it is highly likely that some of the irrigation facilities date back to the Pyu period.

10. Ito Toshikatsu, 'History of the irrigation system of the Meiktila Lake from the ancient time to the Konbaung period', *Toho Gakuhou* (*Journal of Oriental Studies*), No. 20, 1980, pp. 121–173. Thu Nandar, 'Characteristics of land-mortgage contracts in the 18th–19th century Myanmar society: An analysis

246 Money-lending Contracts in Konbaung Burma

based on *thet-kayit* manuscript', PhD dissertation submitted to Tokyo University of Foreign Studies, 2008, p. 14. Michael Aung-Thwin, *Irrigation in the Heartland of Burma*, Northern Illinois University, Occasional Paper No. 15, 1990, p. 29.

11. In Region III, there were some rain-fed paddy fields, as well as paddy fields irrigated by small-scale irrigation facilities managed by the canal heads and cultivators. In the mountainous areas of the Shan, Kachin, and Chindwin regions, there are also many small weirs and canals to lead water to paddy fields. In the central plains there was one variety of rice called *mayin* which grew without irrigation facilities, but it was planted near ponds and lakes. As the yields of *mayin* were very low, the main form of paddy production in Upper Burma was irrigated rice culture.

12. Even in the colonial period, and the period after independence in 1948, the works of the government irrigation department concentrated on the maintenance and repair of existing facilities and partial extension of canals.

13. F. N. Trager and W. J. Koenig introduced *sit-tan*s to the outer world for the first time. F. N. Trager and W. J. Koenig, *Burmese Sit-tans 1764–1826: Records of Rural Life and Administration*, University of Arizona Press, 1979. In Japan, studies using *sit-tan* documents have been conducted by Ito Toshikatsu and Iwaki Takahiro. For a discussion on the two groups in the society at this time, the *ahmudan* and the *athi*, see note 18 of this chapter.

14. Yi Yi, 'Konbaung hkit sit-tan-mya', *JBRS*, Vol. 49, No. 1, 1966, p. 71.

15. According to U Tin, three kings (namely, Tharawadi, Pagan, and Mindon) also conducted *sit-tan*s. However, this cannot be ascertained, as no data or records have yet been discovered. U Tin, *Myanma Min Ok-chok-pon Sadan* (Governance of Myanmar kings), Vol. II, Yangon: Ministry of Culture, 1962 (reprint), p. 108 (hereafter, *MMOS*).

16. Regarding this *sit-tan*, Ito says that, 'soon after his ascension to the throne, [the king] ordered the local lords to submit the interrogation reports. However, the reports sent to him were fraudulent and erroneous, so in 1785, he ordered them to submit the correct reports again.' Ito Toshikatsu, 'Introduction of *thathameida* tax by the Mandalay dynasty and *ahmudan*—cases in Shwebo District' (in Japanese), in T. Ito (ed.), *Studies of the Establishment of Monopolistic Resources Control by the State in the 19th Century Myanmar*, report to the Kaken Project, Japan Society for the Promotion of Science, 2008, p. 9. H. Burney also wrote that the king relieved many local officials of their posts and put some of them to death for their inaccurate or erroneous reports and that the king also sent spies to the various provinces to get an accurate number of households. However, it is likely that Burney's stay in Ava was more than a decade after Bodawhpaya's death, and therefore it was not his actual sighting but indirect information from Burmese court officials. Regardless, it is clear that Bodawhpaya had a strong zeal to ascertain the actual situation of the local

society by the *sit-tan* survey. H. Burney, 'On the population of the Burman Empire', *JBRS*, Vol. 31, No. 1, 1941 (reprint), p. 24.

17. This includes both inland plains and the downstream regions and the coastal delta. The English called the area Burma Proper, and later, under colonial rule, Burma Proper was placed under the direct control of the British Indian government.

18. The *ahmudan* was a hierarchy that was obliged to perform hereditary services to the Crown, and among them the soldier status of cavalry, riflemen, engineers, king's guard, and sailors was prominent. However, a variety of other occupational groups, such as court cooks, entertainers, carpenters, and potters, were included in the *ahmudan* status. They were rewarded for their services to the Crown with a grant of a certain area of land in proportion to their duties. The *athi*, on the other hand, was a hierarchy that did not have such hereditary functions and was, in principle, charged only with taxation. However, they were conscripted into the war effort and were commissioned for construction work under the royal authority. There was no particular distinction between the *ahmudan* and *athi* in terms of status.

19. Than Tun, *The Royal Orders of Burma, A.D. 1598–1885*, Kyoto: The Center for Southeast Asian Studies, Kyoto University (hereafter, *ROB*), Vol. IV, pp. xxvii–xxviii, xxiv. The construction of the Mingun pagoda never reached completion.

20. Toe Hla, *Konbaung Shwe-pyi*, Yangon: Moe Kyi Press, 1993, p. 142.

21. Htun Yee (ed.), *Konbaung hkit Sayin Padeitha, Collection of Sayin* (various lists of Myanmar affairs in the Konbaung period), Toyohashi: Aichi University, 2003.

22. William J. Koenig, *The Burmese Polity, 1752–1819: Politics and Administration, and Social Organization in the Early Kon-baung Period*, Center for South and Southeast Asian Studies, The University of Michigan, 1990, Appendix 2, pp. 245–247.

23. Micheal Aung-Thwin, 1990, op.cit.

24. V. Lieberman, *Burmese Administrative Cycles: Anarchy and Conquest, c. 1580–1760*, Princeton University Press, 1984, p. 20.

25. Maung Baw, *Konbaung Hkit Sittan* (2nd ed.), Yangon: Aman-htit Sape, 2009, p. 75.

26. There are different opinions as for the period of the great famine. However, from the price of paddy, as the price jumped during 1810–13 and calmed down in 1816, we can assume that the great famine subsided at the latest in 1816. The memories of the great famine were handed down generation to generation even at the end of the nineteenth century in Meiktila, Mingyan, and Magwe, where thousands of people died of hunger. J. G. Scott and J. P. Hardiman, *Gazetteer of Upper Burma and the Shan States*, Rangoon: Government Printing, Burma, Part I, Vol. II, 1900, p. 362 (hereafter, GUBSS).

27. Government of Burma, *Report on the Famine in Burma, 1896–7*, Rangoon: Superintendent Govt. Printing, 1898, p. 28.

28. Under the British administration after 1886, several serious food crises occurred in 1889–90, 1891–92, 1895–96, and 1899–1900 in Upper Burma. Government of Burma, *Report on the Settlement Operations in the Magwe District, Season 1897–1903*, Rangoon: Superintendent, Government Printing, 1903, pp. 22–23. Government of Burma, *Report on the Settlement Operations in the Minbu District, Season 1893–97*, Rangoon: Superintendent, Government Printing, 1900, p. 12. Michael Adas, *The Burma Delta: Economic Development and Social Change on the Rice Frontier, 1852–1941*, University of Wisconsin Press, 1974, p. 46.

29. The instructions for fire prevention were as follows. (1) Check the fireplace several times in the day and a few more times at night. (2) Keep five to ten bamboo stakes with one end sharpened, ready on a rack. (3) Pots with full water must be kept on a shelf. (4) Cook food in a pit of 4.5 feet square, in the given time; 5:00 a.m. to 7:00 a.m. and 3:30 p.m. to 5:30 p.m. (5) Use a feather to check the fireplace at non-cooking time and punish the housewife if the feather singes. (6) Seize the smoking pipe when a man is found smoking on the road. (7) Men on fire duty must check points where fire could have started, at least five times a day. (8) Do not allow anyone go out and wander around after 9 p.m., or if he has some important business to attend to after the forbidden hour, let him go by carrying a lamp. *ROB*, Vol. III, pp. 49–50, 204.

30. Royal Orders issued on February 6, 1783; January 28, 1785. *ROB*, Vol. IV, pp. 244, 413. Royal Order issued on January 27, 1788. *ROB*, Vol. V, p. 357.

31. Royal Orders issued on February 3, February 8, and February 13 in 1788. *ROB*, Vol. V, pp. 364, 367, 371.

32. *KBZ*, Vol. III, p. 232.

33. *KBZ*, Vol. III, p. 232.

34. *KBZ*, Vol. III, p. 229.

35. *KBZ*, Vol. III, p. 392.

36. *ROB*, Vol. IV, p. 244 (1788). *KBZ*, Vol. III, p. 232 (1810).

37. The punishment was expressed as 'Put under a log and left in the sun.' However, a royal pardon was given quickly, usually on the same day. *ROB*, Vol. V, p. 853; Vol. VI, pp. 651, 706.

38. The only defensive war in the period was the war against the Chinese army sent by Emperor Qianlong during the time 1765–69, when the Chinese army launched attacks four times on the northern Shan Plateau. Burma succeeded in driving the army back to China in all battles.

39. *ROB*, Vol. III, p. 54.

40. In Burmese, Manipur is known as Kathe, Assam as Arthan, and Cachar as Ekkapa.

41. Michael Symes, *An Account of an Embassy to the Kingdom of Ava, in the Year 1795*, Vol. II, Edinburgh, 1827, pp. 57–58. Henry Yule, *A Narrative of the Mission to the Court of Ava in 1855*, Kuala Lumpur: Oxford University Press, 1968, pp. 153–156.

42. *ROB*, Vol. X, p. 194.

43. Yi Yi Hkin, *Yodaya Naing Mawgun (by Letwe Nawyahta)*, Yangon: Htun-Hpaun Dei-shin-Ban Sape Komati, 2011, p. 194.

44. Burmese royal chronicles and history books cited the figure given by Letwe Nawyahta as it was, but Letwe Nawyahta himself wrote another figure in the same poetry that the Burmese army took more than 100,000 war captives from Vientiane and Ayutthaya to Burma. So it is not easy to judge which figure is more reliable. See *KBZ*, Vol. I, p. 415. U Sein Lwin Lay, *Myanma Sit Hmat-tan-mya hnit Thaningabyuha-mya*, Yangon: Khit-hmi Sape Taik, 1968, p. 121.

45. Prince Damrong Rajanubhab, *Our Wars with the Burmese: Thai-Burmese Conflict 1539–1767*, Bangkok: White Lotus, 2001 (reprint), p. 356.

46. Maung Baw, 2009, p. 118.

47. Viewed from Siam side, the last wars against Burma seem to be the unsuccessful attacks on Kyaington in the Shan Plateau in 1849 and in 1852 that were commanded by King Rama III and Rama IV, respectively. See Ishii Yoneo and Iijima Akiko, *The King and I, Another Story* (in Japanese), Mekong Publishing, 2015, pp. 117–122.

48. *ROB*, Vol. VIII, p. 134.

49. Saito Teruko, 'Responses to modernity—socioeconomic changes and reformist thought' (in Japanese) in Saito Teruko (ed.), *History of Southeast Asia*, Vol. 5, Iwanami Shoten, 2001, pp. 53–54.

50. Tun Wai, *Economic Development of Burma from 1800 till 1940*, Rangoon: Department of Economics, University of Rangoon, 1961.

51. Cheng Yi Sein, 'The Chinese in Upper Burma before A.D. 1700', *The Journal of Southeast Asian Researches*, Vol. II, 1966, p. 89.

52. *GUBSS*, Part I, Vol. II, p. 429.

53. Many examples of royal orders granting monopoly rights to specific merchants can be seen in *ROB*, Vol. V–VI.

54. *ROB*, Vol. V, pp. 270–319. These cases are particularly concentrated in the second half of 1806; *ROB*, Vol. V, pp. 270–319.

55. Toe Hla, 'Money-lending and contractual "thet-kayit": A socio-economic pattern of the later Kon-baung period, 1819–1885', PhD dissertation submitted to Northern Illinois University, 1987, pp. 94–95.

250 Money-lending Contracts in Konbaung Burma

56. O. Pollak, *Empires in Collision: Anglo-Burmese Relations in the Mid-nineteenth Century*, Westport, Connecticut: Greenwood Press, 1979, pp. 124, 129.

57. Pollak, 1979, pp. 124, 129.

58. Pollak, 1979, p. 201.

59. Pollak, 1979, p. 201.

60. Taw Sein Ko, *Selections from the Records of the Hlutdaw*, Rangoon: Government Printing, 1898, pp. 88–89.

61. Symes, 1827, p. 250. V. Sangermano, *A Description of the Burmese Empire: Compiled Chiefly from Burmese Documents*, translated by William Tandy, London: Susil Gupta, NY: Augustus M. Kelly, 1969 (reprint), p. 218.

62. J. Crawfurd, *Journal of an Embassy from the Governor General of India to the Court of Ava, in the Year 1827*, Vol, II, London: Waren and Whittaker, 1829, p. 198.

63. Howard Malcom, *Travels in South-eastern Asia: Embracing Hindustan, Malaya, Siam, and China; With Notice of Numerous Missionary Stations, and a Full Account of the Burman Empire; With Dissertations, Tables, etc.*, Vol. I, Boston: Gould, Kendall and Lincoln, 1839, p. 74.

64. After the Treaty of Yandabo in 1826, trade negotiations were held between J. Crawfurd and a high official in the Bagyidaw government. The Burmese government sought the free import of arms and ammunition from British Burma, but this request was rejected by Crawfurd, and the British demand for the free export of gold and silver from Burma was also rejected by the Burmese government. As a result, the commercial treaty, although signed, had no substantial results for either side. Anna Allot, *The End of the First Anglo-Burmese War: The Burmese Chronicle Account of How the 1826 Treaty of Yandabo Was Negotiated*, Bangkok: Chulalongkorn University Printing House, 1994, pp. 77–78. In the Anglo-Burmese Commercial Treaty of 1867, negotiated between H. E. Fitche, the Commissioner of Burma, and the King's Government of Mindon, the British envoy succeeded in the abolishment of the royal monopoly on all goods except crude oil, timber, and precious stones. In return, the Burmese government was allowed to buy arms and ammunition freely, but with the consent of the British Commissioner of Burma. However, successive commissioners rarely agreed to export arms, and King Mindon's government relied mainly on smuggling to secure arms.

65. *Ngapyi* is fermented fish paste, which is indispensable for the Burmese diet.

66. Yule, 1968, Appendix H, pp. 359–60.

67. Yamamoto Kumiko, The *Descendants of Chinese Muslims: From Yunnan to Myanmar*, Tokyo: Shogakukan, 2004, p. 199.

Notes   251

68. According to Sun Laichen, large quantities of jade obtained from Mohnyin were transported to China via Yunnan for the Ming court as early as the fifteenth century. Sun Laichen, 'Shan gems, Chinese silver and the rise of Shan principalities in northern Burma, c. 1450–1527' in Geoff Wade and Sun Laichen (eds.), *Southeast Asia in the Fifteenth Century, The China Factor*, Singapore: National University of Singapore Press, and Hong Kong University Press, 2010, pp. 169–196.

69. Yoshimatsu Kumiko, 'The Pandee in Myanmar, trade and immigration from the late 19th century to the early 20th century' (in Japanese), *Islamic World*, No. 61, 2003, pp. 7–10, pp. 22–25.

70. Chen Yi Sein, 1966, p. 87.

71. Wil O. Dijk, *Seventeenth-century Burma and the Dutch East India Company, 1634–1680*, Singapore: NIAS Press, 2006, pp. 46–48.

72. Symes, 1827, Vol. II, p. 64.

73. When the British won the Second Anglo-Burmese War, they called the occupied area the Province of Pegu, which covers the whole area of Lower Burma except Arakan and Tenasserim. Arthur Phayre was the first Commissioner of the Province of Pegu.

74. Yule, 1968, p. 149.

Chapter 2

1. Robert S. Wicks, *Money, Markets, and Trade in Early Southeast Asia*, Ithaca, New York: Cornell University, Studies on Southeast Asia, 1992, pp. 135–136.

2. Than Tun, *Shehaung Myanmar Yazawin*, Yangon: Mahadagon Press, 1964, p. 182. G. H. Luce, 'Economic life of the early Burman,' *JBRS*, Vol. 30, Part 1, 1940, p. 300.

3. V. Lieberman, *Burmese Administrative Cycles: Anarchy and Conquest, c. 1580–1760*, Princeton University Press, 1984, p. 121. M. Robinson and L. A. Shaw, *The Coins and Banknotes of Burma*, Manchester, 1980, p. 23.

4. Bin Yang, 'Horses, silver and cowries: Yunnan in global perspective', *Journal of World History*, Vol. 15, No. 3, 2004, p. 292.

5. Bin Yang, 2004, p. 293.

6. Wil O. Dijk, *Seventeenth-century Burma and the Dutch East India Company, 1634–1680*, Singapore: NIAS Press, 2006, pp. 5–6.

7. Dijk, 2006, Appendix I, Table C, Dutch exports from Burma, 1634–80.

8. Dijk, 2006, p. 6.

9. Robinson and Shaw, 1980, p. 24.

10. Lieberman, 1984, p. 122.

11. Robinson and Shaw, 1980, p. 25. Dijk, 2006, p. 49.

12. R. C. Temple, 'Notes on currency and coinage among the Burmese', Bombay: The British India Press, 1928 (reprinted from *Indian Antiquary*, Vol. XLVIII, 1919), p. 21.

13. For examples, see DMSEH, Vol. 5, No. 1210 (1.5 *kyat ke* alloy), Pyi Myo Shwebonpwin Museum Library; DMSEH, Vol. 11, No. 2889 (1.5 *kyat ke* alloy), Mandalay; Salin *Thet-kayit* Collection (Toe Hla), *Ko-nei thet-kayit*, No. 1, 2, 15 (1.6 *kyat ke* alloy, 20 *kyat ke*), Salin; KUMF, Reel No. 82, Vol. 9, No. 8~28 (2 *kyat ke alloy, ngwe mwe ywet ni*), Mandalay; KLTLST (Byan-gya collection), No. 5 (2 *kyat ke*, 30 *kyat ke*, 50 *kyat ke*). These currencies of various qualities were all called *ywet-ni* in the contracts.

14. Meiktila *Thet-kayit* Collection, *Thet-kayit* No. 20.

15. Toe Hla, *Konbaung Hkit Leya Thet-kayit Pa Luhmu Sibwayei Thamaing* (unpublished typescript, Rangoon, 1977–81), 1979, p. 61 (hereafter, *KLT*). Toe Hla, 'Money-lending and contractual "thet-kayit": A socio-economic pattern of the later Kon-baung period, 1819–1885', PhD dissertation submitted to Northern Illinois University, 1987, pp. 255–256.

16. Toe Hla, *KLT*, 1979, p. 59. Toe Hla, 1987, p. 256–257.

17. Henry Yule, *A Narrative of the Mission to the Court of Ava in 1855*, Kuala Lumpur: Oxford University Press, 1968 (reprint of 1855 ed.), p. 261. Yule noted that, in Ava, the low-quality alloy (i.e., silver ratio below 50%) was liable to confiscation by the king, but was used in the provinces.

18. Robinson and Shaw, 1980, p. 2.

19. Than Tun, *The Royal Orders of Burma, A.D. 1598–1885*, Kyoto: The Center for Southeast Asian Studies, Kyoto University (hereafter, *ROB*) Vol. IV, 1987, pp. 182, 621. U Tin, *Myanmar Min Ok-chok-pon Sadan* (Governance of Myanmar Kings), Government Printing Office, Vol. III, Sec. 395, 1970, p. 128.

20. *ROB*, Vol. IV, pp. 286–287.

21. *ROB*, Vol. IV, p. 69, p. 369.

22. Hiram Cox, *Journal of a Residence in the Burmhan Empire and More Particularly at the Court of Amarapoorah*, British Library, Historical Print Editions, 2011 (reprint), p. 311. Robinson and Shaw, 1980, p. 68.

23. Howard Malcom, *Travels in Southeastern Asia*, Michigan University Library, 1834. Yule, 1968. Temple, 1928. Robinson and Shaw, 1980.

24. Toe Hla, *KLT*, 1978, p. 267.

25. Cox, 2011, p. 310.

26. Cox, 2011, pp. 312–13.

27. Cox, 2011, p. 321.

28. U Tin, 1970, pp. 39–40. 1 *viss* = 100 *kyat*s = 1.63kg.

29. Than Tun, *ROB*, Vol. V, p. xviii.

30. *ROB*, Vol. IV, p. xxvii.

31. *KLT*, Vol. I, p. 88.

32. *KLT*, Vol. I, p. 90

33. J. G. Scott and J. P. Hardiman, *Gazetteer of Upper Burma and the Shan States*, 5 volumes, Washington DC: Government Printing, 1900, Part I, Vol., II, pp. 419–421.

34. V. Lieberman, 'Was the 17th century a watershed in Burmese history?' in Anthony Reid (ed.), *Southeast Asia in the Early Modern Era: Trade, Power, and Belief*, Ithaca, NY: Cornell University Press, 1993, p. 235. His estimate seems quite reasonable, as the main tax on land was payable either in crop or in cash.

35. *ROB*, Vol. IX, p. 366.

36. *ROB*, Vol. IX, p. 391.

37. Here *thet-kayit* means Burmese Era.

38. *ma* is a suffix to express that the person is female. Here, the creditor is one of the female members of Salin *Thugaung* families.

39. *Myo-thugyi* is a hereditary ruler of a *myo*, a provincial socio-administrative unit.

40. Salin *Thugaung* manuscript collection, no. 66.

41. Toe Hla, 1987, p. 267.

42. Robinson and Shaw, 1980, p. 82. Wallace was the founder of the Bombay Trading Co. Ltd, which was renamed The Bombay Burmah Trading Co. Ltd., soon after its foundation in 1863. Robinson and Shaw, 1980, p. 82.

43. After Wyon worked in Mandalay, he went to various places, including Osaka, Bogota, and Canton, to set up mints.

44. U Maung Maung Tin, *Konbaung hset Maha Yazawin-daw-gyi*, Vol. III, Yangon: Tekkatho-mya Thamain Thutei Thana Oozi Htana, 2004 (reprint), pp. 226–227.

45. 5 *mu* gold coin were fixed as equivalent to 1 *kyat* silver coin. Formerly, 1 *kyat* made 10 *mu*s, but it was altered to be equivalent to 8 *mu*s in the reform.

46. Robinson and Shaw, 1980, p. 88.

47. J. S. Furnivall, 'A study of the social and economic history of Burma (British Burma)' (unpublished manuscript submitted to the Office of Prime Minister in 1957–59 and The National Planning Commission, Ministry of National Planning in 1960), Statistical Appendix, 1861–62 to 1867–68, pp. 111, cii.

48. In Mandalay (the royal capital area), *dinga* had been used in money-lending since the 1850s and Salin *Thugaung* families had been using *dinga* since 1864, and switched to the peacock silver coins without problems.

Chapter 3

1. Ohn Kyi, 'Konei Thetkayit mya wa Lu-paung Sagyok', *Magwe Degree College Annual Magazine*, 1991, pp. 48–52.

2. There are 46 duplicates in DMSEH and STM-KT, and nine duplicates within DMSEH itself. As it was a custom to make several copies of a contract, not only for debtors and creditors but also for witnesses, duplication of the contracts were often founded.

3. In KUMF and STM-KT, the original debt-slave contracts and repeated borrowing on the same debt-slave are categorized as debt-slave contracts (*konei thet-kayit*). In DMSEH, repeated borrowings on the same debt-slave are categorized as money-borrowing contracts (*ngwe-kyi thet-kayit*).

4. KUMF, Reel 67, No. 1 (30–31) (referring to images 30 and 31 of the first document in Reel No. 67). (The same applies hereafter.)

5. *Thugaung* was a kind of honorary title given by the king to a person whose contribution to the kingdom was admitted. Unlike *bwe*, which is also an honorary title given by the king to a person for his excellent performance while he remains on service, the *thugaung* title was inherited by the descendant and, for that reason, it is sometimes translated as 'nobility'.

6. Royal capitals in the Konbaung period were Shwebo (1752–60, known as Mokhsobo), Shwebo and Sagaing (1760–64), Ava (1764–83), Amarapura (1783–1823), Ava (1823–37), Amarapura (1837–57), and Mandalay (1857–85).

7. Ohn Kyi, 1991, pp. 48–52.

8. *Taik-soe* was a person who governed *taik*, which was a local administrative unit.

9. STM-KT, no. 12.

10. DMSEH, Vol. 11, No. 2525.

11. *ROB*, Vol. 9, p. 474. There are records showing that a transaction tax was levied on the buying and selling of slaves.

12. The system of appanage lands disappeared with the reforms introduce in 1861 during the reign of King Mindon. Thereafter, remuneration for all *ahmudan* changed to a system of fixed monthly salaries. This reform did not extend to monastic lands. See Saito Teruko, 'Responses to modernity—socioeconomic changes and reformist thought' (in Japanese) in Saito Teruko (ed.), *History of Southeast Asia*, Vol. 5, Iwanami Shoten, 2001, p. 61.

13. The phrase 'like building a pagoda or monastery' is an expression used to stress that once one has made a promise, one will never break it.

14. In a contract from Mandalay written in 1846 (1208 M.E.) and a contract from Kyaukpadaun in 1882 (1244 M.E.), there is one phrase that says, '*Ngwe ma hsoun, lu ma hsoun*' (neither money, nor people would be lost). The implication of the phrase has not yet been clarified.

Notes   255

15. The use of the words *thei* (to die) and *shin* (to live) as a couplet is often found in contracts, especially in money-lending contracts. It is thought to have originated in traditional Burmese law books; for example, a Burmese translation of the Wagaru Dhammathat, which was used by the Mon kings, says, 'There are three kinds of pawned goods (*paung*): *paung thei, paung shin,* and *paung thwin.*' The first two are explained in Burmese, but the last one, *paung thwin,* is not explained in Burmese, leaving the Pali language as it is. It may be inferred that only the concept was introduced without any equivalent to this word being recognized in Burma. Government of Burma, *Manu Dhamma That-htan kho Manu Dhamma That Kyan: King Wagaru's Manu DHAMMA-SATTHAM,* Rangoon: Supdt. Government Printing and Stationery, 1934, pp. 22–23. The Manugye Dhammathat, which was compiled in 1756, also mentions two types of pledged land, *mye shin* (living land) and *mye thei* (dead land), but to the best of my knowledge, there is not a single instance of these words used in the contracts related to land. D. Richardson, *The Damathat, or the Laws of Menoo,* translated from the Burmese, XIV vols. in one (2nd ed.), Rangoon: The Mission Press, 1874, pp. 227–229. Saito Teruko, 'A history of the land system of Upper Burma in the 18th and 19th centuries: A preliminary study', *Asian Economy,* Vol. 30, No. 5, 1989, pp. 5–7. It seems that the concepts of *shin-thei* couplets which did not necessarily conform to the actual conditions of Burmese society were introduced into the world of Dhammathat in the process of accepting the Manu Code from India and remained intact until the Konbaung period.

16. Ohn Kyi, 'Salin Thugaung Thamaing Achyin' (Short history of Salin *Thugaung*) unpublished mimeograph, colleague of Dr. Than Tun (ed.), *Bama Thamaing Hinley: Studies in Burmese History,* History Department, Mandalay University, 1987, p. 73.

17. Ohn Kyi, 1991, p. 51.

18. Ohn Kyi, 1991, p. 209. Government of Burma, *Wagaru Dhammathat,* 1934, p. 23.

19. Okudaira Ryuji, 'The Burmese Dhammathat' in M. B. Hooker (ed.), *Laws of Southeast Asia,* Vol. I, The Pre-Modern Texts, Singapore: Butterworth & Co. Pte. Ltd., 1986, p. 33.

20. Ohn Kyi, 1987.

21. DMSEH, Vol. 2, No. 0177.

22. DMSEH, Vol. 2, No. 0180.

23. DMSEH, Vol. 2, No. 0230.

24. DMSEH, Vol. 10, No. 1305.

25. The 51 contracts are the original contracts of debt-slave mortgage. Other documents such as repeated borrowing contracts on the debt-slave or guarantor's pledge letters are excluded.

256 Money-lending Contracts in Konbaung Burma

26. KUMF, Reel 82, No. 9 (6).

27. In one contract written in 1856, the wife of a village chief pawned her daughter to the wife of an army commander in Mandalay (DMSEH, Vol. 2, No. 0177). However, one-and-a-half months later, the contract was rewritten as the mortgaged girl was not her daughter but a slave girl possessed by the family of the village chief (DMSEH, Vol. 2, No. 0180).

28. DMSEH, Vol. 1, No. 0830; in this contract the wife of the guarantor became a debt-slave. In another contract (DMSEH, Vol. 6, No. 2632), the daughter of the guarantor became a debt-slave in place of the runaway debt-slave.

29. KUMF, Reel 82, No. 9 (8–17).

30. KUMF, Reel 82, No. 9 (17).

31. KUMF, Reel 82, No. 9 (17–2).

32. As the creditor, Min-maha-min-tin-yaza, was a man of high social status, the management of slaves must have been put in the hands of house stewards. It seems that many debt-slaves wanted to move to his residence because they knew the laxity of the control of the slaves, not because they could expect kind treatment in his residence. When a debt-slave ran away, Min-maha-min-tin-yaza confiscated the house and paddy fields of the escapee, and made his wife a debt-slave. KUMF, Reel 82, No. 9 (2 of 17).

33. KUMF, Reel 82, No. 9 (2 of 28).

34. KUMF, Reel 82, No. 9 (6).

35. KUMF, Reel 82, No. 9 (1–3 of 29).

36. KUMF, Reel 82, No. 9 (1, 6–7, 28–2, 33, 34).

37. KUMF, Reel 82, No. 7–1.

38. KUMF, Reel 82, No. 7–1.

39. KUMF, Reel 82, No. 7, 8–20.

40. KUMF, Reel 82, No. 7–6.

41. KUMF, Reel 82, No. 7–16.

42. KUMF, Reel 82, No. 7–8.

43. A *sit-ke* was sent from the central government to assist the governor in military, judicial, and security affairs. Maung Maung Tin (U), *Shwe Nan Thoun Wahara Abidan*, Yangon: Tekkatho-mya Thamaing Thutei Tana Oo-zi Htana, 1975, pp. 206–207.

44. There are 21 debt-slave contracts in Meiktila in DMSEH, Vol. 7. As three are duplicated, the actual number of contracts is 18.

45. DMSEH, Vol. 6, No. 2758.

46. DMSEH, Vol. 6, No. 2605, 2632.

47. DMSEH, Vol. 9, No. 1354, 1361, 1365–67, 1711, 1713~14, 1718–19, 1731–32.

Notes   257

48. The body price was written in Burmese as *kou bou*. There were certain standards for the price of slaves and the body price of a man was a little bit higher than that of a woman.

49. DMSEH, Vol. 9, No. 1718.

50. DMSEH, Vol. 9, No. 1711.

51. DMSEH, Vol. 9, No. 1364.

52. STM-KT, No. 54.

53. DMSEH, Vol. 11, No. 1058, 1059.

54. DMSEH, Vol. 5, No. 0471.

55. Maung Pe said the farmland was his own land. However, it often happened there were many owners on the same land because of the custom of equal inheritance to all heirs. It was quite possible there were other heirs who had rights on this farmland.

56. *Ngwe-mwe 2 kyat 8 mu* coin means coin made of alloy of silver and copper, in which silver purity is 78%. Up to 1865, when varieties of currencies casted privately were circulated, these metal currencies were weighed by a standard weight decided by the royal government. *Hinda* weight is shaped like a legendary sacred bird, *hinda*.

57. DMSEH, Vol. 5, No. 1305.

58. STM-KT, No. 74.

59. DMSEH, Vol. 9, No. 1364.

60. STM-KT, No. 97.

61. In this contract, the debtor promised to deliver 15 baskets of paddy *per year* to the creditor's residence as interest on the loan of 20 *kyat*s. If compared to the second and third contracts, the interest was cheap, as in the second contract the debtor should deliver 15 baskets of paddy *per month* for the loan of 30 *kyat*s, and in the third contract the debtor should pay the same amount of paddy for the loan of 100 *kyat*s. It is not clear why such a low rate of interest was allowed to the mother and her son.

62. DMSEH, Vol. 9, No. 1713.

63. V. Lieberman, *Burmese Administrative Cycles: Anarchy and Conquest, c. 1580–1760*, Princeton University Press, 1984.

64. Lieberman, 1984, pp. 152–153, 155, 164–165.

65. Lieberman, 1984, p. 260.

66. Lieberman, 1984, p. 260.

67. DMSEH, Vol. 11, No. 1059.

68. KUMF, Reel 82, No. 9 (6).

69. DMSEH, Vol. 5, No. 0582.

258 Money-lending Contracts in Konbaung Burma

Chapter 4

1. This chapter is based on the following article. There is no significant change, but some parts that overlapped with Chapter 3 are omitted. In addition, there were two points on money that I did not fully understand at that time, and I have changed the notes to that effect. Saito Teruko, 'Mortgaged slaves in nineteenth-century Burma: The case of the Salin region', *Southeast Asia: History and Culture*, No. 38, 2009, pp. 13–46.

2. Anthony Reid, 'Introduction: Slavery, bondage in Southeast Asian history' in A. Reid (ed.), *Slavery, Bondage and Dependency in Southeast Asia*, St. Lucia, London and New York: University of Queensland Press, 1983, pp. 11–12.

3. Michael Aung-Thwin, 'Athi, Kyun-Taw, Hpaya-kyun: Varieties of commendation and dependence in pre-colonial Burma' in A. Reid (ed.), *Slavery, Bondage and Dependency in Southeast Asia*, St. Lucia, London and New York: University of Queensland Press, 1983, pp. 64–89.

4. Aung-Thwin, 1983, pp. 68–69.

5. On this controversy, see Iwaki Takahiro, 'The idea of pre-modern Burmese history: A comparison of three books by Aung Thwin, Lieberman and Koenig', *Southeast Asia: History and Culture*, No. 21, 1992, pp. 142–160.

6. For historical studies on the Salin region and Salin *Thugaung*, studies to be referred to are as follows. Iwaki Takahiro, 'Local power in the early period of the Konbaung dynasty in Salin: An analysis of the *Sit-tan* documents', *Journal of History*, Vol. 109, No. 9, 2000, pp. 63–79. Iwaki Takahiro, 'Study of the local power and royal control on them in the early Konbaung Burma', PhD dissertation submitted to Tokyo University, 2002. Kyaw Hmu Aung, 'Konbaung Hkit-hnaung Salin Thugaung Thamaing (1819–1885)', MA thesis submitted to History Department, Yangon University, 1992. Htun Yee, 'Cases of headman-ship of Salin Myo in Myanmar during the 19th century', *Journal of International Affairs*, (Aichi University), No. 109, 1998, pp. 91–155. Ohn Kyi, 'Salin Thugaung Thamaing (Achyin)' (Short history of Salin *Thugaung*), colleague of Dr. Than Tun (ed.), *Bama Thamaing Hinley: Studies in Burmese History*, History Department, Mandalay University, 1987, pp. 55–82. As for the irrigation system in the Salin area, Michael Aung-Thwin, *Irrigation in the Heartland of Burma*, Northern Illinois University, Occasional Paper No. 15, 1990, and Ito Toshikatsu, 'Traditional irrigation technology and the development of agriculture', *Shiroku* (Kagoshima University), Vol. 11, pp. 39–80, 1979, provide useful information.

7. Ohn Kyi, 1987, p. 57.

8. The first settlement of the Burmese people who moved from Yunnan to the Ayeyarwady Basin was called *hkayain*. In the Pagan period, there were nine *hkayain*s in Kyause and in Minbu six *hkayain*s, both rice producing areas with river irrigation systems.

Notes 259

9. *Myo-thugyi* is the ruler of *myo*, and *ywa-thugyi* is the village chief. Both *thugyi*s are hereditary in principle.

10. *ROB*, Vol. IV, p. 513.

11. Kyaw Hmu Aung, 1992.

12. Htun Yee, 1998, pp. 96–99.

13. Government of Burma, *Report on the Settlement Operations in the Minbu District, Season 1893–97*, Rangoon: Superintendent, Government Printing, 1900, pp. 43–45.

14. Government of Burma, 1900, pp. 43–45.

15. As already mentioned in Chapter 2, *ywet-ni* was a currency widely circulated up to the monetary reform by Mindon's government in 1865. It was treated as a kind of standard currency which contained silver and copper at the rate of 9:1. But the silver content rate of the currency used in this contract was only 84%, as it was described as 1 *kyat* 6 *mu* alloy. The word *hman-baw* means pure silver, but, like *ywet-ni*, these words were often used just to imply the high quality of money in a transaction.

16. In order to weigh the various currencies cast privately, every king of the Konbaung dynasty made standard weights and ordered the use of the kings' weight in marketplaces. The *hinda* weight, whose shape was the legendary bird, *hinda*, was made during the reign of King Bagyidaw (r. 1819–37).

17. STM-KT, No. 1.

18. STM-KT, No. 2.

19. STM-KT, No. 57, 58, 71, the latter part of No. 74.

20. STM-KT, No. 52, 63, 104.

21. STM-KT, No. 63.

22. Kyaw Hmu Aung, 1992, p. 14.

23. *Sit-ke*s were positioned as assistants to the provincial governor. They were appointed by the king and sent to strategically important *myo*s. They were primarily responsible for security measures such as military, security, and judicial affairs under the provincial governor.

24. *Taik* is a relatively newer local administrative unit than *myo*. *Taik-so* is synonymous with the word *taik-thugyi*, and means the chief of a *taik*.

25. STM-KT, No. 23.

26. There were a few names seen in the contracts suggesting that they might belong to ethnicities other than Burmese, such as Ko Tayo or Mi Shan. However, in rural areas of modern Burma, someone with a white complexion is often called Mi Shan (Miss Shan) or, with narrow eyes, Ko Tayo (Mr. Chinese), regardless of their ethnicities. I suppose the same would be true in eighteenth- and nineteenth-century Burma. At any rate, there was little awareness of the differences in ethnicity in the world of debt contracts.

27. STM-KT, no. 17.

28. STM-KT, no. 18.

29. For the sale of slaves, we have not yet found a single contract in any database, but this is quite natural because, as transactions were settled at once by cash, there was no need to make contracts, even in the case of human trafficking. However, it is certain that in eighteenth-century Burma, there existed slave transactions, as we saw some records on the transaction of slaves. For example, in the *sit-tan* of Pinya Myo in 1783, it was stated that a transaction tax of 1 *viss* of copper (about 1.63 kg) was imposed on the sale of slaves. *ROB*, Vol. IX, pp. 55, 474.

30. STM-KT, No. 64~66.

31. STM-KT, No. 60.

32. STN-KT, No. 1.

33. STN-KT, No. 25.

34. STM-KT, No. 6.

35. STM-KT, No. 20.

36. STM-KT, No. 67, 84, 93.

37. STM-KT, No. 104.

38. STM-KT, No. 74, 97.

39. Kyaw Hmu Aung, 1992, p. 107. Ohn Kyi, 1987, p. 73.

40. A British official who worked as a settlement officer in the region in 1893–97 also claimed that *Thugaung* families treated their tenants generously. Government of Burma, 1900, p. 45. (He thought people working both in the farm and in the household were tenants, but it should be debt-slaves.)

41. STM-KT, No. 31.

42. STM-KT, No. 32.

43. STM-KT, No. 35.

44. STM-KT, No. 49, 50.

45. 20 *kyat* alloy means that the alloy contains silver and copper at the rate of 8:2.

46. STM-KT, No. 25, 26, 29, 30, 37, 42, 53, 61.

47. STM-KT, No. 6, 7, 8, 14, 78~79, 80~81.

48. STM-KT, No. 82, 83, 86.

49. STM-KT, No. 9.

50. STM-KT, the first half of contract No. 34.

51. STM-KT, the latter part of contract No. 34.

52. STM-KT, No. 52.

53. The date corresponds approximately to late November, when the harvest of paddy is over and the rice market is open.

Notes   261

54. STM-KT, No. 55.
55. STM-KT, No. 57~58.
56. Tagu is approximately the period from the middle of April to early May.
57. STM-KT, No. 77.

Chapter 5

1. The author has written two papers using 50 *thet-kayit*s of Byangya from 1791 to 1843 as the main sources (Saito Teruko, 'Changing rural societies in the Konbaung period' in Ikehata Setsuho (ed.), *Changing Images of Southeast Asian Histories*, Yamakawa Shuppan-sha, 1994; Saito Teruko, 'Rural monetization and land-mortgage *thet-kayit*s in Kon-baung Burma' in Anthony Reid (ed.), *The Last Stand of Asian Autonomies: Responses to Modernity in the Diverse States of Southeast Asia and Korea, 1750–1900*, London: Macmillan, New York: St. Martin's Press, 1997). However, as she found another 11 Byangya *thet-kayit*s in the Universities' Central Library (UCL) in Yangon, the time span of the study extended from 52 years to 67 years (1776~1843). This chapter is a new version of the former papers which cover the early stage of the Konbaung period.

2. Shwebo is famous not only for being the birthplace of the founder of the dynasty, but also for being the stronghold of insurgents who often attempted to usurp the throne. There are many examples of rebels who followed the Alaunghpaya tradition of feeding their troops here and recruiting new ones to attack the capital. Many elite soldiers who were taken from Manipur, Kathe, and Assam and organized as the cavalry of the king's army were settled in the vicinity of Shwebo, and it seems to have been a convenient place for mobilizing troops.

3. A. Williamson, *Burma Gazetteer, Shwebo District*, Vol. A, Rangoon: Govt. Printing and Stationary, 1963 (reprint, compiled 1929), p. 113.

4. Williamson, 1963 p. 116; Michael Aung-Thwin, *Irrigation in the Heartland of Burma*, Northern Illinois University, Occasional Paper No. 15, 1990, p. 25.

5. The size of 25 baskets of seed sowing paddy field is estimated at approximately 50 acres. The size of paddy fields was described in many ways and varied by locality.

6. UCL *para-baik* No. 151107.

7. As for the names of currencies used in *thet-kayit*s, please see Chapter 2. The name of each currency denotes the quality.

8. Toe Hla, 'Konbaung Hkit Leya Thet-kayit par Luhmu Sibwaye Thamaing', (unpublished typescript), Appendix, Byangya collection (hereafter, KLT-Bc), No. 50, p. 244.

9. At that time, it was estimated that approximately 1.5 baskets of seeds were sown per acre of paddy field. Toe Hla, 'Money-lending and contractual "thet-

kayit": A socio-economic pattern of the later Kon-baung period, 1819–1885', PhD dissertation submitted to Northern Illinois University, 1987, p. 14.

10. Pagoda slaves were the people donated to Buddhist institutions by the kings or wealthy people for the maintenance and preservation of pagodas and monasteries. They worked on the tax-free monastery land and their surplus labor and products were used for the maintenance of Buddhist institutions. They were not allowed to be redeemed for good.

11. The word *lo'hpet* was also used in the case of share-cropping tenancy. In eighteenth- and nineteenth-century Burma, the word *thi-sa* (tenant) was not yet used, but *lo'hpet* (working partner) was often used on various occasions.

12. The chief of paddy cultivators was called the *le-gaung*. The word *le-gaung* was used for the chief of hereditary cultivators of royal lands called *lamaing*s, as well as the chief of monastery cultivators (i.e., pagoda slaves).

13. *Ahsaun-daw-mye* was the name of an official position, meaning the chamberlain whose duty was to protect the king from assaults or any other danger. This person appeared as Min-kyaw-tin-syi-thu- naw-yata, a honorary title bestowed by the king for his service in later contracts.

14. KLT-Bc, No. 41.

15. KLT-Bc, No. 17.

16. KLT-Bc, No. 45.

17. The term *ti' hku-lat-to* was used in this contract. The term is not heard nowadays, but it appeared frequently in the *thet-kayit*s in the eighteenth to nineteenth centuries. As it means one-half, in this contract, for the loan of 110 baskets of paddy, the interest would be 55 baskets of paddy.

18. KLT-Bc, no. 41.

19. KLT-Bc, no. 11.

20. D. Richardson, *The Damathat, or the Laws of Menoo*, translated from the Burmese, XIV vols. in one (2nd ed.), Rangoon: The Mission Press, 1874, Part 8, Chapters 1~2.

21. *MMOS*, Vol. 5, Part V, Section 12.

22. J. S. Furnivall, *An Introduction to the Political Economy of Burma* (3rd ed.), Rangoon: Peoples' Literature Committee & House, 1957, pp. 83–86.

23. *Lamaing*s were hereditary cultivators on the royal farmland.

24. Since the Pagan period, kings, royalty, and the wealthy people had donated land and slaves to religious institutions at their own will. In the Konbaung period, kings tried to ban the donation of land and slaves by the people, but it was less than successful. See U Tin, *The Royal Administration of Burma*, translated by Euan Bagshawe, Bangkok: Ava Publishing House, 2001, p. 585. Toe Hla, 1987, p. 57.

25. *Pagan-mye* in the context of Byangya *thet-kayit*s denoted monastery lands of the Hsin-mati pagoda in Pagan, the old capital in the Pagan period.

26. KLT-Bc, No. 2.

27. *ROB*, Part IV, pp. 120–23, 460–65.

28. V. Lieberman, *Strange Parallels: Southeast Asia in Global Context, c. 800–1830: Vol. 1, Integration on the Mainland*, Cambridge University Press, 2003, pp. 159–160.

29. *GUBSS*, Part I, Vol. II, pp. 432–433.

30. *GUBSS*, Part I, Vol. II, pp. 441–444.

31. Thu Nandar, 'Characteristics of land-mortgage contracts in the 18th–19th century Myanmar society', PhD Dissertation submitted to Tokyo University of Foreign Studies, 2008, p. 42.

32. *GUBSS*, Part I, Vol. 2, p. 483.

33. W. J. Koenig, *The Burmese Polity, 1752–1819: Politics and Administration, and Social Organization in the Early Kon-baung Period*, Center for South and Southeast Asian Studies, The University of Michigan, 1990, p. 245.

34. *Ywa-sa* was a person who was given a certain percentage of the revenue from a particular village by the royal government.

35. '2 *mat-ke* silver' means an alloy whose percentage of silver content is 95%. 'Flowered silver' was currency made of alloy whose silver content was thought to be 90%.

36. UCL *para-baik* No. 151113.

37. Koenig, 1990, Appendix 1, p. 241.

38. Koenig, 1990, p. 245.

39. *Myo-sayei* is often translated as town clerk, but the position comes next to *Myo-Thugyi*.

40. UCL *para-baik* No. 151107.

41. KLT, Vol. II; p. 18 (Taungdwin Hla Pe collection).

42. *GUBSS*, Part II, Vol. III, p. 87. Aung-Thwin, 1990, p. 22.

43. Ohn Kyi, 'Salin Thugaung Thamaing (Achyin)', colleague of Dr. Than Tun (ed.), *Bana Thamaing Hinley: Studies in Burmese History*, History Department, Mandalay University, 1987, pp. 55–82.

44. Kyaw Hmu Aung, 'Konbaung Hkit Hnaung Salin Thugaung Thamaing', MA thesis submitted to the History Department, Yangon University, 1992, p. 69.

45. *GUSS*, Part I, Vol. II, p. 432.

46. Toe Hla, 1987, pp. 151–152.

47. Toe Hla, 1987, pp. 138–143. Htun Yee (collected and ed.), *Konbaung Hkit Ngwe-hkyi Thet-kayit Sagyok-mya* (Collection of *thet-kayit*—money lending

264 Money-lending Contracts in Konbaung Burma

contracts of Myanmar rural area in Kon-baung period), Vol. 1, Toyohashi: Aichi University, 1999, pp. 45–46.

48. Henry Yule, *A Narrative of the Mission to the Court of Ava in 1855*, Kuala Lumpur: Oxford University Press, 1968 (reprint of 1855 ed.), p. 246.

49. Toe Hla, 1987, pp. 143–147.

50. V. Lieberman, 'Was the 17th century a watershed in Burmese history?' in Anthony Reid (ed.), *Southeast Asia in the Early Modern Era: Trade, Power, and Belief*, Ithaca, NY: Cornell University Press, 1993, p. 235.

Chapter 6

1. V. Lieberman, *Strange Parallels: Southeast Asia in Global Context, c. 800–1830: Vol. 1, Integration on the Mainland*, Cambridge University Press, 2003, p. 179.

2. J. S. Furnivall, *An Introduction to the Political Economy of Burma*, Rangoon: Peoples' Literature Committee & House, 1957, pp. 94–95.

3. KUMF, Reel 60, No. 7, 6.

4. KBZ, I, p. 52.

5. Reel Nos. 52, 53, 54, 55, 60, 61, 62, 63, 67, 68, 82, and 84, for a total of 12 volumes. A small number of *thet-kayit*s are included in volumes 10, 11, 12, 15, 16, 39, 40, and 45, which were mostly collected in the area surrounding the royal capital, including Amarapura and Mandalay.

6. Looking at these 99 debt-slave contracts, 83 are concentrated in volume 82, the creditors of which are the influential Min-maha-min-tin-yaza and his relatives residing in the royal capital, as seen in Chapter 3. Looking further at the contents, only 14 of the 83 items are debt-slave contracts in the narrow sense of the term, and the remaining 69 items are additional loan contracts in which debt-slaves piled up debts to the same creditors without providing new collateral. Thus, in effect, debt-slave contracts are less in number and have a more limited geographical distribution than they appear.

7. Ba U, *Myanmar Ok-chok-ye Pyinnya*, Mandalay: Bahoshi Thadinsa Taik, n.d., p. 155.

8. DMSEH, Vol. 3, No. 2061.

9. *Thet-kayit* collection in the Centre for Documentation & Area Studies, Tokyo University of Foreign Studies (C-DATS), 2005, No. 566.

10. KUMF, Reel 60, No. 15, 14.

11. KUMF, Reel 60, No. 11, 32.

12. DMSEH, Vol. 0621, 0645, 0652, 0655.

13. DMSEH, Vol. 5, No. 0728, 0729, 0801, 0792 (contracts written in 1890, in British Lower Burma), No. 0802 (written in 1897, certificate of exchanging paddy fields).

Notes   265

14. Lieberman, 2003, p. 179.

15. D. Richardson, *The Damathat, or the Laws of Menoo*, translated from the Burmese, XIV vols. in one, Rangoon: The Mission Press, 1874, pp. 71–72. Government of Burma, *Manu Dhamma That-htan kho Manu Dhamma That Kyan: King Wagaru's Manu DHAMMA-SATTHAM*, Rangoon: Supdt. Government Printing and Stationery, 1934, p. 19.

16. For example, the Manugye Dhammathat says, 'When paddy fields, dry fields, or orchards, etc., are handed over to creditors as security for a debt, or even when they are sold outright, the creditors do not have a perfect right to those agricultural lands. If the original owner or his heirs demand repurchase, they must do so'; article 4 , vol. 3, Richardson, 1874, p. 71. The Wagaru Dhammathat also says, 'If the purchasers of such landed property become poor, and by their poverty are compelled to sell the property thus bought, they should in the first instance offer it to the original owner to purchase it back'; Government of Burma, 1934, Chapter 7, article 86, p. 19.

17. DMSEH, Vol. 4, No. 0203.

18. KUMF, Reel 82, No. 8, 20.

19. DMSEH, Vol. 7, No. 0478.

20. DMSEH, Vol. 4, No. 0034.

21. Regarding land-mortgage contracts in Kyaukse during the colonial period, there is an article by Mizuno Asuka, 'Land ownership and land pledging in a village of Upper Burma, in the colonial period—a case study in Kyaukse district', *Toyo Bunka*, No. 82, March 2002, pp. 165–180. Land-mortgage contracts in 1948 in Kyaukse were very similar to those written in the Konbaung period. In addition, the redemption of pledged land was admitted for 10 to 20 years, which was quite different from the practice in Lower Burma in the same period. In Upper Burma, the customs related to mortgaged lands were still maintained in the middle of the twentieth century.

22. KUMF, Reel 60, No. 13–9, 13–12, 13–13, 13–16.

23. Meiktila *Thet-kayit* Collection (MTC), No. 93. Thu Nandar, 'Characteristics of land-mortgage contracts in the 18th–19th century Myanmar society: An analysis based on *thet-kayit* manuscript', PhD dissertation submitted to Tokyo University of Foreign Studies, 2008, Appendix, p. 153.

24. Thu Nandar, 2008, p. 161, No. 133.

25. For example, in the MTC, we found among 268 land-related *thet-kayit*s, 133 pieces of original land-mortgage *thet-kayit*s, 12 land redemption *thet-kayit*s, 18 *thet-kayit*s of changing creditors, and 105 additional-loan *thet-kayit*s, which occupied 40% of all land-related *thet-kayit*s.

26. C-DATS, 2005, No. 0056–22, No. 0249.

27. Me Zat is thought to be the wife of U Lu.

28. C-DATS, 2005, No. 0056–22, No. 0250. Ma Ae is presumed to be the heir of U Lu and Me Zat.
29. C-DATS, 2005, No. 0056–23, 0256.
30. Furnivall, 1937, pp. 94–95.
31. MTC, No. 181.
32. MTC, No. 189.
33. See Figure 2.1. The trend of paddy price in the Konbaung period.
34. MTC, No. 122.
35. MTC, No. 148.
36. MTC, No. 162.
37. MTC, No. 191.
38. MTC, No. 223.
39. MTC, No. 224.
40. In British Lower Burma, a tenant was called not *lok-phet*, but *thi-za*, which is still used today.
41. MTC, No. 39.

Chapter 7

1. See, for example, on the Chinese contract, Kishimoto Mio, *Early Modern Period in Eastern Asia*, World History Librette, No. 13, Yamakawa Shuppan Sha, 1998, pp. 166–168; and, on the European contract, Tanaka Minoru, 'Contract in Europe' in Yamamoto Hiroufumi (ed.), *Dictionary of Historical Studies*, Vol. 9 (Law and Order), Kobun Do, 2002, pp. 168–169. As it is stated that 'the concept of contract has been used to characterize Western and modern society' (Tanaka, 2002, p. 168), the dominant view is that the formation of voluntary consensus among legally equal individuals is based on the premise that people are free from the status system and feudal constraints, and, therefore, it is a phenomenon that has occurred since the establishment of modern society in Western Europe.

2. According to Kishimoto Mio, for more than two thousand years, from the time of Qin Shi Huang to the Xinhai Revolution, small peasants in Chinese society, under a bureaucratic regime headed by the emperor, formed various relationships of production mainly through contracts. Kishimoto, 1998, p. 3.

3. Hiroaki Terada, 'Agreement and contract—contracts in early modern China' in Miura Toru, Kishimoto Mio, and Sekimoto Teruo (eds.), *Comparative History of Asia—Ownership, Contract, Market, and Equity*, Tokyo University Press, 2004, p. 89.

Notes 267

4. Several words were used in *thet-kayit*s to denote a witness, such as *thet-thei* (witness), *thi-shi-dhu* (observer), *thi-kya-myin-dhu* (person who hears, foresees, and understands), and *athi akya* (person with knowledge).

5. According to Thu Nandar, in 330 money-lending *thet-kayit*s found in Meiktila, the names of witnesses were recorded in 235 documents. There were 33 donors, ten administrative officials, 18 relatives of debtors, six traditional medical practitioners, and the rest, as much as 168 persons, were commoners without any titles but were called only by their names. Thu Nandar, 'Characteristics of land-mortgage contracts in the 18th–19th century Myanmar society: An analysis based on *thet-kayit* manuscript', PhD dissertation submitted to Tokyo University of Foreign Studies, 2008, p. 67.

6. Toe Hla, *Konbaung Hkit Myanmar Luhmu Apwe Asyi Hnin Tayahmu-hkin-mya*, (Social organization and litigation in the Konbaung period), Yangon: Thekkatho-mya Thamaing Thutei Thana Oo-zi Htana, 2004, p. 48. He states that out of about 160 written judgments of lawsuits collected from Sagaing, Mandalay, and Magwe divisions, the most common were land disputes, followed by 38 disputes related to inheritances, and, third, 17 disputes related to debts. It is evident that the number of lawsuits over land and debts was outstandingly high.

7. *Hlut-taw* is sometimes translated as the Supreme Council of State, consisting of the king and ministers, issuing royal orders, judging important cases, and making decisions of religious, military, foreign, domestic, and palace affairs. In the case that the king could not attend, the crown prince should be present. Thein Hlaing, *Hkit Haung Myanmar Thamaing Thutei Thana Abidan* (Dictionary of ancient Burmese historical terms), Yangon: Tekkatho-mya Thamaing ThuteiThana Oo-zi Htana, 2000, p. 164.

8. MTC, No. 54.

9. KUMF, Reel 82, No. 7–9.

10. *KBZ*, 2004, Vol. III, p. 243. Ito Toshikatsu, 'Introduction of *thathameida* tax by the Mandalay dynasty and *ahmudan*—cases in Shwebo District' in T. Ito (ed.), *Studies of the Establishment of Monopolistic Resources Control by the State in the 19th Century Myanma*, Japan Society for the Promotion of Science, Report to the Kakenhi Grant, 2008, pp. 1–44.

11. *Bo-ba-baing* land, as mentioned briefly in Chapter 5, means land that has been owned since the *bo-ba* (grandparents). Specifically, it meant land that had been cultivated by the ancestors and cultivated by their descendants for at least three generations in succession, and on the condition that they paid taxes on the land, they had full rights of disposal, as well as use.

12. *MMOS*, Vol. 5, Part V, pp. 20–21.

13. MTC, No. 237.

268 Money-lending Contracts in Konbaung Burma

14. Than Tun, *The Royal Orders of Burma, A.D. 1598–1885*, Kyoto: The Center for Southeast Asian Studies, Kyoto University (hereafter, *ROB*), Vol. III, pp. 63, 229.

15. *ROB*, Vol. IV, p. 16, 246.

16. *ROB*, Vol. IX, p. 408.

17. *ROB*, Vol. IX, p. 410.

18. *ROB*, Vol. IX, p. 412.

19. U Hpo Hlaing, a minister who served King Mindon and King Thibaw, proposed a financial reform to prevent the king from spending the treasury's money privately and to fix a stipend for the king and other members of the royal family. His proposal was met with displeasure from the kings, and he was often put under house arrest. Hpo Hlaing (U), 'Yaza Dhamma Thingaha Kyan' (Books of king's canon) in Maung Htin (ed.), *Yaw Mingyi U Hpo Hlaing Akutho Patti hnin Yaza Dhamma Thingaha Kyan* (2nd ed.), Yangon: Zabe Sape, 1983.

20. The word '*Kalan*' referred to a general *ahmudan* in the Pagan period, but in the Konbaung period it meant a lower-ranking official or village headman. Thein Hlaing, 2000, p. 3. *MMOS*, Vol. 1, pp. 189–90.

21. The second King Naungdawgyi, the eldest son of Alaunghpaya. Bodawhpaya himself was the fourth son of Alaunghpaya. Thein Hlaing, 2000, p. 3. *MMOS*, Vol. 1, pp. 189–190.

22. Hsinbyushin was the second son of Alaunghpaya and the third king, famous for his military successes, such as the Ayuttaya expedition.

23. Singu, the fourth king, was usurped by Maung Maung, the son of the second king, Naungdawgyi. Bodawhpaya captured and destroyed Maung Maung, who had only been on the throne for a week, and also destroyed Singu, his family, and the remnants of his party before ascending the throne. He did not refer to Singu as the old king, but as a *myo-za* in a contemptuous tone.

24. As one *beita* is 100 *kyat*s and weighs about 1.63 kg, 23,000 *beita* silver weighs 37,490 kg and 10 *beita* gold weighs 16.3 kg.

25. *MMOS*, Vol. 3, pp. 39–40.

26. *MMOS*, Vol. 5, p. 176.

27. Thant Myint-U, *The Making of Modern Burma*, Cambridge University Press, 2001.

28. Toe Hla, 'Konbaung Hkit Leya Thet-kayit par Luhmu Sibwaye Thamaing' op.cit., 1981, pp. 136–137.

29. KUMF, Reel 84, No. 8-3, 8-4, 8-5, Toe Hla, 1981, p. 131.

30. *So-bwa* is a hereditary ruler of the small kingdom in Shan States.

31. *ROB*, Vol. III, p. 214.

Notes 269

32. For example, a dispute between the female ruler of Sa-ye village, Mi We, and Nga Aung Kyaw San in 1787 was brought to the Privy Council and handed down to the Minister of Athi Affairs and adjudicated by the Minister. *ROB*, Vol. IV, p. 558.

33. *ROB*, Vol. IV, pp. 228–229.

34. It was written as 'the price given by the king'. This is the only example found in the *thet-kayit*s in the Konbaung period.

35. *Ngwe-wunbwe* was one of the metal currencies used before the monetary reform in 1865. The quality of this currency is unknown.

36. UCL, *para-baik* No. 178505. Written on August 4, 1776. The place where it was written is unknown.

37. KLT, Vol. 1, p. 30, written on May 26, 1811.

38. 2 *mat* alloy means an alloy of 95% silver and 5% copper. See Table 2.1.

39. KLT, Vol. 1, p. 33, Nwa-thein *pe-sa*.

40. Ma Hkain, a member of the Taungzin family lineage in Salin *Thugaung*s, married Maung Ta Tun Aung of the same lineage, who became the *Myo-thugyi* of Salin. From the late 1830s, they had been extensively engaged in finance, lending and collecting loans in the name of *Myo-thugyi* and his wife, but from the late 1840s to the end of the 1860s, Ma Hkain lent and collected loans mainly in the name of herself, went on to search for fugitive debt-slaves, and managed everything necessary for her business. Her daughter, Me Kyi Nyo, married to U Thaw, who also served as *Myo-thugyi*, managed the loan business from the 1860s to the end of the Konbaung era, mostly by herself or with her sons.

41. Ito Toshikatsu, 'Sale of mortgaged local domain—cases of small and medium *thugyi*s in the early Konbaung period', *Toyo Gakuho* (Journal of Oriental Studies), Vol. 82, No. 2, 2000, pp. 97–129.

42. They were called *Shwe Thugyi*. As a gold-mining area, these villages were under the direct control of the royal government, and the gold officer ruled over several gold-producing villages. *Shwe thugyi*s were thought to be the heads of one of these villages that were obliged to pay taxes in gold.

Chapter 8

1. This royal decree was issued by the second king of the Taungoo dynasty, King Anauk-hpetlun, on June 23, 1607, and was reissued in the same text by the fourth king of the Taungoo dynasty, King Tarlun, on June 24, 1634. Successive Konbaung kings also took over the same text as the qualification of judges. *ROB*, Vol. I, pp. 191, 216.

2. *MMOS*, Vol. 1, Sec. III, No. 118, p. 177. For a detailed explanation of the qualities required of judges, see Okudaira Ryuji, *Introduction to the Study of*

Burmese Legal History: The Historical Role of Traditional Law, Japan Book Publishers, 2002, pp. 30–31.

3. Dibeyin is pronounced as Dabayin by not a few people.

4. KLT, Vol. 1.

5. KLT, Vol. 1, p. 85.

6. In this area, the area of the paddy field was expressed by the amount of paddy seed sown. The area of paddy field sown with 1 basket of seed was equivalent to about 1 acre (0.4 ha).

7. The person referred to by this title was said to be a relative of Nga Yan. As he was also Nga Yin's father, Nga Hmu's father-in law, Nga Yan and Nga Yin are not complete strangers, but are loosely related to each other.

8. KLT, Vol. 1, p. 85.

9. KLT, Vol. 1, p. 86.

10. This tea, a pickled tea leaf from the Shan region, played an important role in indicating whether or not the verdict would be accepted by both parties at the conclusion of the trial. If the parties exchanged pickled tea leaves and ate them, they agreed and the case was concluded; if one of them did not eat the tea and expressed his disagreement with the verdict, the case was still ongoing.

11. KLT, Vol. 1, p.86.

12. UCL *para-baik* No. 151105.

13. KLT, Vol. 1, p. 87.

14. KLT, Vol. 1, p. 88.

15. KLT, Vol. 1, p. 89.

16. When the army or any taskforce was organized in ancient Myanmar, there was a custom that each member (soldier) drunk the blood of the other members as an oath of solidarity. Because of this ceremony, the infantry soldiers were called *thwe-thau* (blood drinker). A *thwet-thauk-gyi* means the captain of 50 soldiers. Maung Maung Tin, *Shwe Nan Thoun Warhaya Abidan* (3rd ed.), Tekkatho-mya Thamaing Thutei Thana Oo-zi Htana, 2005, p. 298.

17. KLT, Vol. 1, p. 90.

18. KLT, Vol. 1, p. 91.

19. KLT, Vol. 1, p. 92.

20. *Ein-oo* means the entrance of the house, but here, it seems to denote the house of the captain of the infantry, who judged the disputes.

21. KTL, Vol. 1, p. 93.

22. The Eastern Court of Justice was a court set up in the Royal Palace, which examined crimes and disputes in the capital area. It was one of the five depart-

ments established under the Privy Council. There was another court in the palace, called the Nauk-Yon, which delt with crime and disputes related to the queens. *ROB*, Vol. IV, pp. 91–98.

23. KLT, Vol. 1, p. 94, December 9, 1856.

24. KLT, Vol. 1, p. 95, December 16, 1856.

25. KLT, Vol. 1, p. 96.

26. KLT, Vol. 1, p. 97.

27. KLT, Vol. 1, p. 99.

28. For example, see the classical work of Daw Mya Sein, *Administration of Burma: Sir Crosthwaite and the Consolidation of Burma*, Kuala Lumpur: Oxford University Press, 1973 (reprint).

29. Thu Nandar, 'Characteristics of land-mortgage contracts in the 18th–19th century Myanmar society: An analysis based on *thet-kayit* manuscript', PhD dissertation submitted to Tokyo University of Foreign Studies, 2008, pp. 115–116.

30. J. S. Furnivall, *An Introduction to the Political Economy of Burma*, Rangoon: Peoples' Literature Committee & House, 1957, p. 87. He wrote as follows. 'In Mingyan District, and probably elsewhere, it is not uncommon to find a hundred or more collaterals, down to the fifth generation, recognized as co-heirs.' According to Furnivall, there were innumerable heirs also on palm trees, as the product, palm sugar, could be divided into many lumps, and that the right to receive a few lumps of palm sugar was regarded as a test of kinship.

31. MTC, No. 199.

32. MTC, No. 204.

33. MTC, No. 197.

34. MTC, No. 137.

35. C-DATS, 2005, No. 216, and MTC, No. 45. These two documents were copies of the same judicial case. It was a custom to make plural copies of a *thet-kayit*, and in not a few cases errors in writing happened. In the record of C-DATs, the amount of money Maung Pyu should pay was 14 *kyat*s 8 *pe*s.

36. C-DATS, 2005, No. 526.

37. KLT, Vol. 1, p. 53.

38. Toe Hla, 1981, p. 99. The figure for 1847 was taken from the Le-gain area, and that of 1849 was from Byangya village.

Conclusion

1. Ninomiya Hiroyuki, *Reconsidering Historiography: from Daily Life to Power System*, Japan Editors' School Press, 1994, p. 4.

2. Kishimoto Mio, *Ming-Qing Hansheng and Jiangnan Society: The Problem of Order in the 17th Century China*, Tokyo University Publishing, 1999, p. xiii. This was introduced as a point of discussion in the report of Mr. Masao Mori at the symposium on 'Community perspectives: Local society and leaders' at Nagoya University in 1981.

3. Tamaki Akira, *Climate: History of the Earth and Human Being*, Tokyo: Heibon Sha, 1974.

4. However, all criminal cases related to kings were judged by the royal court and sentenced in the form of royal edicts. Naturally, pickled tea leaves were never served after the sentence. See Okudaira Ryuji, *Introduction to the Study of Burmese Legal History: The Historical Role of Traditional Law*, Japan Book Publishers, 2002, pp. 19, 42.

5. The Burmese customary law texts, known as *Dhammathat*, are 'a kind of compilation of laws and regulations to which indigenous customs were codified and to which precedents, such as court cases, were added as time went by. They are not so-called statute law. The main reason for the lack of statute law in Burma resided in the concern that the statute would become rigid, making it inappropriate for the contemporaries and creating complex interpretive problems'; Okudaira Ryuji, 2002, pp. 29–30. Furthermore, as it is said, 'In making the decision, if the provisions of the Dhammathat conflicted with the Yazathat (king's law, criminal law) the Yazathat took precedence over the Dhammathat, and if the provisions of the Yazathat conflicted with customs and practices, customs and practices took precedence over the Yazathat'; Okudaira Ryuji, 2002, p. 41. In the Burmese judiciary system, great emphasis was placed on the customs and practices prevalent in that era.

Bibliography

Manuscripts

Debt-slave contracts (*Lu-baung Sa-gyok*)

Kagoshima University Burma Research Mission microfilm (KUMF)

Toyo Bunko, Tokyo University of Foreign Studies Library (duplicate)
Reel No.–Document No.–Image No. (number of evidences in one image)

52. 3–2, 7.
53. 8–19. 10–2, 3. 19–3.
54. 9–1, 4, 7, 15.
67. 1–23, 26, 29–34, 8-1.
82. 8–3. 9–1, 3–7, 8 (4), 9 (5), 10 (6), 11 (6), 16 (3), 17 (2), 18, 20 (6), 21 (5), 22 (5), 23 (5), 24 (4), 25 (4), 26, 27 (4), 28 (2), 29 (4), 30, 33 (2), 34 (4), 35.
84. 8–15 (2), 19.

Salin Thugaung Manuscripts, 'Ko-nei Thet-kayits', Volume 10 (STM-KT)

Handwritten transcription. Private collection of Toe Hla (U) and collection of Universities Historical Research Centre (UHRC). Debt-slave contracts No. 1–104.

Documents of Myanmar Socio-Economic History (DMSEH)

Aichi University, taweb.aichi-u.ac.jp/DMSEH/
Volume – Image No.

Vol. 1 0480–81, 0703, 0728, 0751, 0830.
Vol. 2 0177, 0180–82, 0206, 0209–10, 0230, 0569.
Vol. 3 0835–36, 0846, 0848, 0856, 1087–88, 1090, 1093, 1096, 1101, 1103, 1105, 1108, 1110, 1113–15, 1119, 1125, 1127–28, 1130, 1132, 1134, 1136–37, 1140, 1142, 1146, 1148, 1150–51, 1156,1158, 1161, 1163, 1166, 1168,1171–74, 1176, 1118, 1145, 1186–88, 1275, 1293, 1299, 1308, 1310, 1437, 1690, 1979, 1983–84, 1160, 1165, 1856–1857.
Vol. 4 0324, 0873–74, 1009–10, 1013, 1015, 1020, 1039–40, 1044, 1050, 1052, 1058, 1064, 1248, 1392, 1395, 1501, 1503, 0250, 0321.
Vol. 5 0130, 0134, 0548, 0558, 0563–64, 0568, 0580, 0648, 1089, 1210, 1256–58, 1260, 1267, 1271, 1273, 1293, 1295–96, 1298, 1305, 1331–34, 1338, 1383, 0205, 0471, 0557, 0582.
Vol. 6 2490–93, 2623, 2625–26, 2750–52, 2754–55, 2757–64, 2605, 2632.
Vol. 9 1360–61, 1364–66, 1711–14, 1718–19, 1731–32, 2458, 2737, 2797.

274 Money-lending Contracts in Konbaung Burma

Vol. 10 1305.
Vol. 11 1058–1059, 1285, 1583, 1585, 2525, 2700, 2889.

Land-mortgage contracts

KUMF

Reel No.–Document No.–Image No. (number of evidences in one image)

16	6–17, 8–30.
39	8–38.
40	1–10, 2–30.
45	6–36, 7–17, 10–45.
46	1–30.
50	7–18.
52	3–1, 3. 4–3. 5–1, 4, 6–12, 15–22, 24–37, 39–40, latter part of 40~54. 6–2–5. 7–1. 9–1~4. 10–3, 9~11, 16~18, 20, 23, 26. 11–1. 12–3~5. 13–2. 14–20, 29.
53	1–3. 6–1–2. 7–1–12. 9–10. 10–6, 7. 11–7. 15–3. 17–1–2.
54	9–5. 18–10.
55	4–2.
60	5–2. 7–2, 6 (4), 10, 14, 20. 10–1~7, 9, 10, 12~16, 18, 22, 23~25, 26~29, 30~31. 11–3, 6, 7~11, 13, 15, 17~18, 20, 24, 26, 28~31, 32~33. 12–3~4. 13–2 (4), 3–7 (14), 8 (3), 9, 10 (3), 11 (4), 12 (3), 13 (4), 15 (2), 16 (5), 17 (3), 18, 21 (4), 22 (3), 23 (5), 25 (3), 26 (3), 27, 28 (4), 30 (4), 31 (2), 32 (2), 33 (4), 34 (4), 35 (3), 36 (4). 14–1, 2 (3), 3 (2), 4 (2), 6 (2), 7 (3), 8, 9 (2). 15–1 (2), 2 (4), 3 (4), 4 (5), 5 (3), 6 (4), 14 (4), 15 (3), 16 (5), 17 (2), 17 (2), 18 (4).
61	1–2 (2), 3, 6 (2), 7 (3), 8 (2), 9 (4). 3–1 (2), 2, 3 (3), 4 (2), 5 (2), 6 (2), 7 (2). 14–4. 15–2, 3, 4 (4).
62	8–9, 10. 14–5.
63	15–1.
67	2–1, 2. 3–3 (2). 4–2. 5–2. 6–2. 7–2, 3 (4), 6. 8–2, 3, 6. 10–1.
68	10–2.
82	6–1, 7–1~2, 4~6, 8~13, 16. 8–2, 5, 7, 10~11, 15~17, 20, 20 (2), 22, 23 (2), 24, 26.
84	3–1, 2 (2), 3 (2), 4, 5 (3), 6 (2). 4–6 (2), 7 (3), 8~9, 13, 20 (2). 5–1 (2), 3, 4 (2), 6 (2), 7, 9. 6–5, 7, 9, 18 (2), 19–21. 7–7 (4), 8 (2), 9~10, 14 (2). 8–3 (3), 4 (3), 5, 7~9, 11~12, 16 (2), 17, 20~21. 9–17~18. 10–13 (2).

Bibliography 275

Konbaung Hkit Leya Thet-kayit Pa Luhmu Sibwayei Thamaing (KLT)

Toe Hla (U) (ed.), 1977/78–78/79. 'Socioeconomic history in the land mortgage contracts of the Konbaung period', two volumes, typescripts, Yangon, undated. 1075 contracts.

Meiktila Thet-kayit Collection (MTC)

Land mortgaged contracts in Meiktila region. Burmese handwritten manuscript collection, Mandalay University, History Department, undated. 364 contracts.

English translation by Thu Nandar, 'Characteristics of land-mortgage contracts in the 18th–19th century Myanmar society', PhD theses submitted to Tokyo University of Foreign Studies, 2008, Appendix B, pp. 137–199.

&Contracts No. 39, 45, 54, 93, 122, 137, 148, 162, 181, 189, 191, 19, 199, 204, 223, 224, 237.

Tokyo University of Foreign Studies, Center for Documentation & Area Studies of Historical Materials (C-DATS) Project

C-DATS 2004–2005, *para-baik*s, CD-ROMs, and microfilms.

1) 75 volumes of *para-baik*s from monasteries in central Myanmar.

2) *para-baik*s in the collection of Mr. Toe Hla (55 volumes)

Tokyo University of Foreign Studies Library.

C-DATS 2005 no. 0056-22, 0056-23, 0249, 0250, 0256, 0352-01, 216, 526, 566, 624.

Universities' Central Library (Yangon) (UCL)

Para-baik no. 151107, no. 151113, no. 178505.

DMSEH

Vol.	Image Number
Vol. 1	0108–12, 0001–05, 0009, 0011–12, 0020, 0022, 0106, 0126, 0163, 0165, 0197, 0204, 0207, 0209, 0212, 0215–16, 0218–0221, 0223, 0227–28, 0231–32, 0237, 0258, 0288, 0289, 0293, 0310, 0313, 0328, 0336, 0392, 0402, 0405, 0408, 0410, 0415–16, 0441, 0443, 0466, 0491, 0499–0501, 0506–08, 0510–11, 0513–15, 0517–18, 1520–23, 0526–29, 0602, 0605, 0611, 0618, 0622, 0627, 0634, 0637, 0640–41, 0643, 0648–49, 0651–52, 0655–56, 0702, 0705–06, 0709–10, 0714–17, 0724, 0726, 0838, 0840–41, 0843–46, 0849, 0851, 0914, 0936, 0937, 0943–44, 0953, 0954–55, 0970, 1038, 1044, 1050, 1081, 1083,

1087, 1089, 1092, 1094, 1131–32, 1153, 1167–69, 1172,1283, 1284, 1286,1296, 1299, 1355, 1360, 1391, 1407–08, 1424, 1426, 1439, 1443, 1486, 1511–13, 1520, 1528–29, 1550, 1569–71, 1578, 1580, 16041688–90, 1610–11, 1654–55, 1658, 1662, 1666, 1684–86, 1690, 1693–95, 1701, 1703, 1744, 1745, 1747, 1750, 1753, 1756, 1761, 1763, 1768, 1771, 1787, 1794, 1798–99, 1808, 1810–12, 1814–15, 1820, 1824, 1828, 1832, 1835–36, 1838–39, 1841, 1845, 1847, 1857, 1859, 1861, 1863, 1865–66, 1870, 1872–74, 1880. (Agricultural land mortgage) 0056, 0502–03, 0505, 0509, 1037, 1422, 1326. (Agricultural land sales)

Vol. 2 1109. (Agricultural land mortgage)

Vol. 3 1044, 1358, 1878, 1879, 0858, 0869, 0926, 0941, 0949, 0247, 0253–56, 0323, 0353–54, 0359, 0379, 0541, 0544, 0644, 0645, 0685, 0745, 0859,0862, 0920, 0925, 0928–29, 0978, 0983–84, 0988, 0990, 0992–94, 0995, 1040–41, 1043, 1049–50, 1297, 1306, 1360, 1747, 1761, 1786, 1790, 1804, 1807, 1817, 1935, 1945–47, 1949, 1960, 1963, 2010, 2016, 2018, 2021–22. (land mortgage) 0662–63, 0680, 0690, 0691, 0743, 0746–47, 0762, 0767, 0796–97, 0799, 0837, 0933–34, 1053, 1721, 1746, 1752, 1983–84, 1941–44, 1961, 1993, 2003–04, 2015, 2023, 1891, 1927, 1918–20, 1958–59, 1990–01. (land sale)

Vol. 4 0391, 0400, 0405, 0905, 0945, 1355, 1435, 1350, 0001, 0003, 0007, 0011, 0013, 0015, 0017, 0020, 0022, 0024, 0026, 0030–32, 0036, 0040–43, 0045, 0049, 0051–53, 0056, 0059, 0062–65, 0068, 0071, 0073, 0081, 0085, 0087, 0090–92, 0094, 0097, 0099, 0102, 0104, 0160, 0116, 0122, 0123, 0124, 0131–32, 0135, 0141, 0143, 0145, 0147, 0151–52, 0154, 0257–58, 0162, 0165–67, 0169, 0171–72, 0174, 0176–78, 0183–85, 0187–89, 0191–93, 0196–97, 0199–0201, 0207, 0216, 0220, 0246, 0275, 0278, 0280, 0282, 0287, 0292, 0297, 0334, 0401, 0458, 0485, 0495, 0511, 0518, 0520–22, 0591, 0604, 0772, 0861, 0864–68, 2854, 0870–71, 0949, 1002, 1011, 1128, 1132,1138, 1140, 1146, 1146, 1147, 1170, 1178, 1182, 1183, 1200, 1208, 1211, 1328, 1335–36. (land mortgage) 1143, 1627, 0004–06, 0008, 0019, 0034, 0078, 0083–84, 0086, 0100, 0120–21, 0125–26, 0130, 0142, 0153, 0164, 0203, 0223, 0294–96, 0346, 0394, 0445, 0472, 0513, 0548, 0550–51, 1187, 1405. (land sale)

Vol. 5 0458, 0915, 1799, 1121, 1559, 1625, 1938, 1971, 1977, 2201, 2204, 2539–41, 2679, 2681, 2839, 2854, 2909, 2922, 2960, 2992, 3002, 0136, 0138, 0145, 0200, 0222, 0225, 0360, 0362, 0365, 0404, 0412, 0423, 0431, 0444, 0447, 0468, 0473, 0476, 0482, 0489, 0492, 0497, 0503–04, 0507, 0512, 0514, 0520, 0529, 0534, 0545, 0549, 0571, 0577, 0595, 0678, 0792, 0874, 0898, 0909, 0912, 0914, 0919, 0926–27, 0932, 0934, 1019, 1021, 1053–54, 1076, 1078,

Bibliography   277

1080, 1094, 1098, 1100, 1108, 1113, 1123, 1127, 1129, 1132, 1134, 1142, 1149, 1151–52, 1156, 1173, 1182, 1186, 1190, 1198, 1204, 1218–19, 1221, 1246, 1250, 1252, 1254, 1306, 1320, 1326–27, 1329, 1336, 1358, 1379, 1380, 1401, 1403, 1417, 1421,1432–33, 1435–36, 1441–42, 1444, 1455, 1463, 1488, 1492, 1510, 1563, 1566, 1569, 1573, 1630, 1632, 1641, 1647, 1649, 1696, 1707–09, 1723, 1731, 1736, 1794, 1796,1894, 1936, 1943, 1949–50, 1959, 1963, 1966, 1991, 1996, 2004, 2014, 2021, 2043, 2046–47, 2051, 2054, 2055, 2173, 2183, 2185, 2187, 2192, 2198–99, 2205, 2210, 2212, 2217, 2256, 2258, 2265, 2267, 2269, 2336–38, 2342, 2394–95, 2399, 2419, 2477, 2533, 2642, 2690, 2694, 2711, 2717, 2829, 2836, 2838, 2849, 2864, 2873, 2880–81, 2912, 2919, 2924, 2944–45, 2948, 2953, 2967, 2970, 2975, 2979, 2986, 2999, 3004, 3010, 3015, 3020, 3033, 3042, 3051, 3054, 3058, 3065, 3075, 3090, 3091, 3093, 3095–99, 3101, 3105, 3117–19, 3126, 3129, 3137–38, 3158, 3161, 3164–67, 3172–75, 3177, 3179, 3183–84, 3187, 3194, 3200–01, 3204, 3207–10, 3215–18, 3220, 3222. (land mortgage) 1,826, 0067, 0483, 0798, 0861, 1177, 1431, 0449, 0547, 0802, 1631. (land sale)

Vol. 6   0468, 0471, 0478, 0066, 0077, 0091, 0092, 0171, 0188–90, 0221, 0224, 0239, 0266, 0291, 0342, 0575, 0580, 1052, 1231, 1237, 1608, 1609, 1610, 1656, 1722, 1724, 1733–36, 1745, 1791, 1799, 1810, 1817, 1850, 1859–61, 2030, 2075, 2082, 2095, 2103, 2127, 2136, 2161, 2196, 2279–80, 2288, 2407, 2440, 2443, 2476, 3013, 3023, 0037, 0048, 0094–95, 0100, 0103, 0114, 0147, 0150, 0168–69, 0172, 0186–87, 0195, 0201, 0203–04, 0206, 0211, 0213–14, 0222, 0225, 0227–28, 0230, 0244, 0248–49, 0264, 0267–68, 0292, 0294–95, 0315, 0317, 0325, 0333, 0335–36, 0476, 0487, 0491, 0483, 0496–98, 0540, 0545–46, 0550, 0557, 0559, 0562, 0567, 0571, 0574, 0676, 0680, 0685, 0695, 0788, 0942, 0988, 0990, 1041, 1043–44, 1046, 1049, 1058–60, 1133, 1146, 1148, 1152, 1223, 1226–27, 1229, 1242, 1246, 1353, 1356, 1358, 1361–62, 1365–66, 1474, 1487, 1509, 1514, 1570, 1573, 1580, 1583, 1585, 1631, 1640, 1642, 1647, 1650, 1654, 1672, 1705, 1708, 1711, 1731, 1738–39, 1741, 1742, 1764, 1783, 1833–34, 1836, 1848, 1856, 1884, 1889, 2037, 2077, 2094, 2102, 2156, 2164, 2168, 2179, 2183, 2195, 2216–17, 2219–2220, 2225–26, 2230–31, 2234–35, 2237, 2278, 2444, 2460, 2484, 2591, 2619, 2767, 2769, 2780, 2803, 2892, 2901, 2910, 2912, 2927, 2983, 2952, 2953, 29578, 2961, 3022. (land mortgage) 0059, 0688–89, 0691. (land sale)

Vol. 7   0162, 0295–96, 0534, 0581, 0839, 0842, 0853–54, 0949, 1012, 1715, 1760–61, 1766–67, 1772–74, 1777, 0011, 0030, 0085–86, 0097, 0105, 0142, 0144, 0149, 0166, 0205, 0210, 0213, 0216, 0220, 0229, 0258, 0272, 0309, 0310, 0321,

278   Money-lending Contracts in Konbaung Burma

0352–53, 0414, 0418–19, 0422, 0446, 0454–56, 0486, 0500, 0517, 0531, 0556, 0590–91, 0617, 0639, 0705, 0724, 0726–27, 0729, 0730, 0732, 0735, 0759, 0767, 0772–73, 0777, 0845, 0857, 0859–60, 0864, 0866, 0929, 0935, 0942–44, 0963, 0966, 0981, 0982, 0986, 0991, 0996, 1001–04, 1006, 1019, 1027, 1032, 1065, 1067, 1107, 1712, 1714, 1728, 1737, 1743, 1746, 1748, 1764, 1769–71, 1778, 1780, 1787–89, 1817. (land mortgage) 0858, 0478, 0526, 0535. (land sale)

Vol. 8 0809, 0811–12, 0944, 1476, 1509, 0242, 0814, 0819, 0842, 0952, 0955–56, 0960, 0964, 0971, 0974, 0977, 0978, 0980, 0983, 0986, 1360–61, 1380, 1387, 1399–1400, 1403, 1421, 1443–44, 1460–61, 1520–21, 1523, 1580, 1594. (land mortgage) 0968. (land sale)

Vol. 9 2462, 2546, 3000, 0104, 0124–28, 0199, 0202, 0205, 0208, 0217, 0223, 0323, 0338, 0376, 0399, 0408, 0422, 0425, 0430, 0437–38, 0553, 05587, 25, 0568, 0575, 0630, 0634, 0636, 0948, 0951, 0972, 0976, 0978, 1033, 1063, 1071, 1075, 1096, 1125, 1245, 1248, 1664, 1667, 1766, 1768, 1770, 1776, 1783, 2051, 2053–54, 2056, 2058, 2060–61, 2063, 2086–87, 2118–19, 2129, 2148, 2177–78, 2233, 2238–39, 2241, 2248, 2306, 2308, 2310, 2316, 2323–24, 2471, 2474–75, 2483, 2486, 2489, 2518, 2539, 2544–45, 2553–54, 2558, 2564, 2566, 2573, 2577, 2578–84, 2586–87, 2596, 2579–84, 2586–87, 2591, 2596, 2608–09, 2616, 2626, 2628, 2645, 2647–48, 2699–2700, 2764, 2799–2801, 2803–04, 2816, 2903, 2934, 2940, 2967, 2976–79, 2986, 2990–98, 3002, 3006, 3034, 3049–54, 3057, 3061, 3062, 3064–65, 3067–69, 3071, 3017–19, 3125, 3131, 3220, 3269, 3271–72, 3276, 3286, 3295, 3304–05. (land mortgage) 0200, 1617, 1651, 2878, 2970, 2972–73, 1106, 1447, 1450, 1453, 1455, 1460, 1462, 1467, 1476, 1479, 1481, 1485–90, 1494, 1496, 1498, 1501, 1508–09, 1633–34, 1643, 1646, 1649, 1652, 1655, 1657–60, 1672, 1674–76, 1678, 1680–82, 1707–09, 1716, 1730, 1733, 1735–37, 1922, 1924–28, 1933, 2150, 2404, 2473, 2567, 2765, 2806, 3119. (land sale)

Vol. 10 0267, 0288–89, 0611, 0859, 0995–96, 0998, 1000–02, 1004, 1218, 1298, 0248, 0618, 0621, 0636, 0638, 0640, 0714, 0741, 0886, 0906, 0908, 0914, 0918, 0920, 0987, 1025, 1041, 1265, 1271, 1272–73, 1290, 0056, 0058, 0247, 0253, 0627, 0649, 0716, 0738, 0742, 0744, 0841, 0844, 0849, 0851–52, 0855, 0857, 0860, 0867, 0872, 0892, 0895, 0904, 0991–02, 1013–14, 1035, 1286, 0657, 0740, 0838, 1268. (land mortgage)

Vol. 11 1173, 1286, 1358, 2606, 2615, 0705, 0725, 0956, 0985, 1123, 1209, 1209, 1377, 1381, 1383, 1924, 1961, 2003, 2006, 2254, 2336, 2695–96, 2985, 2987–88,

3059, 3061, 2003, 0073, 0149, 0182–84, 0212, 0313–14, 0345, 0362, 0381–82, 0384–85, 0412, 0437, 0445, 0446–47, 0459, 0505, 0537–38, 0613, 0618, 0620, 0644, 0699, 0700–01, 0703–04, 0706, 0708–10, 0713–14, 0716–17, 0720–23, 0726, 0737, 0741–43, 0792, 0795, 0802, 0813, 0931, 0935–36, 0938, 0941, 0945, 0950, 0952, 0954, 0965–66, 0975, 0979, 0987, 1120, 1128, 1155, 1167, 1175–76, 1184, 1186, 1208, 1212–13, 1215, 1217, 1219, 1254–56, 1277, 1284, 1350, 1352, 1359, 1360, 1366–68, 1371–72, 1380, 1384, 1702, 1705, 1710–11, 1717, 1883, 1891, 1919, 1922, 1926, 1929, 1931, 1942–43, 1951, 1965, 1967, 1969, 1971, 1976, 1979, 2004–05, 2330, 2337, 2341, 2346–48, 2352–55, 2423–24, 2443, 2484, 2492, 2496, 2508–09, 2512, 2555, 2559, 2562, 2567–68, 2582, 2589, 2618, 2647, 2649–52, 2654, 2657, 2659, 2660, 2683, 2687, 2743, 2766, 2950, 2984, 2986, 2993–94, 2999, 3001, 3043, 3055, 3060, 3065. (land mortgage)

Comparative tables of Burmese and English calendars

Irwin, A. M. B., *The Burmese Calendar*, London: Sampson Low, Marston and Company, 1901.

Moyle, J. Copley, *An Almanac of Corresponding English and Burmese Dates: For One Hundred Years from A.D. 1820 to the end of A.D. 1920*, Rangoon: The American Baptist Mission Press, 1905.

Than Tun and Yi Yi, 'Pondaw Pyat-kadein: King's own calendar A.D. 1806–1819' in *ROB*, vol. IV, 1986, 1971, pp. xxxiii–cxi.

Yi Yi, *Mynamar Ingaleik Pyat-kadein, 1710–1820*, 2 volumes, Yangon: Ministry of Culture, Myanmar Naing-ngan Thamaing Komashin, 1969.

Dictionaries of Myanmar historical terms

Maung Maung Tin (U), *Shwe Nan Thoun Wahara Abidan* (Dictionary of the words and terms in the royal palace) (3rd ed.), Yangon: Tekkatho-mya Thamaing Thutei Thana Oo-zi Htana, 2005.

Thein Hlaing (U), *Hkit Haung Myanma Thamaing Thutei Thana Abidan* (Dictionary of ancient Burmese historical terms), Yangon: Tekkatho-mya Thamaing Thutei Thana Oo-zi Htana, 2000.

Yi Yi (Dr.), *Thutei Thana Abidan-mya Hmatsu* (Dictionary for Burmese historical studies), Yangon: Myanmar Naing-ngan Thutei Thana Atin (Burma Research Society), 1984.

280 Money-lending Contracts in Konbaung Burma

Official publications

Furnivall, J. S. and W. S. Morrison, *Burma Gazetteer, Syriam District*, Rangoon: Superintendent, Govt. Printing and Stationery, 1963 (reprint).

Government of Burma, *Report on the Famine in Burma, 1896–7*, Rangoon: Superintendent Govt. Printing, 1898.

—— *Report on the Settlement Operations in the Minbu District, Season 1893–97*, Rangoon: Superintendent, Government Printing, 1900.

—— *Report on the Settlement Operations in the Magwe District, Season 1897–1903*, Rangoon: Superintendent, Government Printing, 1903.

—— *Manu Dhamma That-htan kho Manu Dhamma That Kyan: King Wagaru's Manu DHAMMA-SATTHAM* (text, translation, and notes), Rangoon: Superintendent, Government Printing and Stationery, 1934.

—— *Gazetteer of Burma*, 2 volumes, Delhi: Gian Publishing House, 1987 (reprint).

Ministry of National Planning and Economic Development, *Statistical Yearbook*, Yangon: Central Statistical Organization, 2000.

Pyi-htaung-su Soshelit Thamada Myanmar Naing-ngan-daw, *Pyi-ne hnin Taing-mya shi Myo-ne alai Myo, Yat-kwe, Kyeywa-ousu, Kyeywa-mya, Sit-kaing Taing* (The list of towns, wards, village tracts, and villages in the States and Divisions), Vol. of Sagaing Division, Yangon Kaba-Aye Sataik, 1974.

Scott, J. G. and J. P. Hardiman, *Gazetteer of Upper Burma and the Shan States*, 5 volumes, Rangoon: Government Printing, 1900.

Williamson, A., *Burma Gazetteer, Shwebo District*, Vol. A, Rangoon: Superintendent, Government Printing and Stationery, 1963 (reprint, compiled 1929).

Secondary sources

In Burmese

Ba U., *Myanmar Ok-chok-ye Pyinnya* (Administration of Myanmar Kingdom), Mandalay: Bahoshi Thadinsa Taik, n.d.

Central Committee, Myanmar Socialist Program Party, *Akye-pya Myanmar Nain-ngan Thamaing* (History of Myanmar in detail), Vol. II, Part II, 1978.

Hpo Hlaing (U), 'Yaza Dhamma Thingaha Kyan' (Books of king's canon) in Maung Htin (ed.), *Yaw Mingyi U Hpo Hlaing Akutho Patti hnin Yaza Dhamma Thingaha Kyan* (2nd ed.), Yangon: Zabe Sape, 1983.

Bibliography 281

Htun Yee (collected and ed.), *Konbaung Hkit Ngwe-hkyi Thet-kayit Sagyok-mya* (Collection of *thet-kayit*—money lending contracts of Myanmar rural area in Kon-baung period), Vol. 1, Toyohashi: Aichi University, 1999.

—— (ed.), *Konbaung hkit Sayin Padeitha, Collection of Sayin* (various lists of Myanmar affairs in the Konbaung period), Toyohashi: Aichi University, 2003.

—— (collected & ed.), *Konbaung Hkit Hpyat Sa Paung Chok, Collection of Hpyat Sa* (Judicial cases and decisions), Vol. III, Myanma-hmu Beikman Sape Bank, 2006.

Kyan (Ma), *Konbaung i Naukhsoun Aaman* (The spirit in the last stage of the Konbaung era), Yangon: Myanmar Uadana Sape, 2004.

Kyaw Hmu Aung, 'Konbaung Hkit Hnaung Salin Thugaung Thamaing (1819–1885)', (History of Salin *Thugaung* in the late Konbaung period), MA thesis submitted to the History Department, Yangon University, 1992.

Maung Baw, *Konbaung Hkit Sittan* (Records of the Konbaung period) (2nd ed.), Yangon: Aman-htit Sape, 2009.

Maung Maung Tin (U) (ed.), *Konbaung-hset Maha Yazawin-daw-gyi* (Chronology of successive kings of the Konbaung period) (KBZ), Yangon: Tekkatho-mya Thamaing Thutei Htana Oozi Htana, 2004.

Ohn Kyi (Daw), 'Salin Thugaung Thamaing (Achyin)' (Short history of Salin *Thugaung*), colleague of Dr. Than Tun (ed.), *Bama Thamaing Hinley: Studies in Burmese History*, History Department, Mandalay University, 1987, pp. 55–82.

—— 'Konei Thetkayit mya wa Lu-paung Sagyok' (*Ko-nei thet-kayit* namely, debt-slave contract), *Magwe Degree College Annual Magazine*, No. 1, 1991, pp. 48–52.

Sein Lwin Lay (U), *Myanma Sit Hmat-tan-mya hnit Thaningabyuha-mya* (Records of wars and Myanmar kings), Yangon: Khit-hmi Sape Taik, 1968.

Than Tun, *Shehaung Myanmar Yazawin* (Ancient history of Myanmar), Yangon: Mahadagon Press, 1964.

Thin Kyi et al., *Pyi-thaun-su Myanmar Naingan hnin Kaba Myei-pon Saok* (Myanmar and world maps), U Htun Aung Pon-hnei Htaik, 1956.

Thu Nandar (ed.), *Microfilm hnai Pa-shi-tho Ahtau-Ahta-mya Sayin: The Catalogue of Materials on Myanmar History in Microfilms*, 2 volumes, Tokyo University of Foreign Studies, COE Program, 2004–5.

Tin (of Pagan), *Myanma Min Ok-chok-pon Sadan* (Governance of Myanmar Kings), 5 volumes, Yangon: Ministry of Culture, 1963–83 (reprint) (MMOS).

Toe Hla, 'Konbaung Hkit Leya Thet-kayit pa Luhmu Sibwaye Thamaing' (Socio-economic history looking from land mortgage contracts in the Konbaung period), typescript, Pyin-nya-ye Tekkatho Thamaing Htana i Thutei Thana Siman-kein (1978–81) atwe Tin-thwin-tho Kyan (unpublished typescript), 1981.

—— 'Konbaung hkit Athapya hnin Ale mya' (Money and weight in Konbaung period), *Tekkatho Pinnya Padeitha*, Vol. 16, No. 3, 1982, pp. 81–130.

—— *Konbaung Shwe-pyi* (Royal capitals in the Konbaung period), Yangon: Moe Kyi Press, 1993.

—— *Konbaung Hkit Myanma Luhmu Apwe Asyi hnin Tayahmu-hkin-mya* (Social organization and lawsuits in the Konbaung period), Yangon: Tekkatho-mya Thamaing Thutei Thana Oosi Htana, 2004.

—— *Kon-baung Hkit Kye-let Luhmu Si-bwa Bawa (1762–1885)* (Socio-economic life in the rural areas in the Konbaung period), Yangon: Myanmar Historical Commission, 2004.

Yi Yi, 'Konbaung Hkit Sit-tan-mya' (*Sit-tan*s in the Konbaung period), *JBRS*, Vol. 49, No. 1, 1966, pp. 71–127.

Yi Yi Hkin, *Yodaya Naing Mawgun (Letwe Nawyahta)* (Records of the victory over Siam written by Letwe Nawyahta), Yangon: Htun Hpaun Dei-shin-Ban Sape Komati, 2011.

In English

Adas, Michael, *The Burma Delta: Economic Development and Social Change on The Rice Frontier, 1852–1941*, University of Wisconsin Press, 1974.

Allot, Anna, *The End of the First Anglo-Burmese War: The Burmese Chronicle Account of How the 1826 Treaty of Yandabo Was Negotiated*, Bangkok: Chulalongkorn University Printing House, 1994.

Aung-Thwin, Michael, 'Athi, Kyun-Taw, Hpaya-kyun: Varieties of commendation and dependence in pre-colonial Burma' in A. Reid (ed.), *Slavery, Bondage and Dependence in Southeast Asia*, St. Lucia, London and New York: University of Queensland Press, 1983, pp. 64–89.

—— *Irrigation in the Heartland of Burma*, Northern Illinois University, Occasional Paper No. 15, 1990.

Badgley, John H., 'Preserving Myanmar's manuscripts and historical documents: UCL/Cornell's collaborative projects' in T. Saito & U Thaw Kaung (eds.), *Enriching the Past, Preservation, Conservation and Study of Myanmar Manu-scripts*, Tokyo University of Foreign Studies, CEO Project, 2006, pp. 121–139.

Bin Yang, 'Horses, silver, and cowries: Yunnan in global perspective', *Journal of World History*, Vol. 15, No. 3, 2004, pp. 281–321.

Burney, H., 'On the population of the Burman Empire', *JBRS*, Vol. 31, No. 1, 1941 (reprint), pp. 19–32.

Cheng Yi Sein, 'The Chinese in Upper Burma before A.D. 1700', *The Journal of Southeast Asian Researches*, Vol. II, 1966, pp. 81–94.

Cox, Hiram, *Journal of a Residence in the Burmhan Empire*, London: Gregg International Publishers Ltd, 1971 (reprint).

Cox, Hiram, *Journal of a Residence in the Burmhan Empire and More Particularly at the Court of Amarapoorah*, British Library, Historical Print Editions, 2011 (reprint).

Crawfurd, J., *Journal of an Embassy from the Governor General of India to the Court of Ava, in the Year 1827*, London: Waren and Whittaker, 1829.

Damrong Rajanubhab (Prince), *Our Wars with the Burmese: Thai–Burmese Conflict 1539–1767*, Bangkok: White Lotus, 2001 (reprint).

Dijk, Wil O., *Seventeenth-century Burma and the Dutch East India Company, 1634–1680*, Singapore: NIAS Press, 2006.

Furnivall, J.S., *An Introduction to the Political Economy of Burma* (3rd ed.), Rangoon: Peoples' Literature Committee & House, 1957.

—— 'A study of the social and economic history of Burma (British Burma)' (unpublished manuscript submitted to the Office of Prime Minister in 1957–59 and The National Planning Commission, Ministry of National Planning in 1960), 1957–1960.

Gear, Donald and Joan, *Earth to Heaven: The Royal Animal-shaped Weights of the Burmese Empires*, Chiang Mai: Silkworm Books, 1992.

Grant, Colesworthy, *Rough Pencillings of a Rough Trip to Rangoon in 1846*, Bangkok: White Orchid Press, 1995 (reprint, originally published in Calcutta in 1853).

Hall, D. G. E., *Early English Intercourse with Burma, 1587–1743* (2nd ed.), London: Frank Cass & and Co. Ltd, 1968.

Hall, H. Fielding, *The Soul of a People*, London: Macmillan & Co. Ltd, 1899.

Htun Yee, 'Cases of headman-ship of Salin Myo in Myanmar during the 19th century', *Journal of International Affairs* (Aichi University), No. 109, 1998, pp. 91–155.

Huke, Robert E., *Rainfall in Burma*, Geography Publications at Dartmouth, 1966.

Ito Toshikatsu, 'Preparation and cataloging of old Myanmar manuscripts' in T. Saito and U Thaw Kaung (eds.), *Enriching the Past, Preservation, Conservation and Study of Myanmar Manuscripts*, Tokyo University of Foreign Studies, CEO Project, 2006, pp. 163–183.

Keeton, C. L., *King Thebaw and Ecological Rape of Burma, the Political and Commercial Struggle between British India and French-Indo-China in Burma, 1878–1886*, Delhi: Manohar Book Service, 1974.

Koenig, William J., *The Burmese Polity, 1752–1819: Politics and Administration, and Social Organization in the Early Kon-baung Period*, Center for South and Southeast Asian Studies, The University of Michigan, 1990.

Lieberman, Victor, *Burmese Administrative Cycles: Anarchy and Conquest, c. 1580–1760*, Princeton University Press, 1984.

—— 'Was the 17th century a watershed in Burmese history?' in Anthony Reid (ed.), *Southeast Asia in the Modern Early Era: Trade, Power, and Belief*, Ithaca, NY: Cornell University Press, 1993, pp. 240–249.

—— *Strange Parallels: Southeast Asia in Global Context, c. 800–1830: Vol. 1, Integration on the Mainland*, Cambridge University Press, 2003.

Luce, G. H., 'Economic life of the Early Burman', *JBRS*, Vol. 30, Part 1, 1940, pp. 283–355.

—— *Old Burma—Early Pagan*, Vol. I, New York: J. J. Augustin Publisher, 1969.

Malcom, Howard, *Travels in Southeastern Asia*, Michigan University Library, 1834.

—— *Travels in South-eastern Asia: Embracing Hindustan, Malaya, Siam, and China; With Notice of Numerous Missionary Stations, and a Full Account of the Burman Empire; With Dissertations, Tables, etc.*, Boston: Gould, Kendall and Lincoln, 1839.

Mitchell, B. R., *International Historical Statistics* (3rd ed.), Macmillan, 1998.

Moore, Elizabeth H., *Early Landscapes of Myanmar*, Bangkok: River Books, 2007.

Mya Sein, *Administration of Burma: Sir Crosthwaite and the Consolidation of Burma* (Rangoon: Zabu Meik-swa Pitaka Press, 1938), Kuala Lumpur: Oxford University Press, 1973 (reprint).

Nisbet, John, *Burma under British Rule and Before*, 2 volumes, Westminster: Archibald Constable & Co. Ltd, 1901.

Okudaira Ryuji, 'The Burmese Dhammathat' in M. B. Hooker (ed.), *Laws of Southeast Asia*, Vol. I, The Pre-Modern Texts, Singapore: Butterworth & Co. Ltd (Asia), 1986, pp. 23–142.

Pollak, Oliver, *Empires in Collision: Anglo-Burmese Relations in the Mid-Nineteenth Century*, Westport, Connecticut: Greenwood Press, 1979.

Polo, Marco and Manuel Komroff, *The Travels of Marco Polo*, New York/London: W. W. Norton, 1926.

Reid, Anthony, 'Introduction: Slavery, bondage in Southeast Asian history' in A. Reid (ed.), *Slavery, Bondage and Dependency in Southeast Asia*, St. Lucia, London and New York: University of Queensland Press, 1983, pp. 1–43.

Richardson, D., *The Damathat, or the Laws of Menoo*, translated from the Burmese, XIV vols. in one (2nd ed.), Rangoon: The Mission Press, 1874.

Robinson, M. and L. A. Shaw, *The Coins and Banknotes of Burma*, Manchester, 1980.

Saito Teruko, 'Rural monetization and land-mortgage *thet-kayit*s in Kon-baung Burma' in Anthony Reid (ed.), *The Last Stand of Asian Autonomies; Responses to Modernity in the Diverse States of Southeast Asia and Korea, 1750–1900*, London: Macmillan, New York: St. Martin's Press, 1997, pp. 153–184.

Sangermano, V., *A Description of the Burmese Empire: Compiled Chiefly from Burmese Documents*, translated by William Tandy, London: Susil Gupta, NY: Augustus M. Kelly, 1969 (reprint).

Stuart, J. M. B., *Old Burmese Irrigation Works: Being a Short Description of the Pre-British Irrigation Works of Upper Burma*, Rangoon: Supdt., Govt. Printing, 1913.

Sun Laichen, 'Shan gems, Chinese silver and the rise of Shan principalities in northern Burma, c. 1450–1527 in Geoff Wade & Sun Laichen (eds.), *Southeast Asia in the Fifteenth Century; The China Factor*, Singapore: National University of Singapore Press and Hong Kong University Press, 2010, pp. 169–196.

Symes, Michael, *An Account of an Embassy to the Kingdom of Ava, Sent by the Governor-General of India in the Year 1795*, Edinburgh, 1827.

Taw Sein Ko, *Selections from the Records of the Hlutdaw*, Rangoon: Government Printing, 1889.

Temple, R. C., 'Notes on currency and coinage among the Burmese', Bombay: The British India Press, 1928 (reprinted from *The Indian Antiquary*, Vol. LVI, 1927, LVII 1928).

Than Tun (ed.), 'History of Buddhism A.D. 1000–1300', PhD dissertation submitted to the Faculty of Arts, London University, 1956.

—— *The Royal Orders of Burma, A.D. 1598–1885*, 10 volumes (in English & Burmese), Kyoto: The Center for Southeast Asian Studies, Kyoto University, 1983–1990.

Thant-Myint-U, *The Making of Modern Burma*, Cambridge University Press, 2001.

286 Money-lending Contracts in Konbaung Burma

Thaw Kaung, U, 'Myanmar traditional manuscripts and their preservation and conservation', *Myanmar Historical Research Journal*, No. 1, November 1995, pp. 241–273.

—— 'Unearthed story of Myanmar history: Preserve palm-leaves in digital format', lecture given at Fukuoka Public Forum, September 17, 2005.

Thu Nandar, 'Characteristics of land-mortgage contracts in the 18th–19th century Myanmar society: An analysis based on thet-kayits manuscript', PhD dissertation submitted to Tokyo University of Foreign Studies, 2008.

Tin (U), *The Royal Administration of Burma*, translated by Euan Bagshawe, Bangkok: Ava Publishing House, 2001.

Toe Hla, 'Monetary system of Burma in the Konbaung period', *JBRS*, Vol. LXII, Part I & II, 1979, pp. 53–87.

—— 'Money-lending and contractual "thet-kayit": A socio-economic pattern of the later Kon-baung period, 1819–1885', PhD dissertation submitted to Northern Illinois University, 1987.

—— 'BI-DA-KAT-TAIKS: A brief survey' in T. Saito and U Thaw Kaung (eds.), *Enriching the Past, Preservation, Conservation and Study of Myanmar Manuscripts*, Tokyo University of Foreign Studies, CEO Project, 2006, pp. 82–102.

Trager, F. N. and W. J. Koenig, *Burmese Sit-tans 1764–1826: Records of Rural Life and Administration*, University of Arizona Press, 1979.

Tun Wai, *Economic Development of Burma from 1800 till 1940*, Rangoon: Department of Economics, University of Rangoon, 1961.

Wicks, R. S., *Money, Markets, and Trade in Early Southeast Asia*, Ithaca, New York: Cornell University, Studies on Southeast Asia, 1992.

Yule, Henry, *A Narrative of the Mission to the Court of Ava in 1855*, Kuala Lumpur: Oxford University Press, 1968 (reprint of 1855 ed.).

In Japanese

Iijima Akiko, 'Paper production from mulberry trees and its circulation in Taung-gyi and its suburb', *Utilization of Bio Resources and Its Changes in Border Areas in the Northern Myanmar*, Japan Society for the Promotion of Science, A Report to the Kaken-hi Grant, 2004.

—— 'Searching for hand made paper in the Shan States', *Nature, Culture and Language*, No. 3, Genso-Sha, 2007, pp. 96–105.

Ishii Yoneo and Iijima Akiko, *The King and I, Another Story*, Tokyo: Mekong Publishing, 2015.

Ito Toshikatsu, 'Traditional irrigation technology and the development of agriculture', *Shiroku* (Kagoshima University), Vol. 11, 1979, pp. 39–80.

—— 'History of the irrigation system of the Meiktila Lake from the ancient time to the Konbaung period', Research Institute of Languages and Cultures in Asia and Africa, *Journal of Asian and African Studies*, No. 20, 1980, pp. 121–173.

—— 'Sale of mortgaged local domain—cases of small and medium *thugyis* in the early Konbaung period', *Toyo Gakuhou* (Journal of Oriental Studies), Vol. 82, No. 2, 2000, pp. 97–129.

—— 'Introduction of *thathameida* tax by the Mandalay dynasty and *ahmudan*—cases in Shwebo District' in T. Ito (ed.), *Studies of the Establishment of Monopolistic Resources Control by the State in the 19th Century Myanmar*, Japan Society for the Promotion of Science, Report to the Kakenhi Grant, 2008, pp. 1–44.

Iwaki Takahiro, 'The idea of pre-modern Burmese history: A comparison of three books by Aung Thwin, Lieberman and Koenig', *Southeast Asia: History and Culture*, Vol. 21, 1992, pp. 142–160.

—— 'Local power in the early period of the Konbaung dynasty in Salin: An analysis of the *Sit-tan* documents', *Shigaku Zassi* (Journal of History), Vol. 109, No. 9, 2000, pp. 63–79.

—— 'Study of the local power and royal control on them in the early Konbaung Burma', PhD dissertation submitted to Tokyo University, 2002.

Kinshichi Norio, *Prince Henrique, the Navigator, the Pioneer of the Age of Discovery*, Tokyo: Tosui Shobo, 2004.

Kishimoto Mio, *Early Modern Period in Eastern Asia*, World History Librette, no. 13, Yamakawa Shuppan Sha, 1998.

—— *Ming-Qing Hansheng and Jiangnan Society: The Problem of Order in the 17th Century China*, Tokyo University Publishing, 1999.

—— 'Ten' in Yamamoto Hirofumi et al. (eds.), *Dictionary of Historical Studies*, Vol. 9, Kobundo, 2002, pp. 166–168.

Koizumi Junko, 'Another story of family politics: The start of the modern period in Ratanakosin Siam' in Saito Teruko (ed.), *History of Southeast Asia*, Vol. 5, Iwanami Shoten, 2002, pp. 75–104.

Mizuno Asuka, 'Land ownership and land pledging in a village of Upper Burma, in the colonial period—a case study in Kyaukse district', *Toyo Bunka*, No. 82, 2002, pp. 165–180.

Mitchell, B. R. (ed.), *Historical Statistics of Asia, Africa and Oceania, 1750–1993*, Japanese ed., Toyo Shorin, 2002.

Ninomiya Hiroyuki, *Reconsidering Historiography—from Daily Life to Power System*, Japan Editors' School Press, 1994.

Okudaira Ryuji, *Introduction to the Study of Burmese Legal History: The Historical Role of Traditional Law*, Nihon Tosho Kankou Kai (Japan Book Publishers), 2002.

Ohno Toru, 'Financial forms of rural Burma in the 18th and 19th centuries', *Ajia Keizai*, Vol. 16, No. 5, 1975, pp. 69–77.

Polanyi, Karl, *History of Economic Civilization*, translated and edited by Tamanoi Yoshiro et al., Nihon Keizai Press, 1975.

—— *Great Transformation: Formation of Market Society and Its Collapse*, translated by Yoshizawa Hidenari et al., Toyo Keizai Press, 1975.

Saito Teruko, 'The land tenure system in the early stage of British colonaization,1826–1876', *Southeast Asian Studies*, Vol. 23, No. 2, 1985, pp. 142–154.

—— 'A history of the land system of Upper Burma in the 18th and 19th centuries: A preliminary study', *Asia Keizai* (Asian Economy), Vol. 30, No. 5, 1989, pp. 2–20.

—— 'Changing rural societies in the Konbaung period' in Ikehata Setsuho (ed.), *Changing Images of Southeast Asian Histories*, Yamakawa Shuppan-sha, 1994, pp. 171–194.

—— 'Responses to modernity—socioeconomic changes and reformist thought' in Saito Teruko (ed.), *History of Southeast Asia*, Vol. 5, Iwanami Shoten, 2001, pp. 49–74.

—— 'A brief history of the Burmese archives: From *bidakat-taik* to the archives', *Rekishigaku Kenkyu* (Journal of Historical Studies), No. 789, 2004, pp. 13–23.

—— *Rural Societies in Southeast Asia*, World History Librette, No. 84, Yamakawa Shuppan Sha, 2008.

—— 'Mortgaged slaves in nineteenth-century Burma: The case of the Salin region', *Southeast Asia: History and Culture*, No. 38, 2009, pp. 13–45.

—— 'Introduction to the study of the monetary system in 18th–19th century Southeast Asia: Based upon Burmese experience', *Tonan Asia: History and Culture*, No. 42, 2013, pp. 59–79.

Takahashi Akio, *Myanmar, The Nation and the People*, Akashi Shoten, 2012.

Tamaki Akira, *Climate: History of the Earth and Human Beings*, Heibon Sha, 1974.

Tanabe Akio, *Cast and Equality; A Historical Anthropology of Indian Society*, Tokyo University Press, 2010.

Tanaka Minoru, 'Contract in Europe' in Yamamoto Hiroufumi (ed.), *Dictionary of Historical Studies*, Vol. 9 (Law and Order), Kobun Do, 2002, pp. 168–169.

Terada Hiroaki, 'Agreement and contract—contracts in early modern China' in Miura Toru, Kishimoto Mio, and Sekimoto Teruo (eds.), *Comparative History of Asia—Ownership, Contract, Market, and Equity*, Tokyo University Press, 2004, pp. 89–112.

Tsubouchi Yoshihiro, *Tonan Ajia Jinko-Minzoku-shi*), Keiso Shobo, 1986.

Yamamoto Kumiko, *The Descendants of Chinese Muslims: From Yunnan to Myanmar*, Shogakukan, 2004.

Yoshimatsu Kumiko, 'The Pandee in Myanmar, trade and immigration from the late 19th century to the early 20th century', *Islamic World*, No. 61, 2003, pp. 1–25.

Index

Subjects

additional loan, 84, 89, 92–93, 95, 108–109, 114, 117–118, 121–124, 129, 139–140, 142–143, 146, 164–165, 175, 177–180, 184–186, 193, 226, 263–264

agricultural land, 8, 17, 24, 86, 99, 107, 151, 158, 161, 165–168, 170–177, 185, 187–188, 215, 225, 235, 264

    disputes (farmland disputes), 215, 239

ahmudan, 24–25, 28, 34, 36, 66, 82, 91, 96–99, 116, 124, 129, 136–137, 148, 151–154, 158–161, 196–198, 201–202, 205, 223, 235, 237–238, 245–246, 253, 266–267

    debt enslavement of *ahmudan*, 99

Ahsaun-daw-mye (royal court official), 136, 140, 143, 145–147, 155, 160, 177, 261

Aka-yein *myo*, 208

Alaunghpaya, 29, 31–33, 41, 52, 58, 97, 133, 162, 174, 200, 202–203, 260, 267

Anglo-Burmese War

    First Anglo-Burmese War (1824–26), 30, 33–35, 37, 42, 47, 157, 235, 249

    Second Anglo-Burmese War (1852–53), 30, 33, 35–36, 43, 47, 63, 67, 151, 235–236, 250

    Third Anglo-Burmese War (1885), 25, 33, 36, 103

Arakan, 19, 25–26, 30, 32–35, 47, 50, 55, 63, 103, 111, 235, 244, 250

    Arakan expedition, 33–34, 103

Arakanese coins, 55

Assam, 20, 32–33, 35–36, 152, 235, 248, 260

athi, 25, 28, 99, 136, 156, 171, 201, 245–246, 257, 266, 268

Ayeyarwady River, 19, 39–40, 72, 75, 88, 103, 157, 170

Ayuttaya, 29, 200, 267

Bagyidaw, 27, 40, 62–63, 73, 173–174, 249, 258

ban-da-zo (royal financial steward), 157

Bhamo, 44–45

bidakat-taik, 5–6, 242–243

Bin Yang, 250

Bo-ba-baing-mye (ancestral land), 148

Bodawhpaya, 25–26, 32, 34, 39–40, 42, 45–46, 49, 55–58, 60–62, 66, 73, 103, 106, 111, 149, 151, 153, 156–157, 173–174, 200, 202–204

body price (*kou bou*), 89–90, 92–93, 108–109, 112, 114, 116, 118, 121–127, 256

Bombay-Burma Trading Corporation, 40–41

British Indian rupee, 63–67, 121

bwe (honorary title), 136, 253

Byangya village, 13–14, 133–134, 136–140, 142–145, 147, 151–153, 155, 160–161, 169, 177, 187–188, 207, 213, 216, 222, 270

Cachar, 20, 32–33, 35–36, 235, 248

change of creditors, 142–143, 146, 221

change of masters (in debt-slave contracts), 88, 90, 116

Chiang Mai, 33, 36, 235

Chindwin, 41, 50, 245

Chinese copper coins, 45, 51

civil court, 14, 239

climate, 17–18, 23, 39, 64, 235, 240, 271

co-heirs, 91, 144, 184, 186–187, 199, 212, 224–228, 239, 270

    see also heirs

confiscation of land, 198, 200

contractual society, 191–192

cost of litigation, 80, 227–228, 231

cotton cultivation, 37–38, 46, 184

cotton export to China, 37, 38

daga (donor), 86, 112, 136, 238

daga-ma (donor), 136

292 Money-lending Contracts in Konbaung Burma

debt-slave
   debt-slave contracts (*ko-nei-thet-kayit*), 13, 72–77, 81–82, 85–91, 93–95, 98, 103, 108, 110–113, 115, 117, 119, 121–122, 155, 163, 166, 196, 205, 236
   escape of debt-slaves, 83
   guarantors of the debt-slave, 9
delta area, 19
demographic change, 24–26
dinga (minted coinage), 62–63, 252
drought, 29–31, 47, 58–60, 67, 161, 235
   the worst drought (1810–12), 27, 58, 59
Dutch East India Company, 45, 51, 250

early modern period, 10, 240–241, 265
economic aspects of a litigation, 228
equal inheritance, 180, 212, 224, 256
envoys, 44–45

families (powerful)
   Maha-thaman family, 106
   Poza family, 106, 110
   Taungzin family, 103, 106, 110, 268
   Kainza family, 106
   see also Salin *Thugaung*
famine, 24, 27–31, 58–59, 67, 161, 235, 246–247
   worst famine, 28, 30
farmland disputes, *see* agricultural land disputes
fire, 4, 27, 29–32, 247
   fire prevention, 30, 31, 247
foreign trade, 18, 41, 43–44, 46, 64, 236
   overland foreign trade (with China), 41, 46
   maritime foreign trade, 41, 46
foreign wars, 13, 29–30, 32, 35, 37, 39, 47, 98, 161
fragmentation of farmland (arable land), 188, 239

ganza (currency), 50–52
gold and silver, 28, 37, 42
Gresham's law, 52

Hanthawaddy Mon kingdom, 32
heirs, 8–9, 78, 117, 125, 174, 176, 178–179, 184, 197, 199, 225–228, 231, 239
   reclaimers and their heirs, 171
hierarchy of authority, 111
Hluttaw, 59, 195, 266
Hmon (U) of Poppa, 88, 157
Hsinbyushin, xi, 34, 45, 165, 174, 202
human trafficking, 94, 102, 115, 259

interregional trade, 39, 236
irrigation
   irrigation system, 17–18, 20, 22–23, 29, 37, 74, 86, 94, 104–105, 112, 155, 194, 235, 243–244, 257
   reservoir irrigation, 22
   river irrigation, 20, 22, 257

kaing (alluvial) land, 164, 167–169, 172, 204
kings as creditors, 201
Kyaukpadan, 74–75, 88–91, 94, 165, 172–173, 176, 188
Kyaw Hmu Aung, 61, 110, 257–259, 262
Kyi-gang-shin-gyi, 59

land-mortgage contracts, 5, 8, 13, 17, 71, 86, 95, 107, 112, 139, 141, 146, 151, 163, 166, 173, 182, 193, 244, 262, 264, 266, 270
land-sale contract, 144, 206
legal tender, 51, 63
le-gaung (chief), 149, 151, 261
Letwe Nawyahta, 34, 248
literacy education, 138
litigation, 10, 77, 80, 87, 142, 145, 179, 195, 201, 216, 227–228, 231, 266
   litigation over paddy field, 213, 216
Lower Burma, 19, 21, 25–26, 29–30, 32–33, 36, 39, 43–44, 47, 50, 63–65, 67, 88, 121–122, 165, 170, 185, 225, 235–236, 242, 244, 250, 263–265

Ma Hkaing, 89, 91–93, 109–112, 120, 122–124, 126–127, 130

Index   293

Mandalay, 3, 9, 20, 22, 31, 34, 63–64, 67, 74–76, 78–83, 85–86, 95, 101, 104, 133–134, 156, 165, 169, 171–173, 188, 198, 245, 251–255, 257, 262–263, 266

Manipur, 20, 29, 32–33, 35–36, 152, 235, 248, 260

Manugye Dhammathat (customary law text), 79, 83, 174, 254, 264

maritime trade, 42

market, 18, 37–38, 51–52, 61–62, 86, 127, 143, 203, 207, 231, 259

  market tax, 38–39

  permanent market, 38–39, 159

Me Kyi Nyo, 89–90, 92, 110–112, 118, 122, 125, 127, 130, 156, 175, 268

Meiktila, 2, 12, 22–23, 27, 71, 74–75, 81, 86, 88, 90, 151, 157, 165, 172, 176, 178, 182–183, 197, 199, 224, 228, 242, 244, 246, 251, 255, 264, 266

Mi U, 119–20

Mindon, 6, 40, 49, 60, 62–67, 73–74, 121, 152, 156, 160, 173–174, 197–198, 200, 203, 236, 243, 245, 249, 253, 258, 267

Min-kyaw-tin-sithu-naw-yata, 135–136, 146

Min-maha-min-tin-yaza, 82–85, 98, 175–176, 203, 255, 263

monastery (*pongyi kyaung*), 5, 6, 9, 13, 24, 77, 89–93, 135, 138–139, 142–143, 146, 148–152, 154, 160–161, 175–176, 187–188, 197, 226, 237, 242, 253, 261–262

  donor of monastery, 138, 196

monastery land, 150

monetary reform, 49, 57, 59–60, 62–67, 121, 236, 280

  by Bodawhpaya, 55–58, 61

  by Mindon, 62–63, 121, 236, 258

money market, 61, 250

mortgage tenancy, 162, 180–185, 187–188

Mu River, 22, 41, 133, 152

Myo-sa (ywa-sa), 10, 157, 197, 220, 243, 262

myo-thugyi (hereditary rulers), 11, 63, 93, 103, 107–108, 110–112, 117, 156, 206–208, 224, 252, 258, 262, 268

ngwe-hkan-thu (appraiser of money quality), 62

paddy field mortgage, 3, 139–140, 167, 177, 179–180

paddy prices, 51, 58–59, 66, 230

Pagan period (849–1287), 6, 19, 22–23, 50, 102, 150, 173, 257, 261–262, 267

pagoda slave (*paya-kyun*), 26, 136, 148–151, 261

Panthay (Chinese Muslim traders), 45

para-baik, 1–4, 9–10, 60, 73–74, 103, 137–138, 163, 175, 211, 213, 216, 228–230, 233, 242–243, 260, 262, 268–269

patron–client relationship, 103, 117, 130, 192

paya daga (donor of pagoda), 136

peacock coin, 63

pe-sa (manuscript written in dried palm leaves), 1–4, 60, 206, 233, 243, 268

pickled tea leaves, 159, 215, 218, 222–223, 226–228, 239–240, 269, 271

Privy Council (*bye-daik*), 195, 202, 204, 209, 215, 223, 229, 230, 268, 270

pwe-sa (broker), 56, 62, 90, 155, 241

Pyi, 19–21, 27, 38, 63, 74–75, 88–89, 91, 104, 134, 170, 172, 225–226, 244, 251

Pyinzi (Prince) and his son, 27, 175, 204

royal land, 148, 151–152, 161, 261

Sale (*Myo*), 74–75, 81, 88, 90, 165

Salin (*Myo*), 13, 22, 27, 59–61, 63, 72–75, 79–81, 83, 87–92, 98, 103–109, 111–112, 114, 118–119, 121–123, 126, 129–130, 155–156, 165, 167, 170, 172–173, 175–176, 188, 207–208, 244, 251–252, 254, 257

Salin Myo *Saya-daw*, 59

Salin *Thugaung*, 60–61, 7–75, 80–81, 88–90, 92, 103, 106–109, 111, 114, 118–119, 121, 123, 126, 155, 167, 173, 207, 252, 254, 257, 262, 268

sa-mye (land for eating), 153

scarce commodity, 47, 170, 235

Shan Plateau, 1–2, 33, 39, 43, 45, 159, 203, 244, 247, 248

share-cropping tenant, 85, 156

shin ma pwa, thei ma hsoun, 92–93, 108, 119, 121, 125

294 Money-lending Contracts in Konbaung Burma

shin-pwa, thei hsoun, 75
Shwebo, 9, 13, 20, 22, 32, 74–75, 82, 133–134, 162, 164, 169, 171–173, 175–176, 188, 213, 223, 237, 245, 253, 260, 266
silver, *see* gold and silver
sit-tan, 4, 24–28, 107, 242, 245–246, 257
    of 1783, 25–28, 245, 259
    of 1802, 25–28, 107, 245
    of 1826, 27–28, 245

Tabinshwehti (r. 1531–50), 32
Taungoo period, 29, 37, 41, 45, 52, 97, 99–100, 116, 129, 170, 196
    first Taungoo period (1531–99), 50
    second Taungoo period (1604–1752), 13, 29, 96, 159, 196, 237
tax farming, 40–41, 46
Thayetmyo, 43–44
thet-kayit, 1, 4–5, 7–14, 21, 52–54, 71–72, 86, 110, 133, 134–149, 151–155, 158, 160–165, 167–180, 182–183, 185–188, 191–198, 201, 203–208, 210, 213–215, 221–223, 225–226, 228, 230–231, 233–234, 238, 240, 242, 244, 260–264, 266, 268
    legal validity of *thet-kayit*, 194
    sales of *thet-kayit*s, 177

thon hni thon thi (three years three harvests), 142
Treaty of Yandabo, 35, 37, 249

Vientiane, 33, 36, 105, 152, 235, 248

Wagaru Dhammathat (traditional law book), 174, 254, 264
war captives, 32, 34, 36–37, 98, 152, 235, 248
witness, 9, 11, 14, 75–76, 83, 87–88, 91, 108–109, 112, 128, 135, 137, 142–145, 147, 149, 154, 178–180, 182–184, 186, 193–194, 197, 207, 210, 212, 217–219, 222, 225, 227, 238, 253, 266

Yandabo Treaty, 33
Yangon port, 41, 43
Ye-U, 133, 164, 168–169, 171–173, 175–176
ywet-ni (currency), 52–58, 109, 135, 144–145, 162, 175, 178, 183, 186, 197, 229, 251, 258

zaba-hkyi (paddy-borrowing), 163–164
zaba-pe, 164

Personal Names

Adas, Michael, 30, 247
Aung-Thwin, Michael, 22, 29, 102, 104, 115, 245–246, 257, 260, 262
Burney, Henry, 25–28, 245–246
Cox, Hiram, 56–58, 61–62, 67, 251
Damrong Rajanubhab, 34, 248
Dijk, Wil O., 250–251
Fedrici, Cesare, 50
Furnivall, J. S., 148, 162, 180–185, 187–188, 224, 244, 252, 261, 263, 265, 270
Gouger, Henry, 40
Htun Yee, 25, 27–28, 38, 246, 257–258, 262
Ibrahim, Moola, 40
Ito, Toshikatsu, 208, 243–245, 257, 266, 268

Iwaki Takahiro, 245, 257
Kishimoto Mio, 265, 271
Koenig, William J., 25, 27–28, 245–246, 257, 262
Lieberman, Victor, 11, 29, 61, 96–97, 102, 129, 150, 159, 162, 170–171, 243, 246, 250, 252, 256–257, 262–264
Malcom, Howard, 56, 249, 251
Maung Nay (cavalry captain), 152–154
Mya Sein, 270
Nga San and Mi Dei Ba, 126–127
Nga San Hla, 153–54, 222
Nga Shwe, 116, 123–126
Ninomiya, Hiroyuki, 270

Ohn Kyi (Daw), 72, 78–79, 110, 119, 253–254, 257, 259, 262
Okudaira, Ryuji, 254, 268, 271
Ono, Toru, 10, 243
Phayre, Arthur, 46, 64, 250
Polanyi, Karl, 17, 244
Symes, Michael, 56, 248–250
Tamaki, Akira, 271
Temple, R. C., 52–53, 56–57, 251
Terada, Hiroaki, 191, 265

Thaung (U), 9
Thu Nandar, 12, 151, 224, 244, 262, 264, 266, 270
Toe Hla (Dr.), 5, 9, 10–12, 27, 53–54, 57, 59, 137–138, 156, 213, 229–230, 242–243, 246, 248, 251, 252, 260–263, 266–267, 270
Tun Wai (U), 37, 248
Wallace, William, 63–64, 252
Wyon, Edward, 64, 252
Yauk (U), 156, 186, 225
Yule, Henry, 44, 46, 56, 157, 248–251, 263

Printed in the USA
CPSIA information can be obtained
at www.ICGtesting.com
LVHW020324101124
795914LV00001B/3